The
Educational Reform Movement
of the 1980s

PERSPECTIVES
and CASES

Edited by
JOSEPH MURPHY,
Vanderbilt University

𝕸𝖈𝕮𝖚𝖙𝖈𝖍𝖆𝖓 𝕻𝖚𝖇𝖑𝖎𝖘𝖍𝖎𝖓𝖌 𝕮𝖔𝖗𝖕𝖔𝖗𝖆𝖙𝖎𝖔𝖓
P.O. Box 774
Berkeley, California 94701

ISBN 0–8211–1261–9
Library of Congress Catalog Card Number 89–63476

Printed in the United States of America

Linda Stickler Lotto
—my star

Contents

Contributing Authors

Ted Bartell. Assistant Vice President and Director, Western Regional Office, American College Testing, Sacramento, California.

William L. Boyd. Professor, Educational Policy Studies, The Pennsylvania State University.

H. Dickson Corbett. Codirector, Applied Research, Research for Better Schools, Philadelphia, Pennsylvania.

William A. Firestone. Associate Professor, Department of Educational Administration, The State University of New Jersey, Rutgers. Senior Research Fellow, Center for Policy Research in Education, Rutgers.

Susan Fuhrman. Director, Center for Policy Research in Education, The State University of New Jersey, Rutgers.

Rick Ginsberg. Associate Professor, Department of Educational Administration, University of South Carolina.

Ann Weaver Hart. Assistant Professor, Department of Educational Administration, University of Utah.

K. Forbis Jordan. Professor, Department of Educational Administration, Arizona State University.

Michael W. Kirst. Professor, Department of Administration and Policy Analysis, Stanford University.

Martha M. McCarthy. Professor, Department of Educational Administration, Indiana University. Director, Consortium on Educational Policy Studies, Indiana University.

Mary P. McKeown. Director, Strategic Planning, Arizona State University.

David Marsh. Professor, Department of Educational Policy, Planning, and Administration, University of Southern California.

Joseph Murphy. Professor and Chair, Department of Educational Leadership, Peabody College, Vanderbilt University. Senior Research Fellow, National Center for Educational Leadership.

Michael Murphy. Professor, Department of Educational Administration, University of Utah.

Julie Noble. Assistant Director, Research and Statistical Services Department, American College Testing, Iowa City, Iowa.

Allan Odden. Professor, Department of Educational Policy, Planning, and Administration, University of Southern California. Director, Southern California Policy Analysis for California Education Center.

David N. Plank. Assistant Professor, Department of Administrative and Policy Studies, University of Pittsburgh.

Allan D. Walker. Lecturer, Department of Management Studies, Singapore Institute of Education, Singapore.

Donald Warren. Professor and Chair, Department of Education Policy, Planning, and Administration, University of Maryland, College Park.

Bruce L. Wilson. Codirector, Applied Research, Research for Better Schools, Philadelphia, Pennsylvania.

Foreword

A good deal of attention has been devoted to educational reform in the last ten years. Since the onslaught of reform reports in the early part of the 1980s, a sustained effort has been undertaken to fix, restructure, and rethink the U.S. educational enterprise. This book is designed to improve understanding of those efforts. We are particularly interested in grounding the reform movement in the longer history of educational reform and the philosophical underpinnings of that history, as well as the perspectives and strategies that have dominated educational improvement efforts in the 1980s. Chapters 1 through 7 provide that foundation. We are also concerned with tracking the effects of the educational reform movement—with getting beyond polemics about the appropriateness of reform strategies to rich descriptions of and explanations for actual effects. Chapters 8 through 15 provide a good deal of insight into this hithertofore lightly charted territory.

I here express my special thanks to all the authors of these chapters for agreeing to engage in this cooperative venture. The book rests ultimately on their dedication and perspicaciousness. I also thank Michael Kirst, series editor for McCutchan, who provided wholehearted support for this project from its inception.

Introduction

CHAPTER 1

The Educational Reform Movement of the 1980s: A Comprehensive Analysis

Joseph Murphy

The nation's public schools are in trouble. By almost every measure—the commitment and competency of teachers, student test scores, truancy and dropout rates, crimes of violence—the performance of our schools falls far short of expectations. . . . [T]oo many young people are leaving the schools without acquiring essential learning skills and without self-discipline or purpose. (Twentieth Century Fund, 1983, p. 3)

In the early 1980s Americans awoke to discover that their public schools were failing them. Student test scores, declining for nearly two decades, showed America trailing the rest of the world's democracies in mathematics and science achievement. Young people were dropping out of high school at rates that had not changed since the mid-1960s. The public had lost faith in its schools and, enduring the worst economic recession since the 1930s, worried whether the nation possessed the intellectual talent to revitalize its industries and compete with the technological sophistication of east Asia. A flurry of prestigious reports, most notably *A Nation at Risk*, validated and perhaps even inflated these fears. (Chubb, 1988, p. 50)

The authors in this book provide a rich treatment of the educational reform movement of the 1980s. They supply valuable perspectives on the political, economic, and historical dimensions of reform. They analyze the macro-level impact of reform proposals across our nation and also show, for the first time, the effects of recent reform initiatives at the district and school levels. And they provide a thorough analysis of reform activity to date and chart paths for future improvement initiatives.

In this introductory chapter, we examine the whole garment of educational reform in the 1980s—as opposed to employing a specific disciplinary lens or analyzing a discrete aspect of the movement. Our intention is to provide a context—a gestalt—for reviewing the investigations in later sections of this book. The opening part of the chapter treats two issues. It places the current reform movement within the longer history of educational reform in the United States. It also discusses similarities and (especially) differences between the current and earlier eras of reform; for example, the use of policy tools such as testing in new ("high-stakes") ways, and deeper thrusts into the technical core operations of schools.

The second section of the chapter traces the origin of the reform movement. It examines education effects—the decline in student outcome measures and the reduced economic competitiveness of the United States in world markets—that form the basis of calls for reform. Backward mapping is used to uncover the conditions in education and schooling—the indices of internal malice—that are reportedly responsible for these effects.

The locus of the reform movement is taken up next. This section includes a discussion of the actors and processes—the catalysts—that transformed knowledge of effects and internal conditions into demands for action. It then examines the state role in the reform movement. It gives specific attention to analyzing the top-down nature of the first wave of reform and also presents reasons why the state has taken a larger role in educational reform.

The fourth section of the chapter unpacks the content of the reform proposals. This is done by filtering the state reform packages through the following rubrics: assumptions, topic areas, reform philosophy, change model, focus, policy mechanisms, and predominant metaphors. The same set of categories are used to uncover the content or imbedded meaning of Wave 1 (1982–1985)[1] and Wave 2 (1986–1988) reform initiatives. Where possible, emerging Wave 3 reform perspectives are examined using the same framework. An analysis of key content differences among the three waves of reform is presented.

The fifth part of the chapter tracks the effects of the reform movement. The first half of this section provides a comprehensive analysis of the expected effects—the rationale for the expected failure of reform policies. The second half of this section provides an explanation for the unexpected success of Wave 1 reform. A review of the literature on organizational theory, on the politics of education and educational policy analysis, and on school improvement and change provides the foundation for the analysis on reform success and failure. The final section of the chapter briefly reviews seven issues within and around the current reform movement that need further exploration. These include the need for a better understanding of (1) the actual and opportunity costs of individual reform measures; (2) the benefits of investing in differing reform measures; (3) the effects of current reforms on intergovernmental relations and local support for education; (4) context and multiple reform initiative effects on the implementation of proposals; (5) the dynamic conflict between the logically inconsistent organizational perspectives that undergird first-wave (bureaucratic) and second-wave (professionalism) reform proposals; (6) the conflicts and changing balance of power among teachers, administrators, and parents suggested by the various reform initiatives; and (7) the data bases that policymakers need.

COMMONALITIES WITH AND DIFFERENCES FROM PRECEDING REFORM MOVEMENTS

The reform movement of the 1980s has dominated the educational agenda for the last decade, pushing nonreform issues aside in its wake. Although this most recent cycle of reform has a surprising number of unique characteristics, it is important to remember that this cycle is part of the larger fabric of reform that has shaped U.S. education for the last hundred years (see Passow, 1984; Powell, Farrar, & Cohen, 1985, pp. 233–308; Warren, Chapter 2 in this book). Analysts have noted a rather cyclical pattern of major reform movements—they erupt noisily every decade or so, often only to recede quietly into the background, leaving the larger educational landscape only slightly altered and producing nearly indistinguishable changes in educational practice (Elmore, 1987; Ginsberg & Wimpelberg, 1987; Passow, 1984). Keeping this larger perspective in mind is helpful as we review educational reform in the 1980s. William Firestone (Chapter 6) reminds us that employing this wide-angle lens allows us to see streams of continuity, to comprehend the incremental nature of proposals that at first may seem radical. Equally important, we are less likely to mistakenly attribute causality to change initiatives. We are encouraged to look for the connections between suggestions for reform and ongoing activities. When we do so, we find that in many ways the current era of reform has reinforced and accelerated practices that were already underway in many states, districts, and schools (see especially Chapters 4, 6, and 8 in this book).

At the same time, it is important to acknowledge the uniqueness of the reform program of the 1980s.[2] The *scope and momentum* of the movement are unparalleled (see Chapter 8, by McCarthy; and Odden & Marsh, 1988): "The level of concern and amount of energy being expended in thinking about public elementary and secondary schooling are more intense now than at any other previous time in our history" (Sedlak, Wheeler, Pullin, & Cusick, 1986, p. ix). The attack on a host of identified problems and deficiencies has been more comprehensive, directed more at the general student population (and less at targeted groups), of greater concentrated intensity, and has spawned more activity than at any time in the past (Guthrie & Kirst, 1988; Odden & Marsh, 1988; Underwood, 1989). The reform agenda also has been sustained longer than previous efforts, actually shifting into a second generation or wave of change with the possibility of a third movement of improvement already on the horizon.

The sustaining *source* of reform is also different. There is greater public attention and a wider coalition of reform actors than often has been the case in the past (Underwood, 1989). Commission reports that served as the catalysts for change were penned by a different mix of reformers: "educationists" were displaced by "a growing number of business representatives, university faculty who were not directly associated with elementary and secondary education, and politicians" (Ginsberg & Wimpelberg, 1987, p. 348). Among these political and economic elites, there was also agreement about the kind of changes needed and consensus about the need for immediate action (see Chapter 7). Finally, and most importantly, "for the first time in a reform movement, state legislators were heavily involved in legislating school improvement . . . and even in reorganizing the teaching profession" (Association for Supervision and Curriculum Development 1986, p. 10; see also Passow, 1984).

Perhaps the most significant differences between current and former reform movements concern the *focus* of the proposals. For the first time in history, legislators made a serious incursion into the technical core operations of schools "and other educational issues that formerly had been reserved for local boards" (Guthrie & Kirst, 1988, p. 55; Kirst, 1984; Mitchell, 1984). Coupled with this incursion has been a shift away from a historical focus on legislating minimum competencies (Campbell, Cunningham, Nystrand, & Usdan, 1975) toward mandating and prescribing excellence (Porter, 1988). Evaluation foci used to judge reform efforts have also changed in an important way—from reliance on procedural assessments toward product or outcome accountability (Boyd & Hartman, 1987; Murphy, 1989a, 1989b; National Governors' Association, 1987). Accompanying this last change has been a major shift in the locus of quality control from school districts and colleges of education to the state.

All the changes just noted have contributed to the evolution of two improvement *perspectives* that distinguish the 1980s from earlier reform eras.

First, the policy role of educational interventions has been greatly enhanced. Testing is perhaps the clearest example of this change:

> Testing has changed dramatically from its former role as an index of educational progress to its current role as an aggressive force in the establishment of educational priorities and practices . . . informing the public has taken a back seat to driving policy and influencing practice. (McClellan, 1988, pp. 769–770)

See also Shepard & Kreitzer, 1987; Chapters 10 and 8, this book; for discussions of the effects of the use of tests as policy instruments, see Chapter 10, this book; Guthrie and Kirst (1988); Odden and Marsh (1988); Shepard and Kreitzer (1987).

Second, although most academics refuse to acknowledge the fact, "unlike the educational reform movement . . . in the late 1950's, this call for excellence casts teachers as professional decision makers and not as technicians" (Freeman, Martin, Brousseau, & West, 1988, p. 3). In the current era of concern for technical core operations, excellence, and accountability, teachers are being seen, for the first time, as the solution rather than the problem (Porter, 1988). This shift has been especially true of the second wave of the current reform era.

Finally, the most noteworthy difference between this era of educational reform and its predecessors may lie in its *effects*. For a number of reasons that we discuss later, the reform program of the 1980s appears to be bringing about more institutionalization of change content than historical analysis would lead one to expect (see Elmore, 1987; Ginsberg & Wimpelberg, 1987). In any case, it has led to the most comprehensive effort in our history to map and track policy initiatives.[3]

ORIGINS OF REFORM

Major periods of educational reform in the United States have historically been initiated by forces external to the public schools (Coombs, 1987). They generally occur in response to a crisis, perceived[4] or real (or a mixture of both), and are designed to promote certain value positions or goals (see Mitchell & Encarnation, 1984). In this section, we examine the forces that propel and shape the current reform agenda as well as its predominant value structure.

Macro-Level Conditions

In Figure 1-1, we trace the path of discontent that is at the heart of the educational reform movement of the 1980s. The fundamental condition, or crisis, that gave life to reform was crystallization of the belief that "the U.S. is falling behind other industrialized countries in technological development, productivity, and product quality" (Underwood, 1989). The language of the various reform reports is particularly descriptive on this point:

> Our nation is at risk. Our once unchallenged preeminence in commerce, industry, science, and technological innovation is being overtaken by competitors throughout the world. (National Commission on Excellence in Education, 1983, p. 5)

> Today, however, our faith in change—and our faith in ourselves as the world's supreme innovators—is being shaken. Japan, West Germany and other relatively new industrial powers have challenged America's position on the leading edge of change and technical invention. In the seventies, productivity in manufacturing industries grew nearly four times as fast in Japan, and twice as fast in West Germany and France, as in the United States.
> The possibility that other nations may outstage us in inventiveness and productivity is suddenly troubling Americans. (Education Commission of the States, 1983, p. 13)

> Already the quality of our manufactured products, the viability of our trade, our leadership in research and development, and our standards of living are strongly challenged. Our children could be stragglers in a world of technology. We must not let this happen; America must not become an industrial dinosaur. (National Science Board, 1983, p. v)

> America's ability to compete in world markets is eroding. The productivity growth of our competitors outdistances our own. The capacity of our economy to provide a high standard of living is increasingly in doubt. (Carnegie Forum on Education and the Economy, 1986, p. 2)

> Educational reform in the eighties was born out of a national consensus that America could not maintain its economic, political, or military leadership in the world or continue to offer its own children the promise of a brighter tomorrow without much better schools. (Clinton, 1987, p. 5)

School Outcomes

It did not take reformers long to make the connection between this economic impotence and the educational system,[5] specifically its failure to

Macro-Level Condition: • Failure of the United States to compete successfully
with other industrialized nations

School Outcomes: • Declining student achievement
• Students unprepared for further education, the
workplace, and general citizenship responsibilities
• High dropout rates

School Conditions: • Bureaucratic organizational structures
• Poor quality of and commitment by staff
• Lack of standards for students

Figure 1-1
**Tracing the Origins and Manifestations of Demands for Educational
Reform in the 1980s**

properly educate and train U.S. youth. Nor was the potential for education
to restore U.S. economic preeminence ignored. Again, the language of reform
reports and analyses describes these connections graphically:

> Public education consumes nearly 7% of our gross national product. Its
> expenditures have doubled or tripled in every postwar decade, even when
> enrollments declined. I can't think of any other single sector of American
> society that has absorbed more money by serving fewer people with steadily
> declining service. (Kearns, 1988a, p. 566)

> The 1980s will be remembered for two developments: the beginning of a
> sweeping reassessment of the basis of the nation's economic strength and an
> outpouring of concern for the quality of American education. The connection
> between these two streams of thought is strong and growing. (Carnegie Forum
> on Education and the Economy, 1986, p. 11)

> If only to keep and improve on the slim competitive edge we still retain in
> world markets, we must dedicate ourselves to the reform of our educational
> system. (National Commission on Excellence in Education, 1983, p. 7)

> Sinking economic productivity, national debt, international commercial com-
> petition, trade deficits, and a declining dollar placed the nation, and thus
> California, in increasing economic jeopardy. Schooling was seen as part of the
> problem and part of the solution. (Guthrie & Kirst, 1988, p. 4)

> Many reforms reflect the assumption that quality education is a key element in
> the development of a stable national economy, which in turn is a critical factor
> in our national security. American productivity has become a political issue,
> and education is seen as a·major factor in improving productivity. (Association
> for Supervision and Curriculum Development, 1986, p. 2)

No pains were spared to document the extent of the failure of U.S. public schools. Seven outcome measures were targeted for special attention: (1) academic achievement in basic subject areas—compared to historical data about the United States and to student performance in other countries; (2) functional literacy; (3) preparation for employment; (4) the holding power of schools (dropout rates); (5) knowledge of specific subject areas such as geography and economics; (6) mastery of higher-order skills; and (7) initiative, responsibility, and citizenship. Indices of less-than-satisfactory student performance in each of these outcome areas are found in Table 1-1. The overall picture does not fill the reader with either optimism or respect for public education. To make matters worse, political analysts have pointed out that the changing demographic patterns in the United States—"the dual challenge of a rapidly expanding body of retired, senior citizens and a growing body of at-risk students, soon to constitute one-third of all American students" (Boyd & Hartman, 1987)—coupled with an accelerating demand for more highly skilled workers (Kearns, 1988a, 1988b; National Commission on Excellence in Education, 1983; National Science Board, 1983) will make the job of reversing this pattern of failure both more difficult and more imperative.

School Conditions

If the rapidly declining economic status of the United States could be accounted for by the poor quality of U.S. schools, measured by an assortment of student outcomes, then it merely remained for reformers to uncover those conditions in schools and classrooms that were causing this undesirable state of affairs. They engaged in their mission with a vengeance. It is difficult to think of a single aspect of schooling that escaped examination and condemnation.[6] Analysis revealed that teachers and administrators were drawn from the bottom of the intellectual barrel and then poorly trained for their roles. Conditions of employment for teachers were unprofessional and stifling. The basic operating structure of schools was reported to be inadequate. The management of the enterprise was discovered to be wanting, especially in providing leadership. The curriculum was a mess, lacking both rigor and coherence. Instruction was poor; materials (textbooks) worse. Students were allowed to drift through school unchallenged and uneducated. And, as bad as school was, it was even worse for less advantaged and minority pupils. Everywhere were intellectual softness, a lack of expectations and standards, and the absence of accountability. In short, it was not difficult to figure out why students subjected to these conditions should fare so poorly in comparison to (1) students from other nations, (2) their peers from other eras, and (3) acceptable standards of performance.

Table 1-1
Indices of School Failure Used to Explain Declining U.S. Productivity

Area	Source
Student Achievement (historical and cross-national comparisons)	
"The National Assessment of Educational Progress (NAEP) revealed a dismal record for 17-year-olds between 1971 and 1982. Test scores reported by the NAEP showed steady declines in vocabulary, reading, and mathematics."	Association for Supervision and Curriculum Development (1986, p. 19)
"International comparisons of student achievement, completed a decade ago, reveal that on 19 academic tests American students were never first or second and were last seven times."	National Commission on Excellence in Education (1983, p. 8)
"U.S. eighth graders' math skills rank ninth among twelve major industrialized countries of the world."	National Governors' Association (1986, p. 5)
"United States 13-year-olds finished last in a six nation study of math and science skills."	*USA Today* (1 February 1989, p. 1)
"Average achievement of high school students on most standardized tests is now lower than 26 years ago when Sputnik was launched."	National Commission on Excellence in Education (1983, p. 8)
"America's top high school science students ranked below those of nearly all other countries in a new comparison of scores from an international test released here last week."	*Education Week* (19 March 1988, p. 4)
"American 12th graders studying biology scored below students from the 16 other countries included in the analysis, which examined data from a 24-nation science assessment administered in 1986."	
"In chemistry, the study found students from all other countries except Canada and Finland outscored their U.S. counterparts."	
"And in physics, only those two countries and Sweden ranked below the United States."	

(*continued*)

Table 1-1 (*continued*)
Indices of School Failure Used to Explain Declining U.S. Productivity

Area	Source
"The achievement levels are particularly 'discouraging,' the study's authors note, since the American students in the comparison were drawn from the small proportion of the nation's high-school students enrolled in advanced science courses."	
"At a time when economic growth is increasingly dependent on mastery of science and technology, U.S. eighth graders' knowledge and understanding of mathematics is below that of most of their counterparts in other industrialized countries (12 out of 14)."	Carnegie Forum on Education and the Economy (1986, p. 16)
"Despite achievement gains over the past decade, particularly among minority students, American high-school students display a 'dismal' level of mathematics proficiency, the National Assessment of Educational Progress reported last week."	*Education Week* (15 June 1988, p. 1)
"About half of all 17-year-olds tested in 1986 were unable to perform 'moderately complex' procedures usually taught in junior high school, such as finding averages and interpreting graphs, the assessment found. Only 6 percent were able to solve multi-step problems."	
"In addition, NAEP's report says, an 'alarming' number of 13-year-olds lack the skills in whole-number computation needed for everyday tasks, and approximately 7,000,000 of the 3rd and 4th graders who took the test 'have not yet acquired an understanding of rudimentary mathematical skills and concepts.'"	
"These results, which federal officials last week called 'tragic' and 'sobering,' are consistent with those of a 1982 international mathematics assessment, which found that U.S. students lagged far behind those of other industrialized nations."	
"The data suggest, according to the report, that students'—and the nation's—economic future may be in jeopardy."	

Table 1-1 (*continued*)

Indices of School Failure Used to Explain Declining U.S. Productivity

Area	Source
"Moreover, contrary to widespread opinion, it isn't clear that our top students compare well with the top students of other nations. As Magnet (1988, p. 86) notes, 'the top 5% of the U.S. 12th-graders who took international calculus and algebra tests in 1982 came in dead last among the top 12th-graders of nine developed countries.'"	Boyd & Hartman (1987)

Basic Literacy

Area	Source
"It is not unusual for one-third of college freshman in the U.S. to read below a seventh grade level."	National Governors' Association (1986, p. 5)
"As we move into another Presidential election year, it's sobering to note that America's public schools graduate 700,000 functionally illiterate kids every year—and that 700,000 more drop out. Four out of five young adults in a recent survey couldn't summarize the main point of a newspaper article, read a bus schedule, or figure their change from a restaurant bill."	Kearns (1988a, p. 566)
"About 13 percent of all 17-year-olds can be considered functionally illiterate. Functional illiteracy among minority youth may run as high as 30 percent."	National Commission on Excellence in Education (1983, p. 8)
"Some 23 million American adults are functionally illiterate by the simplest tests of everyday reading, writing, and comprehension."	National Commission on Excellence in Education (1983, p. 8)

Preparation for Employment

Area	Source
"The business community blamed the schools for failing to prepare students adequately in basic skills. In fact, business leaders charged that the decline in achievement paralleled the decline in performance of American workers."	Association for Supervision and Curriculum Development (1986, p. 20)
"I believe the success of that second wave of reform is critical, because public education has put this country at a terrible competitive disadvantage. The American workforce is	Kearns (1988a, p. 566)

(*continued*)

Table 1-1 (*continued*)
Indices of School Failure Used to Explain Declining U.S. Productivity

Area	Source
running out of qualified people. If current demographic and economic trends continue, American business will have to hire a million new workers a year who can't read, write, or count. Teaching them how—and absorbing the lost productivity while they're learning—will cost industry $25 billion a year for as long as it takes. And nobody I know can say how long that will be. Teaching new workers basic skills is doing the schools' product-recall work for them. And frankly, I resent it."	
"As a major contributor of tax dollars to public education, corporate America is getting a lousy return on its investment. Not only are schools today not preparing kids for jobs, they aren't even teaching them to read and write."	Perry (1988, p. 38)
"In the U.S., 30% of all high school students—one million teenagers each year—drop out before graduating. Most are virtually unemployable. Of those who do graduate, many do not have the problem-solving skills to function in an increasingly complex information society."	
"Illinois employers have little confidence in the skill levels of high-school graduates who apply to them for jobs, a new study suggests."	*Education Week* (24 February 1989, p. 22)
"In its survey of 360 employers, the Illinois Manufacturers Association found that 45 percent characterized their job applicants as 'poorly educated.' Fifty-five percent of those surveyed said the applicants generally had 'average skills.'"	
"The education community has been allowed to float along," said William Dart, vice president of the 5,000-member trade group, 'but the fact that the product coming out is not sufficient is disturbing.'"	
"The USA's most powerful business leaders today tackle a crisis that threatens everyone's future: a near-total breakdown in our public schools."	*USA Today* (3 February 1989, p. 1B)

Table 1-1 (*continued*)
Indices of School Failure Used to Explain Declining U.S. Productivity

Area	Source
"'We simply don't have any more time to wait,' says Owen 'Brad' Butler, retired chairman of Procter & Gamble Co."	
"U.S. corporations spend $25 billion a year teaching employees skills they should have learned at school. Motorola spends $50 million a year teaching seventh-grade math and English to 12,500 factory workers—half its hourly employees. Kodak is teaching 2,500 how to read and write."	
"CEOs are starting to attack the education crisis with a vengeance. Says Butler: 'The momentum this has gained is beyond my wildest dreams.'"	
"Business and military leaders complain that they are required to spend millions of dollars on costly remedial educational and training programs in such basic skills as reading, writing, spelling, and computation. The Department of the Navy, for example, reported to the Commission that one-quarter of its recent recruits cannot read at the ninth grade level."	National Commission on Excellence in Education (1983, p. 9).
Holding Power	
"Large numbers of American children are in limbo—ignorant of the past and unprepared for the future. Many are dropping out—not just out of school but out of productive society."	Carnegie Forum on Education and the Economy (1986, p. 2)
"Large numbers of drop-outs have become a serious problem."	Association for Supervision and Curriculum Development (1986, p. 9)
"In the U.S., 30% of all high school students—one million teenagers each year—drop out before graduating."	Perry (1988, p. 38)
Knowledge of Specific Subject Areas	
Geography: "A 1987 survey of 5,000 high school seniors in eight major cities produced equally	Kearns (1988a p. 566)

(*continued*)

Table 1-1 (*continued*)
Indices of School Failure Used to Explain Declining U.S. Productivity

Area	Source
dismal results. In Boston, 39% of the students couldn't name the six New England states; in Minneapolis-St. Paul, 63% couldn't name all seven continents; in Dallas, 25% couldn't identify the country that borders the U.S. to the south."	
Economics: "Only one out of three high school students in its 41-state poll could define such basic concepts as profit and the law of supply and demand. The 8,205 eleventh and twelfth graders who took the 40-minute multiple-choice test correctly answered less than 40% of the 46 questions. Declared William Walstad, a co-author of the study: 'Our schools are producing a nation of economic illiterates.'"	Joint Council on Economic Education (cited in *Time*, 9 January 1989, p. 48)
History: "Results of the history test were, in Mr. Finn's words, 'accurate but reprehensible.' Overall, public-school students answered 54 percent of all questions correctly, with college-bound public-school students answering 60 percent correctly."	*Education Week* (9 March 1988, p. 7)
"For nonpublic schools, the results were only slightly better, he said, with an overall average of 60 percent and an average for independent-school students of 63 percent."	
Literature: "On the literature assessment, public-school students answered an average of 51 percent of the questions correctly, with college-bound public-school students averaging 57 percent. The average score for students in nonpublic schools was 58 percent, and for those in independent schools 60 percent."	*Education Week* (9 March 1988, p. 7)
"'I consider a score in the low 60's on this a D minus,' Mr. Finn said."	
Science: "There was a steady decline in science achievement scores of U.S. 17-year-olds as measured by national assessments of science in 1969, 1973, and 1977."	National Commission on Excellence in Education (1983, p. 9)

Table 1-1 (*continued*)
Indices of School Failure Used to Explain Declining U.S. Productivity

Area	Source
Science: "Only about 1 in 20 American adults is 'scientifically literate' and can answer such basic questions as whether the earth revolves around the sun, whether antibiotics kill viruses, and whether astrology is scientific, a federally funded study has found."	*Education Week* (25 January 1989, p. 25)
"The findings, released here last week at the annual meeting of the American Association for the Advancement of Science, are similar to those of two previous U.S. studies, in 1979 and 1985."	
Science and Mathematics: "American 13-year-olds performed at or near the bottom on a new six-nation international mathematics and science assessment, according to a federally funded study released here last week."	*Education Week* (8 February 1989, p. 5)
"Their performance on the math assessment was the poorest recorded, and on the science assessment narrowly surpassed only that of test takers from Ireland and the French-speaking portions of Ontario and New Brunswick."	
Science: "American students' 'distressingly low' levels of achievement in science may signal the need for fundamental changes in the way the subject is taught, according to a study released last week by the National Assessment of Educational Progress."	*Education Week* (28 September 1989, p. 1)
"The study showed that, despite gains over the past four years, particularly among minorities, a majority of high-school students 'are poorly equipped for informed citizenship and productive performance in the workplace.'"	
"And, it said, only 7 percent have the knowledge and skills necessary to perform well in college-level science courses."	
"In addition, the study found that almost half of the 13-year-olds tested lacked a grasp of the basic elements of science, and that nearly 30	

(*continued*)

Table 1-1 (*continued*)
Indices of School Failure Used to Explain Declining U.S. Productivity

Area	Source
percent of the 9-year-olds—representing 1 million students—'have not yet developed some understanding of scientific principles and a rudimentary knowledge of plants and animals.'"	
"'The data in this report present a situation that can only be described as a national disgrace,' said Bassam Z. Shakhashiri, director of the science- and engineering-education directorate of the National Science Foundation, at a press conference here."	
Mastery of Higher-Order Skills	Carnegie Forum on Education and the Economy (1986, p. 2)
"As jobs requiring little skill are automated or go offshore, and demands increase for the highly skilled, the pool of educated and skilled people grows smaller and smaller and the backwater of the unemployable rises."	
"Many of the 17-year-olds do not possess the 'higher order' intellectual skills we should expect of them. Nearly 40 percent cannot draw inferences from written material; only one-fifth can write a persuasive essay; and only one-third can solve a mathematics problem requiring several steps."	National Commission on Excellence in Education (1983, p. 9)
"Between 1971 and 1982, there was a net loss of 9-, 13-, and 17-year-olds' knowledge about and ability to use scientific principles. And there has been no improvement in advanced mathematical problem-solving ability."	National Governors' Association (1986, p. 5).
"The Nation that dramatically and boldly led the world into the age of technology is failing to provide its own children with the intellectual tools needed for the 21st century."	National Science Board (1983, p. v)
Initiative, Responsibility, Citizenship	
"Too many young people are leaving the schools without . . . self-discipline or purpose."	Twentieth Century Fund (1983, p. 3)
"Student behavior and attitudes, ranging from lack of motivation to large number of drop-outs, became a serious problem."	Association for Supervision and Curriculum Development (1986, p. 9)

LOCUS OF REFORM

As the watchword shifted almost overnight from "equity" to "quality," the
states assumed the role of primary change agent in American education. They
became the vehicle by which the demands of business for a concerted national
effort in the development of human capital would be turned into school policy.
. . . States that historically had been the watchdogs became the lead dogs on
the sled of education reform. (Coombs, 1987, pp. 4–5)

Two aspects of the reform movement capture our attention in this
section—(1) the catalysts that transformed concern into reform actions and
(2) the vehicles used to translate findings from the reform reports and studies
into specific strategies for improvement.

Reform Catalysts

The forces that galvanized economic concerns and dissatisfaction with
schooling into action agendas were neither professional educators nor the
general public, but rather "spokesmen in the business community, the
media, and the government" (Coombs, 1987, p. 5; also Doyle & Hartle,
1985; Kirst, 1987). Two major forms served as conduits for these concerns—
studies of schooling and commission reports (Chapter 5 in this book). In fact,
most analysts have coupled the start of the current reform movement to the
publication of these reports and studies, especially of the National Commission on Excellence in Education's (1983) *A Nation at Risk* (Chubb, 1988;
Hawley, 1988), making them in effect the principal catalysts for educational
improvement in the 1980s.[7]

State Role

A number of political analysts have pointed out that the reform movement
in the 1980s has been largely a state show (Doyle & Hartle, 1985; Kirst,
1984, 1987; Mitchell & Encarnation, 1984). This state locus has resulted in
important changes in intergovernmental activities.[8] To begin with, states
have replaced the federal government as the unit of reform action (Doyle &
Hartle, 1985). State government officials have displaced educational interest
groups in the policy-setting arena: "Now state government officials create
education policies, and local interest groups react to them. Educators lost
control of the state agenda quite a while ago" (Kirst, 1987, p. 161). As noted
earlier, states have also pushed into areas of responsibility, especially curricular and instructional matters, that have historically been the province of

local school boards (Institute for Educational Leadership, 1986; Cuban, 1984; Guthrie & Kirst, 1988).[9] From the local perspective, an obvious corollary of this change is that reform edicts "emanate mainly from state legislatures far removed from the schools" (Chubb, 1988, p. 58; also Boyd, 1987; Cuban, 1984).[10] Underwood (1989) captures this change nicely when she reports that "the state legislatures [are] acting as superschool boards, and telling the school districts and administrators how to manage the schools."

Mitchell and Encarnation (1984, p. 4) note that "a wide variety of political, economic, and social forces have been responsible for shifting the initiatives in educational policy formation away from local and federal actors to state-level policy systems." One of the most important of these conditions has been the reduction of federal interest in education (see especially Clark & Amoit, 1981). The connection between the election of President Reagan and the decline in federal-level ideological support for education has been drawn by many analysts (for example, see Association for Supervision and Curriculum Development (ASCD), 1986; Coombs, 1987; Mitchell & Encarnation, 1984). The limited success of many federal programs (ASCD, 1986), the traditional reluctance of the federal government to become involved in current areas of reform emphasis, such as instruction (Coombs, 1987); and a steady reduction on federal regulatory prescriptions (Doyle & Hartle, 1985), all combined with the decentralization philosophy of the Reagan administration to push matters of schooling to the state level. The U.S. Congress's engagement with educational issues has also declined over the last decade (Underwood, 1989). In addition, federal courts, because of their changing philosophical compositions and "the lack of an adequate constitutional basis for sustaining an expansive federal involvement" (Mitchell & Encarnation, 1984, p. 4) have assumed a stance of greater deference in educational topics (Underwood, 1989).

Forces were also at work pushing educational decisions upward from the local to the state level. To help ensure greater fiscal equity among districts and to offset the diminished capacity of local school districts to finance education adequately (Mitchell & Encarnation, 1984), state funding of education increased significantly during the 1970s (Doyle & Hartle, 1985). Not surprisingly, as their share of the financial obligation for schooling increased, state interest in education, including demands for accountability for their money, expanded (Association for Supervision and Curriculum Development, 1986; Guthrie & Kirst, 1988), while "flexibility and autonomy of local school districts gradually diminished" (Doyle & Hartle, 1985, p. 21). Another force in this upward shift of educational policymaking and control has been identified by Mitchell and Encarnation (1984). They report that a variety of factors—fluctuating economic conditions, changing population patterns, and significant political and social conflicts—have combined to overwhelm many local educational agencies. This sense of helplessness, and the need to turn to the state for possible solutions, have been accentuated in recent years by attempts of educational interest groups to have their agenda issues resolved at the state level, rather than in the many diverse districts throughout the state.[11]

Finally, a variety of conditions have encouraged state actors to pursue a more vigorous role in the educational policy arena than they have in the past. In many states, consolidation efforts have permitted states to reach local districts more effectively (Strang, 1987). There has also been a dramatic increase in the capacity of state governments to engage in educational issues: "legislative reapportionment and the professionalization of legislative and state department staff have given state agencies the political legitimacy and technical capacity to pursue policy leadership" (Association for Supervision and Curriculum Development, 1986, p. 14). This professionalization has been facilitated by a large influx of federal dollars to state education agencies (Coombs, 1987). In addition, the growing acceptance of two positions has kindled state interest in educational matters. The first is the belief that there is a body of research on school effects showing that school quality can be influenced by policy[12] (Doyle & Hartle, 1985; Murphy & Hallinger, 1984). The other is the re-emergence of faith in the connection between education and the economic well-being of the states, at a time when many of them find themselves in financial jeopardy and when they are being asked more and more by the federal government to solve their own problems. Finally, states have had both a historical interest in equity and a responsibility for developing redistributive policies in order to ensure equity across district boundaries (Musgrave & Musgrave, 1976). As the definition of equity has changed over time (see Murphy & Hallinger, 1989; Murphy, 1988)—from access to schooling, to access to financial resources, to access to conditions of learning[13]— pressures have increased on the states, both to expand their level of involvement in education and to direct more attention to technical core issues historically left to local school districts.

REFORM CONTENT

The educational reform movement of the late 1980s looks significantly different from the reform agenda of the early and middle 1980s. Important differences affect the areas charted for change as well as the methods deemed most appropriate to ensure improvement. Therefore, in this section we discuss the content of educational reform for each of what we see as three distinct waves of improvement efforts. We organize that analysis around the following seven dimensions (see Table 1-2): metaphor, philosophy, assumptions, change model, policy mechanisms, focus, and areas of emphasis.

Table 1-2

Comparing the Different Waves of Educational Reform in the 1980s

	Wave 1	Wave 2	Wave 3
Metaphor	Fix the old clunker (repair)	Get a new car (restructure)	Rethink view of transportation (redesign)
Philosophy	Expand centralized controls	Empower professionals and parents	Empower students
Assumptions	Problems traceable to low standards for workers and low quality of production tools	Problems traceable to systems failure	Problems traceable to fragmented, uncoordinated approaches for taking care of children
Change model	Top-down (bureaucratic model)	Bottom up (market model); lateral (professional model)	Interorganizational (interprofessional model)
Policy mechanisms	Prescription (rule making and incentives); performance measurement	Power distribution	
Focus	The system; incremental improvement	The people (professionals and parents); radical change	The child; revolutionary change
Areas	Specific pieces of quantitative requirements—standards	Governance and work structures	Delivery structure

Wave 1 (1982–1985)

If we choose our metaphors in this section from the vernacular of transportation, "Fix the old clunker" would aptly describe the first wave of educational reform. We have already traced the connections between calls for change and the reported failure of schools to produce the work force needed to maintain America's competitive economic edge. The philosophical infrastructure of early suggestions to repair this situation was highly mechanistic, being comprised mainly of centralized controls and standards (Boyd, 1987):

> The major response of the 1980s is to emphasize the supervision and control of internal processes. Present reform efforts are characterized by a tightening of the organization and an increased supervision and evaluation for both teachers and students. (Sedlak et al., 1986, p. 175)

This approach assumes that the conditions of schooling contributing to poor student outcome measures are attributable to the poor quality of the workers and to the inadequacy of their tools, and that they are subject to revision through mandated, top-down initiatives—especially those from the state. Using the bureaucratic model to institute improvement proposals led in turn to the emphasis in early reform efforts on policy mechanisms such as prescriptions, tightly specified resource allocations, and performance measurements that focused on repairing components of the system (such as writing better textbooks) and raising the quality of the work force by telling employees how to work—for example, specifying instructional models (see Coombs, 1987; Hawley, 1988; Underwood, 1989). A dizzying array of reform initiatives were discussed in reform reports and studies and subsequently passed into law by the various states (see Table 1-3).[14]

Table 1-3
Initiatives from the First Wave of Educational Reform

Teachers and Teaching

- Salaries—establishing or raising minimums
- Career advancement
  - · Merit pay
  - · Career ladders
  - · Supervision of beginning teachers
- Recruitment
  - · Higher standards
  - · Scholarships and loans (general, minorities and women, critical subject areas)
  - · Special progrms in high schools
- Preparation
  - · Degree structure (liberal arts degree)
  - · Clinical training
  - · Changes in coursework

(continued)

Table 1-3 *(continued)*
Initiatives from the First Wave of Educational Reform

- Testing and certification
  - · Entry tests for degree programs
  - · Exit tests for degree programs
  - · Certification test for beginning teachers
  - · Certification test for veteran teachers
  - · Alternative certification
- Beginning teacher induction
- Professional development and continuing education
  - · Peer visits
  - · Staff development plans
  - · Sabbaticals
  - · Fellowships and summer employment
  - · Teaching methods
  - · Evaluation

Curriculum

- Increased requirements for graduation
- Core curriculum
- Greater academic focus
- More sequenced coursework
- Higher-order skills
- Citizenship component
- Computer and technology courses
- Better textbooks

Time

- Longer school year
- Longer school day
- Better use of time
- Increased student attendance

Monitoring, Testing, and Accountability

- Evaluation of staff (principals and teachers)
- Promotion and retention standards for students
- School report cards
- Educational bankruptcy programs
- School improvement incentives and awards
- State-centered student testing programs
- State-centered testing program for professionals

New Programs

- Gifted students
- At-risk students

Table 1-3 *(continued)*
Initiatives from the First Wave of Educational Reform

· Alternative programs
· Recapture programs
· Substance abuse
· Early identification of students with problems
· Teenage parents

Extended Concepts

• Exemplary practice schools (key schools)
• Demonstration schools
• Clinical schools
• Curriculum research and development centers
• School-university partnership

Wave 2 (1986–1989)

No sooner had the ink dried on these early reform measures than they came under attack. A wide variety of scholars and practitioners found the entire fabric of the Wave 1 reform agenda to be wanting (see, for example, Boyd, 1987; Chubb, 1988; Cuban, 1984; Sedlak et al., 1986; Sizer, 1984):

> The first wave of reform has broken over the nations' public schools, leaving a residue of incremental changes and an outmoded educational structure still firmly in place. (Kearns, 1988b, p. 32)

> I don't think we've gotten to the heart of the problem. We're still talking about testing everybody and putting the screws on the existing system even more. The problem is the existing system. And until we face up to that unpleasant fact—that the existing system has to change—we're not going to get the kinds of changes that everybody wants. (Sizer, in Olson, 1988, p. 21)

Finding the earlier suggestions inadequate at best and wrongheaded at worst, reformers clamored for fundamental revisions in the way schools were organzied and governed:

> If we accept the existence of standard practices, and see their resilience as a symptom of organizational failure, then solutions seem to lie in fundamentally changing the organizational form of schools, the characteristics of the people who work in them, and the incentives under which they work. (Elmore, 1987, p. 66)

> The task before us is the restructuring of our entire public education system. I don't mean tinkering. I don't mean piecemeal changes or even well-intentioned reforms. I mean the total restructuring of our schools. (Kearns, 1988b, p. 32)

Using the metaphor of transportation once more, the label for the second wave of reform is "Get a new car." Reformers in this group believe that continued repairs of the old system are not only unlikely to get us to our desired destination but may actually be counterproductive:

> We are doing better on the old goals, often at the expense of making progress on the goals that count the most. Because we have defined the problem of the schools in terms of decline from earlier standards, we have unwittingly chosen to face backwards when it is essential that we face forward. (Carnegie Forum on Education and the Economy, 1986, pp. 15, 20)

> As current standards-raising proposals were compiled and analyzed, it became clear that none addressed the element of the high school program which we had identified previously as the critical component in academic learning, the bargain struck between students and educators. Indeed, our conclusion is that in many instances the proposed reforms have not only failed to address the bargain, but may also in fact exacerbate its current consequences. (Sedlak et al., 1986, p. xi)

These reformers called for a major overhaul—a restructuring—of the current educational system:

> Much of the rhetoric of the recent education reform movement has been couched in the language of decline, suggesting that standards have slipped, that the education system has grown lax and needs to return to some earlier performance standard to succeed. Our view is very different. We do not believe the educational system needs repairing; we believe it must be rebuilt to match the drastic change needed in our economy if we are to prepare our children for productive lives in the 21st century. (Carnegie Forum on Education and the Economy, 1986, p. 14)

The major philosophical foundation of Wave 2 reformers is that educational improvement is contingent on empowering teachers to work more effectively with students (Carnegie Forum on Education and the Economy, 1986; Holmes Group, 1986). A less well-ingrained but still persistent theme is that real change also depends on empowering parents (Chubb, 1988; Kearns, 1988a, 1988b). The major policy mechanism employed in Wave 2 reforms has been "power distribution"—a perspective that

> assume[s] that schools can be improved by distributing political power among the various groups who have legitimate interests in the nature and quality of educational services. Reforms that seek to reallocate power and authority among various stakeholders are based on the belief that when power is in the

right hands, schools will improve. (Association for Supervision and Curriculum Development, 1986, p. 13)

Unlike the strategy employed in the earlier era of reform, this change model is designed to capitalize on the energy and creativity of individuals at the school site level:

Perhaps most importantly, however, the individual school is the focus of the second wave of reform. While previous reports called for leadership, it was generally at the state level; now the cry is for local involvement and reforms that improve what happens in the classroom itself. (Green, 1987, p. 4)

Putting policy changes into effect—actually implementing what the reformers have called for—is a responsibility that will fall on local schools. That is where the leadership must come from if the promise of education reform is to be realized. (Doyle & Hartle, 1985, p. 24)

Underlying almost all second-wave proposals is the assumption that the problems in education can be ascribed to the structure of schooling—"that the highest impediment to progress is the nature of the system itself" (Carnegie Forum on Education and the Economy, 1986, p. 40). The bureaucratic infrastructure of education has been subjected to close scrutiny and has been found to be failing (Clark & Meloy, 1989; Frymier, 1987; Green, 1987; Kearns, 1988a, 1988b; Sedlak et al., 1986; Sizer, 1984):

We are learning, for instance, that deeply ingrained "ways of organizing," often written into statutes and legally binding regulations, are more clearly attributable to educator self interest, prevailing prejudice, and the deeply ingrained mythology of schooling, than to any firm knowledge base. (Erickson, 1979, p. 9)

It is not surprising that the focus of improvement in this era of reform has been on the professionals who populate schools and the conditions they need to work effectively, including basic changes in the organizational arrangements of schooling—a shift from mechanistic, structure-enhancing strategies to a professional approach to reform and from "regulation and compliance monitoring to mobilization of institutional capacity" (Timar & Kirp, 1988, p. 75). Nor is it surprising that reformers who consider the basic structure of schools as the root of education's problems should propose more far-reaching and radical solutions than their predecessors, who believed that the current system could be repaired (Boyd, 1987; Perry, 1988):

We recommend nothing less than a revolution in the role of the teacher and the management of schools in order to upgrade the quality and professionalism of the U.S. teacher work force. (Committee for Economic Development, cited in the Carnegie Forum for Education and the Economy, 1986, p. 36)

Three broad content areas are stressed in Wave 2 reform reports: (1) the professionalization of teaching, (2) the development of decentralized school management systems, and (3) the enactment of specific reform topics overlooked in the early 1980s (such as programs for at-risk students). Strategies to foster greater professionalism within the existing teacher core most often focus on upgrading the quality of the work environment, increasing collegial interaction, and redistributing authority from the administration to the teaching core (see, for example, American Association of Colleges for Teacher Education, 1988; Carnegie Forum on Education and the Economy, 1986; Holmes Group, 1986; National Commission for Excellence in Teacher Education, 1985). A redistribution of authority is also a defining characteristic of the second content area—school-based management. Shifts of power and influence here generally flow in three directions: from district offices to individual school sites;[15] from administrators to teachers; and (sometimes) from professional educators to parents—"empowering teachers and increasing the level of cooperation between schools and community members" (Jennings, 1988, p. 10).[16] Programs to provide parents with greater choice, to "break up the complacent, consumer-insensitive, monopoly relationship that public schools enjoy in relation to most of their clients" (Boyd, 1987, p. 96; see also Kearns, 1988a), are an important component of Wave 2 reforms that are designed to radically change existing organizational structures through site-based governance and control. The third broad content area of Wave 2 reforms are new program thrusts designed to compensate for gaps in Wave 1 proposals. Measures have been developed to promote higher-order thinking and problem-solving skills (Guthrie & Kirst, 1988; Michaels, 1988; Porter, 1988), to treat the needs of at-risk students (Green, 1987; Hawley, 1988), and to address issues of equity (Green, 1987).

Wave 3 (1988–)

The third wave of educational reform began, as did its predecessor, with a critique of reform proposals to date:

There are two general reasons why the current reform agenda is incomplete. First, the proposals that comprise the second wave reforms are encumbered both by an undertow of first wave proposals and assumptions and by stated justifications for significant proposals that are unlikely to gain popular support. Second . . ., the second wave proposals now on the policy agenda fail to address two major problems: (a) the separation of schools and families and (b) the need to develop, beyond the goals policy makers have heretofore owned, the cognitive *capabilities* of our young people. (Hawley, 1988, p. 416)

Because this third wave of educational reform is so new,[17] we know considerably less about it than we do about earlier efforts at change. What we do have are the initial planks of an infrastructure culled from the thinking of a small group of scholars.

Returning to the metaphor of transportation, "Rethink the entire view of transportation" would aptly describe the third wave of reform. Unlike measures in the two earlier eras, those in Wave 3 go beyond schooling to encompass a comprehensive system for the delivery of services to children. Wave 3 reformers speak in terms of "children's policy" (Kirst, 1987; Odden, 1989) rather than of school policies:

> The new report [*Conditions of Children in California*] was conceived after it became increasingly apparent to us that it is insufficient to talk about schools unless we also talk about the environmental factors that surround kids. (Snider, 1989a, p. 10)

These reformers are interested in replacing the uncoordinated and unconnected series of approaches for taking care of children (Olson, 1989) with an integrated interorganizational, interprofessional service model.[18] They envision a major redesign of programs for children with both the family and the school at the hub of the service wheel. Whereas all three eras of reform in the 1980s are concerned with helping children, the primary activities of earlier waves centered on conditions that were believed to lead to improved situations for students—Wave 1 on the educational system and Wave 2 on teachers. The focus in Wave 3 is directly on children. The underlying philosophy is that children should be empowered to contribute successfully to the needs of a rapidly changing society. The current change model is more revolutionary, or transformational (T. D. Deal, December 1988, personal communication), than those of the two preceding eras of reform. Change is both more fundamental and more comprehensive in nature. Finally, the specific areas emphasized in inchoate Wave 3 thinking focus on the structures for the delivery of services to children rather than on the work and governance structures of adults (see Cohen, 1989; Jennings, 1989).

EFFECTS OF THE REFORM MOVEMENT[19]

Trying to sort out the effects of the educational reform movement is difficult business indeed. The number of reform initiatives is overwhelming.

States have selected different strategies to implement similar reforms. Furthermore, the definition of impact (success and failure) is difficult to pin down, because it depends as much on the perspective of the analyst and the time of the observation as on pre-established standards. Still, certain patterns are discernible in the literature on educational reform. By and large, the literature suggests that, based on our understanding of previous attempts at change and because of glaring deficiencies in the strategies underlying current reforms, educational change in the 1980s should have emerged from its cocoon of public discontent, flown briefly and erratically, and departed leaving little noticeable influence on the schooling system. Yet many of the reform initiatives of the 1980s—especially Wave 1 measures—have been successfully implemented on a widespread basis and are having an important influence on the schooling process. In addition, although it is too early to assess the effects of Wave 2 reforms, there is reason to believe that proposals such as school-based management and shared leadership may be more widely implemented than the general literature suggests.

In this section, we analyze what we know about the impact of Wave 1 reform initiatives. We begin with a review of the financial, political, and organizational factors that normally support the position that reform measures are likely to result in few substantive improvements. Next we argue that educational reform reommendations have been surprisingly successful, presenting what we believe are the reasons for this unexpected outcome.

Why the Reform Movement Was Expected to Fail

> A common theme of the literature on educational reform is that these large cycles of reform and reaction have had little effect on the way teachers teach, the way students are expected to learn, and the way knowledge is defined in schools . . . most students of educational reform see these large, glacial changes as masking an enduring continuity in what teachers and students do in classrooms. "Plus ça change, plus c'est la meme chose" [The more things change, the more they stay the same], is carved over the archive of research on school reform. (Elmore, 1987, p. 61)

> In short, state educational reformers [in the 1980s] face an army of skeptics and a consensus—at least among educators and educational researchers—that state education reform "would not work." (Odden & Marsh, Chapter 7 in this book)

Critics of the current reform movement have usually taken one of two paths to arrive at the conclusion that the reforms would not work. A number of analysts have concluded that, because of their top-down nature, initiatives would probably fail to be implemented. Worse, if they were implemented, they would not only fail to produce the outcomes claimed by their developers, but would also lead to many unintended negative consequences (Cuban, 1984; Sedlak et al., 1986). Others maintained that, regardless of whether they were enacted, Wave 1 reform measures would fail because they were limited (Hawley, 1988; Plank, 1987), left current organizational arrangements largely unaltered (Chubb, 1988; Sedlak et al., 1986), and failed to touch the central activity of schooling, the teaching-learning process:

> Not only does it [the standards-raising reform movement] ignore the personal nature of the learning and teaching processes and the power of either party to subvert them toward other ends, but it is also condescending because it implies that not only teaching and learning, but also teachers and learners, can always be manipulated toward predictable ends by altering rather superficial variables. (Sedlak et al., 1986, p. 185)

Financial Arguments. Supporting the positions of scholars in each of these camps are financial, political, and organizational explanations. On the financial front, it was held that insufficient funding (Jordan & McKeown, Chapter 4 in this book; Rossmiller, 1986) would lead to widespread rejection of reform measures. Indeed, some evidence suggests that this has occurred. For example, in 1988 nearly one-quarter of the districts in Illinois took preliminary steps toward initiating a lawsuit claiming that the State Board of Education was powerless to force them to implement mandated but unfunded reform proposals (*Education Week*, 17 February 1988, 11 May 1988). Other states have shifted funds for current reform initiatives from proposals adopted in the early 1980s (Walker, 1988) or simply ignored the knotty problem of where funding for programs would come from (Perry, 1988; Plank, 1987).

Political Arguments. On the political side of the ledger, a host of positions have been developed to suggest why reform measures would miss the mark. Many felt that the absence of a comprehensive approach to change—relying on fragmented, disparate strategies (Timar & Kirp, 1988)—would hinder implementation. Plank (1987, p. 13) pointed out that the process of relying on commission reports to fuel the reform agenda ensured that "little in the way of significant change" would occur.[20] There was also considerable support for the position that inappropriate policy mechanisms—regulations and compliance monitoring—were being used (Chubb, 1988; Timar & Kirp, 1988). In addition, serious doubts were raised about the selection of specific policy tools to address recognized problems; for example, student retention rather than student remediation programs to address the problem of social promotion (Smith & Shepard, 1987). Finally, scholars questioned whether the responses to the problems were too small and too indirect to be effective and whether unexpected consequences might undermine targeted objectives (Cuban, 1984; Peterson, no date; Timar & Kirp, 1988).

Organizational Arguments. The most pervasive rationale for the unlikely success of reform measures has focused on the organizational nature of schools, especially on the ability of highly bureaucratized systems simply to deflect initiatives and to "take shelter from reform by constructing routines" (Elmore, 1987, p. 75; also Timar & Kirp, 1988). This organizational explanation is comprised of a series of interrelated analyses. One of the simplest is that the adults who populate schools have too much to lose from changes and too few incentives to make them. The *intransigence of professionals* would ensure that the reforms produced cosmetic changes at best. Depending on the biases of the particular analyst, board members, administrators, and teachers are all viewed as obstacles to reform:

> Significant gains in student achievement may well require basic changes in the ways schools are governed and organized—in the authority entrusted to them, the objectives imposed upon them, and the professional discretion they are granted. Such changes would, however, threaten the security of political representatives and education administrators whose positions are tied to the existing system and who now hold the reins of school reform . . . their responsibilities would be radically changed and likely reduced under alternative systems of control, whose enactment they have enough political influence to prevent. The reforms that are most promising are therefore the ones least likely to be adopted. (Chubb, 1988, pp. 29–30)

> The Secretary's report reiterates his assault on the "education establishment," and teachers' unions in particular. Mr. Bennett blames the slow progress of reform on "the narrow, self-interested exercise of political power" by "those with a vested interest in the educational status quo." (Olson, 1988, p. 20)

Analysis of *organizational culture* has led others to conclude that the educational reform movement is unlikely to result in significant changes in schools. According to this view, certain deep-rooted or "sacred" norms (Corbett, Firestone, & Rossman, 1987) exist in the general culture of education, such as egalitarianism, professionalism, and teacher autonomy (see Lortie, 1975; Cusick, 1983). Other "sacred" norms are part of the cultures of particular schools (see Corbett, Firestone, & Rossman, 1987). Reform initiatives that conflict with these deep-seated macro- and micro-level values are attacked and neutralized in much the same way transplanted organs are rejected by the body. Shepard and Kreitzer (1987) have provided us with a good example of this conflict—between the control-oriented philosophy of the Texas Teacher Test for practicing teachers and the enduring value of teacher professionalism. Malen and Hart (1987) have also painted a portrait of this tension—between the merit-oriented, state-initiated career ladder program in Utah and the "sacred" values of teacher autonomy and egalitarianism:

> With rare exception, a proposal aimed at differentiating salaries, creating hierarchical positions, and generating opportunities for ongoing professional growth and career advancement has produced an egalitarian distribution of benefits, minimal staff differentiation, and support for familiar work patterns. (Malen & Hart, 1987, p. 1)

Teachers simply readjusted and reinterpreted reform measures to be "more congruent with cherished norms and established practices" (Malen & Hart, 1987, p. 35).

A third organizational explanation that predicts only marginal impact of reform measures is based on our understanding of the *institutional character* of schools. Goffman (1969) and others have shown that the institutional aspect of schooling—the fact that "public schools are expected to provide universal access, daytime custody, and education to large numbers of students who are, for the most part, required or expected to attend school regardless of their interest or aptitude for academic learning" (Elmore, 1987, p. 63)—results in the need to batch-process students. These requirements imposed on schools almost guarantee that standard institutional routines—large groups of students performing similar activities at the same time—will control school operations. Reforms that threaten these routines (for example, class periods of varying length) have very little chance of being successfully incorporated into schools. Without fundamental reconfigurations of institutional patterns, isolated efforts at reform simply cannot be grafted successfully into schools.

Analyses of the *bureaucratic nature* of school organizations are also employed to explain how educational reforms are likely to be deflected.[21] The portrait of the school as a failed public monopoly is central to this line of explanation (see Kearns, 1988a, 1988b). Downs (1967) has shown how bureaucracies can evolve into organizations that displace system and client goals with strategies designed to enhance the welfare of the work force. Since the monopoly nature of schools provides few incentives to change, reform initiatives (such as full-year school programs) that clash with the operant goals—maintaining the self-serving routines of employees—are rejected out of hand with little consideration of their potential impact on official organizational goals. In the words of Kearns (1988b, p. 32), "results are sacrificed to bureaucratic convenience."

The most widely cited organization rationale for the expected failure of the educational reform movement of the early 1980s draws on our understanding of schools as *loosely linked systems*. Research on change and improvement efforts as well as information about the success of reform measures in earlier periods of this century caused many to conclude that top-down reforms, especially regulatory ones, did not produce much improvement in the past and were unlikely to do so now (see Odden & Marsh, Chapter 7 in this book, for a review; also Combs, 1988; Cuban, 1984; Sedlak et al., 1986). The fundamental building block of this position is that top-down reform is inconsistent with basic structural conditions in schools; that is, loose coupling. Without tight connections among components of the organization, top-down change strategies that are not consistent with the predilections of personnel in those units, or that are not predicated on their goodwill and support, can simply be ignored or implemented in form only:

> Both types of reform—the menancing and the benign—look much the same from inside a school. They look like someone else's ideas about what a school should be. Life in schools becomes an attempt simply to maintain a predictable existence in the face of periodic external disturbances. (Elmore, 1987, p. 75)

Because, as noted earlier, exactly this state-directed, regulatory approach has characterized Wave 1 reforms, many critics have afforded them little chance of success.

In fact, some analysts have concluded that reforms—no matter how meritorious—will yield meager returns because they are built on and reinforce existing organizational arrangements. They criticize the reforms for failing to acknowledge that the structure itself is, to a large extent, the cause of the problem. Thus, they claim that these types of efforts to foster improvements are, by definition, more likely to lead to harm than good:

> Interest groups and elected officials have responded to the crisis in education by proposing reform packages that give the appearance of comprehensive, in-depth reform. When disaggregated, however, their common parts, as they affect the critical aspects of teaching, become too little and even potentially damaging. (Sedlak et al., 1986, p. 152)

> I don't think we've gotten to the heart of the problem yet. We're still talking about testing everybody and putting the screws on the existing system even more. The problem is the existing system. And until we face up to that unpleasant fact—that the existing system has to change—we're not going to get the kinds of changes that everybody wants. (Sizer, in Olson, 1988, p. 20)

Why the Reform Movement May Succeed

The most appropriate standards would be the specific recommendations included in *A Nation at Risk*. If progress were assessed on these terms, the reform effort would receive relatively high marks.

Alternative standards would be the individual philosophies of such major public figures as U.S. Secretary of Education William J. Bennett, or the advocates of a second wave reform to follow *A Nation at Risk*, commonly described as "restructuring" or "teacher professionalism." By these standards, the reforms would fall far short of the stated objectives. (Kirst, 1988, p. 40)

Our analysis leads us to a conclusion similar to Kirst's. To a large extent—to a much larger extent than most analysts anticipated—proposals called for in early reform reports have been enacted and successfully implemented. In addition, indicators show that some of these state-initiated structures have produced meaningful changes in schools and districts. More importantly, available data support the contention that reforms, both individually and collectively, are connected to improvement in measures of student performance.[22] There is, of course, no doubt that some Wave 1 reform proposals were probably better left unenacted, and that the implementation of others has been far from successful. We do not deny that people using other criteria to evaluate impact may reach different conclusions. Nor do we claim that different criteria (such as redistributing authority to teachers and parents) may not provide more appropriate measures of reform success or failure in the future. Yet, given these caveats, the evidence does suggest that educational reform in the 1980s is working. We also argue that rather than inhibiting second- and third-wave reform as many critics have argued, the Wave 1 reform agenda is an essential stage in the path to a comprehensive, fundamental reform of U.S. public education.[23] We attempt to account for these unanticipated results in the following analysis.

Consistency with School Operations and Processes Linked to Achievement. One reason why many reform initiatives have been successful is that they built improvement efforts on existing organizational structures—in the words of Goodlad (1984), they were designed to improve the schools we have. Although critics view this as a serious problem, we maintain that the yields provided by the early reform agenda are partially attributable to the fact that they did not call for major upheaval of current operations (see Plank, 1987). They emphasized quantitative increases in areas such as curriculum requirements and time for learning. Improvements were not predicated on dramatic changes in the quality of people employed in schools nor on the ways they worked or the task structures under which they operated.[24]

After studying all the analyses of the problems in these early reform proposals, it is easy to lose sight of one of the most important factors behind their successful implementation and subsequent effects on students: they were primarily directed to the conditions of schooling that have been shown by research to help explain student learning. For the first time in memory, calls from scholars in organizational theory (Erickson, 1979) and educational policy (Boyd, 1983) to direct policy tools to educational effects were being heeded. Problems with standards-raising, regulatory approaches to change notwithstanding, opportunity to learn (time plus content covered) remains the most powerful predictor of student learning.[25] Whether done in the most appropriate manner or not, or formed with the best available policy tool or not, the reform agenda could not help but bring about some meaningful improvement by its redirection of attention, resources, and energy toward important conditions of learning.

Consistent with the line of analysis presented so far, we argue that the reform agenda has been successful because it has tightened organizational linkages in existing school structures, especially those dealing with curriculum and instruction. It has recoupled the various actors in education around the core mission of schooling. Although we agree with critics who maintain that there are other (perhaps even more appropriate) methods to strengthen organizational linkages (see, for example, Firestone & Wilson, 1985a) and that there are inherent problems in emphasizing bureaucratic couplings (see, for example, Sizer, 1984), we believe that many of these observers have, in their analyses of the methods and tools employed, overlooked the significance of the recoupling itself. We also argue that these linkages are the key to unlocking more fundamental types (Wave 2 and Wave 3) of educational change.

Conditions for success also appear to be more prevalent in the current as opposed to earlier eras of reform. We already noted the widespread support for reform. More importantly, to a large extent, the directions in which current reformers were pushing schools were quite consistent with where many schools and districts preferred to go and with paths on which many of them had already embarked:

> Thus, education reform, while state initiated, nevertheless reinforced and bolstered—in the main—substantive foci on which local educators were already working. While there obviously were several differences between local foci on curriculum and instruction and state initiatives, the fact remains that both levels of government targeted the same issue for action. (Odden & Marsh, Chapter 7 in this book)

Recipe for Failure Predicated on Inadequate Understanding of the Evolution of School Organizations. Analysts who believed that state-initiated, top-down reform would fail overlooked important changes in the organizational structure of schools that rendered them much more receptive to rationalistic, mandated change than in the past (see Murphy, Hallinger, & Mesa, 1985). They formulated judgments on a set of conditions that no longer dominated the decision model. In short, schools were becoming more tightly linked in the 1970s and 1980s. The defining characteristics of loosely coupled systems were less stark than before.[26] Not only was our knowledge of the educational production function solidifying for the first time in history, but also schools were acting as if they understood how to improve the teaching-learning process. Although subjected to vigorous criticism in both the academic and practitioner communities, tightly defined and uniform teaching models were being widely implemented in school systems throughout the United States.[27] For the first time in memory, curriculum was being specified *and* used to shape classroom instruction. Widespread implementation of programs designed to align curriculum objectives, instructional materials and strategies, and assessment tools helped lend a sense of surety to the technology of schooling—curricular and instructional validity became meaningful terms for practitioners. At the same time, the goals or purposes of schooling were narrowing,[28] becoming clearer and more tightly linked to academics.[29] Educators were beginning to talk about doing one task well rather than a host of activities in a mediocre fashion. Notions of measurement and accountability were being seriously discussed.[30] A focus on student outcomes, both in terms of quality and equity, became the defining characteristic of the widely accepted "effective schools" movement. Tests were no longer simply sources of information to file in students' cumulative folders but suppliers of data about the effectiveness of teachers, administrators, and schools.

The important point here is that the changing nature of the organization of schools greatly enhanced the potential for successfully implementing top-down reform strategies. Information about the inappropriateness of top-down change and the need for buy-in, ownership, and bottom-up strategies was derived from studies of reform and improvement in loosely linked schools. Under the conditions that characterize loosely coupled organizations, regulatory approaches are poor mechanisms to infuse reform throughout a system. Goodwill and personal ownership are essential prerequisites for change in these situations. Loose coupling, however, was not nearly so dominant a part of the fabric of school organizations in the 1980s as it had been when earlier mandated change strategies were found to have produced so limited an array of effects. Many critics who argued that reform would fail missed this important evolution in school organizational structure. They predicted an effect from a set of conditions that were no longer operant.

Claims for Failure Based on Limited Views of Policy Tools. Not only did critics base their arguments on organizational propositions that, at least to some extent, were incongruent with school systems in the 1980s, but they also drew lessons about implementation from types of policies different from those being employed in the current reform movement. According to Odden and Marsh (see Chapter 7), data supporting the "no effect" school of thought were drawn from implementation studies on "redistributive policies"—those that "require local educators to focus on issues to which they had not been giving sufficient attention." Because these policies require school people to do things differently, allocate important resources in new ways, and often challenge fundamental values and deeply ingrained work patterns, it is nearly impossible to expect them to be implemented successfully in the absence of strong local support. And this, of course, is exactly what was found in earlier studies on school reform and improvement. However, Odden and Marsh correctly note that redistributive policies were not the primary mechanisms dominating the reform agenda of the 1980s. Because the current reform agenda focused on "developmental policies"—"initiatives in areas in which local governments (school districts in the case of education) are already involved" (Chapter 7)—top-down changes were much more likely to be implemented successfully than in earlier eras when redistributive policies were emphasized. Many critics who predicted that the movement of the 1980s would fail, largely missed this point:

> At least in part because of this redirective nature, redistributive programs have a much more contentious implementation process and take longer to "put into place." Since most of the "conventional wisdom" about education policy implementation was drawn from research on the early years of redistributive policy implementation, when local resistance was strongest, it was inappropriate to apply it to the more developmental education reform initiatives. (Odden & Marsh, Chapter 7 in this book)

Failure as an Artifact of the Definition of Success. The belief that the reform agenda would fail grew to a certain degree from the employment of inappropriate measures of success and faulty timelines for assessment. Critics ignored important aspects of the same organizational literature (such as schools as loosely linked systems) from which they constructed the funeral pyre for educational reform. We know from the work of such scholars as Meyer and Rowan (1975) that the "rational" response of a decoupled organization in trouble is to create new, more legitimate categories (such as competency tests for teachers) to replace discredited ones (such as teacher credentialing), without undue concern for whether the new categories increase anything but acceptance of the legitimacy of the categories themselves.[31] Consistency for those who employ loose linkages as an explanation for the probable failure of Wave 1 reform initiatives would suggest that the passage of reform measures themselves is an important criterion of success, regardless of whether changes occur in schools and classrooms. Yet few of the critics seem to be willing to define reform success in this manner. Furthermore, they adopt highly rational lenses to scrutinize the reform agenda, even as they discredit the power and usefulness of rational models to explain organizational phenomena. Definitions of success look quite different depending on the perspective from which activities are examined. What would pass for success using a bargaining or a cultural model would most likely be seen as only a partial success, at best, from a structural-functional frame of reference. Critics grounded in nonrational perspectives of organizations have, by and large, not analyzed the actual or potential impact of the reform agenda in a manner consistent with their primary orientations—they have emphasized instrumental analysis to the near exclusion of other frameworks for assessment.

To make matters worse, analysts often select instrumental criteria more on the basis of personal values than on the basis of the inherent structure of the reforms. For example, critics are apt to label the reform agenda a failure because it has not improved students' higher-order thinking skills as measured on various tests. The problem here is that the criterion selected to define success—increased scores on tests measuring higher-order thinking skills—although rational and instrumental, is not only decoupled from the instrumentality of the reform, but also overlooks important evidence that the intent of reform initiatives—increased scores on tests of basic skills—is being realized (Snider, 1989b). It is not surprising that reform proposals should be judged inadequate if only very narrow instrumental conceptions of success—and ones that are often decoupled from reform intent—are employed.

Finally, it is important to remember that many critics use a very short time perspective when evaluating reform efforts, thereby overlooking the importance of successive approximation in the process of achieving more fundamental changes. For example, a number of observers have lamented the fact that reform policies in the area of testing are failing because they have focused interest on those matters of schooling that are of least importance (that is, basic skills). In addition to serving as a textbook example of replacing personal values for reform intent, such assessments generally ignore the important role Wave 1 policies in the area of testing have played in focusing attention on outcome measures in general. They also fail to realize that the types of tests they prefer are much more likely to become a reality in the future because these initial policy tools were enacted, implemented, and debated.

Predictions of Failure Neglecting Shifts in Values. We have asserted that analysts who predicted little or no effect from Wave 1 reform measures missed the target because they misdiagnosed the context in which the reform agenda was enacted. They also failed to take into account two important shifts—in the organizational structure of schools and in the type of policy tool emphasized—that made top-down change more likely to succeed than in the past. Finally, we argued that the definitions critics used to reach their conclusions were flawed, in terms of both (1) fidelity to the predominant models of analysis they championed and (2) consistency with the intents of the reform agenda itself. Although our analysis of this last point is somewhat less firm than that of the other points made so far, we believe that predictions of "no effect" may have missed subtle shifts, possibly portending significant changes, in the fundamental values underlying schooling and teaching. For example, while egalitarian aspects of reform initiatives have not fared particularly well, they are receiving more attention and being implemented on a larger scale than our earlier treatment of values would suggest. The same can be said about other measures that differentiate schools and teachers, for example, parental choice. It may be that Wave 1 reforms have been enacted at a time when, even though they run counter to extant values of education, they are consistent with an incipient metamorphosis of those values.[32]

ISSUES FOR FURTHER EXPLORATION

In this final section of the chapter, we outline a number of reform issues that require further exploration. The topics examined are designed to identify (1) matters that have received insufficient attention to date as well as (2) logical avenues for future research on educational reform.

Cost Information

Treatments of the costs of educational reform measures have been inadequate. Ginsberg and Wimpelberg (1987, p. 358) concluded that "little, if any, attention is paid to the financial or procedural requirements for putting [educational commission] recommendations into practice." Even when expenditures are clearly specified,[33] they usually do not include opportunity costs. In the absence of data on the real costs of educational programs, policymakers are ill informed, and educators and students are ill served. Shepard and Kreitzer (1987) found, for example, that the actual public costs to develop and deliver the Texas Examination of Current Administrators and Teachers (TECAT)—to assess the skills of licensed teachers—were ten times ($35.6 million) greater than the direct costs ($3.0 million) included in the official state reports. In addition, the test resulted in more than $42 million in private costs, including materials and supplies and projected wages for preparation time. In their summary on the issue of costs, Shepard and Kreitzer (1987, p. 29) reported,

> A one-time test for practicing teachers was considered to be one of the cheapest of all the likely reforms. Data on the real public costs of TECAT indicate that it was an expense more on the order of a programmatic intervention.

Their analysis of the private costs of this test reinforces a point made by others—the need to examine the less obvious costs of reform measures. For example, one of the most popular reform proposals is to increase the amount of homework assigned to students (see Murphy & Decker, 1989, for a review). Although such proposals generally require no outlay of funds, Epstein and Pinkow (1988, p. 4) remind us that real costs are associated with homework:

> Even "time" has greater subtleties. For example, homework is a "cost-less" resource, but it is not a "cost-free" resource. It "costs" teachers when they use planning time, class time, or personal time to prepare, explain, correct, comment on, return, and review homework assignments. Too much homework or inappropriate homework "costs" students if it is boring, frustrating, or repetitive of skills already well mastered. It may limit time spent on other useful activities, such as the development of skills and talents that the school does not or cannot teach. If homework is just busywork, both teachers and students have wasted their time.

Cost-Benefit (Effectiveness) Information

If information on the costs of reform initiatives is limited and somewhat misleading, data to compare the cost-benefits of different reform measures are conspicuous by their absence (Levin, 1988).[34] Our concern here is twofold. First, because the amount of money that state legislatures have supplied to date and are projected to provide in the future for reform programs is limited (see Jordan & McKeown, Chapter 4, in this book), it is important to understand the benefits of investing public funds in differing reform strategies. Without this information, it is difficult for policymakers to make appropriate decisions (Levin, 1984, 1988). Second, the welfare gains (benefits) *and* the welfare losses (costs) that accompany forced collective consumption of government services (such as a mandated curriculum for all students, a statewide salary schedule for teachers) should be considered (see Oates, 1972). For example, the benefits of mandating a statewide testing program in terms of increased student achievement may be offset by the costs in terms of teacher commitment and the richness of the curricular experiences that students would lose (Coombs, 1987; Wilson & Corbett, Chapter 10 in this book; Cuban, 1984):[35]

> But new policies and programs that require service delivery personnel to abandon familiar and comfortable routines to benefit someone else also are redistributive, even if only psychic costs are involved. When there is a unilateral imposition of costs on semiprofessionals they also experience a loss in autonomy and self-respect on top of other costs. Moreover, much more may be at stake than just psychic costs and the violation of the "psychological contract" (Schein, 1965) with the employer. Employees may well feel they are being deprived of a real "property right" they have in their job. (Boyd, 1987, p. 92)

Intergovernmental Relations

Throughout this chapter, we have discussed shifts in activities among the various levels of government. We reported on the decline in the federal role in education. More importantly, we noted the major increase in state activity in educational policymaking, governance, and control. The result has been that the "relationships among the various levels of school governance have grown more complex in recent years, and the boundaries between these levels have become less distinct" (Guthrie & Kirst, 1988, p. 54). Yet the changes in intergovernmental relations resulting from the educational reform movement of the 1980s have received little empirical attention. Only in the last three years have analyses been conducted of reform measures across governmental layers. Examinations of the changes these initiatives have fostered in the macro-level context of intergovernmental relations are more rare. Analyses of the effects of these altered relationships are even scarcer. However, hypotheses for investigation are beginning to be developed. For example, Coombs (1987, p. 8) has argued that the new alignment in governmental arrangements may lead to a diminution in financial and political support for public education:

> The proximity effect creates a more favorable basis of support for public schools within the local political arena than is likely to endure at the state or national levels. Should the funding of public education and decisions with respect to public schools be absorbed into the state political arena, the continued support of citizens may waver.

Coombs has noted another potential welfare loss associated with state-mandated educational systems—the alienation of parents in affluent districts and the privatization of schooling (see also Boyd, 1987). Thus, the move to greater state control in education may contribute to the evolution of a dual-class educational system in our country—one for the poor and one for the rich.[36] Others have suggested that this fundamental shift in governmental responsibilities may significantly reduce the representative nature of educational decision making (Guthrie & Kirst, 1988); foster the perpetuation of school bureaucracy (Strang, 1987); increase uncertainty and instability (Guthrie & Kirst, 1988) and frustration (Coombs, 1987) in local schooling operations; and discourage systematic planning on the part of school officials (Guthrie & Kirst, 1988). These and other matters concerning the changed relationship between governmental units clearly need much more analysis than they have received to date.

Issues Affecting the Unfolding of Reform Proposals

A host of factors interact with and influence the implementation of reform measures. School improvement literature leads us to believe that two of these issues need considerable exploration. To begin with, little attention has been paid to the contexts within which reforms are implemented. An initiative in California is transported to Tennessee with little consideration for the unique educational environments of the two states. More importantly, varying district and school contexts have generally been ignored in the policymaking processes of the current reform movement. All schools are treated the same, and policies are assumed to have identical effects everywhere. Willower (1987, p. 16) has cautioned us about this approach:

> In the politics of education different policies to resolve similar problems could have similar results just as similar policies could have different outcomes depending on the contingencies involved which are seen as a key to exploration.

More investigators also need to study the effects of simultaneous implementation of multiple reform measures (Guthrie & Kirst, 1988; Odden & Marsh, 1988).[37] Colvin (1987, p. 7) has captured the issues of the situation nicely:

> The state-generated reforms of the 1980s have an interactive effect that is comparable to giving dozens of medicines at once. Doctors cannot always predict how a battery of chemicals will affect the body as they become coefficients of change in a complex psychological equation. The equation for educational remedies now confronting schools and a growing number of researchers are as complicated.

Conflicting Perspectives

The first two waves of educational reform in the 1980s seem, on the surface, to have adopted diametrically opposed perspectives—the bureaucratic, mechanistic, top-down approach of Wave 1 versus the professional, bottom-up strategy of Wave 2 (Boyd & Hartman, 1987). Most of the analysis of this issue has focused on the incompatibility of these two perspectives and, depending on one's beliefs and values, the inability of one or the other approach to promote real educational improvement. The usefulness of this type of analysis is limited, however. More thoughtful attempts are needed to show how these different philosophies and strategies can be combined to draw on the best of both while limiting the negative dimensions of each. Important work on this area has been initiated by Boyd (1987); Firestone and Wilson (1985b); McLaughlin (1987); Murphy, Hallinger, and Mesa (1985); and Timar and Kirp (1988). Porter's thinking is especially enlightening:

> The challenge to external standard setting activities is to set standards which guarantee good teaching of worthwhile content to all students. To do this will require standard setting activities which somehow preserve (or strengthen) the responsibility that teachers and students accept together for student learning. One way to do this might be to shift external standard setting away from reliance on rewards and sanctions (power) and toward reliance on authority. External standard setting activities would become matters of persuasion, not issues of compliance.
>
> Simply telling teachers what to do is not likely to have the desired results. Neither is leaving teachers alone to pursue their own predilections. A productive middle ground might be to seriously involve teachers in the business of setting standards for student achievement. The result would still be external standards set at state and/or district levels (or perhaps even nationally, as may be done by the National Board of Professional Teacher Standards). Through the process of teacher representative participation in these external standard setting activities, the standards would take on authority. Teachers would become involved in the task of telling teachers what to do. Rosenholtz (1987) refers to this approach as delegated authority and Benne (1986) calls it anthropological authority. (Porter, 1988, pp. 22–23)

More scholars should begin to investigate how loose *and* tight organizational linkages, pressure *and* support, and autonomy *and* direction support successful implementation of reform initiatives.

Conflicts over Power and Authority

One common thread running through the entire fabric of the reform movement of the 1980s is the redistribution of authority. The only consistent theme in reports on this topic is that district offices will (and should) lose power. Depending on the particular report, one or more of the other actors in the schooling process—states, teachers, administrators, parents—should be granted more authority over educational issues. These recommendations are often contradictory, sometimes self-serving (see, for example, Holmes Group, 1986), and almost never grounded on a knowledge base sufficiently strong to support the proposals. What is needed here is less advocacy and more analysis. As with the issue of professionalization and bureaucracy, it is probable that the best work in this area will examine various (seemingly contradictory) ways that authority and influence can be shared, especially among professionals and between professionals and parents.

Data Bases

These reforming tests . . . are not well understood by either measurement specialists or policy makers. Laws to create these tests are passed based on beliefs about their effects; opponents have different beliefs but no more compelling evidence. (Shepard & Kreitzer, 1987, p. 22)

The information base on which the educational reform agenda rests must be strengthened (Ellwein, Glass, & Smith, 1988). As Shepard and Kreitzer (1987) reported earlier, large amounts of money have been invested in reform measures simply on the basis of beliefs and hunches. We have already noted the less than adequate specification of cost data and the virtual absence of information on the benefits of reform proposals. Equally important, our ability to learn from early reform measures and to make more informed decisions about the shape of the agenda for the future is being severely compromised by the "pathetically small" amount of money states are spending to assess the effects of their reform initiatives (Kirst, 1987, p. 163).[38] There is a great need for additional money to fuel data collection activities designed to more effectively inform the educational reform policy development process.

NOTES

1. These time periods are estimates and are consistent with prevailing thought (see, for example, Green, 1987; Plank & Ginsberg, Chapter 5 in this book). Reform

waves in the 1980s are, however, defined more by their assumptions, policy mechanisms, and change models than by their date of publication (see Table 1-2).

2. Note that one unique aspect of the current era of reform is the extent to which it is being studied, especially during the policy development and implementation phases of improvement efforts. It is possible that some of the unique aspects discussed in this section may result as much from this intensive analysis as from actual differences with less thoroughly analyzed reform eras.

3. See Haenn and Houser (1988) for a methodology to track educational reform; Mitchell (1984) for a taxonomy of major topics in education policy research; and Mitchell and Encarnation (1984) for a framework on state policy mechanisms for influencing school performance. In addition to the chapters in this book, see Malen and Hart (1987) and Shepard and Kreitzer (1987) for elegant treatments of specific reform initiatives.

4. See Hawley (1985, 1988) for a discussion of the mythological aspects of the current reform debate.

5. The Association for Supervision and Curriculum Development (1986, p. 48) panel on state policy initiatives reminds us that "the link between education and economics is complex."

6. It is beyond the scope of this chapter to provide indicators of inadequacy in all the areas of schooling discussed in the reform literature. Five works that examine schooling processes in general are particularly useful in providing an overview of these conditions: Boyer (1983); Goodlad (1984); Powell, Farrar, and Cohen (1985); Sedlak et al. (1986); Sizer (1984). In addition, all the commission reports supply examples of poor school quality. Some treat specific topics (for example, school management) while others address a variety of subject areas.

7. It is important to note that many states and districts had already begun work on a variety of the reform proposals contained in these reports before their publication (see Firestone, Chapter 6 in this book).

8. Analysis of resulting changes in intergovernmental relations in response to these shifts in activities has been slow in coming; we discuss this issue in the concluding section of this chapter.

9. See Guthrie and Kirst (1988, pp. 5–7) for one story of the increasing centralization of decision making in education at the state level.

10. The implications of this pattern for the likely success of reform proposals are discussed later in this chapter.

11. Collective bargaining is a good example of this desire of interest groups to resolve issues at the state level.

12. For reviews of the effects research at the classroom level, see Brophy and Good (1986) and Rosenshine (1983); at the school level, see Purkey and Smith (1983a) and Murphy, Weil, Hallinger, and Mitman (1985). The work on the manipulativeness of factors influencing school outcomes was noted early on by such scholars as Bloom (1980) and Erickson (1979). For discussions of the state role in translating effects research into policy initiatives, see Murphy, Hallinger, and Mesa (1985); Murphy, Mesa, and Hallinger (1984); and Purkey and Smith (1983b). For a more general discussion of state policy mechanisms for influencing the quality of schooling, see Mitchell and Encarnation (1984).

13. There is a growing body of research on this third-generation conception of

equity; that is, equity as access to learning opportunities. See, for example, Cicourel and Kitsuse (1963), Eder (1981), Evertson (1982), Goodlad (1984), Hanson and Schutz (1978), Oakes (1985), Page (1984), Schwartz (1981), and Weinstein (1976).

14. For example, the Illinois reform package contained 161 new initiatives (Illinois State Board of Education, 1985); the South Carolina Improvement Act had 61 new or expanded initiatives (Peterson, 1988).

15. Most reformers see a drastic reduction in the role of district offices. For example, Kearns (1988a, p. 567) sees them becoming "service centers—helping schools, instead of dictating to them" (see also Kearns, 1988b; Carnegie Forum on Education and the Economy, 1986).

16. The Schools for the 21st Century Project in Washington is a good example of a site-based management program. Recent changes in Minnesota, Chicago, and the East Baton Rouge Parish School System also provide useful examples of attempts at instituting school-based management programs.

17. The first two major reports of the third wave of reform were released in 1989: the National Governors' Association's *America in Transition: Report of the Task Force on Children* and *Conditions of Children in California* by Policy Analysis for California Education (PACE)—cited in Olson (1989) and Snider (1989a). Also, the National Commission on Children, a congressionally created group charged with developing a set of recommendations on children's policy in a wide variety of areas, began its work in February 1989.

18. The work of L. L. Cunningham and his colleagues at The Ohio State University is perhaps the most advanced exemplar of an interprofessional approach to children's policy. Although it is too early to tell, the shift in focus from the "disciplines" to the "professions" that is embedded in Cunningham's work (1988) may represent a significant change in how we prepare professionals to work with children.

19. This section of the chapter is taken entirely from a paper entitled "Educational Reform in the 1980s: Explaining Some Surprising Success" published in *Educational Evaluation and Policy Analysis*, Fall 1989. Copyright 1989 by the American Educational Research Association. Reprinted by permission of the publisher.

20. Plank's (1987, p. 15) point is that the inclusive process used in the formation of the commissions "limit[s] reform proposals to those that can win the approval of all interested groups, with the consequence that changes in the structure and operation of state educational systems have not been seriously considered."

21. It is also important to note that many reformers in this group turn the discussion around and argue that the professional, not the bureaucratic, nature of schools may account for the failure of reform measures. According to this line of thought, schools are really professional organizations. As such, regulatory reforms are likely to fail because "they are incongruent with teachers' cultivated understandings and deliberate judgments about how to teach" (Elmore, 1987, p. 65).

22. There is also preliminary evidence that at-risk students have not been left behind by Wave 1 reforms, as many observers had anticipated (see Murphy, 1989a, 1989b, for reviews).

23. As a matter of fact, we argue that it would be impossible to implement Wave 2 and Wave 3 agendas without first experiencing the reforms prevalent in earlier proposals. We base this argument on our understanding of reform as an incremental process (see Firestone, Chapter 6 in this book; McLaughlin, 1987; Plank, 1987).

24. Critics have argued that the overall yield available from these types of reforms is not likely to be significant—or at least not as significant as the yield from more fundamental reform initiatives. Although attacks on the likely success of Wave 1 measures are quite well developed, empirical evidence on the yield from more fundamental reforms is conspicuous by its absence.

25. See Murphy and Hallinger (1989) and Murphy (1989c) for reviews.

26. We are not arguing that the particular types of tightening of organizational linkages discussed in the section are either good or bad, only that they are occurring and that they have important implications for implementing reform initiatives.

27. The widespread implementation of instructional models based on Hunter's work is a good example of this movement.

28. A number of the critics have missed the point on this issue. It is not the reform movement that is leading to a narrowing of the educational agenda, but the narrowing of the educational agenda that is supporting reform proposals.

29. See Goodlad (1984) for another point of view.

30. Accountability was going beyond the development of new categories (such as student proficiency tests) for discredited ones (the high school diploma). Schools and the professionals who populated them were beginning to be assessed on measures of student outcomes.

31. Indeed, evidence shows that some of the reforms may fit this pattern. For example, Ellwein, Glass, and Smith (1988, p. 8) reached the conclusion that "competency tests and standards function as symbolic and political gestures, not as instrumental reforms."

32. If this line of analysis is accurate, it supports one of the basic positions of this chapter: that Wave 1 reforms are an essential first step in the evolution to more fundamental types of educational change. It also suggests that successive approximations of reform trends be given more serious consideration.

33. Jordan and McKeown (Chapter 4 in this book) remind us that cost data can be difficult to ascertain because "reform" has been poorly defined; that is, it is often difficult to determine whether additional funding is for reform or maintenance of current programs (see also Firestone, Chapter 6 in this book). They also caution us that, because of varying fiscal practices, comparing costs among the states can be misleading.

34. John Folger and his colleagues at Vanderbilt are one of the only groups we know that is analyzing the benefits of reform expenditures.

35. For a thorough analysis of the welfare loss associated with teacher tests, see Shepard and Kreitzer (1987).

36. Some evidence suggests that we are already evolving in this direction (Braddock, 1989).

37. In his AERA (American Educational Research Association) presentation to the AERA School Effectiveness special-interest group, Michael Fullan (1987) drew a similar conclusion about the need to study the effects of multiple school improvement initiatives being implemented concurrently.

38. A variety of organizations are attempting to fill the void left by the state in this area (see Pipho, 1988). The most well known and successful is Policy Analysis for California Education (PACE), under the direction of James Guthrie and Michael Kirst. A consortium of these organizations has been developed through the guidance

and direction of Martha McCarthy at Indiana University. Also, a number of the federal laboratories and centers are examining issues related to the reform agenda of the 1980s (see Chapter 10, by Wilson and Corbett, and Chapter 6, by Firestone, in this book).

REFERENCES

American Association of Colleges for Teacher Education. (1988). *School leadership: A preface for action.* Washington, DC: American Association of Colleges for Teacher Education.

Association for Supervision and Curriculum Development. (1986, September). *School reform policy: A call for reason.* Alexandria, VA: Association for Supervision and Curriculum Development.

Bloom, B. S. (1980, February). The new direction in educational research: Alterable variables. *Phi Delta Kappan, 61*(6), 382–385.

Board will defy Illinois mandates. (1989, 17 February). *Education Week, 8*(23).

Boyd, W. L. (1983, March). What school administrators do and don't do: Implications for effective schools. *Canadian Administrator, 22*(6), 1–4.

Boyd, W. L. (1987, Summer). Public education's last hurrah? Schizophrenia, amnesia, and ignorance in school politics. *Educational Evaluation and Policy Analysis, 9*(2), 85–100.

Boyd, W. L., & W. T. Hartman. (1987). The politics of educational productivity. In D. Monk & J. Underwood, eds., *Distributing educational resources within nations, states, school districts, and schools.* Cambridge, MA: Ballinger.

Boyer, E. L. (1983). *High School: A report on secondary education in America.* New York: Harper and Row.

Braddock, D. (1989, 12 February). Education and human development: The future. Presentation made to the faculty of Peabody College, Vanderbilt University.

Brophy, J., & T. L. Good. (1986). Teacher behavior and student achievement. In M. W. Wittrock, ed., *Handbook of research on teaching,* 3rd ed. New York: Macmillan.

Campbell, R. F., L. L. Cunningham, R. O. Nystrand, & M. D. Usdan. (1975). *The organization and control of American schools.* Columbus, OH: Merrill.

Carnegie Forum on Education and the Economy. (1986, May). *A nation prepared: Teachers for the 21st century.* Washington, DC: Carnegie Forum on Education and the Economy.

Carnegie Foundation for the Advancement of Teaching. (1988). *Report card on school reform: The teachers speak.* Princeton, NJ: Carnegie Foundation for the Advancement of Teaching.

Chubb, J. E. (1988, Winter). Why the current wave of school reform will fail. *Public Interest,* No. 90, 28–49.

Cicourel, A. V., & J. I. Kitsuse. (1963). *The educational decisionmakers.* Indianapolis: Bobbs-Merrill.

Clark, D. L., & M. A. Amoit. (1981, December). The impact of the Reagan administration on federal education policy. *Phi Delta Kappan, 63*(4), 259–262.

Clark, D. L., & J. M. Meloy. (1989). Renouncing bureaucracy: A democratic structure for leadership in schools. In T. J. Sergiovanni & J. H. Moore, eds., *Schooling for tomorrow*. Boston: Allyn & Bacon.

Clinton, B. (1987, July). *Speaking of leadership*. Denver: Education Commission of the States.

Cohen, D. L. (1989, 22 February). Virginia Assembly approves child-services agency. *Education Week, 8*(22), 12.

Colvin, R. (1987, August–September). Studying the effects of reform. *Educational Researcher, 16*(6), 7.

Combs, A. W. (1988, February). New assumptions for educational reform. *Educational Leadership, 45*(5), 38–40.

Coombs, F. S. (1987, April). The effects of increased state control on local school district governance. Paper presented at the annual meeting of the American Educational Research Association, Washington, DC.

Corbett, H. D., W. A. Firestone, & G. B. Rossman. 1987, November). Resistance to planned change and the sacred in school cultures. *Educational Administration Quarterly, 23*(4), 36–59.

Cuban, L. (1984, November). School reform by remote control: SB 813 in California. *Phi Delta Kappan, 66*(3), 213–215.

Cunningham, L. L. (1988, October). Discussant comments. Invited symposium of the annual conference of the University Council for Educational Administration, Cincinnati, Ohio.

Cusick, P. (1983). *The egalitarian ideal and the American high school*. New York: Longman.

Downs, A. (1967). *Inside bureaucracy*. Boston: Little, Brown.

Doyle, D. P., & T. W. Hartle. (1985, September). Leadership in education: Governors, legislators, and teachers. *Phi Delta Kappan, 67*(1), 21–27.

Eder, D. (1981, July). Ability grouping as a self-fulfilling prophecy: A microanalysis of teacher-student interaction. *Sociology of Education, 54*(3), 151–162.

Education Commission of the States. (1983). *Action for excellence*. Denver: Education Commission of the States.

Ellwein, M. C., G. V. Glass, & M. L. Smith. (1988, November). Standards of competence: Propositions on the nature of testing reforms. *Educational Researcher, 17*(18), 4–9.

Elmore, R. F. (1987, November). Reform and the culture of authority in schools. *Educational Administration Quarterly, 23*(4), 60–78.

Epstein, J. L., and Pinkow, L. (1988, April). *Homework: U.S. and international studies, issues, and models*. Paper presented at the annual meeting of the American Educational Research Association, New Orleans.

Erickson, D. A. (1979, March). Research on educational administration: The state-of-the-art. *Educational Researcher, 8*, 9–14.

Evertson, C. M. (1982, March). Differences in instructional activities in higher-and-lower-achieving junior high English and math classes. *The Elementary School Journal, 82*(4), 329–50.

Firestone, W. A., & B. L. Wilson. (1985a, Spring). Using bureaucratic and cultural linkages to improve instruction: The principal's contribution. *Educational Administration Quarterly, 21*(2), 7–30.

Firestone, W. A., & B. L. Wilson. (1985b, July). *Management and organizational outcomes: The effects of approach and environment in schools.* Philadelphia: Research for Better Schools, Inc.

Freeman, D. J., R. J. Martin, B. A. Brousseau, & B. West. (1988, April). Do higher program admission standards alter profiles of entering teacher candidates? Paper presented at the annual meeting of the American Educational Research Association, New Orleans.

Frymier, J. (1987, September). Bureaucracy and the neutering of teachers. *Phi Delta Kappan, 69*(1), 9–14.

Fullan, M. (1987, April). An agenda for research on school change. Paper presented at the annual meeting of the American Educational Research Association, Washington, DC.

Ginsberg, R., & R. K. Wimpelberg. (1987, Winter). Educational change by commission: Attempting "trickle down reform." *Educational Evaluation and Policy Analysis, 9*(4), 344–360.

Goffman, E. (1969). The characteristics of total institutions. In A. Etzioni, ed., *A sociological reader on complex organizations.* New York: Holt, Rinehart and Winston.

Goodlad, J. I. (1984). *A place called school: Prospects for the future.* New York: McGraw-Hill.

Green, J. (1987). *The next wave: A synopsis of recent education reform reports.* Denver: Education Commission of the States.

Guthrie, J. W., & M. W. Kirst. (1988, March). *Conditions of education in California 1988.* Policy Paper No. 88–3–2. Berkeley: Policy Analysis for California Education.

Haenn, J. F., & J. M. Houser. (1988, April). A study of educational reform in the Southeast: Application of a methodology to map and track educational reform. Paper presented at the annual meeting of the American Educational Research Association, New Orleans.

Hanson, R. A., & R. E. Schutz. (1978). A new look at schooling effects from programmatic research and development. In D. Mann, ed., *Making change happen?* New York: Teachers College Press.

Hawley, W. D. (1985, Summer). False premises and false promises: The mythical character of public discourse about education. *Peabody Reflector, 60*(1), 2–3.

Hawley, W. D. (1988, November). Missing pieces of the educational reform agenda: Or why the first and second waves may miss the boat. *Educational Administration Quarterly, 24*(4), 416–437.

Holmes Group. (1986, April). *Tomorrow's Teachers.* East Lansing, MI: Holmes Group.

Illinois State Board of Education. (1985). *Reform package.* Springfield: Illinois State Board of Education.

Institute for Educational Leadership. (1986). *School boards: Strengthening grass roots leadership.* Washington, DC: Institute for Educational Leadership.

Jennings, L. (1988, 22 June). "Schools for the 21st century" project is taking off. *Education Week, 7*(39), 10.

Jennings, L. (1989, 22 February). Tally of homeless should be viewed "with caution," department concedes. *Education Week, 8*(22), 15.

Kearns, D. L. (1988a). A business perspective on American schooling. *Education Week, 7*(30), 32, 34.

Kearns, D. L. (1988b). An education recovery plan for America. *Phi Delta Kappan*, *69*(8), 565–570.

Kirst, M. (1984, November). The changing balance in state and local power to control education. *Phi Delta Kappan, 66*(3), 189–191.

Kirst, M. W. (1987, October). PEER, An interview with Michael Kirst. *Phi Delta Kappan, 60*(2), 161–164.

Kirst, M. W. (1988, 22 June). On reports and reform: *Nation at risk* assessed. *Education Week, 7*(39), 40.

Levin, H. M. (1984, Summer). About time for educational reform. *Educational Evaluation and Policy Analysis, 6*(2), 151–163.

Levin, H. M. (1988, Spring). Cost-effectiveness and educational policy. *Educational Evaluation and Policy Analysis, 10*(1), 51–69.

Lortie, D. C. (1975). *Schoolteacher.* Chicago: University of Chicago Press.

Malen, B., & A. W. Hart. (1987, April). Shaping career ladder reform: The influence of teachers on the policy making process. Paper presented at the annual meeting of the American Educational Research Association, Washington, DC.

McClellan, M. C. (1988, June). Testing and reform. *Phi Delta Kappan, 69*(10), 768–771.

McLaughlin, M. W. (1987, Summer). Learning from experience: Lessons from policy implementation. *Educational Evaluation and Policy Analysis, 9*(2), 171–178.

Meyer, J. W., & B. Rowan. (1975). Notes on the structure of educational organizations: Revised version. Paper presented at the annual meeting of the American Sociological Association, San Francisco.

Michaels, K. (1988, February). Caution: Second-wave reform taking place. *Educational Leadership, 45*(5), 3.

Mitchell, D. E. (1984, Summer). Educational policy analysis: The state of the art. *Educational Administration Quarterly, 20*(3), 129–160.

Mitchell, D. E., & D. J. Encarnation. (1984, May). Alternative state policy mechanisms for influencing school performance. *Educational Researcher, 13*(5), 4–11.

Murphy, J. (1988, Spring). Equity as student opportunity to learn. Findings and implications. *Theory into Practice, 27*(2), 145–151.

Murphy, J. (1989a, February). Is there equity in educational reform? *Educational Leadership, 46*(5), 32–33.

Murphy, J. (1989b, March). Educational reform and equity: A reexamination of prevailing thought. Paper presented at the annual meeting of the American Educational Research Association, San Francisco.

Murphy, J. (1989c). Principal instructional leadership. In L. S. Lotto & P. W. Thurston, eds., *Recent advances in educational administration*, Vol. 1. Greenwich, CT: JAI Press.

Murphy, J., & K. Decker. (1989, May–June). Teachers' use of homework in high schools. *Journal of Educational Research, 82*(5), 261–269.

Murphy, J., & P. Hallinger. (1984, Spring). Policy analysis at the local level: A framework for expanded investigation. *Educational Evaluation and Policy Analysis, 6*(1), 5–13.

Murphy, J., & P. Hallinger. (1989, March–April). Equity as access to learning: Curricular and instructional treatment differences. *Journal of Curriculum Studies, 21*(2), 129–149.

Murphy, J., P. Hallinger, & R. P. Mesa. (1985, Summer). School effectiveness: Checking progress and assumptions and developing a role for state and federal government. *Teachers College Record*, 86(4), 615–641.

Murphy, J., R. P. Mesa, & P. Hallinger. (1984, October). A stronger state role in school reform. *Educational Leadership*, 42(2), 20–26.

Murphy, J., M. Weil, P. Hallinger, & A. Mitman. (1985, Spring). School effectiveness: A conceptual framework. *Educational Forum*, 49(3), 361–374.

Musgrave, R. A., & P. B. Musgrave. (1976). *Public finance in theory and practice*. New York: McGraw-Hill.

National Commission for Excellence in Teacher Education. (1985). *A call for change in teacher education*. Washington, DC: American Association of Colleges for Teacher Education.

National Commission on Excellence in Education. (1983, April). *A nation at risk: The imperative of educational reform*. Washington, DC: U.S. Government Printing Office.

National Governors' Association. (1986). *The governors' 1991 report on education—time for results*. Washington, DC: National Governors' Association.

National Governors' Association. (1987). *The governors' 1991 report on education—time for results: 1987*. Washington, DC: National Governors' Association.

National Science Board. (1983). *Educating Americans for the 21st century*. Washington, DC: National Science Board.

Oakes, J. (1985). *Keeping track: How schools structure inequality*. New Haven, CT: Yale University Press.

Oates, W. E. (1972). *Fiscal federalism*. New York: Harcourt Brace Jovanovich.

Odden, A. (1989, 15 February). The future of colleges of education and human development. Presentation made to the faculty of Peabody College, Vanderbilt University, Nashville.

Odden, A., & D. Marsh. (1988, April). How comprehensive reform legislation can improve secondary schools. *Phi Delta Kappan*, 69(8), 593–598.

Olson, L. (1988, 4 May). Reform: Plaudits for staying power, prescriptions for new directions. *Education Week*, 7(32), 1, 20–21.

Olson, L. (1989, 22 February). Governors say investment in children can curb "long-term costs" for states. *Education Week*, 8(22), 10.

Page, R. N. (1984, April). Lower-track classes at a college-preparatory high school: A caricature of educational encounters. Paper presented at the annual meeting of the American Educational Research Association, New Orleans.

Passow, A. H. (1984, April). *Reforming schools in the 1980s: A critical review of the national reports*. New York: Institute for Urban and Minority Education, Teachers College, Columbia University.

Perry, N. J. (1988, 4 July). The education crisis: What business can do. *Fortune*, 118(1), 70–81.

Peterson, P. E. (No date). "Economic and policy trends affecting teacher effectiveness in mathematics and science." Unpublished manuscript, Center for the Study of American Government, Johns Hopkins School for Advanced International Studies.

Peterson, T. K. (1988, April). Building, passing, implementing and assessing educational reform in South Carolina. Paper presented at the annual meeting of the American Educational Research Association, New Orleans.

Pipho, C. (1988, 27 April). Information and state education policy making. *Education Week*, *7*(31), 29.

Plank, D. N. (1987, April). Why school reform doesn't change schools: Political and organizational perspectives. In William Lowe Boyd & Charles Kerchner, eds., *The politics of education and choice: The first annual politics of education yearbook*. Philadelphia: Taylor and Francis.

Porter, A. C. (1988, April). External standards and good teaching: The pros and cons of telling teachers what to do. Paper presented at the annual meeting of the American Educational Research Association, New Orleans.

Powell, A. G., E. Farrar, & D. K. Cohen. (1985). *The shopping mall high school: Winners and losers in the educational marketplace*. Boston: Houghton Mifflin.

Purkey, S. D., & M. S. Smith. (1983a, March). Effective schools: A review. *Elementary School Journal*, *83*(4), 427–452.

Purkey, S. D., & M. S. Smith. (1983b, October). *Educational policy and school effectiveness*. Madison: Center for Educational Research, University of Wisconsin.

Rosenshine, B. (1983, March). Teaching functions in instructional programs. *Elementary School Journal*, *83*(4), 335–351.

Rossmiller, R. A. (1986, Winter). Some contemporary trends and their implications for the preparation of school administrators. *UCEA [University Council for Educational Administration] Review*, *27*(1), 2–3.

Schwartz, F. (1981, Summer). Supporting or subverting learning: Peer group patterns in four tracked schools. *Anthropology and Education Quarterly*, *12*(2), 99–121.

Sedlak, M. W., C. W. Wheeler, D. C. Pullin, & P. A. Cusick. (1986). *Selling students short: Classroom bargains and academic reform in the American high school*. New York: Teachers College Press.

Shepard, L. A., & A. E. Kreitzer. (1987, August–September). The Texas teacher test. *Educational Researcher*, *16*(6), 22–31.

Sizer, T. R. (1984). *Horace's compromise: The dilemma of the American high school*. Boston: Houghton Mifflin.

Smith, M. L., & L. A. Shepard. (1987, October). What doesn't work: Explaining policies of retention in the early grades. *Phi Delta Kappan*, *69*(2), 129–134.

Snider, W. (1989a, 22 February). California's child services badly fragmented, study finds. *Education Week*, *8*(22), 10.

Snider, W. (1989b, 22 February). NAEP finds basic skills up, higher-order skills lacking. *Education Week*, *8*(22), 7.

Strang, D. (1987, September). The administrative transformation of American education: School district consolidation, 1938–1980. *Administrative Science Quarterly*, *32*(3), 352–366.

Thompson to back a tax hike for schools. (1988, 11 May). *Education Week*, *7*(33).

Timar, T. B., & D. L. Kirp. (1988, Summer). State efforts to reform schools: Treading between a regulatory swamp and an English garden. *Educational Evaluation and Policy Analysis*, *10*(2), 75–88.

Twentieth Century Fund. (1983). *Making the grade*. New York: Twentieth Century Fund.

Underwood, J. (1989). State legislative responses to educational reform literature. In L. S. Lotto and P. W. Thurston, eds., *Recent advances in educational administration*, Vol. 1. Greenwich, CT: JAI Press.

Walker, R. (1988, 2 March). Educators, lawmakers rap Kentucky Governor's budget. *Education Week, 7*(23).

Weinstein, R. (1976). Reading group membership in first grade: Teacher behaviors and pupil experience over time. *Journal of Educational Psychology, 68*(1), 103–116.

Willower, D. J. (1987, Winter). Inquiry into educational administration: The last twenty-five years and the next. *Journal of Educational Administration, 25*(1), 12–28.

CHAPTER 2

Passage of Rites: On the History of Educational Reform in the United States

Donald Warren

In the 1980s, educational reform became a worldwide phenomenon. The U.S. effort actually began at the end of the previous decade, as various states moved to raise high school graduation requirements, particularly in mathematics and the sciences, standardize assessments of students' academic performance, and develop quantitative measures of teacher competence (see Firestone, Chapter 6 in this book). The publication of *A Nation at Risk* (National Commission on Excellence in Education, 1983) caught these waves as they crested and propelled educational reform onto the front pages of newspapers across the country. By capturing in a single word— *excellence*—both widespread dissatisfaction with public schools and diverse

I am grateful to Ronald E. Butchart for providing extensive and thoughtful comments on an earlier version of this chapter.

hopes for their improvement, this brief report seemed responsible for generating a movement. Heated debate ensued, touching on virtually every aspect of education policy and practice in the United States.

In countries where ministries of education presided over national systems, momentum may have moved in the opposite direction, but move it did. Japan and Korea, whose schools many Americans eyed covetously, launched national commissions to formulate comprehensive reform agendas (Korean Educational Development Institute, 1985; National Council on Educational Reform, 1986). Sri Lanka, too, developed plans for a general reorganization of its schools (National Institute of Education, 1988). Following a two-year study, India began to implement a new national education policy in 1988, hoping schools would contribute toward greater national cohesiveness as they became more responsive to the diversity of languages and cultures in the states (Government of India, 1986). Reform strategies in Great Britain appeared to be self-canceling. The Thatcher government sought to promote administrative decentralization on one hand, and a national school curriculum on the other (Haydon, 1987). The Saudi Arabian reform effort seemed to arise initially from the kingdom's novel experience with limited funds, but it quickly encompassed programmatic initiatives at all educational levels, not merely budgetary reductions (Kingdom of Saudi Arabia, 1986). Egypt commenced a comprehensive strategy to strengthen elementary, secondary, and teacher education and to draw university students into programs preparing specialists who were in short supply (National Centre for Educational Research, 1986).

These represent only a sample of the sorts of educational improvement initiatives that one could find underway around the world. Nations of all sizes and at various stages of development joined a process that bore the signs of an international movement. Cross-national comparisons of student achievement became especially popular (see Murphy, Chapter 1 in this book). In many countries, reformers took cues from their counterparts in the United States, despite the relatively low achievement scores posted by U.S. students. Ironically, while our reforms moved toward more centralized modes of organization and control, nations with strong educational ministries looked for ways to decentralize their school systems.

One aim of this chapter is to place this centripetal turn of U.S. education policy against historical background. The tradition of local control of schools in the United States has long expressed popular political values. Yet over the years, centralization has occurred, especially at the state levels. The history of educational reform may help us understand these developments. Another aim is to explore why educational reform has generated such controversy. Finally, using resources from social and intellectual history, the chapter attempts to establish a broad historical framework for the subsequent sections of this book. Emphasis falls on the reform environment rather than the distant origins of particular proposals. These aims are pursued in three sections. The first treats conceptual and epistemological difficulties that arise when we try to reconstruct the history of educational reform in the United States. The middle section sketches the political contexts and major goals of three past episodes of reform. The third section discusses common themes and elements that have linked reform initiatives over time.

EDUCATIONAL REFORM AS HISTORICAL PROBLEM

Several complications muddy the history of educational reform in the United States. One arises from a curious trait of school improvement campaigns in this country: They have tended to lack a memory. Current proposals illustrate the point. State legislators who find the idea of career ladders for teachers attractive seem unmindful of its earlier versions. Applauded in the press, various states and school districts have inaugurated merit salary plans for teachers, the aim being to reward those judged to be effective, while encouraging "deadwood" to seek some other line of work. The new policies have political resonance. They impress school administrators and taxpayers alike as necessary for devising reasonable and just personnel management strategies. Why, indeed, would anyone object to rewarding meritorious teachers or conversely to cleansing schools of incompetents? Unexpected answers might be found in the past, because various types of merit salary schedules have been adopted and subsequently discarded in school districts across the country for more than a century. Curriculum reform, which is much discussed nowadays, also has a long history. Over the years, we have tested different configurations of the core studies concept, debated the goals and content of vocational education, and altered high school diploma requirements. Knowledge of these efforts and an inkling of why changes endured or lapsed would seem to represent resources that curriculum planners need. At least we would learn more precisely what qualifies today as an innovation. Similar instances of reforms being proposed or enacted without reference to—or a search for—possible antecedents can be found in earlier periods.

This ahistorical tradition in U.S. educational reform not only places improvements on a sandy foundation conceptually, but also isolates reforms in different eras from each other. They become time-bound, programmed for obsolescence. Perhaps this temporariness helps to explain the ritual quality of educational reform in the United States. Sentiment for change has broken out periodically over the past two centuries, but the repetition seems not to have enabled us to identify enduring educational goals and values. The complication boils down to a question: What understanding of the history of

U.S. educational reform can we hope to achieve when reformers and policy-makers have themselves made so little use of history? At best, they have often seemed to be refighting the last educational war, as they labored to correct the previous swing of the reform pendulum. Writing the history of educational reform threatens to impose a rationality on the enterprise, a connectedness, that has been lacking.

Nonetheless, considerable work on the history of educational reform has been completed. A brief historiographical review may help us identify other complications in this field of study. Not so long ago, the history of U.S. education tended to be organized as a history of school reform. Ellwood P. Cubberley (1934) and his cohorts wrote epic accounts of educational expansion and improvement, focusing on the friends and enemies of public schools, victorious battles, and temporary defeats. There could never be any doubt about their viewpoint. Advocates of public schools, they championed the formation of systems, professional hierarchies, and manageable curricula. Most overlooked the negative effects of bureaucracy and the nagging ambiguities about race, gender, social class, religion, and region that might have made the tale less laudatory. Although exceptions to this whiggish approach to educational history can be seen in the work of scholars such as Horace Mann Bond (1966), R. Freeman Butts (1939), Merle Curti (1935), and Bessie Pierce (1930), throughout the first half of the twentieth century writers on the history of U.S. education gave an untroubled and reassuring rendition of progressive school reform from the colonial period to the present. It dominated the curricula of teacher education programs and provided a handy reference for scholars seeking historical prologs for school surveys, student achievement studies, and other topical research. Emphasizing names, dates, and places in chronological order, this was a history of famous white men, their educational intentions, the institutional systems they promoted and managed, and the service to the republic credited to their efforts. It was history by and for the victorious.

As was the case with U.S. history in general, the history of education began showing the effects of two revisionist efforts by the 1960s. Cultural and intellectual historians shifted attention from public schools to an array of educative agents, including families, museums, and television (Bailyn, 1960; Cremin, 1965). Exploring the various modes of learning at work in the society, they sought to explain the range, depth, and evolution of public knowledge, in effect, to test the "intelligence of the people" (Calhoun, 1973). Hard on their heels came social historians with case studies of state and urban school systems; educational histories of black people, women, immigrants, and working-class groups; and regional studies highlighting educators whose contributions had been considered minor (Tyack, 1974; Kaestle, 1976). The timeliness of this research to social justice crusades in the 1960s, its closer affinity to the social sciences than to the humanities, and its more direct challenge to the old survey histories combined to eclipse the work of cultural and intellectual historians. But both endeavors had the effect of unraveling the familiar consensus accounts. Social historians in particular tried to assess the effects of education policies and practices on students, families, and communities, those on the receiving end of reforms promulgated by others. Typically more interested than cultural and intellectual historians in the distribution and use of power and status, they produced a body of literature that attempted to move from inside defined arenas of educational action (Tyack & Hansot, 1982; Tyack, 1989). Both revisionist efforts generated heated controversy among historians over sources, evidence, and interpretations. More important, a dramatic expansion of knowledge about educational institutions and processes resulted, along with greater sophistication in identifying and measuring the variety of learning outcomes.

Some expected this new knowledge to deflect attempts to return to the consensus histories of old. That path, after all, offered merely the comforts of nostalgia, history's natural enemy. It also avoided a challenging conceptual problem posed at least tacitly by the recent findings: Can we integrate the disparate histories without rounding off their substantive edges? Attempts by contemporary historians in various specializations to address this dilemma have generated controversy of their own (Bender, 1985). Noting the instrumental role of history in fostering political community and adherence to majoritarian values, some scholars have bemoaned the fragmenting effects of social history on the formerly apparent consensus (Bloom, 1987; Hirsch, 1987). Unfortunately, these protests appear to suggest that patriotism can be simpleminded and that we should somehow forget what we now know about educational experience in the United States. They also relax pressure on historians to undertake the difficult labor of trying to formulate conceptual bases for comprehensive narratives about the public education of a pluralistic people.

We now know with utter certainty that differences within the U.S. population represent a mix of cause and effect. Our diversity of races, cultures, creeds, and classes hardly comes as news, although we have acquired fresh data and surprising perspectives on the variety of values, traditions, and rituals at work in the society. We are far better informed about the attitudes of particular groups and communities toward education and the ways they have influenced schools. We have equally telling evidence of another sort. Through formal and informal policies, including their modes of organization, schools and school systems have ignored conditions of culture and circumstance among the people, catered to these conditions uncritically, and discriminated against teachers and students solely on the wealth, gender, or some other singular characteristic. In education, we have not only treated some people differently, but have also treated them unjustly, thereby adding alienation to their sense of uniqueness and banking the social dynamite that threatens democratic community (Kaestle, 1988).

Now that we can more fully document this complex diversity, we find it has raised a formidable barrier to recounting our history in customary ways. Or to make the same point from a different angle, the new historical knowledge requires fresh thinking about how to recall our educational past. Its substantive contribution is also formidable. It permits the construction of fuller, more complete stories, and in that sense more accurate ones (Bailyn, 1982; Bender, 1985).

This brief incursion onto the private preserve of historians pinpoints two other complications that arise from the history of educational reform. Recall that the first complication emerges from the ahistorical character of U.S. school reform. The second complication has to do with the conceptual work entailed in reconstructing the history of these efforts. The third complication pertains to the problem of perspective. Like all such enterprises, the history of educational reform takes on different configurations depending on the vantage point from which it is viewed.

A need to untangle the ways and contexts in which we have invoked "reform" has already been suggested, but clarifying the meanings that have been attached to the word *education* also seems essential. The term has been used to refer both to institutions and the processes that cannot be confined to particular kinds of institutions. Have there been schools that were not educational? If so, have we witnessed reforms calculated to improve schools that either by design or misadventure rendered them less educational? Schools have been likened to businesses, and the educational process to production modes of the sort one might find in a manufacturing plant (Callahan, 1962). Are these analogies legitimate or illuminating? What might be appropriate metaphors for education or for schools? What are they *like*? On what historical grounds can we analyze the goals of proposed reforms? Given changes in the social context, can we compare particular reforms in different eras? Such questions probe fundamental issues regarding the purposes, authority, organization, and control of U.S. public schools. Unless all we have in mind is a catalog of past efforts, these issues—along with questions of the sort just posed—confront those who want to understand the history of educational reform.

But whose perspectives count? The question suggests a third complication in the history of educational reform. Cubberley (1934) and his colleagues wrote from the vantage point of reformers, professional educators, and the "friends" of public schools. Their accounts tended to omit teachers and to castigate opponents of educational reform as narrow-minded, short-sighted, or tight-fisted, in all respects an unattractive lot (Elsbree, 1939; Warren, 1989). They stressed reform intentions, and the victories they celebrated had to do with laws, policies, and organizational characteristics of school systems. These achievements constituted only parts of the story, the parts on view to those looking at education from the outside. If, however, the purpose of a reform is to enhance student learning, judging the success or failure of the venture requires information from the inside. We need to know something about the processes of teaching and learning from more centrally located actors—teachers, students, and perhaps parents as well (Cohen, 1989; Tyack, 1989). Testimony from these sources may be difficult to collect, yet without it the history of educational reform is left with a gaping hole.

Outsiders may see these complications as little more than family squabbles among historians. But more is at stake than arcane matters of historiography. In somewhat different form, the dilemmas faced by historians of educational reform confront a broader audience of educational researchers, reformers, and professional educators. If the history of educational reform is problematic because of tenuous links among reform efforts over time, reform itself threatens to become an exercise in unfounded optimism. Quite literally, there cannot be a reform without a past. And if we don't know where we have been with regard to educational improvement, and why we went there, we are left to chart our direction in the shallow waters of contemporary comparisons and current political moods. We may want our schools to be more like those of the Japanese but lack grounds for assessing the material, social, and cultural costs of pursuing such a goal or for understanding what the Japanese find attractive in our schools. One could argue that the difficulty historians have in conceptualizing the purpose of education pales beside that facing those who are concerned about contemporary reform efforts. My point, however, is that reformers and historians face similar conceptual tasks. Reformers must also address the matter of perspective, the problem that knowledge accrues from particular angles of light cast on the educational enterprise. Like historians, they must find ways to heed insiders and outsiders in formulating reform proposals and in assessing outcomes, assuming they want their plans and strategies to have positive effects. History and the ways historians work are thus relevant to their projects. But other worries remain. In driving toward educational reform, do we want the kind of disruptive knowledge that history can deliver? Would we prefer a laundered version? The questions warrant attention because there seems to be no shortage of people willing to tell us the history we want to hear.

EPISODES OF EDUCATIONAL REFORM

With these complications in mind, let us turn to three narratives from the history of educational reform. The episodes have been selected because, first, they are somewhat remote from the present and thus more amenable to historical analysis. Second, each has generated a large body of historical research. As familiar educational reform efforts, they lend themselves to brief summaries. Third, each in its own time was highly controversial. Finally, although in each case somewhat different goals and strategies were dominant, the three episodes seem to be linkable, at least in terms of their themes and outcomes. They suggest continuity.

The Common School Movement

At best loosely coordinated, strategies emerged across the country in the 1840s and 1850s to promote the establishment of what we today call "elementary schools." Although the most frequently noted of these campaigns occurred in Massachusetts, and enthusiasm in the South remained muted, if not hostile, no state or territory was left unaffected by this first truly nationwide educational reform initiative. Looking back on it, R. Freeman Butts (1978) saw the formative period of public education in the United States, when the idea of tax-supported, tuition-free schools, accessible to all, was entered into policies, laws, and state constitutions. By contrast, Michael B. Katz (1975) placed the movement in a much less favorable light. For him, it began a long tradition of imposed school reform that resulted in bureaucratic, rigidly controlled educational systems. Its aims were inspired not by democratic values but by the needs of an emerging capitalist economy for a pliant work force. Notwithstanding their starkly different interpretations, both seemed to view the common school movement as larger than life. And in many respects it was.

Two basic goals prevailed. One goal sought to place teachers and schools where none had existed, the other to make schools more comparable with regard to such essential features as curricula, teacher preparation, and the length of school terms. Reformers pursued both aims simultaneously and with considerable doggedness, although it is important to note that the effort to increase the number of schools coincided with a growing trend in the 1830s. Looking back from the late twentieth century, we may not appreciate fully the difficulty of the reformers' undertaking or why it provoked such controversy. However, there was much about the common school movement that subsequent generations could recognize.

We can begin to grasp these familiar elements by pretending that we do not know how the story of this initial educational reform effort ended. To play this game, we must imagine ourselves in the formative period of U.S. political institutions. With regard to education, the federal Constitution was silent, and no national agency or congressional committee existed to provide educational leadership (Warren, 1974). Interest by the states varied regionally. In the mid-1830s, none had an agency solely responsible for promoting the establishment of schools, although the idea of such an entity had been discussed and tested in several states. Massachusetts created a school agency in 1837, and other states followed suit over the next two decades. Most of these new agencies had a full-time administrator with the title of *superinten- dent, commissioner,* or—in Massachusetts' case—*secretary of the board of edu- cation,* but their budgets and mandates were modest (Tyack, Kirst, & Hansot, 1980). None exercised control over schools. Their assignments, rather, included collecting statistics and information on the schools of their states and submitting annual reports to governors and legislatures. With regard to the common school movement, therefore, we must imagine a crusade that spread across the country without the help of central govern- ments, political institutions, or organization infrastructures (Tyack & Han- sot, 1982). It "moved" by way of local initiative, aided and abetted by emerging informal networks that linked educational activists within regions and states and across the country.

As might have been anticipated, even schools within a section of the same state varied greatly. School terms, teachers' salaries, textbooks and equip- ment, and the buildings themselves reflected local wealth and commitment. Recent research on the history of teachers gives us glimpses of these institu- tions from the inside out (Kaufman, 1984; Clifford, 1989; Finkelstein, 1989). Students of all ages, ranging perhaps from three to over twenty years old, attended them for brief terms that were organized to avoid planting and harvesting seasons. Teachers typically fashioned the curriculum, often rely- ing on reading material the students brought from home. The local com- munity exercised accountability, which helped to explain the prevalence of public rituals in which students demonstrated newly acquired skills. The vast majority of these new institutions functioned in agricultural districts, which were cash-poor, isolated, and by necessity more or less self-sufficient. These were invented schools, the early ones formed without benefit of precedents or experience (Warren, 1989).

These conditions underscored for reformers the importance of their other principal objective. They wanted less dissimilarity and more commonality among the schools. Although a few envisioned the need for a national educational agency, whether public or private, most worked within the states to systematize education (Tyack & Hansot, 1982). General consensus emerged on the issues and topics that required attention: oral and written examinations of teachers, school architecture and furniture design, curricu- lum, pedagogy, teacher training, and measures of student achievement. For the most part, these wide-ranging concerns about the details of schooling were to be addressed through local initiative and policy formation, but growing support was also evident for the proposition that state governments should help fund common schools. The annual meetings of newly formed regional and national organizations of educational leaders became settings for debating proposals and sharing information on local developments. Periodicals that were devoted to educational topics also helped to disseminate information about schools. These strategies, originating in different locations yet increasingly modeled after each other, gave the common school movement its sense of a concerted effort.

But what made the common school an idea whose time had come? From the nation's founding years, political leaders had worried about the effects of regional loyalties on its future. Many of them included schools among the devices that might be employed to weld its sections into a union. Throughout the early years of the nineteenth century, the number of schools increased steadily. Frontier settlements in new states and in the territories often viewed the hiring of a teacher and the construction of a schoolhouse as visible signs of civilization. There is little evidence that the common school movement accelerated this process. For the reformers, however, it left too much to chance. By the 1830s, several plans for coordinated strategies to produce school systems had been formulated. The new ingredient, then, was not the idea of schooling *per se* or even of school systems, but rather something else that lent it urgency.

The diversity of "principles, opinions, and manners" among U.S. citizens that had distressed George Washington and his contemporaries became even more pronounced a few decades later (Richardson, 1908, p. 202). Regional loyalties sharpened, cities grew exponentially, and they competed fiercely for regional economic dominance. Irish Catholic immigrants unsettled the presumed Protestantism of the U.S. ethos. The growth of jobs in manufacturing lured young people off the farms. New patterns of work emerged, as people went "out" to their jobs rather than work at home as part of a family unit. Amid economic, religious, and cultural change came an alteration of the political equation, as universal white manhood suffrage became the norm. Voting was no longer merely a gentleman's prerogative. The idea began to catch on that education offered a way to prepare the new ruler—the common man—for citizenship.

The rationale for schooling thus acquired a sharp edge. Borrowing ideas and plans from the much-envied Prussian educational system, reformers portrayed schools as efficient means to promote morality, loyalty, and economic sufficiency among the people. Schooling became a matter of "public" necessity, to be treated by policy and law, not of individual preference alone. As such, it required funding by taxes, not tuition. Because it benefited society, all should contribute to its financial support, not parents alone. No community or district could be permitted to choose not to have schools. Reformers spoke openly about a "law of external pressure," which advised that parents and communities should be cajoled or, if need be, coerced into establishing schools and sending their young to them (Warren, 1974, chap. 1). Furthermore, the English concept of charity schools was specifically rejected. All children, not merely those of the lower classes, should attend. For openly strategic reasons, common school reformers advocated the necessity of both excellence and equity in public education, to use twentieth century terminology. Without the former, the upper classes would continue to patronize private schools; without the latter, children of the lower classes would not be properly prepared for citizenship or productive labor. At risk was the nation's political tranquility, its economy, and its future as a republic. Their perceptions of these larger stakes in the advancement of schools served to shape the reformers' practical vision. In the curriculum, the modes of instruction, and the organization of schools themselves, emphasis actually fell on the common moral development of children.

By the end of the 1850s, something akin to state systems of public elementary schools could be detected in the northern regions of the country. The vast majority of children attended them (Kaestle, 1983). School terms became longer and more uniform, and a consensus over the curriculum emerged. Not surprisingly, the textbook-publishing industry mushroomed. A revolution had occurred in the teaching force. Initially a male occupation, teaching became women's work, due to both dysfunctional policies and deliberate strategies by local and state authorities. Women teachers could be paid lower salaries than men, and unlike men, who had other, more lucrative employment opportunities, they were available to fill the rapidly growing number of positions (Carter, 1989; Rury, 1989). Teacher-training institutions existed in several localities, although preservice preparation was rare. Most began their jobs with little academic background beyond the level of elementary schooling (Warren, 1985).

Few of these developments can be adequately described as evolutionary. Intense opposition arose at several junctures. The proposition that taxpayers should pay for the schooling of other people's children, not merely their own, proved especially controversial. In 1840, the Massachusetts legislature narrowly defeated a move to abolish the state education agency (Kaestle & Vinovskis, 1980). There as elsewhere, political leaders looked askance at suggestions that local school control should be diluted by state authority. Catholics objected strenuously to the Protestant tone of common schools and most pointedly to the anti-Catholic bias often found in textbooks (Tyack & Hansot, 1982). Also, unexpected policy effects occurred. Reformers working to lengthen school terms and to make teaching more of a full-time occupation were surprised to discover that their attempts to professionalize public schooling discouraged men from accepting teaching positions. So long as teaching remained a part-time job that could be scheduled in conjunction with farming or other employment opportunities, men were available. But the low salaries of teachers sent them to other occupations (Carter, 1989; Rury, 1989).

As settlements spread westward, newer states experienced their own version of the common school movement. This was one of the effects of our first educational reform effort: a model of the stages of the institutionalization of elementary schooling. Another was the formulation of a rationale that linked schooling to national needs and aspirations. The common school movement promoted the habit of going to school and made it a sign of good citizenship. It also articulated the idea that effective schooling in the United States must be inclusive. The rationale permitted no exception based on race, gender, religion, or social class. Such language, to be sure, braved unsettling realities. As Horace Mann (1870, p. 841), the best-known leader of the movement, put it, the schools must be "open to all, good enough for all, and attended by all." But they were not.

Education for National Reconstruction

No educational reform effort of the scope and magnitude of the common school movement occurred again in the United States until the turn of the century. However, for a brief period following the Civil War, a fresh wave of educational reform seemed imminent. In this case, as in the past, schools gained attention obliquely via concern over particular social issues, in this case those related to rebuilding the union.

Well before the outbreak of hostilities, northern common school advocates had castigated the South as educationally backward. The criticism had merit only in a limited sense. Although their region included some of the nation's oldest and best-known colleges and academies, southerners had been relatively inactive in the network of educational associations and publications that had been formed to advance the goals of the common school movement. They also tended to reject the movement's inclusive ideology. The long-held southern view of education placed it among the prerogatives and responsibilities of families and communities. A sense of public responsibility might be expressed in charity schools for orphans and children of the poor, but it did not justify invoking state authority to require local folk to establish schools for the general population. Schools of this latter sort emerged in the South, typically in the few urban centers, but in virtually every case they resulted from local initiative and funding. A notable exception to this *laissez-faire* approach concerned the slaves. Following an outbreak of revolts in the 1820s and 1830s, state laws proscribing the education of slaves became common throughout the South. On this point, there was no local prerogative.

It was the absence of educational *systems* in the South that aggravated northern school advocates. They viewed southern opposition to governmental efforts to disseminate educational opportunity as evidence of antirepublican sentiment and ultimately of national disloyalty. Secession provided all the confirmation they needed. But southerners in Congress had lent credence to northern suspicions during the first debate on the land grant college bill in 1858 and 1859. They viewed the proposal as unconstitutional, because it dealt with education, and as an ominous precedent. As a Virginia senator warned, passage of the bill might permit "a majority in Congress to fasten upon the southern States that peculiar system of free schools in New England" (Warren, 1983, p. 161). White southerners generally did not see the absence of policies and laws providing for general education as a problem. On the contrary, they judged the diffusion of basic learning, especially among black people, as a likely source of social upheaval. For good reason, many viewed the common school as a seed bed of abolitionist sentiment in New England and wanted no part of it in their region. White southerners thus tended to reject the two clearest achievements of the common school movement: the inclusive, albeit unrealized, rationale for public education and the emerging state school systems. Although common school reformers overlooked the point, the attitudes of northern whites toward blacks differed at best in degree, not in kind, from that of their southern counterparts. The citizenship status and educational opportunities of blacks in the Union states remained problematic throughout the Civil War and Reconstruction periods.

These complications aside, once they saw that the Union would be victorious, northern school reformers prepared to launch an educational crusade against the South. They traced the Secession to the dearth of basic schooling in the states that had formed the Confederacy. If the people had been educated, the argument went, southerners would have resisted their leaders' call to break the Union apart. Their sense of patriotism would have overwhelmed regional loyalties. Needed, the reformers insisted, were armies of teachers who would see the South as their "missionary ground." They would "reconstruct" the Union on the appropriate foundation of republican values, literacy, and national unity (Warren, 1974, chap. 2).

Although such language permeated speeches delivered at northern educational gatherings in the mid-1860s, congressional debates took a pragmatic turn of a different sort. Earlier in the decade, they emphasized educational strategies that could advance the war effort. By 1864, the focus had shifted to the tasks of reconstruction. Education could serve these aims, too, but certain constraints had to be respected. Traditional readings of the U.S. Constitution had blocked direct federal involvement in general schooling, and among the Republicans, who held large majorities in both houses of Congress, many still professed this interpretation. Even those who agreed that the Civil War and its destructive aftermath justified unprecedented policy initiatives—the so-called Radical Republicans—argued among themselves about appropriate strategies. Some wanted immediate social change in the South, including the redistribution of land and the extension of voting privileges to black people. Others favored long-range projects, the promotion of education among them. One notable development caught nearly everyone in Congress by surprise: the high, widespread, and insistent demand for schools and teachers among the former slaves (Eaton, 1907). Whatever their disagreements, congressional Republicans tended to rest their hopes for a reconstructed South on the growth of the Republican Party in the Confederate states. For all practical purposes, this meant winning the hearts and minds—and votes—of black people.

Of the three federal education initiatives taken in the 1860s—the acts providing for land grant colleges, the U.S. Department of Education, and the Bureau of Refugees, Freedmen, and Abandoned Lands—only the last could reasonably be expected to respond to the clamor of black people for basic learning and to other pressing educational needs in the South. Originally, the Freedmen's Bureau, as it was popularly called, had no authority to engage in educational activities, but supplemental legislation expanded its mandate somewhat. It appointed superintendents to oversee teachers hired by philanthropic organizations, and financed the construction and renting of buildings to be used as schools. By the time it ceased operation in 1872, the bureau had presided over a network of state school superintendents and supervisory personnel responsible for over 5,000 teachers in day and Sunday schools, scattered across the South (Butchart, 1983; Warren, 1983). Some of the schools charged tuition. Given heated opposition by whites to any form of race mixing, virtually all of them were segregated. In fact, the vast majority of students were black. Yet despite its far-flung operation, the bureau served no more than 10 percent of the school-age black population of the South. Although they challenged the traditional southern opposition to general schooling, its programs were more precisely intended as reconstruction strategies. They reflected at best temporary policy. In no case was full federal funding of schools envisioned. The aim rather was to augment philanthropic efforts, which operated outside the policy realm altogether.

These private initiatives, which antedated and outlived the bureau's efforts, had more powerful effects on the distribution of schooling among southern black people than any of the federal programs. They brought scores of teachers into the region, most of them women, who took up their duties with missionary zeal (Jones, 1980). They worked under primitive, often dangerous conditions. School buildings tended to be crude affairs, and organized threats from white vigilante groups became common. But the educational aims of the various aid societies tended to aim low. Philanthropy provided support for both schools and colleges to serve southern blacks. In most of the institutions, however, the curriculum stressed the acquisition of basic literacy skills and the preparation of blacks for laboring and service occupations, not their intellectual growth (Butchart, 1983; Anderson, 1988).

The reconstruction programs ended not because they failed or succeeded but because federal funds became unavailable. The aid societies lasted longer, but their effects were shaped by distorted notions about the capabilities and needs of blacks. Eventually, philanthropy too fell victim to diminishing financial support. Nevertheless, southern education changed its appearance. State school agencies were established throughout the region in the postwar years. More schools, more widely dispersed, became available, and a semblance of state educational systems could be detected. For rural and low-income whites, these organizational developments promised at least the possibility of an inclusive public education. In effect, southern legislatures endorsed the goals, if not the rationale and core concept, of the antebellum common school movement. Evidence suggests that this partial commitment to public education served a southern white strategy to head off northern advocates of more fundamental social reform and in the process to gain control over the education of blacks (see Butchart, 1988).

Looking back on the period, W. E. B. DuBois (1935) concluded bitterly that with regard to education policy, the South had won the Civil War. Left to state and local governments with at best ambivalent commitments to the needs and aspirations of black people and low-income whites, schooling in the South began its long march toward separate and unequal public education.

The Progressive Education Movement

Several developments converged toward the end of the nineteenth century to set the stage for one of the most pervasive social reform campaigns witnessed in the United States. An accumulation of industrial wealth and power within an elite group sharpened social class distinctions. Large businesses dominated the economy, a trend that both stimulated and was supported by technological advance. Industrialization also shaped the job market. Its structure became more overtly pyramidal and less elastic, with openings at the bottom more distinctly defined and possibilities of advancement more narrowly circumscribed. Long a fixture in U.S. mythology, the frontier vanished as a geographical reality, and cities swelled in size. Immigrants from southern and eastern Europe poured into the country, many settling in urban centers. Depending on one's point of view, cultural pluralism grew richer or more threatening. In the popular mind, poverty, political graft, and crime became associated with such places as New York and Chicago. In the daily newspapers, indignant muckrakers bared the sorry state of life in big cities. Intellectual developments at once mirrored and abetted the changes. The scientific study of society surfaced in major universities, a new breed of researchers—social scientists—appeared, and confidence spread that their concepts and findings should guide human affairs, from the formulation of public policy to the management of industrial workers. It was a time in which few aspects of society seemed to be functioning properly and yet confidence remained high that social problems would bend before reason and science applied with moral certitude.

From the turn of the century through the period of the Great War, roughly 1895–1920, a wide spectrum of "progressive" reforms swept the country. This was the era of Teddy Roosevelt's presidency, child labor laws, trust busting, big-city political reform, and Americanization campaigns aimed at newly arrived foreigners. Walter Rauschenbusch's (1917) "theology for the social gospel" inspired countless missions among the urban poor; voluntary associations, like the YMCA and Jane Addams's Hull House in Chicago, ministered to the needs of body, mind, and soul—the "whole person"— among those crowded in inner-city tenements and immigrant enclaves. The principal organizers of these efforts tended to come from "the managing, leading, guiding class," the elite of the "four layers in civilized society," to borrow descriptors coined by Harvard University president Charles Eliot in 1908 (Tyack, 1974, p. 129). In cities all across the country, they formed "blue-ribbon" commissions to organize progressive reform campaigns.

The progressive education movement was a wing of this more extensive effort. Like the common school movement, it was loosely coordinated nationally, and yet its champions in various localities interacted frequently and shared similar goals. One of their clearest objectives was to cleanse the schools of political taint. Another was to organize and manage them according to sound business principles—efficiently, scientifically, professionally. A third goal sought a differentiated curriculum that could respond to student interests and abilities. Vocational education and high school "tracks" emerged as a consequence. Finally, public schools were perceived as effective dispensers of a wide range of social services on the grounds that hungry, ill, or poorly clothed children could not be expected to concentrate on their studies.

For progressive reformers, these aims addressed the deplorable conditions they found in schools. Most alarming, the political organizations that dominated big-city governments across the country had also taken charge of educational matters, where reason advised that professional expertise ought to prevail. Large, unwieldy school boards, some with upward of fifty members, each representing a different ward or some other power base, encouraged the existence of equally unwieldy urban school systems (Tyack, Kirst, & Hansot, 1980). Political favoritism infected all manner of educational operations, ranging from the appointment of teachers and principals to the letting of contracts for heating fuel. City schools, especially, became overcrowded polyglots, where almost every language seemed to be represented among the students *except* English. Confusion and disorganization reigned. Too many teachers lacked appropriate training or motivation for their work, and the ablest were demoralized. Here were conditions that cried out for order and immunity from political interference.

Within these unsavory circumstances, the old notion of the common curriculum functioned as an effective disincentive. When children could escape school, they did, although the alternative might be working long hours under dispiriting, even dangerous conditions. As Charles Eliot (see Tyack, 1974, pp. 129–130) argued, new, responsive curricula were needed, because the children brought different abilities and interests to school and because their social stations and job prospects could usually be predicted. These more tailored programs would give schooling a practical bent, whatever the student's future prospects, enabling it to retain a broader spectrum of young people and thus to be more inclusive. In addition to the diverse curricula, an extra curriculum of sports, clubs, and student government would offer inviting opportunities for students to participate in school life and to join in fashioning a model society. Also, the progressive curricula required teachers who knew both what and how to teach. Pedagogy too aspired to the status of science.

To bring these expectations to fruition, progressive reformers placed their trust in professionalism and the application of social science research. Students would be sorted into appropriate curricula. A new profession of school administrator emerged, its members university trained and confidently armed with the expertise needed for their tasks. Unsoiled by political bias and self-interest, theirs were the proper hands to be entrusted with the operation of schools. Like the professional businessmen they wanted to emulate, school administrators would organize both their systems and individual schools in a carefully arranged hierarchy (Callahan, 1962). Each actor—whether a superintendent, principal, teacher, or one of the growing number of central office specialists—had a defined role to play in keeping the organization operating efficiently and effectively.

Perhaps even this brief summary suggests the range and complexity of the progressive education movement and the mixed motives that inspired it. Americans living at the end of the twentieth century can locate in its goals and plans the spiritual ancestors of their own schools. David Tyack (1974) has given us a name for these reformers. They were "administrative progressives," those who plotted the early outlines of the sorts of schools most of us have attended. From their efforts followed increased centralization and bureaucratization of school organization and control, confidence in professional expertise and in tests of student aptitude and achievement, steadily increasing high school enrollments and graduation rates, a variety of curricula for different ability groups and vocational interests, and the development of teacher education within postsecondary institutions. For teachers, progressive education meant a growing disengagement from decisive roles in curriculum development, textbook selection, and school leadership roles as these duties were assigned to specialists within school systems. Although the reforms tended to focus on urban education, their impact spread to rural areas. Small, sparsely populated school districts were merged to form more cost-efficient units. Children of farmers were more likely to study agriculture in schools, on the assumption that requiring them to do so served their current and future interests (Fuller, 1989).

Opponents stressed the political character of the changes. Some parents watched with palpable disapproval as professionalization resulted in the distancing of local schools from their immediate constituencies. Others objected to the specialized curricula that were intended to respond to students' interests, fearing the vocational tracks would impose inescapable ceilings on the aspirations and opportunities of working-class youth. Within black communities, a teacher's race was often as important as professional credentials. Long before social scientists, black parents understood the salutary effects of positive adult role models on children. Country and city teachers alike complained about the "factoryizing" of schools, to borrow a term favored by Margret Haley, the outspoken leader of the Chicago Teachers' Federation (Tyack, 1974, p. 257). Many complained that progressive reforms ignored teachers or, worse, held them in contempt. Other opposition came from the urban political machines that the reformers had hoped to supplant. In several cities, political bosses never lost power; in others, they made successful comebacks. In both cases the search for patronage encompassed schools, and the notion of "nonpolitical" education fell by the wayside. The concept had no factual basis, in any case. Their claims notwithstanding, progressive reformers merely proposed to replace one mode of school politics with another.

Readers may have noticed that John Dewey has not been mentioned in this discussion. The omission was deliberate, even though his name is virtually synonymous with progressive education. Throughout his long life (he died in 1952 at the age of ninety-two), he returned frequently to his core argument with regard to education: Dichotomous approaches, whereby things to be learned were perceived as objects outside the student's sense of self, produced many effects, but growth—the primary aim of education—was not among them. He explored this thesis in *Interest and Effort in Education*, a terse and crystalline book even by Deweyan standards. It first appeared in 1913. By "sheer power," Dewey (1975 [1913], p. 7) observed, adults can force children to repeat facts, even bodies of knowledge, but through the process students learn the "habit" of divided attention (p. 9). They simulate attention, performing as expected, or in a fit of self-assertion refusing to do so, while their real interests pursue other matters or, worse, lie fallow. Students may acquire "well-disciplined habits" while their deeper nature "has secured no discipline at all" (p. 10).

Nor can learning be accomplished through the opposite approach. When teachers with great ingenuity make things interesting, they merely confirm that "interest itself is wanting" (p. 11). Dewey rejected any conception of education that disjoined subject matter from pedagogy or learners from what they learned. Curriculum was not "stuff to be learned" (p. 94) but the route to the development of the self. The point was not to impose interest, by force or ruse, but to nurture "the conditions that lie back of it and compel it" (p. 94). It was not enough, he warned "to *catch* attention; it must be *held*. It does not suffice to arouse energy; the *course* that energy takes, the results that it effects are the important matters" (p. 91, emphasis in original).

Looking backward from the late twentieth century, we may miss the originality of Dewey's analysis of educational principles. It also cut against the grain of established approaches to education policy and practice in the United States. Administrative progressives, however, worked within that tradition by affirming the "law of external pressure" articulated earlier by common school reformers. Ironically, then, Dewey can be counted among the opponents of the progressive education movement as it shaped the spirit, purposes, and organization of U.S. public schools. He left educational reform—its goals and methods—on the horns of a dilemma: If learning cannot be imposed without diverting the process from its desired outcomes, do imposed institutional forms and modes of control threaten to render schools similarly dysfunctional?

PATTERNS OF EDUCATIONAL REFORM

A recent episode in the public school system of Montgomery County, Maryland, illustrated the sorts of knots we try to untangle with educational reform. As reported in the *Washington Post* (Goldstein, 2 March 1989), a fourth-grade teacher gave her students the following social studies assignment: "Pretending you are a plantation master in the Old South, plan a week's schedule of activities required to keep your operation successful." One student decided that on the first day he would free the slaves. Unsure of what to write for the rest of the week, he took the problem to his mother. After complaining to the school principal that the assignment encouraged toleration for slavery, she filed a formal protest with the superintendent's office. Someone alerted the press. The story would have taken an ironic turn if the teacher had been black and the student's family white, but the opposite was the case. Confronted with the resulting furor, the teacher was dismayed. Sensitive to reform proposals urging greater emphasis on history and critical thinking skills, she had intended to help students progress beyond textbook descriptions by grappling with aspects of life and work in antebellum

Maryland. Furthermore, she added, the assignment appeared in the school system's curriculum guide as an approved optional activity. Indeed, it did. Black leaders and the student's mother remained outraged. They were particularly galled that the assignment had been given during Black History Month. The superintendent was quoted as saying, "What is in history needs to be taught . . . [but] what is important is how it is taught, and what messages it gives kids. You have to be sensitive" (Goldstein, 2 March 1989, p. B6).

Educators have not always been so candid about the extent to which educational reform has been a kind of juggling act. Fewer balls in their air make the work easier but from several perspectives less enthralling. As this episode in Montgomery County, Maryland, suggests, good intentions and technical proficiency, important as they may be in education, cannot alone guarantee success. The teacher, the school system, the student, and his mother endorsed the values of academic achievement, and yet cognitive development alone remained insufficient.

Although too general to satisfy the interests of historians, the three narratives in the previous section were intended to focus on the multilayered character of educational reform in the United States. The familiar adage "What you see is what you get" has not applied. Beneath specific objectives, educational reform has organized occasions in which we Americans teach ourselves about the values and expectations that we have lodged with schools. If debate is sufficiently acrimonious and far-flung, a kind of national seminar occurs. Such was the case every twenty-five years or so in the nineteenth century and more frequently in recent memory. Educational reform has functioned as a means of civic learning, a form of macro public schooling. As we can see, the results in terms of both education policies and practices have not always been edifying.

Two other general features of the pattern deserve mention. Educational reform has tended to arise from perceived failures of schools to serve certain social goals adequately. Rarely has it affirmed education as intrinsically valuable. Typically, we have thought of schools as means to other ends. Finally, educational reform has been relentlessly solemn. Its persistent lack of a sense of humor suggests that reformers may have inflated their own importance and coincidentally forgotten the targets of their strategies— children and youth.

In addition to these general characteristics of educational reform, the three narratives point toward the kinds of concern that have animated efforts to improve schools. A pattern emerges. First came seismic social change that threatened established values and structures of authority, followed by strategies focused on schools that sought to restore order. In the three examples, educational reform did not serve merely as a proxy for social reform, for it arose within more comprehensive improvement efforts. Still, it clearly functioned as a vehicle for political reform. Its driving force was not intellectual goals and values but social conflict. In these instances, educational reform was about power and its distribution. No one should be surprised that it generated controversy. This part of the pattern sheds light on the persistent struggle over the control and finance of public education, the argument being that those who paid the taxes should exercise authority over schools. The "law of external pressure" served to justify this point of view. If U.S. society needed public schools to promote political cohesiveness, cultural compatibility, and economic productivity, quite apart from any benefit they offered to individuals, reformers tended to agree that these larger purposes should guide both educational practice in schools and classrooms and the formation of education policy. The rationality of school centralization seemed unassailable. John Dewey's error, if it can be called that, was in thinking that with regard to schools and their reform, educational goals and values ought to prevail.

Neither have we pursued social benefit goals consistently. Reviewing the history of educational reform in the United States, one might draw from the numerous speeches, reports, and exposés, even with allowances for hyperbole, that national interests dictate a public schooling devoted to both academic excellence and social equity. Waffling on the latter, we have failed to achieve the former. Relaxing educational standards, particularly with regard to working-class and minority populations, has made a mockery of our rhetorical commitments to inclusiveness. Over the years, the reform pendulum has swung from one emphasis to the other. To switch metaphors, our schools and our education policies have rarely succeeded in juggling these two balls simultaneously, despite a great deal of talk about the profound national interests that have warned us to do so.

The reforms of the 1980s—the so-called excellence in education movement—repeated the pattern. In apparent reaction to an emphasis on equality of educational opportunity in the 1960s, reformers undertook to raise standards. The measured achievement of U.S. students was reported to have declined sharply over the past two decades. International comparisons placed them well below students in several other countries. Reformers in the United States wanted greater rigor in mathematics and science curricula, more homework, longer school days, and extended academic years. Conversely, fewer electives should be permitted. A core curriculum would expose students to a body of essential knowledge. In history, for example, they would confront those events, ideas, and leaders that have shaped the nation, not accounts that underscored our diversity (Hirsch, 1987). Participation in extracurricular activities, including athletic teams, would be linked to a student's grades. In short, education was to be made tougher. High school diploma requirements were raised accordingly.

As in the past, educational reform in the 1980s represented strategies to reach social objectives. In this case economic dysfunctions provided the stimulation. Other nations, Japan especially, were proving to be more productive, and U.S. reformers located the causes of our decline in the failure of schools to promote academic achievement. Strengthening the United States' competitive edge in the world economy provided the compelling rationale. With the nation at risk, schooling must become a more serious business. Limited educational funds would be invested in those programs and students that could advance the commitment to excellence. As one group of reformers put it in 1984,

> [T]he money and resources being thus reallocated do not belong to teachers, pupils, or parents. They are the money and resources of voters and taxpayers. There needs to be some connection between the welfare of these "paying" groups and decisions on school expenditures. (Quoted in *Education Week*, 5 September, 1984, p. 12)

Thus, once again, educational reform undertook the Herculean task of juggling one ball at a time. Those with a sense of history might have predicted that waiting offstage was a similar act with a different ball to toss around.

And yet, as several chapters in this book attest, the excellence movement has drawn a strongly positive public response. Some of the authors speak of an unprecedented popular endorsement of the reform goals. Historians tend to be more guarded about isolating the present from the past, for left to their own devices, they can nearly always find antecedents. In any case, because the history of educational reform has had little apparent influence on the formulation of current proposals, arguments over the dawning of a new day do not seem to pose fruitful lines of inquiry relative to the widely acknowledged need to improve schools. Rather, some old but fundamental questions still warrant the attention of reformers and policymakers: What purposes guide U.S. public education? Whom do they benefit? Do we intend to provide schools of excellence for all the people, and if so, what commitments of intellect, energy, imagination, and material resources are required?

Perhaps, however, educational reformers over the years have resorted to what today would be labeled a "marketing ploy." In selling education as a solution to social conflict and economic problems, they formulated focused rationales for public schooling that people in a particular era wanted to believe. Despite differences in the educational opportunities available across social class, racial, gender, and geographical lines, schools became the common institution. People aspired to its idealized benefits. The repetitious occurrence of educational reform thus kept an experiment alive. Like ritual dancers who had not yet learned their steps, we continued to debate which movements could approximate these ideals formulated long ago. It may be this spectacle, with its fits and starts and ragged edges, that has so intrigued foreigners. For other countries too need to find a uniting thread of education policy for their pluralistic populations—even Japan, which tends to deny its own diversity. Perhaps they suspect that our recurring struggles over educational reform may be instructive. They need to confront as well the prices we have paid when the struggle subsided and lost its memory.

For them and for the United States, John Dewey's (1975 [1913]) conclusion to *Interest and Effort in Education* has offered both hope and a warning:

> If we can discover a child's urgent needs and powers, and if we can supply an environment of materials, appliances, and resources—physical, social, and intellectual—to direct their adequate operation, we shall not have to think about interest. It will take care of itself. For mind will have met with what it needs in order to *be* mind. The problem of educators, teachers, parents, the state, is to provide the environment that induces educative or developing activities, and where these are found the one thing needful in education is secured. (p. 96, emphasis in original)

Writing these words over seventy-five years ago, Dewey articulated what may qualify as the enduring aim of educational reform in the United States.

REFERENCES

Anderson, J. D. (1988). *The education of blacks in the South, 1860–1935*. Chapel Hill: University of North Carolina Press.

Bailyn, B. (1960). *Education in the forming of American society: Needs and opportunities for study*. Chapel Hill: University of North Carolina Press.

Bailyn, B. (1982). The challenge of modern history. *American Historical Review, 87*(1), 1–25.

Bender, T. (1985, 6 October). Making history whole again. *New York Times Book Review*, pp. 1, 42–43.

Bloom, A. (1987). *The closing of the American mind*. New York: Simon & Schuster.

Bond, H. M. (1966). *The education of the Negro in the American social order*. New York: Octagon Books. (Reprint of the 1934 edition by Prentice-Hall.)

Butchart, R. E. (1983). Bureau of Refuges, Freedmen, and Abandoned Lands. In D. R. Whitnah, ed., *Government agencies*, pp. 41–46. Westport, CT: Greenwood Press.

Butchart, R. E. (1988). "Outthinking and outflanking the owners of the world": A historiography of the African American struggle for education. *History of Education Quarterly, 28*(3), 333–366.

Butts, R. F. (1939). *The college charts its course*. New York: McGraw-Hill.

Butts, R. F. (1978). *Public education in the United States: From revolution to reform, 1776–1976*. New York: Holt, Rinehart & Winston.

Calhoun, D. (1973). *The intelligence of a people*. Princeton, NJ: Princeton University Press.

Callahan, R. E. (1962). *Education and the cult of efficiency*. Chicago: University of Chicago Press.

Carter, S. B. (1989). Incentives and rewards to teaching. In D. Warren, ed., *American teachers: Histories of a profession at work*. New York: Macmillan.

Clifford, C. J. (1989). Man/woman/teacher: Gender, family, and career in American educational history. In D. Warren, ed., *American teachers: Histories of a profession at work*. New York: Macmillan.

Cohen, D. K. (1989). Practice and policy: Notes on the history of instruction. In D. Warren, ed., *American teachers: Histories of a profession at work*. New York: Macmillan.

Cremin, L. A. (1965). *The wonderful world of Ellwood Patterson Cubberley: An essay on the historiography of American education*. New York: Teachers College Press.

Cubberley, E. P. (1934). *Public education in the United States: A study and interpretation of American educational history*. Rev. ed. Boston: Houghton Mifflin.

Curti, M. (1935). *The social ideas of American educators*. New York: Scribner's.

Dewey, J. (1975). *Interest and effort in education*. Carbondale: Southern Illinois University Press. (Originally published by Houghton Mifflin in 1913.)

DuBois, W. E. B. (1935). *Black reconstruction in America*. Philadelphia: Saifer.

Eaton, J. (1907). *Grant, Lincoln, and the freedmen*. New York: Longmans, Green.

Education Week. (1984, 5 September), pp. 1, 12.

Elsbree, W. S. (1939). *The American teacher: Evolution of a profession in a democracy*. New York: American Book Company.

Finkelstein, B. (1989). *Governing the young: Teacher behavior in popular primary schools in nineteenth-century United States*. Philadelphia: Falmer Press.

Fuller, W. E. (1989). The teacher in the country school. In D. Warren, ed., *American teachers: Histories of a profession at work*. New York: Macmillan.

Goldstein, A. (1989, 2 March). Lesson on slavery called insensitive. *Washington Post*, pp. B1, B6.

Government of India, Ministry of Human Resource Development, Department of Education. (1986). *National policy on education: Programme of action*. New Delhi: Ministry of Human Resource Development.

Haydon, G., ed. (1987). *Education for a pluralist society: Philosophical perspectives on the Swann Report*. London: Institute of Education, University of London.

Hirsch, E. D., Jr. (1987). *Cultural literacy: What every American needs to know*. Boston: Houghton Mifflin.

Jones, J. (1980). *Soldiers of light and love: Northern teachers and Georgia blacks, 1865–1873*. Chapel Hill: University of North Carolina Press.

Kaestle, C. F. (1976). Conflict and consensus revisited: Notes toward a reinterpretation of American educational history. *Harvard Educational Review, 46*(3), 390–396.

Kaestle, C. F. (1983). *Pillars of the republic: Common schools and American society, 1790–1860*. New York: Hill & Wang.

Kaestle, C. F. (1988). Literacy and diversity: Themes from a social history of the American reading public. *History of Education Quarterly, 28*(4), 523–549.

Kaestle, C. F., & M. A. Vinovskis. (1980). *Evolution and social change in nineteenth-century Massachusetts*. New York: Cambridge University Press.

Katz, M. B. (1975). *Class, bureaucracy, and schools: The illusion of educational change in America*. New York: Praeger.

Kaufman, P. W. (1984). *Women teachers on the frontier*. New Haven, CT: Yale University Press.

Kingdom of Saudi Arabia, Ministry of Higher Education. (1986). *The educational policy in the Kingdom of Saudi Arabia*. Riyadh, Saudi Arabia: Ministry of Higher Education.

Korean Educational Development Institute. (1985). *Educational reform: A review of international trends and tasks for advancement of Korean education*. Seoul, Korea: KEDI Press.

Mann, H. (1870). Oration delivered before the authorities of the City of Boston, July 4, 1842. *American Journal of Education, 19*, 837–850. (Originally published in Boston, 1842.)

National Centre for Educational Research. (1986). *Development of education in the Arab Republic of Egypt, 84/85–85/86*. Cairo: Arab Republic of Egypt.

National Commission on Excellence in Education. (1983). *A nation at risk: The imperative for educational reform*. Washington, DC: U.S. Government Printing Office.

National Council on Educational Reform. (1986). *Second report on educational reform*. Tokyo: Government of Japan.

National Institute of Education. (1988). *Forum, 1*(2), 1–8. Maharagama, Sri Lanka: NIE Research Division.

Pierce, B. L. (1930). *Civic attitudes in American school textbooks*. Chicago: University of Chicago Press.

Rauschenbusch, W. (1917). *A theology for the social gospel*. New York: Macmillan.

Richardson, J. D., ed. (1908). *A compilation of the messages and papers of the presidents: 1789–1908*, Vol. 1. Washington, DC: Bureau of National Literature and Art.

Rury, J. L. (1989). Who became teachers? The social characteristics of teachers in American history. In D. Warren, ed., *American teachers: Histories of a profession at work*. New York: Macmillan.

Tyack, D. (1974). *The one best system: A history of American urban education*. Cambridge, MA: Harvard University Press.

Tyack, D. (1989). The future of the past: What do we need to know about the history of teaching? In D. Warren, ed., *American teachers: Histories of a profession at work*. New York: Macmillan.

Tyack, D., & E. Hansot. (1982). *Managers of virtue: Public school leadership in America, 1820–1980*. New York: Basic Books.

Tyack, D., M. Kirst, & E. Hansot. (1980). Educational reform: Retrospect and prospect. *Teachers College Record, 81*(3), 253–269.

Warren, D. (1974). *To enforce education: A history of the founding years of the United States Office of Education*. Detroit: Wayne State University Press.

Warren, D. (1983). The federal interest: Politics and policy study. In J. H. Best, ed., *Historical inquiry in education: A research agenda*, pp. 158–179. Washington, DC: American Educational Research Association.

Warren, D. (1985, December). Learning from experience: History and teacher education. *Educational Researcher, 14*, 5–12.

Warren, D. (1989). Messages from the inside: Teachers as clues in history and policy. *International Journal of Educational Research*.

Perspectives on Reform

CHAPTER 3

Balancing Control and Autonomy in School Reform: The Politics of *Perestroika*

William Lowe Boyd

Worldwide social, economic, and technological trends have generated needs that few existing school systems can meet. At the least, these developments require major reform efforts. In reality, they seem to require a fundamental restructuring of education systems. Unfortunately, even modest reforms are hard to achieve. Still more so is the ambitious idea, now spreading across national boundaries, of restructuring educational systems. These notions are difficult to realize partly because we often want to simultaneously maximize competing values, such as equity, excellence, efficiency, and liberty or choice (Boyd, 1984; Garms, Guthrie, & Pierce, 1978).

American reformers today are facing a need to strike a new and more educationally effective balance between competing values that have played a central role in the evolution of our education system. We began with a highly decentralized education system that was high on local participation, but low on central control, standards, and equity. Since the 1950s, there has been a steady movement to raise standards, enhance equity, and reduce fragmentation. But this movement toward more centralized control has come at substantial cost to local control and participation, and it has alternated in a tradeoff between an emphasis on excellence and an emphasis on equity.

Of course, although every society has to pick a particular policy mix or balance among competing values, no choice is final. Whatever choice is made favors some values over others, thereby sowing the seeds for tomorrow's reform movements (Kaufman, 1963). In time this leads to what, in the spirit of the Gorbachev era, can be called the politics of *perestroika*; that is, the maneuvering to determine whose interests and preferred reform agenda will shape the round of restructuring or reform that is unfolding. Whether radical restructuring or modest reforms are pursued, however, no program, even if fully achieved, will prove a panacea. Instead, the cycle of reform will continue, driven by the need for periodic adjustments in the balance of competing values (Kaufman, 1963).

CONTROL VERSUS AUTONOMY

In the United States today, Dan Lortie's (1969) classic discussion of the balance of control and autonomy in elementary schools can be extended as a shorthand for the current tensions in the education reform movement. An irony of the reform movement is that the well-known first and second "waves" of reform are driven by competing impulses. The first wave emphasized control; the second, autonomy. The conflict between the standardization and centralization embodied in the first, and the emphasis on teacher autonomy and professionalism embodied in the second, has been called the "San Andreas fault" in the reform movement.

Following the prescriptions of *A Nation at Risk* (National Commission on Excellence in Education, 1983), the first wave of reform efforts centralized control at the state level. It focused on the pursuit of "excellence" through state mandates intensifying much of what already was being done—such as higher graduation requirements, more testing, a more standardized curriculum. When carried to the extreme, this approach has tended to "deskill" teachers by reducing opportunities for professional discretion (McNeil, 1986).

By contrast, the second wave builds on the notion of professionalizing teaching and restructuring schools. Epitomized in the Carnegie Forum report, *A Nation Prepared* (1986), and the National Governors' Association report, *Time for Results* (1986), the second wave argues that decentralization, flexibility, and autonomy are essential, both to foster engagement in teaching and learning and to meet the diverse needs of our increasingly heterogeneous student bodies. Remarkably, "parental choice" (that is, autonomy for consumers—parents and students), a component of the second wave that was dismissed initially by many observers, has been gaining support rather dramatically.

Still, there can be little doubt that the conflicting "undertow" from the first wave of reform has impeded the progress of the second-wave reforms (Hawley, 1988). Now there is talk of the coming of a "third' wave, but its character is still unclear. One candidate might be even more pronounced "nationalizing" and centralizing forces. Certainly, the momentum behind the curriculum alignment and state- and national-level testing movement is growing. Some see us evolving toward a *de facto* national curriculum (Doyle, 1988), which is now being pursued *de jure* in the United Kingdom.

Whether movement toward a national curriculum is developing or not, it is significant that at the first annual meeting of the Business Roundtable to be devoted to a single topic (education) "a recurring theme in both [President] Bush's speech and the panel discussion was the need for an overarching national strategy for reform" (Walker, 1989, pp. 1, 17). Corporate leaders at the meeting agreed that fundamental reforms and restructuring were needed, not incremental improvements here and there. But Ernest Boyer emphasized the challenge, in developing a national strategy, of balancing "this need for coordination with the need for more school-based innovations" (Walker, 1989, p. 17).

Even though we don't seem to know quite how to achieve this balance—between control and autonomy—remarkably, we already have simultaneous efforts to increase both the centralization (to the state level) and decentralization (to the school level) of governance arrangements in education. In fact, this is a worldwide phenomenon, as noted by the foremost international expert on school-based management, Brian Caldwell, of the University of Tasmania:

> In general, governments in many countries are adopting a more powerful and focused role in terms of setting goals, establishing priorities and building frameworks for accountability—all constituting a centralizing trend in the centralization-decentralization continuum—at the same time as authority and responsibility for key functions are being shifted to the school level—a decentralizing trend. Much uncertainty arises because these trends, almost paradoxically, are occurring simultaneously or in rapid succession. (Caldwell, 1989, p. 3)

Local school boards may well feel caught in a no-man's land between these diverging thrusts. Must we choose between them, or can they coexist effectively?

TOWARD A NEW BALANCE OF CONTROL AND AUTONOMY

When properly understood, I believe that these diverging thrusts reflect not schizophrenic tendencies, but simultaneous imperatives for organizational improvement (see Caldwell & Spinks, 1988). Unlike private schools, public schools are not independent islands. They are, and must remain, part of a larger system serving broad social interests. To accomplish their purposes, they need a balanced combination of autonomy and coordinated control. If each school were allowed to go entirely its own way, local whims and biases could undercut educational coherence and equity. Thus, to realize the simultaneous imperatives, the interconnected system of public school governance is needed as much as ever—but in a revised form. Schools, school districts and their boards, and state departments and state boards of education need one another; none are likely to be complete and adequate without the other.

In this view, a key role for district and state-level boards of education is the collaborative development of (1) a strategic plan for educational improvement and (2) a broad, overall scheme for encouraging, supporting, and assessing the implementation of the goals of this plan. Research shows that schools seldom become and remain effective and innovative solely on their own. They need impetus and support from higher levels (Coleman, in press). Leithwood and Jantzi (in press, p. 16) remark that

> Research on effective districts suggests considerable involvement of school staffs and "experts" in district-level decision making. Such involvement is often delegated within a strong, centrally developed framework, which may take the form of a strategic plan. Feedback channels are developed which permit central coordination, monitoring, and long-term planning activities. Decision making in effective schools parallels that of effective districts. Teachers are involved in school-level policy decisions often including, for example, the assignment of students to classes. Effective schools have considerable school-level discretion for determining the means to be used in addressing problems of increasing academic performance. Effective secondary schools are organized and managed to support the purposes of the curriculum and the requirements for instruction implied by the school's philosophy of education.

Further support for the strategic planning responsibility is found in the experience of other nations. Reflecting on the international experience, a recent Organization for Economic Cooperation and Development (OECD) report (1987, p. 89) on the quality of schooling concludes that

> However great the autonomy enjoyed by schools, they are still answerable to administrative authorities at local, regional, and national level that have responsibility for

1. Setting quality targets and providing the means of attaining them;
2. Monitoring the implementation of appropriate strategies;
3. Conducting regular appraisals of performance in association with the schools concerned.

In all this, however, policymakers and administrators must remember the modern management adage that "to manage is not to control, but rather to get results." It is all too easy to become unnecessarily prescriptive and intrusive, even when pursuing a strategic planning approach. After all, as Ellen Goodman (1989) asks, "How can you manage flexibility? Is that a contradiction in terms? Businesses want plans and controls. The new workers want options and individual treatment." Can we have both?

The way toward a resolution of this tension is shown by Peters and Waterman's (1982) observation that excellent companies were characterized by "simultaneous loose–tight properties." That is, they were "both centralized and decentralized" (p. 15) and distinguished by "the co-existence of firm central direction and maximum individual autonomy" (p. 318). The firm central direction sets the key values and parameters that guide activiy, but the sphere of activity has an openness that encourages individual initiative and creativity. Firm guidelines, accountability arrangements, and staff socialization processes advance and protect the core values, such as equity. Exemplary practice in school administration already demonstrates the merits of this approach (see, for example, Hill, Wise, & Shapiro, 1989, p. 26; Murphy, 1989).

RESTRUCTURING VIA SCHOOL-BASED MANAGEMENT

Although restructuring covers a range of possibilities, much of the discussion has focused on school-based management and various schemes to improve and "empower" the teaching profession. Success in achieving the latter goal depends heavily on effective movement toward school-based management. As with all restructuring arguments, the claim is that fundamental improvement in school and student performance cannot be achieved without significant changes in the traditional structure and operation of public schools. If this claim is valid—and I believe it is—we need to carefully consider the arguments and issues involved in this matter.

Why School-Based Management Is Needed

The critical ingredients in successful education occur where students, teachers, and parents actually come together. Consequently, school-based management is founded on the belief that many key decisions inescapably must be made at the school level. This is where the people closest to the students and their distinctive needs can decide what needs to be done and how general goals and policies set at higher levels can be best implemented.

In the past, we perhaps assumed that school principals could accomplish these purposes. However, the traditional view of the school principal, as a kind of "superteacher" with all the answers, is giving away to a more realistic view of what principals can and should try to accomplish. Although most principals subscribe to the ideal of providing "instructional leadership," research documents that few principals have the skills, or can find the time, to execute this phase of their role successfully. Indeed, as Sykes and Elmore (1989) argue, the traditional conception of the principal's role creates a nearly impossible job. Consequently, the role needs to be reconceptualized to facilitate and share leadership opportunities with the teaching staff.

Thus, school-based management typically involves the creation of a school council, composed of the principal and members representing the teachers and parents, which is responsible for a variety of programmatic and operational decisions as well as the allocation of a small budget. Obviously, this shared decision-making model modifies the role of the school principal. This approach requires some careful negotiation and delineation of the new spheres of responsibility and authority and the ground rules for decision making, all of which is grist for the politics of *perestroika*.

School-based management is consistent with trends in modern business management that emphasize the advantages of maximum delegation of decision making to the operational level within a centrally coordinated framework—the "loose–tight" approach popularized by Peters and Waterman (1982). It also builds on the widely documented finding that effective schools are characterized by active staff involvement in school improvement efforts, involvement that fosters commitment and a sense of ownership. By contrast, highly prescriptive, "top-down" approaches to school governance diminish the professionalism and commitment of educators and may even result in their performing substantially below their capacity (McNeil, 1986).

Implementing School-Based Management

Experts agree that it is far easier to recommend school-based management, within a "loose–tight" framework, than to implement it. It is by no means a "quick fix" for what ails the schools. Indeed, this innovation must be approached as a developmental process requiring fundamental changes in roles and relationships that can be achieved only over a period of years, even when there is continuous and strong support from system-level leaders. For example, in the Edmonton Public School District, in Alberta, Canada, the process has been underway almost ten years. Begun with a three-year trial of school-based budgeting, it now has reached a stage in which

> The elected school board sets priorities each year which must be addressed in all schools. Budget preparation and staff selection are wholly decentralized to schools. Accountability in an education sense is addressed through a system-wide set of standardized tests in language, mathematics, science and social studies at two points in elementary schooling and at one point in secondary. Target levels of performance are set each year. (Caldwell, 1989, p. 14)

A key reason why a substantial period of time is needed for implementing school-based management is that its implications ultimately may affect so many stakeholders: parents, teachers, and school principals; superintendents, central office personnel, and local school boards; and state boards and departments. Ideally, collaborative planning and deliberation on the governance issues involved should be carried out in a spirit of cooperation and trust. At the least, they must try to move in this direction. Safeguards need to be built into school-based management schemes to protect a variety of equity considerations, such as guaranteed access and equity across neighborhood boundaries. A collaborative, professional relationship between teachers and school principals must be forged. If policymakers and the public believe that meaningful citizen participation in school councils is important, then vigilance will be required to prevent the councils from being dominated by the professional educators (Malen & Ogawa, 1988). The greater fear in governance circles, generally, is that school councils could become the captives of narrowly based, external interest groups. School-based decision-making rules and system-level accountability requirements must be designed to minimize this danger.

The Politics of Perestroika

Having sketched out the objectives and implementation of school-based management, as a key step in contemporary restructuring of school systems, we need to consider the politics of perestroika that are likely to ensue despite admonitions to the contrary. To begin with, school administrator associations have taken a very leery view of the Carnegie recommendation, in *A Nation Prepared*, for empowering teachers and sharing school decision-making more broadly (Thomson, 1986a, 1986b). Issues of power, turf, authority, and labor-management relations abound here. And apart from the power issue, there is no guarantee that the changes, by themselves, will lead to better performance. Hawley (1988, p. 434) remarks that "the idea that teachers will change the way they teach because we free them from bureaucratic constraints and provide them with opportunities to shape school policies and practices has a mystical quality to it." Without doubt, in the absence of positive leadership, there is a danger that school-based management ventures could bog down in power grabs and fractious relationships. As noted earlier, educators fear that if parents and community members are involved, further dangers of politicization will be opened up. What is more likely, as Malen and Ogawa (1988) found, is that citizen involvement in school-based management usually will remain perfunctory and ineffective.

Significantly, in a prescient discussion of school-based management a decade ago, Garms, Guthrie, and Pierce (1978, pp. 278–294) emphasized that parental choice of public schools may be needed to bolster and make effective parental political voice in school councils. Indeed, in my view, discussions of the problem of balancing control and autonomy in teaching and school management, now and in the past, have tended to leave students and parents as the odd men out. As I've argued elsewhere (Boyd, 1989), there are at least three legs on the schoolhouse stool and meaningful student and parental choice of public schools is needed to counterbalance the strong current thrusts toward managerial control and professional autonomy.

A persistent theme in the study of educational politics is the power of professional interests to triumph over parental preferences (Boyd, 1976, 1982; Guthrie & Thomason, 1975; Tucker & Zeigler, 1980; Zeigler & Jennings, 1974). Even when school boards resist the strong tendency toward conversion into "rubber stamps" for approving professional recommendations (Kerr, 1964), they are blunt instruments, at best, for representing and protecting the interests of individual families. Moreover, political "voice" through the ballot box is of limited value when dealing with public school systems that enjoy near monopoly status and that may still prefer to offer a "one best system" approach to education (Tyack, 1974). Thus, an increasingly diverse set of groups, from left, right, and center, is emerging to demand that far greater choice in public schooling arrangements be made available to parents and students. Given the inclination of professional educators, many of whom hope that demands for choice will go away, it is not surprising that the politics of choice is being played out largely outside of professional circles.

Greater choice for consumers of educational services can go a long way toward reducing the problems, in focus and goal displacement, that plague public schools. Choice not only restores an element of consumer sovereignty in public education, but at the same time increases the effectiveness of political voice (Hirschman, 1970). The power of consumer choice alters the political economy and dynamics of behavior within bureaucracies. Perhaps most important of all, choice facilitates movement toward building communities of shared values and educational purpose (Powell, Farrar, & Cohen, 1985; Coleman & Hoffer, 1987). However, this goal requires that educators, as well as clients, have greater freedom of choice in devising educational programs or choosing the kind of program with which they wish to affiliate. Indeed, Elmore (1987) shows that demand-side choice for consumers requires greater supply-side choice on the part of public providers, if they are to be able to respond successfully to public demands. Moreover, greater choice and, hence, discretion for teachers are essential for the real professionalism now being sought for the occupation by the "second wave" of the reform movement. Clearly, the more that communities of shared educational values and purpose can be created through reciprocal choice, the less will be the need for the kind of compulsion and coercion in teaching and learning that critics of schools have long deplored. The dramatic success story provided by Community School District No. 4, serving a low-income population in Spanish Harlem in New York City, is based on exactly the dynamics and advantages that such programs of educational choice enable (Fliegel, 1989; U.S. Department of Education, 1987, p. 60).[1]

In working toward a new balance of control and autonomy, we have to recognize that the reality of professional work in publicly controlled and funded schools requires a compromise between professional and bureaucratic models of control. Neither the entirely professionalized nor the entirely bureaucratized model is workable or desirable, although it seems clear that we need a new compromise that is more professional and less bureaucratic. Yet, because parents and the public at large can be frozen out, even from a better compromise of these two models, one of our vital concerns has to be for the creation and enhancement of governance models that effectively combine politics and markets (in other words, voice and choice) along with elements of professionalism and bureaucracy. School site management plans, involving parental choice and parental representation alongside teachers and administrators in the governance of schools, offer one promising model for public education in the future.

CONCLUSION

It will not be easy to achieve a new, more effective balance of control and autonomy that includes the consumers as well as the producers of education. School-based management schemes are not the only alternatives for restructuring, but it is hard to see how school improvement can be widespread without adopting many elements of these schemes, regardless of what one

calls them. The benefits that a coordinated approach to school-based management can bring, when properly implemented, justify the time and complications that inevitably are involved in pursuing this form of restructuring.
More effective schooling cannot be mandated or legislated. Nor is it fruitful
to intensify or continue pursuing a standardized, "one best system" of
education. Instead, a school improvement process that involves choice, as
well as bottom-up and top-down forces, must be brought into play. Coupled
with choice, school-based management is an ideal vehicle for increasing the
professionalism and creative engagement of teachers and school principals,
and for gaining the involvement and commitment of students and parents
that are needed for effective education. When school-based management is
linked to a well-designed strategic plan, to comprehensive and focused efforts
to improve instruction, and to the community and commitment that can flow
from reciprocal choice, the result can be true improvement of teaching and
student learning.

NOTE

1. Obviously, unrestricted and promiscuous choice could lead to a number of
serious problems, including those detailed in *The Shopping Mall High School* (Powell,
Farrar, & Cohen, 1985). Any system of choice within public education will need
provisions to ensure equity, to protect and promote a sound, basic curriculum, and to
protect client welfare, particularly in light of the growing proportion of the student
body that is composed of minoriy and "at-risk" students.

REFERENCES

Boyd, W. L. (1976). The public, the professionals and educational policymaking:
    Who governs? *Teachers College Record, 77*, 539–577.
Boyd, W. L. (1982). Local influences on education. In H. Mitzel, J. Best, & W.
    Rabinowitz, eds., *Encyclopedia of educational research.* 5th ed. New York: Macmillan
    and Free Press.
Boyd, W. L. (1984, Spring). Competing values in educational policy and governance:
    Australian and American developments. *Educational Administration Review, 2(2)*,
    4–24.
Boyd, W. L. (1989). School reform policy and politics: Insights from Willard Waller.
    In D. Willower & W. Boyd, eds., *Willard Waller on education and schools.* Berkeley,
    CA: McCutchan.
Caldwell, B. J. (1989, 29 March). Paradox and uncertainty in the governance of
    education. Paper presented at the annual meeting of the American Educational
    Research Association, San Francisco.

Caldwell, B. J., & J. M. Spinks. (1988). *The self-managing school*. New York: Falmer Press.

Carnegie Forum on Education and the Economy. (1986, May). *A nation prepared: Teachers for the 21st century*. Washington, DC: Carnegie Forum on Education and the Economy.

Coleman, J. S., & T. Hoffer. (1987). *Public and private high schools: The impact of communities*. New York: Basic Books.

Coleman, P. (In press). School district or regional management and school improvement. In Supplement 2 to the *International encyclopedia of education*. Oxford, England: Pergamon Press.

Doyle, D. P. (1988). The excellence movement, academic standards, a core curriculum, and choice: How do they connect? In W. L. Boyd & C. T. Kerchner, eds., *The politics of excellence and choice in education*. New York: Falmer Press.

Elmore, R. F. (1987). Choice in public education. In W. L. Boyd & C. T. Kerchner, eds., *The politics of excellence and choice in education*. New York: Falmer Press.

Fliegel, S. (1989). Parental choice in East Harlem schools. In J. Nathan, ed., *Public schools by choice*. St. Paul, MN: Institute for Teaching and Learning.

Garms, W. L., J. W. Guthrie, & L. C. Pierce. (1978). *School finance: The economics and politics of public education*. Englewood Cliffs, NJ: Prentice-Hall.

Goodman, E. (1989, 17 March). Mommy track poses risks, possibilities. *Centre Daily Times*.

Guthrie, J. W., & D. K. Thomason. (1975). The erosion of lay control. In National Committee for Citizens in Education, *Public testimony on public schools*. Berkeley, CA: McCutchan.

Hawley, W. D. (1988). "Missing pieces of the educational reform agenda." *Educational Administration Quarterly, 24*(4), 416–437.

Hill, P. T., A. E. Wise, & L. Shapiro. (1989, January). "Educational progress; cities mobilize to improve their schools." RAND Report R-3711-JSM/CSTP. Santa Monica, CA: Rand Corporation.

Hirschman, A. O. (1970). *Exit, voice, and loyalty*. Cambridge, MA: Harvard University Press.

Kaufman, H. (1963). *Politics and policies in state and local government*. Englewood Cliffs, NJ: Prentice-Hall.

Kerr, N. D. (1964). The school board as an agency of legitimation. *Sociology of Education, 38*, 34–59.

Leithwood, K. A. & D. Jantzi. (In press). Organizational effects on student outcomes. In Supplement 2 to the *International encyclopedia of education*. Oxford, England: Pergamon Press.

Lortie, D. C. (1969). The balance of control and autonomy in elementary school teaching. In A. Etzioni, ed., *The semi-professionals and their organizations*. New York: Free Press.

Malen, B., & R. T. Ogawa. (1988, Winter). Professional-patron influence on site-based governance councils. *Educational evaluation and policy analysis, 10*(4), 251–270.

McNeil, L. M. (1986). *Contradictions of control: School structure and school knowledge*. New York: Routledge & Kegan Paul/Methuen.

Murphy, J. T. (1989). The paradox of decentralizing schools: Lessons from business, government, and the Catholic Church. *Phi Delta Kappan*, June.

National Association of State Boards of Education (NASBE). (1988). Effective accountability: Improving schools, informing the public. Report of the Accountability Study Group, National Association of State Boards of Education, Alexandria, Virginia, October.

National Commission on Excellence in Education. (1983). *A nation at risk: The imperative for educational reform.* Washington, DC: U.S. Government Printing Office.

National Governors' Association. (1986). *Time for results.* Washington, DC: National Governors' Association.

Organization for Economic Cooperation and Development. (OECD). (1987). Quality of schooling: A clarifying report. Restricted Secretariat Paper ED(87)13. Paris, France: Organization for Economic Cooperation and Development.

Peters, T. J., & R. H. Waterman. (1982). *In search of excellence: Lessons from America's best-run companies.* New York: Harper & Row.

Powell, A. G., E. Farrar, & D. K. Cohen. (1985). *The shopping mall high school: Winners and losers in the educational marketplace.* Boston: Houghton Mifflin.

Sykes, G., & R. F. Elmore. (1989). Making schools manageable: Policy and administration for tomorrow's schools. In J. Hannaway & R. Crowson, eds., *The politics of reforming school administration.* New York: Falmer Press.

Thomson, S. D. (1986a, September). School leaders and the Carnegie agenda. *American School Board Journal, 173*(9), p. 32.

Thomson, S. D. (1986b, 28 May). Strengthen, don't diffuse, school leadership. *Education Week,* p. 28.

Tucker, H. J., & L. H. Zeigler. (1980). *Professional versus the public: Attitudes, communication, and response in school districts.* New York: Longman.

Tyack, D. (1974). *The one best system.* Cambridge, MA: Harvard University Press.

U.S. Department of Education. (1987). *Schools that work: Educating disadvantaged children.* Washington, DC: U.S. Government Printing Office.

Walker, R. (1989, 14 June). Bush to appoint group to proffer education ideas. *Education Week,* pp. 1, 17.

Zeigler, L. H., & M. K. Jennings. (1974). *Governing American schools.* North Scituate, MA: Duxbury Press.

CHAPTER 4

State Fiscal Policy and Education Reform

K. Forbis Jordan and Mary P. McKeown

For the past five years, public and media attention has been directed toward the need for reform of the public elementary and secondary schools and higher education in the United States. Starting with Secretary of Education Bell's National Commission on Excellence in Education and its 1983 report, entitled *A Nation at Risk*, approximately thirty national reports have called for a variety of reforms of the U.S. educational system. Many of the reports also have contained recommendations calling for changes in the preparation programs for elementary and secondary school teachers.

Efforts to understand and respond to the call for reform have been confused because of the lack of agreement on what should be classified as an educational reform. In the various reform reports released since 1983, the term "education reform" has been used to refer to a variety of state actions. Examples include increased graduation requirements for students, competency testing for teachers, increased state accreditation standards for schools, state takeover of schools because of fiscal or educational deficiences, new status titles and higher salaries for classroom teachers, revisions in teacher certification patterns, reductions in class size, and longer school days and years.

The impact of reform efforts may be immediately evident or difficult to observe or identify. Some reforms may be immediately observable, such as a longer school day, special programs for students, lower pupil-teacher ratios, increased graduation requirements, or state takeover of schools. Others, such as higher teacher salaries or staff development training programs, may not result in immediate changes. Even though these latter reforms may not be immediately evident, the likelihood is great that they will have positive long-term effects on teaching and learning.

The definition of an education "reform" is a continuing problem. State-required public school kindergarten programs provide an easily understood example. This action may represent a "reform" in one state, but be a long-established tradition in another. Concepts such as the "master teacher" or "career ladders" for teachers may be viewed as a reform in one state, but may be a discarded practice in another. Thus, the operational definition of an education "reform" may depend on the setting and the analyst-observer.

The challenge of determining what is a "reform" was illustrated in the reports on the actions in several states. In Alabama, reform funds included new state dollars for textbooks, instructional supplies, and school maintenance (Gold, 1988). Louisiana provided $15 million in additional state equalization dollars to poor parish school districts ("Louisiana reform package signed," 1988). Georgia allocated over $200 million, about 10 percent of total state funds, to reduce revenue disparities per pupil among local school districts ("State capitals," 1986b). Another example is the Kentucky action raising state aid to low-wealth local school districts to reduce disparities in expenditures per pupil among school districts. State appropriations were increased by 16 percent; provisions included dollars to equalize revenues among districts, mandated reductions in class size, and higher teacher salaries ("State capitals," 1986d). General state aid also was increased in Maryland, but limited funding was provided for new initiatives that might be classified as education "reforms" ("State capitals," 1986c).

A specific reform definition issue is whether reduction of class size should be considered to be an education "reform." Alabama (Gold, 1988), New Mexico (Snider, 1986a), and Kentucky ("State capitals," 1986d) provided funds for reduction of class size. An example of the differences among states is shown by statewide implementation of kindergarten programs being considered a "reform" in New Mexico (Snider, 1986a) and Mississippi ("Mississippi hikes school budget," 1986).

FOCUS OF THE EDUCATION REFORM
RECOMMENDATIONS

The thrust of the 1980 education reform recommendations has been quite different from the 1970 efforts to reform state school finance programs or the earlier calls for curricular reform in the schools. The goal of the 1970 efforts was to provide equal fiscal inputs for all students, and the intent was to increase the level of fiscal equity, or access to funds per pupil, in the methods used to finance a state's elementary and secondary schools.

The 1980 school reform reports have emphasized school graduation requirements, student performance, and improvement of teaching. The focus of this discussion is on analyzing the recent reform reports in terms of changes in inputs for schools. From a macro fiscal perspective, the problem is to ascertain if the funding commitment has been consistent with the rhetoric. From the micro perspective, the challenge is to identify fiscal resources for programs and activities that might be classified in some manner as education "reform." From the school finance perspective, the question is to determine if the schools again have fallen victim to "unfunded, or underfunded, mandates."

As indicated later in this discussion, some interesting developments have been identified in studies and analyses of state actions. Dougherty (1986), Inman (1987), and Odden (1986), as well as the case studies reported in this chapter, suggest that overall state funding for public elementary and secondary schools has increased in absolute dollars and in the proportion of total revenues from state and local sources.

The issue then becomes whether these "new" funds can be appropriately classified as dollars for school reform. In some instances, local school districts have been directed to use the additional state dollars to raise teachers' salaries. In other cases, the intent of the state legislation has been to increase the level of equalization in funding among local school districts. More fiscal resources have been provided for low-wealth/high-tax-effort school districts. In other cases, to ensure that local school districts respond to legislative intent, some states have enacted categorical programs that require local school districts to use the "new" state dollars for specific school reform initiatives.

Even with the additional funding and expressions of support for schools, the more crucial question may be what impact the reforms have had on the day-to-day work of the classroom teacher. Results from a recent survey of 13,500 teachers by Ernest Boyer (Carnegie Foundation, 1988) suggest that teacher morale has declined rather than increased over the past five years. The respondents also reported that they felt less "empowered" than at the start of the school reform movement. However, the same teachers indicated that student achievement levels had increased; goals for schools had been clarified; classrooms were more orderly; uses of technology had increased; availability of textbooks and instructional materials had improved; and teachers' salaries had increased. Even with these changes, many teachers reported that working conditions had not improved. Classes were larger in many cases; nonteaching duties remained; and less time was available to meet with other teachers (Jennings, 1988).

DATA ISSUES

Even though the literature is replete with studies of educational reform, inconsistency among data sources has been a continuing problem in interpreting the impact of educational reform. This report includes an analysis of two national studies, a national telephone survey, revenue projections for the states, and other accounts. The national reports include an unpublished survey conducted by the Education Commission of the States, or ECS (Dougherty, 1986), and a published survey from New York University's Center for Education Finance (CEF) study of the fiscal impact of educational "reform" (Inman, 1987). News accounts provided summaries of actions by state legislatures; and detailed analyses of a selected group of states were obtained from state education agencies and legislative bodies. The telephone survey we did provided information concerning state actions related to additional funding for teacher education programs. The actual dates covered in the reports varied somewhat, but did contain comparable data. The ECS study reports funding for the 1984–85 and 1985–86 school years; the New York University study reports funding for the years 1983–1987; the summaries are for 1986–88; the case studies covered 1985–89; and the phone survey covered 1985–1989.

FUNDING FOR ELEMENTARY AND SECONDARY SCHOOL REFORM

The most comprehensive study of funding for education reform since release of *A Nation at Risk* was the ECS study (Dougherty, 1986). Fiscal data on "reform" activities were secured from forty-seven states; activities were classified into the five categories shown in Table 4-1. From a total of $67 billion in state dollars for local school districts, the forty-seven states in the ECS survey reported total "school reform" appropriations in 1985–86 of less

Table 4-1
State Funds (in millions) for "Education Reform" Activities

Type of Activity	1984–85		1985–86	
	Dollars	Percent	Dollars	Percent
Teacher initiatives	$588	42.4	$796	40.1
Graduation requirements	9	0.6	11	0.5
Curriculum and programs	379	27.3	552	27.8
Student testing	54	3.9	72	3.6
School-classroom structure	357	25.8	554	28.0
	$1,387	100.0	$1,985	100.0

Source: V. Dougherty. (1986, 1 April). Funding education reforms. Unpublished draft. Denver: Education Commission of the States.

than $2 billion, or about 3 percent of the state total for all states (Sirkin, 1986).

The possibility of misconceptions concerning the magnitude of state funding for school reform also was evident in 1988 legislative action in West Virginia in which a measure for fiscal 1989 referred to as "school reform" originally was funded at the same level as provided for local schools in the previous two fiscal years. However, the level of state funding later was reduced from $717 million to $712 million in a special session of the West Virginia legislature (Mirga & Mathis, 1988).

Even though the actions cannot be construed as being specifically for school reform, results from the 1988 general election suggest a continuing base of public support for elementary and secondary education. In passing a statewide referendum, California voters guaranteed the state's elementary and secondary schools either a minimum of 39 percent of the state's general fund budget or the same amount they had received the previous year after adjustments for inflation and enrollment changes. Observers suggest that one possible impact would be a reduction in revenues for higher education if the state experiences a revenue shortfall (Colvin, 1988).

Public education advocates found additional relief in the 1988 election with the defeat of tax limitation proposals in Colorado, South Dakota, and Utah. In another instance, Illinois voters rejected a measure calling for a constitutional convention; opponents feared that the session might try to limit or freeze local property taxes, thereby restricting fiscal resources for schools (Walsh, 1988b).

Data from the ECS survey on funding for school reform are summarized in Table 4-1. Funding is reported in five major categories, and these provide the framework for the following discussion.

Teacher Initiatives

In 1985–86, funding for teacher initiatives reached almost $800 million, or 40 percent of the "reform" dollars, and about 90 percent (of the 40 percent) for teacher initiatives was targeted for teacher compensation. The principal legislative actions were to fund career ladder plans, across-the-board raises for all teachers, pilot merit pay programs, increase in the minimum salary schedule for all teachers, or higher salaries for beginning teachers (Hume, 1986). In 1986, states' appropriations for this approach to "reform" were reported in Arizona ("State capitals," 1986a), Georgia ("State capitals," 1986b), Kentucky ("State capitals," 1986d), Mississippi ("State capitals," 1986e), New Mexico (Snider, 1986a), and Virginia ("State capitals," 1986f). During the same time period, the largest portion of New York's reform was the provision of $96.5 million through a discretionary grant program to increase salaries of teachers in Grades 1–3 when the district salaries were below the state or regional average (Snider, 1986b).

From fiscal year 1983 through fiscal year 1987, twenty-five states reported efforts to increase salaries, but only sixteen states provided additional funds. Career ladder and merit pay programs were proposed in twenty-one states, but state appropriations were provided in only fifteen states (Inman, 1987).

In 1988, several states enacted additional legislation concerning teacher compensation. Mississippi provided from state dollars a $3,700 increase in teachers' salaries ("Legislative update," 1988b). Kansas also earmarked $38 million for teacher salary increases ("Legislative update," 1988a). In passing a $2.4 billion appropriation for precollegiate education in 1988, Alabama allocated $93 million for a 7.5 percent pay raise for teachers (Gold, 1988).

From a $1.46 billion appropriation for precollegiate education, Louisiana provided $66 million for a 5 percent increase in teachers' salaries and $15 million in state equalization dollars to poor parish school districts ("Louisiana reform package signed," 1988). In a somewhat similar manner, the North Carolina legislature appropriated $110.7 million to raise teachers' salaries by 4.5 percent; this amount represented about 0.4 percent of the total state appropriation for precollegiate education ("Legislative update," 1988e).

In 1988, Tennessee raised the state minimum teacher salary amount and revised its career ladder system to permit all teachers to apply for eleven- and twelve-month contracts ("Legislative update," 1988e). In a more drastic action than Tennessee's relaxation of requirements for its extended-school-year salary for teachers, Florida terminated its incentive pay master teacher program before the expiration of the state's career ladder law. The state legislature failed to fund the program even though forty of the state's sixty-seven school districts had submitted plans for the career ladder program (Mathis, 1988).

Graduation Requirements

Of the forty-one states that had raised their graduation requirements between 1983 and 1986, only two states had provided any additional dollars to meet the costs associated with these increased standards (Hume, 1986). Some relief may have been obtained through using classes with larger numbers of students and reducing the number of electives. Direct funding for higher graduation requirements accounted for less than 0.5 percent of the total 1985–86 "reform" dollars (Dougherty, 1986).

Curriculum and Programs

Over $550 million, or about 27 percent of the 1985–86 state "reform" dollars, were for school curriculum and educational programs (Dougherty, 1986). Target areas included basic skills; mathematics, science, and computer education; early childhood education; programs for "at-risk" students; and programs for gifted and talented students. For these target groups, thirteen states allocated $67.3 million for programs to serve "at-risk" youth, and twenty-three states allocated $131 million for programs to serve gifted and talented youth. Over 80 percent of the dollars for "at-risk" students was in a single state (Inman, 1987).

In 1988, interest continued concerning special funding for at-risk and gifted and talented students. Missouri funded summer programs as well as programs to serve gifted and talented students ("Legislative update," 1988a). From a total state appropriation for elementary and secondary education of $1 billion, the Colorado legislature appropriated $1 million for a pilot preschool program for 2,000 disadvantaged children considered to be handicapped or "linguistically different" ("Legislative update," 1988c). North Carolina allocated $4.2 million for before- and after-school programs for latchkey students and $3 million for programs to serve academically gifted students ("Legislative update," 1988e). From $1.09 billion for K–12 schools in Arizona, $3 million was provided to reduce class size and improve instruction in Grades K–3 and $1.5 to implement a dropout prevention program ("Legislative update," 1988e). In Mississippi, $2 million of the total of $747 million for grades K–12 was earmarked for a new mathematics-science residential high school ("Legislative update," 1988b). In Alabama, sufficient funds were provided to reduce the kindergarten pupil-teacher ratio to 17 to 1, as required by a new state mandate (Gold, 1988).

The 1988 trend of providing small appropriations for specific projects also was found in Maine, where ten schools have received state funding to experiment with flexible scheduling and interdisciplinary study projects

("Across the nation," 1988). Connecticut followed this trend of using special grants by providing $1 million for fifteen extended-day kindergarten programs ("Report's sampling of state initiatives," 1988).

Student Testing

In 1985–86, $72 million—less than 4 percent of the total reform dollars—were allocated for student-testing programs. State actions were limited; for example, two states accounted for about 60 percent of the $72 million. One funded incentive grants, and the other supported remedial programs (Dougherty, 1986).

Recently, a somewhat different use of student test scores has been enacted in Connecticut. Starting in the 1989–90 school year, a portion of the state school aid will be provided on the basis of the number of students who score below the remedial level on the state's mastery tests ("Connecticut to link aid, test scores," 1988).

School and Classroom Structure

About 28 percent, or over $550 million, of the 1985–86 state "reform" dollars was allocated for classroom and organizational structural changes. The two principal areas were reduction of class size and extension of the school day and/or school year. Over 60 percent of the dollars were expended in a single state to extend the school day and the school year. Funds to reduce primary-grade class size in three states represented over 10 percent of the resources expended for changes in school and organizational structure (Dougherty, 1986). To encourage schools to offer an additional mathematics-science period in high schools, Florida allocated $29 million in 1983–84 and $69 million in 1984–85, but no funds in 1985–86 (Florida Legislature, 1986). However, for 1988–89, the Florida legislature appropriated $108.6 million for an extended day and a seventh period in secondary schools ("Statistical report," 1988).

Interest in structural reforms also was evident in 1988. Minnesota authorized an extended day program for Grades K–6, but provided no funding ("Legislative update," 1988a). With $2.5 million, Washington funded twenty-one projects to encourage schools and school districts to experiment with reforms of their own design ("State capitals," 1988). From a total K–12 state appropriation of $346 million, Rhode Island created two $2 million education block grants for a new early childhood initiative and additional dollars for special education, limited-English-speaking (LES) students, gifted students, and administrator training ("Legislative update," 1988d).

States have included in their reports of "education reforms" such diverse and traditional items as additional state equalization aid to poor school districts, higher minimum teachers' salaries, and special categorical aid for special populations, summer camps, and administrator training programs. This diversity of programs and activities illustrates some of the difficulties with developing definitions of "reform" of classroom or organizational structure.

ACTIONS IN SPECIFIC STATES

Summary information on legislative actions from specific states provides additional insight into the level and purposes of funding for school "reform." Florida, Illinois, and Texas were selected because their legislative actions illustrate two different responses to "reform"—increased dollars for the basic state aid program or targeted funds for special purposes. Florida has increased its relative funding for both the regular education program and school reform; however, the percentage of the state appropriations for reform has not increased significantly. Faced with economic problems, increases in general school aid were limited in Illinois, and funding for reform was also limited. Texas has focused its new funding on the state's foundation program, and only limited fiscal resources have been provided for reform.

Florida

As a state with increasing numbers of students attending the public schools and with high-density urban areas as well as a large number of rural school districts, diverse pressures influence the policymakers who determine funding levels for Florida schools. Even with the interest in special reform activities, additional dollars have been provided for the state share in the funding of operational costs in the schools. The trend is shown in the following chart of the state appropriation for Florida's basic state equalization program in selected years:

Fiscal year 1984	$2.123 billion
1985	$2.373 billion
1986	$2.576 billion
1989	$3.539 billion

The amounts listed here do not take into account categorical funding. When these dollars are included, total state dollars increased by $256 million between fiscal years 1985 and 1986. Of these additional state monies, $203 million was for the state's basic school aid, or foundation, program. Between fiscal years 1984 and 1986, categorical funds for special programs including reforms increased by about $100 million from $315 million to $425 million, and total state appropriations for education increased by $500 million over the same period (Florida Legislature, 1984, 1986).

Between fiscal years 1986 and 1989, the state added over $1.2 billion for elementary and secondary schools. Over the same period, categorical funding increased by more than $140 million, of which $40 million was earmarked for pupil transportation. More reform-related funds included a $55 million increase for K–3 programs, $19 million for middle childhood education, $10 million for instructional materials, and $7 million for writing skills instruction. By fiscal year 1989, the principal reforms were K–3 improvement, writing skills, middle childhood education, compensatory education, and merit schools, and the total for the five programs in fiscal year 1989 was about $250 million, or almost 6 percent of total state appropriations for education. This amount was an increase from the $160 million allocated for the same programs in FY 1986, when reform funds comprised 5.4 percent of the total state dollars ("Statistical report," 1988).

As shown in Table 4-2, funding patterns have not been consistent for programs. Funding levels for compensatory education, instructional materials, K–3 improvement, student development services, student transportation, and writing skills instruction have increased incrementally. Funding for middle schools improvement suggests an additional area of emphasis. Support for reading resource specialists, safe schools, and summer inservice institutes has tended to remain constant.

Illinois

Differences in definitions for reform were evident in information from Illinois. In the 1985–86 school year, the state appropriation included approximately $2.4 billion for Illinois school districts. About $114 million of the total could be classified as new state funds for education "reform." In the same year, the increase in general state aid was $213 million. The principal "reform" initiatives were summer schools for gifted students at $23.5 million, preschool programs at $12.1 million, K–6 reading improvement at $38 million, and improvement of instruction in mathematics and science at $20 million (Illinois State Board of Education, 1985, 1986).

For fiscal 1989, the state appropriated $2.53 billion for students in K–12, a $110 million increase over the amount for 1985–86. News reports classified $27 million of the 1988–89 dollars as being for education reform. The bulk of these funds was for early childhood education programs. Other reform

Table 4–2
State Funds for Categorical Programs to Florida Public Schools for Fiscal Years (FY) 1984, 1986, and 1989

Program	FY 1984	FY 1986	FY 1989
Community schools	0	$3.3	$2.6
Compensatory education	$32.8	36.1	41.5
Comprehensive health program	0	1.4	2.1
Computer lab equipment	10.0	0	0
Diagnostic resource centers	0	2.2	2.0
Dropout prevention	0	1.6	1.5
Instructional materials	38.6	46.8	57.4
K–3 improvement program	79.9	89.5	145.3
Master teacher	0	6.6	0
Merit schools	0	10.0	10.0
Middle grades improvement	0	4.5	23.8
Migrant education	0	2.2	3.1
Reading resource specialists	4.6	4.8	5.8
Safe schools	10.0	10.4	11.2
School bus replacement	8.0	8.0	15.0
School lunch match	0	9.1	9.1
Science lab equipment	2.0	2.1	2.4
Student development services	20.3	23.7	31.1
Student transportation	75.6	100.0	148.2
Summer camps	0	1.0	1.0
Summer inservice institutes	9.2	9.5	9.7
Teachers as advisors	0	3.6	5.3
Writing skills instruction	20.3	22.7	29.5
Other	4.5	25.4	9.7
TOTAL	$315.8	$424.5	$567.3

funding included $3.5 million for dropout prevention and $2 million for a mathematics and science academy ("Legislative update," 1988e).

Texas

The impact of changes in a state's economic conditions is illustrated in the response to school reform in Texas. Even though Texas has the reputation for having enacted significant school reforms, the fiscal commitments have been very limited. When adjustments have been made for inflation and increases in pupil enrollments, the state appropriations for reform have been rather insignificant, and the tendency has been for state-level funding to remain stable, decrease, or be "folded into" the basic program.

From fiscal year 1985 to fiscal year 1986, the total regular education foundation program state and local sources increased by $322 million from $5.526 billion to $5.848 billion, an increase of about 6 percent. Required local funds increased by $336 million, resulting in a $14 million decline in state foundation aid for schools. The major change enacted in the new formula was to shift from a personnel-based state school finance formula to a pupil-based formula. The weighted student approach was used to provide funds for special popula⁺ions, and factors were included to recognize differences in the cost of delivering education and the additional costs associated with small schools (Texas Education Agency, 1985).

From fiscal year 1987 to fiscal year 1989, total state and federal funding for elementary and secondary schools increased by $340 million, almost 6 percent of the $5.7 billion base for fiscal 1987. Approximately $100 million was attributable to increases in federal dollars. Appropriations for particular programs did not follow a pattern. The basic allotment under the foundation program for elementary and secondary education from the state increased by less than $70 million to a 1989 level of $4.4 billion, less than a 2 percent increase. Funding for special education increased by just over $100 million (21+ percent); funding for compensatory education increased by $36 million (10 percent); funding for bilingual and vocational education remained constant. Pupil transportation increased by $14 million (7 percent). Fiscal 1989 funding for education improvement, including the career ladder program, increased by about $7 million to $423 million (less than 2 percent). Required local effort for the state foundation program increased by $148 million (8 percent), and state funds for local district equalized enrichment increased by $82 million—less than 5 percent (Texas Education Agency, 1988).

If the change in the state school aid distribution formula is not considered, Texas allocated about 10 percent of state funds for education "reform." Reform-related items included $416 million in state and local dollars for the career ladder program, $57 million in state and local funds for prekindergarten programs, and $3 million from the state for school district summer school activities (Texas Legislature, 1985; Texas Education Agency, 1988).

One of the principal Texas school reforms has been a mandated maximum class size of 22 to 1 for Grades K–4; however, no specific funding has been provided to cover either the instructional or facilities costs of the mandate. This issue was addressed in recent proposals from a consortium of Texas educational organizations. The group recommended that additional fiscal resources be provided for this program through the state's school aid formula. Annual costs for the proposal are estimated to be $300 million or more (School Finance Working Group, 1988).

FUNDING FOR TEACHER EDUCATION REFORM

Proposals for changes in teacher education have been a major emphasis in many school reform reports. However, information is limited concerning the actions taken by state legislatures and executive bodies to provide additional funding for improvement of teacher education. States provide funds for higher education through complex funding formulas, incremental appropriations, and special appropriations (McKeown, 1987). In addressing teacher education reform, states used one of these three approaches. Much of the following information was secured by telephone interviews with professional staff members in state agencies responsible for higher education.

Between the 1986 and 1989 academic years, states took several different approaches in their efforts to address problems related to teacher education programs. Areas included financial aid for students, entrance standards, and curricular "reform" for teacher education programs.

Financial Aid

In 1986–87, financial aid packages for prospective teachers were provided by thirty-five states.[1] By 1988–89, special financial aid packages were available in forty-four states.[2] Table 4-3 lists the states that did provide some type of financial aid in 1988–89. Special scholarship programs for teacher education students were provided in twenty-one states. The scholarship amount varied from about $1,500 per year to $10,000 per year in Nevada. The highest number of potential scholarships reported in the survey was 312 in New York, and the lowest number was 6 in Colorado.

As shown in Table 4-3, in 1988–89, loans were available in thirty-six states, up from twenty-six states in 1986–87. Of these thirty-six states, twenty-seven had some type of forgiveness provisions. Some loans were completely forgiven on a year of teaching for a one-year loan basis, while other states forgave a specified percent of the loan amount each year. Forgiveness clauses typically included interest on that portion of the loan that was forgiven.

Although in 1988–89, more states reported some type of financial aid to attract potential students to teacher education programs, the majority of these programs were forgivable loans. Since research on financial aid indicates that minority students are unlikely to use loans, this form of financial aid may be questionable (Wagner, 1986).

Table 4-3
List of States by Type of Financial Assistance Provided for Teacher Education Students in 1988–89

Type of Assistance		
Scholarships	**Forgivable Loans**	**Loans**
Alabama	Alaska	Georgia
Colorado	Arizona	Iowa
Florida	Arkansas	Kentucky
Idaho	California	Louisiana
Illinois	Connecticut	Maine
Iowa	Delaware	Massachusetts
Kentucky	Florida	New York
Louisiana	Hawaii	North Carolina
Maryland	Indiana	
Missouri	Kansas	
Nebraska	Maine	
Nevada	Maryland	
New York	Mississippi	
North Carolina	Montana	
Oklahoma	New Hampshire	
Pennsylvania	New Jersey	
South Carolina	Ohio	
Tennessee	Oklahoma	
Utah	Oregon	
Washington	Pennsylvania	
West Virginia	South Carolina	
	Tennessee	
	Texas	
	Vermont	
	Virginia	
	Washington	
	Wisconsin	

Entrance Standards for Teacher Education Programs

Entrance standards for applicant students desiring to enter teacher education programs have been established as a second component in the effort to improve the quality of students pursuing teaching careers. As shown in Table 4-4, as of 1988, at least forty-seven states reported some type of entrance standards for admission to teacher education programs. Approximately half of the states had initiated entrance standards since 1980.

The survey results reported in Table 4-4 indicate that only four state

Table 4-4
Type of Entrance Standard Used by States and Source of Funds for Administration

State	Type of Entrance Standard	Cost Paid by
Alabama	GPA, test	Student
Arizona	Test	Student
Arkansas	GPA, test	Student
California	Test	Student
Colorado	GPA, test	Student
Connecticut	GPA, test	Student
Delaware	Test	Student
Florida	Test	Student
Georgia	GPA	NA
Hawaii	GPA	NA
Idaho	GPA	NA
Illinois	Test	State funds
Indiana	Determined by institution	Student
Kansas	Test	State funds
Kentucky	Test	State funds
Louisiana	Test	Student
Massachusetts	Test	Student
Minnesota	Test[a]	Student
Mississippi	GPA, test	Student
Missouri	Test	Student
Montana	GPA	NA
Nebraska	Test	Student
Nevada	GPA, test	Student
New Jersey	GPA, test	Student
New Mexico	Test	Student
New York	Determined by institution	Varies
North Carolina	Test	Student
North Dakota	GPA	NA
Ohio	Test	State funds[b]
Oklahoma	GPA, test	Student
Oregon	Test	Student
Pennsylvania	Test	Student
Rhode Island	GPA	NA
South Carolina	Test	Student
South Dakota	GPA, test	Student
Tennessee	Test	Student
Texas	Test	Student
Utah	GPA, test	Student
Vermont	GPA	NA
Virginia	GPA	NA

(continued)

Table 4-4 *(continued)*
Type of Entrance Standard Used by States and Source of Funds for Administration

State	Type of Entrance Standard	Cost Paid by
Washington	Test	Student
West Virginia	Test	Student
Wisconsin	GPA, test	Student
Wyoming	GPA, test	Student

Note: GPA, grade-point average; NA, not applicable.
ᵃ Testing program to be started in 1991.
ᵇ Special state appropriation provided for development of testing program.

legislatures had made an appropriation for test development and/or test administration. As a result, the test makers have limited incentive to devote resources to test development. Either the student or the institution must pay for administration of the test. Such actions can have interesting implications for the quality of the tests being used to screen students, and the testing fee for the student may have a discriminatory impact. The expense may affect the choices made by economically deprived students—as well as other applicants—with the ability and performance record that permits them to choose alternative careers.

Curricular Reform in Teacher Education

In addition to providing financial aid for students and establishing standards for people who want to pursue teaching careers, states also have initiated changes in teacher education programs. Some type of "reform" of the teacher education curriculum was reported in twenty-seven states in 1986. In 1988–89, forty-five states reported "reforms" in this area. (See Table 4-5.)

In some states, reform initiatives were being taken independently by the teacher education institutions; in others, actions were required by state legislatures or executive agencies. Special funding for these activities was being provided in only six states in 1986–87 and by only two states in 1988–89. Even though no special state appropriations were provided for the study and design of reform of teacher education programs, the costs of operating the program likely would be covered by funding formulas in states with those formulas. Additional funds would be made available by adjustments to the components of the state's funding formula. Responses from twelve states indicated that additional dollars likely would be available

Table 4–5
Type of Curricular Change in States and Source of Funds for Implementation

State	Type of Curricular Change	Funding Source
Alabama	Subject area revision	No new revenues
Arizona	Unspecified	No new revenues
Arkansas	Unspecified	State appropriation
California	5-year program	State appropriation
Colorado	M.Ed./subject area revision	No new revenues
Connecticut	Subject area revision	No new revenues
Delaware	Revision of core	No new revenues
Florida	Individual institution	State formula
Georgia	Revision of program core	State formula
Hawaii	Unspecified	Regular budget
Idaho	Subject area revision	No new revenues
Illinois	Individual institution	No new revenues
Indiana	Individual institution	No new revenues
Iowa	Unspecified	No new revenues
Kentucky	Unspecified	State formula
Louisiana	Unspecified	State formula
Maine	Unspecified	No new revenues
Maryland	Subject area	State formula
Michigan	Individual institution	No new revenues
Minnesota	Outcome measures	No new revenues
Mississippi	Unspecified	State formula
Missouri	Unspecified	Regular budget
Montana	Unspecified	No new revenues
Nebraska	Institution specific	No new revenues
Nevada	Program core revision	No new revenues
New Hampshire	Academic major	No new revenues
New Jersey	Academic major	Regular budget
New Mexico	Unspecified	No new revenues
New York	5-year program	No new revenues
North Carolina	Unspecified	No new revenues
North Dakota	Unspecified	No new revenues
Ohio	Core and subject area revised	State formula
Oklahoma	Unspecified	State formula
Oregon	Subject area revision	No new revenues
Pennsylvania	Study of 5-year program	No new revenues
South Carolina	Unspecified	State formula
Tennessee	Unspecified	State formula
Texas	Subject area revision	State formula
Utah	Unspecified	No new revenues
Vermont	Unspecified	No new revenues

(continued)

Table 4-5 *(continued)*
Type of Curricular Change in States and Source of Funds for Implementation

State	Type of Curricular Change	Funding Source
Virginia	Some 5-year programs	State formula
Washington	M.Ed. proposed	No new revenues
West Virginia	Unspecified	No new revenues
Wisconsin	Unspecified	No new revenues
Wyoming	Under study	No new revenues

through the state's higher education funding formulas. In addition to the funds available under the regular state's higher education funding formula, a special state appropriation provided additional fiscal resources for the teacher education reforms in Florida and Louisiana. Respondents from an additional three states indicated that increased funding would be available through nonformula appropriations.

In the remaining states, any programmatic changes would have to be supported through regular funding. However, to illustrate the confusion over what is a "reform," in eight of these latter states that reported no new funding for reform activities, special appropriations had been provided for improving teacher education programs. "Centers for Excellence" were being funded in five states; dollars for pilot projects or competitive grants were provided in three additional states. Private foundation funding had been secured by Idaho in 1986–87, but did not continue into 1988–89.

Formal report documents, media releases, and subsequent state actions have given considerable attention to "reform" of teacher education programs. However, state legislatures and executive agencies appear to have taken the position that "reform" in this area can be achieved without additional dollars or by reallocating existing resources.

The lack of designated funding for reform of teacher education programs adds further importance to the call for action referred to as "the Spring Hill letter." The essence of this letter was a recognition by top campus administrators that reform of teacher education will require a commitment of fiscal and intellectual resources by the total institution as well as leadership from the chief executive officers in each institution. This statement, signed by thirty-seven college presidents and chancellors, was sent to every college and university president in the nation ("Spring Hill: The letter thirty-seven presidents write . . .," 1987). Subsequently, the American Association for Higher Education received a $500,000 grant to launch a "President's Forum on Teaching as a Profession" (Edgerton, 1988).

FISCAL PROJECTIONS OF FUNDING FOR REFORM

Even though public officials, educational leaders, and members of the business community may make eloquent statements concerning the need for education reform, the test for a policy statement is the extent to which public funds are allocated for the activity. The previous discussion illustrates two dilemmas about this examination of funding for education reform. First, only marginal amounts of state dollars have been provided for those activities that the individual states have classified as reforms. Second, the issue of whether funding is for reform or maintenance of the current educational system often cannot be answered because of the diversity in funding practices and the absence of agreement about what constitutes an educational reform. This dilemma has resulted in the labeling of new dollars for ongoing educational programs as funding for ongoing educational reform (Odden, 1986).

In a recent survey of state-level legislative fiscal officers by the National Conference of State Legislatures (NCSL), education was listed as one of the leading fiscal issues for the 1989 legislative session in twenty-eight states. This finding differed from the survey prior to the 1988 session in which tax reform was *the* leading fiscal issue. Elementary and secondary education was listed as *the* highest-priority issue in thirteen states, and higher education was listed as *the* highest-priority issue in two states. Taxation was listed as a leading fiscal issue in twenty-one states, and as *the* leading issue in ten states. The third most frequent fiscal issue was budget policy; it was listed as a leading fiscal issue in twelve states, and as *the* leading issue in eleven states. In thirty-six, *the* leading issue was listed as elementary and secondary education, higher education, or budget policy. However, the trend appears to be that, as state-level fiscal conditions improve, state policymakers broaden their range of fiscal concerns to address more diverse issues (Gold, Eckl, & Fabricius, 1988).

Most education reforms have a direct and an indirect cost. For example, higher salaries will require additional dollars or fewer teachers; smaller class size will lead to more funds or lower salaries; and increased graduation requirements will result in more teachers or reduced course offerings. Because of the disparities in assessed value of taxable property per pupil—or fiscal capacity—among local school districts, if the state does not provide dollars for the education reforms, initiatives likely will not be implemented without curtailing education programs. Thus, the capacity of a state to implement education reforms will be affected by the availability of "new" state fiscal resources for education.

Overall, among the states, the possibilities of increased state appropriations for education in fiscal year 1988 appear to be better than for 1989; the

NCSL attributed this projection to the impact of new state taxes and the strength of the economy. However, conditions vary, and depressed conditions in agriculture and energy likely will have a negative fiscal impact on some states. The greatest indicator for caution is that the average of the end-of-year balances for all states was marginal at 2.6 percent of the total budget, less than the average balance a few years ago and only half the 5 percent level recommended by many fiscal analysts. For fiscal year 1988, twenty-seven states estimated that their year-end balances would exceed 5 percent of their general fund, but in 1989, only fifteen states projected that their year-end balances would be that high (Gold, Eckl, & Fabricius, 1988).

The overall current economic conditions among the states appear to be better than anticipated in a 1986 report from the National Governors' Association (1986). In this report, only ten states were projected to have in excess of the five percent benchmark in 1986, and only eight states in 1987. However, in 1987, the actual number of states with year-end balances in excess of 5 percent was seventeen (Gold, Eckl, & Fabricius, 1988).

Overall state funding for elementary and secondary education had a larger rate of increase than higher education between fiscal years 1988 and 1989, and the rate was greater than between 1987 and 1988. The 1989 increase in funding for elementary and secondary was 7.4 percent compared to 6.5 percent in 1988. Placed in a longitudinal perspective, this rate of increase for elementary and secondary education is less than in the years prior to 1988. For higher education, the trend among the states is less positive; the fiscal 1989 increase was 4.9 percent, about two-thirds of the increase for fiscal 1988. The effect of a state's fiscal conditions on the capacity to increase funding is illustrated in Wyoming. The proportion of that state's general fund allocated to education increased by 18.2 percent, but funding for education at both levels decreased by about 1.0 percent (Gold, Eckl, & Fabricius, 1988).

Regional patterns of funding for education illustrate the differences in fiscal conditions among the states. Appropriations for elementary and secondary schools in "oil states" such as Oklahoma (6.5), Texas (2.2), and Wyoming (−0.6) either decreased or increased at less than the average percentage for all states, while Louisiana reported an 11.3 percent increase for elementary and secondary education and a 7.4 percent decrease for higher education. Higher education funding for Texas (3.6 percent) and Wyoming (−0.9 percent) followed the same trend, but Oklahoma reported increased state funding for higher education: 12.1 percent (Gold, Eckl, & Fabricius, 1988).

Because of different fiscal practices among the states, information on state fiscal allocations for education can be misleading. For example, federal dollars may be reappropriated by the state and reported as state dollars; local spending is not included for elementary and secondary education;

community college monies may be reported separately or included in the data of either level; and student tuition may or may not be included in the higher education data.

Even though education has been classified as the leading fiscal issue by most states, this may more reflect the expectations and the pressures on both local and state revenues sources, than a commitment or the fiscal capacity to increase funding for education. Because of the lack of a significant fiscal surplus in most states, the pressures on the local property tax, and local sensitivity to unfunded and underfunded state mandates, significant funding for education reforms appears unlikely without increases in state taxes.

CONCLUSIONS

Fiscal projections and past state practices do not suggest that state legislatures will provide significant increases in funding for the reform of education. Much of the new state money labeled as "funding for education reform" has been earmarked for increases in teacher salaries or for greater fiscal equalization among local school districts. Once again, the question of a definition for education reform becomes relevant. If education reform is to be interpreted as changing a school's organization or system for teaching students, then very little additional dollars have been provided by the state for "reform" of education. This conclusion has been used in developing the following insights about funding for school reform:

1. Estimates of funding for school "reform" will continue to vary because of differing interpretations and varying conditions among the states. A "reform" in one state may be a tradition in another and discarded practice in another. Efforts to raise teachers' salaries and increase fiscal resources in poor school districts may be well intended, but may have minimal impact on either school organization or classroom practices.
2. State commitments of funds for educational "reforms" have varied. The tax effort in some states and the level of funding for education historically have been relatively low, and much of the new money in these states must be classifed as "gap closing."
3. Except for a few instances, the level of new state funding has not been sufficient to support the actions called for by the advocates for "reform" of the public schools and teacher education programs. To secure visibility for the reform agenda, limited funding has been allocated to specific "high-visibility/low-cost" educational programs or activities.
4. Of the additional fiscal resources that have been made available for public elementary and secondary schools, large portions have been in

the form of general state aid and have not been aimed at either specific programs or groups of students. Even in those states that have provided special funding for school reform, reform funding has represented less than 10 percent of total state appropriations for elementary and secondary education.

5. Efforts to achieve reform through higher standards and increased requirements may benefit gifted and talented and/or highly motivated students; however, these efforts may have an adverse effect on efforts to increase success levels for low-achieving students. These students may find themselves confronted with increased in-school performance requirements and higher expectations without additional support.

NOTES

1. The District of Columbia, and Hawaii, Idaho, Kansas, Massachusetts, Michigan, Minnesota, Montana, Nebraska, New Hampshire, New Mexico, North Dakota, Oregon, Rhode Island, South Dakota, and Wisconsin do not provide financial aid packages for perspective teachers.

2. In 1988–89, no programs were being provided in Minnesota, Michigan, New Mexico, North Dakota, Rhode Island, and South Dakota.

REFERENCES

Across the nation. (1988, 21 September). *Education Week*, p. 2.

Carnegie Foundation for the Advancement of Teaching. (1988). *Report card on school reform: The teachers speak*. Princeton, NJ: Carnegie Foundation for the Advancement of Teaching.

Colvin, R. (1988, 16 November). California voters back "guarantee" for school funding in constitution. *Education Week*, *1*, 11.

Connecticut to link aid, test scores. (1988, 25 May). *Education Week*, p. 10.

Dougherty, V. (1986, 1 April). Funding education reforms. Unpublished draft. Denver: Education Commission of the States.

Edgerton, R. (1988, November). Help wanted: "Education presidents." *AAHE Bulletin*, pp. 8–9.

Florida Legislature. (1984). Florida's fiscal analysis in brief. Tallahassee Florida Legislature.

Florida Legislature. (1986, 20 May). Working documents, public school budget 1986–87. Tallahassee: Florida Legislature.

Gold, D. (1988, 21 September). "The best": $2.4 billion budget for Alabama schools gets a go-ahead. *Education Week*, p. 12.

Gold, S. G., C. L. Eckl, & M. A. Fabricius. (1988, September). *State budget actions in*

1988. Legislative Finance Paper No. 64. Fiscal Affairs Program. Denver: National Conference of State Legislatures. Pp. 32–33.

Hume, M. (1986, 1 May). Career ladders boosted as response to "A Nation at Risk." *Education Daily*, p. 6.

Illinois State Board of Education. (1985). *State, local and federal financing for Illinois public schools*. Springfield: Illinois State Board of Education.

Illinois State Board of Education. (1986). *State, local and federal financing for Illinois public schools*. Springfield: Illinois State Board of Education.

Inman, D. (1987). *The fiscal impact of educational reform*. New York: Center for Education Finance, New York University.

Jennings, L. (1988, 25 May). Survey finds teachers "dispirited," uninvolved in reform. *Education Week*, p. 7

Legislative update. (1988a, 11 May). *Education Week*, p. 15.

Legislative update. (1988b, 18 May). *Education Week*, p. 11.

Legislative update. (1988c, 8 June). *Education Week*, p. 13.

Legislative update. (1988d, 22 June). *Education Week*, p. 13.

Legislative update. (1988e, 3 August). *Education Week*, p. 27.

Louisiana reform package signed. (1988, 3 August). *Education Week*, p. 24.

Mathis, N. (1988, 12 June). Florida incentive-pay experiment dies quietly. *Education Week*, p. 11.

McKeown, M. (1987). Funding formulas. In M. McKeown and K. Alexander eds., *Values in conflict: Funding priorities for higher education*. Cambridge, MA: Ballinger, pp. 63–90.

Mirga, T., and N. Mathis. (1988, 3 March). West Virginia governor signs massive reform measure. *Education Week*, p. 22.

Mississippi hikes school budget. (1986, 23 April). *Education Week*.

National Commission on Excellence in Education. (1983). *A nation at risk: The imperative for educational reform*. Washington, DC: U.S. Government Printing Office.

National Governors' Association. (1986, March). Fiscal survey of the states. Washington DC: National Governors' Association.

Odden, A. (1986, January). Sources of funding for education reform. *Phi Delta Kappan, 67*(5), 335–340.

Report's sampling of state initiatives. (1988, 21 September). *Education Week*, p. 15.

School Finance Working Group. (1988, 14 November). Texas guaranteed yield program: Blueprint for the future. Austin: Office of the State Comptroller.

Sirkin, J. R. (1986, 23 April). Education spending rate slows: salary gains made, N. E. A. finds. *Education Week*, p. 4.

Snider, W. (1986a, 5 March). New Mexico lawmakers pass wide-ranging school reform act. *Education Week*, pp. 5, 13.

Snider, W. (1986b, 16 April). Oil and education budgets: It's feast and famine. *Education Week*, pp. 1, 9.

Spring Hill: The letter 37 presidents write. . . . *AAHE Bulletin*. (1987, November). Pp. 10–14.

State capitals. (1986a, 28 May). Arizona: Salary hike voted, but cap remains. *Education Week*, p. 6.

State capitals. (1986b, 9 April). Georgia: New funds for education reform. *Education Week*, p. 6.

State capitals. (1986c, 9 April). Maryland: 11 percent hike for schools passed. *Education Week*, p. 14.

State capitals, (1986d, 16 April). Kentucky education reforms win full funding. *Education Week*, p. 8.

State capitals. (1986e, 23 April). Mississippi hikes school budget. *Education Week*, p. 16.

State capitals. (1986f, 19 March). Virginia legislature funds education package. *Education Week*, p. 6.

State capitals. (1988, 22 June). "Schools for 21st Century Project" is taking off. *Education Week*, p. 10.

Statistical report. (1988, August). 1988–89 Florida Education Finance Program. MIS Series 89–04. Tallahassee: Division of Public Schools, Florida Department of Education.

Texas Education Agency. (1985, 5 August). State Summary Table. Austin: Texas Education Agency.

Texas Education Agency. (1988, November). State Board of Education Budget Materials. Summary Table. Fiscal 1990 and 1991 Budget Materials. Austin: Texas Education Agency.

Texas Legislature. (1985). Supplement to the House Journal, Sixty-Ninth Legislature, Text of Conference Report, House Bill No. 20. Austin: Texas Legislature.

Wagner, A. (1986). Financial aid. In M. McKeown and K. Alexander, eds., *Values in conflict: Funding priorities for higher education*. Cambridge MA: Ballinger, pp. 157–182.

Walsh, M. (1988a, 15 June). 3 states must trim budgets in wake of revenue shortfalls. *Education Week*, p. 10.

Walsh, M. (1988b, 11 November). Tax limits defeated in Colorado, South Dakota, and Utah. *Education Week*, p. 11.

CHAPTER 5

Catch the Wave: Reform Commissions and School Reform

David N. Plank and Rick Ginsberg

The school reform movement has recently met increasing skepticism with respect both to its accomplishments and to the effects of recent reforms on students and schools. A wide array of scholars and policymakers, including William Bennett, Albert Shanker, Terrence Deal, and Theodore Sizer, has begun to question whether the reform movement has yet brought about significant changes in schools, and whether the changes that have been made (standardization of curriculum, centralization of control) really portend improvements in the quality of U.S. education (Nienhuis, 1987; Rodman, 1987a; Snider, 1987; Olson, 1987b; see also Boyd, 1987). These and other critics have dismissed most recent reforms as symbolic or cosmetic, and they have begun to call for "structural" changes in the way schools are organized and operated.[1]

The call for structural educational reforms represents the so-called second wave of the school reform movement. Reports like those recently published by the Carnegie Forum on Education and the Economy's Task Force on

The original version of this chapter was written while Plank was supported by a Spencer Fellowship from the National Academy of Education, and he would like to express his gratitude to the Academy and to the Spencer Foundation. Research assistance was provided by Diane Kirk, Anella Nickolas, and Dave Smith, and we are grateful to them as well.

Teaching as a Profession (1986), the Holmes Group (1986), and the National Governors' Association (1986) call for changes in the U.S. educational system that go well beyond the reforms adopted—or even proposed—in the first wave of the reform movement. Proposals to professionalize teaching, to decentralize administrative control, and to expand parental choice would, if enacted, require major changes in the distribution of power and authority within the U.S. school system. It remains to be seen, however, whether any of these proposals can attract sufficient political support to be adopted or implemented.

One striking similarity between the first and second waves and the present school reform movement is the extent to which both have relied on commissions of experts and distinguished citizens to focus public attention on educational issues and to generate proposals for change. The first wave of the reform movement was shaped to a great extent by the reports of a multitude of reform commissions, including the National Commission on Excellence in Education (*A Nation at Risk*), the Twentieth Century Fund Task Force on Federal Educational Policy (*Making the Grade*), the Task Force for Economic Growth (*Action for Excellence*), the National Science Board Commission (*Educating Americans for the 21st Century*), and the Carnegie Foundation for Advancement of Teaching (*High School*). In an early survey of these reports, the Education Commission of the States identified sixteen national reform commissions, and noted that more than 175 state task forces were simultaneously considering educational reform issues (Education Commission of the States, 1983).

The second wave of the school reform movement has also been defined to a great extent by the activities and reports of educational reform commissions. Reports from the Carnegie Forum on Education and the Economy, the Task Force on Teaching as a Profession (*A Nation Prepared*), the Holmes Group (*Tomorrow's Teachers*), the National Governors' Association (*Time for Results*), the National Commission on Excellence in Educational Administration (*Leaders for America's Schools*), and the Committee for Economic Development (*Investing in Our Children, Children in Need*) have attempted to set the terms of the continuing debate on educational reform. Each of these commissions has put forward a variety of proposals for further changes in the organization and operation of U.S. schools.

In this chapter, we investigate the relationship between educational reform commissions and educational reforms. We put forward two related hypotheses:

1. The number of structural educational reforms proposed by a reform commission is inversely related to the number of constituencies represented on the commission.
2. The political viability of the reforms proposed by a reform commission

(as measured by subsequent adoptions in state legislatures, for example) is positively related to the number of constituencies represented on the commission.

We also propose a third hypothesis, based on the chronology of the first and second waves of the reform movement:

3. First-wave reform reports were characterized by the use of dramatic, "agenda-setting" rhetoric, while second-wave reports presented policy alternatives in more straightforward prose.

We test these hypotheses with data on commission membership, reform rhetoric, and reform proposals from a sample of national commissions from the first and second waves of the school reform movement. Then we discuss the theoretical bases for our hypotheses. We subsequently present data on the constituencies represented among the members of five first-wave and five second-wave school reform commissions, categorize the reform proposals put forward by each of these ten commissions, and analyze the rhetoric of the reform reports. In the sixth section of the chapter, we present some preliminary evidence on the extent to which reform proposals from first- and second-wave commissions have been adopted at state and district levels. In the concluding section, we assess the relationship between commission membership and commission proposals for reform, and we discuss the implications of our findings for the future prospects of the school reform movement.

THEORETICAL FRAMEWORK

It is a commonplace to observe that the U.S. educational system is highly decentralized, with power and authority fragmented and widely diffused within the system (Campbell, Cunningham, Nystrand, & Usdan, 1986; Guthrie, 1985. See also Weick, 1976). Consequently it is difficult if not impossible to change the educational system without wide agreement on the necessity and utility of reform among those at lower levels of the system, including local administrators, teachers, and parents. The lack of authoritative central control in the U.S. educational system imposes a common character on national school movements, which must rely on symbolic appeals, exhortations, and the rhetoric of "crisis" to generate support for change (see, for example, Meyer, 1983; Deal, 1985).

Lacking more efficacious instruments, school reformers have for nearly a century relied on "blue-ribbon" panels of educators and notables to establish the symbolic and rhetorical context in which educational reform might become possible. Reform commissions foster a sense of urgency about the state of the schools and promote symbols (such as "excellence" or "standards") that define the nature of the current crisis and point the way to its resolution. Commissions commonly urge the adoption of specific changes, but often the main product of their labor is a climate of opinion favorable to educational reform. This may in turn encourage (or allow) state and local education officials to adopt and implement changes in the schools (Ginsberg & Wimpelberg, 1987).[2]

The U.S. educational system is also exceptionally open to its environment, and susceptible to political and other influences from a diverse array of internal and external constituencies (Wirt & Kirst, 1983). Many groups have a stake in the system, and something to win or lose from changes in its current operation and structure. As a result, reforming U.S. schools is a highly pluralistic and problematic process (Fullan, 1982). Constituencies ranging from teachers and parents to politicians and business leaders take part, and the fragmentation of power and authority within the system multiplies the number of points (from courts to Congress to classrooms) at which each group can intervene. Many of these constituencies are able to modify or block reforms that they perceive to be contrary to their interests, either prior to adoption or during the process of implementation (Adams, Cornbleth, & Plank, in press).

To succeed, therefore, school reformers need to win support for their proposals from a variety of interests. In those states that have recently adopted comprehensive reform packages, for example, the reformers' success depended on the support of strong and diverse coalitions (Chance, 1986). The membership of educational reform commissions commonly reflects this fact. In an effort to take diverse and sometimes competing interests into account, commission members are often recruited from the full array of the educational system's internal and external constituencies. Giving all these groups a voice in the preparation of the commission's report ensures at least some degree of prior political support for reform proposals, and may improve the chances that the commission's recommendations will be approved and implemented. (For a related argument, and some evidence, see Pfeffer, 1972, 1973.)

The disadvantage of recruiting commission members from diverse constituencies is that the representation of all affected interests virtually guarantees that only marginal changes in the present structure and operation of the education system will be proposed, because of the veto accorded to all members by the informal norm requiring unanimity in commission recommendations (Peterson, 1983). Only those reforms that offend no significant interest can win universal approval. Structural reforms that would alter the prevailing distribution of power and authority or advance some interests at the expense of others are rarely if ever proposed by commissions.

To the extent that reformers take the rhetoric of "crisis" seriously, therefore, they face strong pressures to dispense with the consensus building that typifies most reform commissions. Panels recruited from among the like-minded, or from a single constituency, are better able to agree on a forthright diagnosis of the school system's ills, and they are not constrained by the need to balance competing interests in their prescriptions for reform. In consequence, such commissions are more likely to produce recommendations for structural changes in the educational system than are more widely representative panels.

Regrettably, panels recruited from a relatively narrow base may alienate constituencies who are not represented, or those who fear that their interests would be harmed by the commission's recommendations. Insofar as excluded groups retain the power to modify or block changes that they oppose, it will prove difficult to gain widespread support or legislative approval for proposals for structural reform.

In sum, the fragmentation of authority within the U.S. educational system makes "blue-ribbon" commissions a useful instrument for school reformers. The openness of the school system to the influence of diverse constituencies argues in favor of broadly based recruitment, but the need to balance competing interests within widely representative commissions virtually rules out recommendations for reforms that promise significant shifts of power and authority. Reform commissions recruited from a narrower base are more likely to produce recommendations for structural changes, but they may face strong opposition as they seek the adoption and implementation of their proposals.

The use of different kinds of rhetoric may help to resolve these dilemmas. We hypothesized earlier that the rhetoric of the first-wave reform reports was more dramatic than that of reports from the second-wave. The use of inflammatory language may help reform commissions to raise educational issues onto the policy agenda and to build support for their policy recommendations, by fostering a perception of "crisis" in the educational system (Polsby, 1984). Such a rhetorical strategy may be particularly effective when the anticipated opposition to the reformers' proposals is relatively weak, as when most interested constituencies are represented on reform commissions. Second-wave commissions, in contrast, may not need to dramatize educational issues, which are already on the policy agenda, but seek rather to present alternative courses of action to policymakers (Kingdon, 1984). Moreover, the use of relatively straightforward rhetoric may serve to make proposals for structural changes less threatening and therefore more palatable to affected constituencies.

In the following sections, we present data on the composition and recommendations of commissions from the first and second waves of the current school reform movement. We examine the choices that reformers have made with respect to these contrasting approaches to commission recruitment, and we assess some of the consequences of these choices. We also analyze differences in the rhetoric used in reports by first- and second-wave reform commissions.

ROUND UP THE USUAL SUSPECTS: COMMISSION MEMBERSHIP

Table 5-1 presents data on the membership of five first-wave reform commissions, all of which published reports in 1983. Nearly 90 percent of the 120 members of these five commissions are included in the twelve occupational groups identified in the table, which represent the principal constituencies of the public educational system. ("Other" groups include journalists, entertainers, former Cabinet officials, lawyers, and foundation representatives.)

Two related features of these data deserve emphasis. The first is the broad array of interests represented on the first-wave commissions. Four of the five commissions included representatives from at least nine of the twelve identified interest groups. The exception is the Twentieth Century Fund Task Force on Federal Educational Policy (*Making the Grade*, 1983), which included representatives from only four groups. Commission sponsors and organizers plainly sought to acknowledge the multiple constituencies of the educational system in the composition of these groups into their proposals for reform.

The second notable feature of the first-wave commissions (which follows almost by definition from the first) is the virtual uniformity of membership structure across commissions. Three groups (state superintendents, local superintendents, and university faculty members) were represented on all five panels, and three others (local school boards, principals, and business executives) were included on four. Only the Twentieth Century Fund Task Force departed significantly from the modal pattern.

Table 5-2 presents data on the membership of five second-wave reform commissions, which published their reports between 1985 and 1987. (The Commission for Economic Development sponsored two reform commissions in this period, and membership data for both are reported together in the last column of the table.) To an even greater extent than on the first-wave reform commissions, the members of these commissions were drawn from the twelve identifed occupational groups. Barely 3 percent of the members of second-wave commissions represented other interests.

Table 5-1

Membership of "First-Wave" Reform Commissions, by Occupational Categories

	AfE[a]	EA[b]	MtG[c]	NaR[d]	HS[e]
Politicians	16	1	0	1	0
Business	14	3	0	1	1
State-level education Administrators					
Superintendent	1	1	1	1	1
School board	1	0	0	1	0
Local-level education Administrators					
School board	1	1	0	2	1
Superintendent	1	1	1	1	2
Principal	1	1	0	2	4
Teachers	1	1	0	1	0
Union officials	1	0	0	0	2
Parents	0	0	0	0	1
Education schools	0	1	4	0	3
Other academic	2	8	6	7	6
Other[f]	3	1	0	1	8

[a] *Action for Excellence* (Education Commission of the States, Task Force on Education for Economic Growth, 1983).

[b] *Educating Americans for the Twenty-first Century* (Commission on Precollege Education in Mathematics, Science, and Technology, 1983).

[c] *Making the Grade* (Twentieth Century Fund Task Force on Federal Education Policy, 1983).

[d] *A Nation at Risk* (National Commission on Excellence in Education, 1983).

[e] *High School* (Boyer, 1983).

[f] Journalists, entertainers, lawyers, foundation employees, unidentified.

In other respects, however, the second-wave commissions were quite different from their first-wave counterparts. Only one of the later commissions (the National Commission on Excellence in Educational Administration) included representatives from as broad an array of interests as the earlier commisions. Two of the second-wave commissions comprised members from single constituencies (governors and education school deans), and a third included members from only two groups (business leaders and university faculty members). Five important constituencies (state and local superintendents, state and local school board members, and principals) had representatives on only one panel.

Table 5-2
Membership of "Second-Wave" Reform Commissions, by Occupational Categories

	TT[a]	TfR[b]	ANP[c]	LAS[d]	CED[e]
Politicians	0	54	3	1	0
Business	0	0	2	1	27/13
State-level education Administrators					
Superintendent	0	0	2	0	0
School board	0	0	0	1	0
Local-level education Administrators					
School board	0	0	0	1	0
Superintendent	0	0	0	3	0
Principal	0	0	0	1	0
Teachers	0	0	0	0	0
Union officials	0	0	2	1	0
Parents	0	0	0	0	0
Education schools	38	0	1	12	0
Other academic	0	0	1	5	6/1
Other[f]	0	0	3	1	1

[a] *Tomorrow's Teachers* (Holmes Group, 1986).
[b] *Time for Results* (National Governors' Association, 1986).
[c] *A Nation Prepared* (Carnegie Forum on Education and the Economy, Task Force on Teaching as a Profession, 1986).
[d] *Leaders for America's Schools* (National Commission on Excellence in Educational Administration, 1987).
[e] *Investing in Our Children* (Committee for Economic Development, 1985), *Children in Need* (Committee for Economic Development, 1987).
[f] Journalists, entertainers, lawyers, foundation employees, unidentified.

The five second-wave commissions were also far more diverse in their membership structure than the first-wave commissions. No single interest group was represented on as many as four of the commissions, and only five groups were represented on three. The second-wave panels tended to focus their attention on particular parts of the educational system (such as teacher training or preschool programs) rather than on the system as a whole, and they were often dominated by groups sharing that focus. These differences in the composition of the first- and second-wave commissions were associated with differences in the reform recommendations that they produced, as shown in the following sections.

RIDING THE WAVE: PROPOSALS FOR REFORM

In Table 5-3, we present data on the recommendations of reform commissions from the first and second waves of the school reform movement.[3] These data indicate that second-wave commissions were indeed more likely to propose structural reforms than first-wave commissions. First-wave commissions proposed an average of 2.0 structural reforms, while the average for second-wave commissions was 3.0. The data also suggest, however, that differences between first- and second-wave commissions in their proposals for structural reforms were less significant than we initially hypothesized.

All but one of the commissions in each wave proposed at least one structural reform. In the first wave, four commissions recommended the introduction of career ladders or merit pay for teachers, or both. Similar proposals were put forward by five of the second-wave commissions, of which three added calls for increased delegation of administrative authority to the school site and school- or district-based performance incentives. Additional structural reforms including public sector vouchers and state intervention in "educationally bankrupt" school districts were proposed by one second-wave commission.

Our first hypothesis thus receives weak support from these data. We argued that because of (1) the variety of interests represented on the first-wave commissions and (2) the informal norm demanding unanimous support for commission recommendations, the first-wave commissions could have been expected to propose only minor changes in the structure and functioning of the U.S. educational system. The second-wave commissions, in contrast, were relatively unconstrained by the obligation to take account of competing interests, and thus were free to put forward radical proposals for structural changes in the educational system.

The second-wave commissions did put forward more proposals for structural change than did the first-wave commissions, but for reasons other than those we originally hypothesized. In fact, it appears that the array of structural reforms available for consideration by school reform commissions is largely fixed in any given period. Rather than developing their own proposals for change, commission members make choices from a menu that is defined more by prevailing notions of political and fiscal possibilities (and by the consensus about these possibilities fostered by expert consultants, some of whom served more than one commission) than it is by their own efforts. The reformers' menu was somewhat more extensive in the second wave, having come to include proposals for school site management and more sophisticated performance-based reward systems, but commissions from both waves appear to have made their choices in similar ways.[4]

The differences in the composition of first- and second-wave panels noted

Table 5-3
Recommendations of the Reform Commissions, First and Second Waves

Report	Focus of the Report	Number of Recommendations	Structural Changes Proposed[a]	Dissent Acknowledged
First Wave				
Action for Excellence (1983)	None	29	1	No
Educating Americans (1983)	Science/math education	26	2	No
Making the Grade (1983)	Federal policies	12	1	Yes
Nation at Risk (1983)	None	38	2	No
High School (1983)	Secondary education	87	4	No
Second Wave				
Tomorrow's Teachers (1986)	Teacher preparation	5	2	No
Time for Results (1986)	None	64	7	No
A Nation Prepared (1986)	Teaching	40	4	Yes
Leaders for America's Schools (1987)	Administration	34	0	No
Investing in Our Children (1985)	None	60	4	Yes
Children in Need (1987)	Disadvantaged children	38	1	Yes

[a] School-based management, differentiated staffing/career ladders, performance-based rewards for teachers and/or schools, public sector vouchers, state intervention in "educationally bankrupt" districts.

in the previous section had additional consequences for the commissions' recommendations. The structural similarities in the membership of the first-wave commissions caused them to generate remarkably similar reform proposals. Despite their ostensible focus on specific aspects of the educational system, first-wave panels typically called for changes throughout the system, and their proposals tended toward uniformity across panels. Because of the diverse memberships of the second-wave commissions, however, the reforms proposed by one commission bore relatively little resemblance to those proposed by the others. Second-wave commissions defined their work more narrowly and were more likely than their first-wave counterparts to restrict their attention and recommendations to their chosen area of emphasis. As a result, second-wave panels tended to propose more specific reforms, and these differed significantly across commissions.

However, proposals for structural reform were generally similar across commissions in both the first and second waves of the reform movement. As we noted earlier, most first-wave commissions called for career ladders and merit pay for teachers, while second-wave panels echoed these proposals and added recommendations for school site management and performance-based incentives for school and districts. There was considerably less variation across panels in these recommendations than in subordinate suggestions. In our view, this consistency provides additional support for the argument that the structural reform agenda in a particular period is defined independently of the efforts of reform commissions.

A quantitative summary of reform recommendations does an obvious injustice to some of the commissions' reports, especially to those from the second wave. *Tomorrow's Teachers* and *A Nation Prepared*, for example, are predicated on the need for sweeping changes in the careers of teachers, and the professionalization that they advocate would necessarily bring about structural reforms in the U.S. educational system. At the same time, though, it is often hard to see how specific reform proposals (such as a national certifying board, fifth-year teacher certification programs) will in themselves contribute to the attainment of the structural changes the commissions seek, or indeed to see precisely how the proposed structural changes are to be brought about. Our aim in this chapter is to assess the likely consequences of the commissions' work for U.S. schools, and we have therefore chosen to focus on their specific recommendations rather than on their ultimate objectives.

THE RHETORIC OF REFORM

In Table 5-4, we present a categorization of the rhetoric used by each reform commission, along with some representative language from each report. Our third hypothesis suggested that first-wave commissions would be more likely than second-wave commissions to use the relatively dramatic rhetoric of crisis in their reports, in order to raise educational issues onto the policy agenda and to solidify political support for their proposed reforms. We also suggested that second-wave commissions would make use of a more straightforward rhetoric of policy alternatives, for two reasons. First, educational issues were already on the policy agenda as a result of the efforts of the first-wave commissions. Second, the more reasoned, less inflammatory language might be expected to soothe potential opponents of the commissions' proposals for change.

Table 5-4
**Two-Way Categorization of Reform Rhetoric from Eleven Reports
(dramatic versus straightforward)**

First-Wave Reports	Language Use	Examples
1. *Nation at Risk* (1983, p. 5)	Dramatic	"Our nation is at risk . . . what was unimaginable a generation ago has begun to occur—others are matching and surpassing our educational attainments. . . . If an unfriendly foreign power had attempted to impose on American the mediocre educational performance that exists today, we might well have viewed it as an act of war."
2. *Making the Grade* (1983, p. 3)	Straightforward	"The nation's public schools are in trouble. By almost every measure—the commitment and competency of teachers, student test scores, truancy and dropout rates, crimes of violence—the performance of our schools falls far short of expectations."
3. *Action for Excellence* (1983, p. 3)	Dramatic	"There are few national efforts that can legitimately be called crucial to our national survival. Improving education in America—improving it sufficiently and improving it now—is such an effort. Our purpose is to reach as many citizens as possible and persuade them to act."
4. *Educating Americans for the 21st Century* (1983, p. 1)	Dramatic	"The nation is failing to provide its children with the intellectual tools needed for the 21st century. By 1995 the nation must provide for all its youth, a level of mathematics, science and technology education that is the finest in the world."
5. *High School* (1983, p. 1)	Straightforward	"The time for renewing education has arrived. We believe that today America has the best opportunity it will have in this century to improve the schools. There is a growing national consensus that our future depends on public education. . . . There is an eagerness to move beyond the alarming headlines, to begin to rebuild, with confidence, the public schools."

Table 5-4 *(continued)*
**Two-Way Categorization of Reform Rhetoric from Eleven Reports
(dramatic versus straightforward)**

Second-Wave Reports	Language Use	Examples
1. *Nation Prepared* (1986, p. 2)	Dramatic	"America's ability to compete in world markets is eroding. The productivity growth of our competitors outdistances our own. The capacity of our economy to provide a high standard of living for all our people is increasingly in doubt."
2. *Tomorrow's Teachers* (1986, p. 3)	Straightforward	"America's dissatisfaction with its schools has become chronic and epidemic. Teachers have long been at the center of the debates, and they still are today. Many commentators admit that no simple remedy can correct the problems of public education, yet simple remedies abound. . . . America's students' performance will not improve much if the quality of teaching is not much improved."
3. *Time for Results* (1986, p. 2)	Dramatic	"Better schools mean better jobs. Unless states face these questions Americans won't keep our high standard of living. To meet stiff competition from workers in the rest of the world, we must educate ourselves and our children as we never have before."
4. *Leaders for America's Schools* (1987, p. xiii)	Dramatic	"For almost four years, the American public has been listening to various segments of society call for changes in the educational system, from preschool to postgraduate study. . . . From these discussions, it became obvious that the needed agenda was not merely change but a revolution in the way schools are organized, in the quality of those who teach, in the expectation for every child who enters the educational system, and in the regard given by all of society . . . a revolution in education requires competent, skilled, visionary leadership as has never been available before."

(continued)

Table 5-4 *(continued)*
Two-Way Categorization of Reform Rhetoric from Eleven Reports
(dramatic versus straightforward)

Second-Wave Reports	Language Use	Examples
5. Committee for Economic Development • *Investing in Our Children* (1985, p. xii)	Straightforward	"The strategy for educational reform we present in this statement is based on the common sense view that real and meaningful changes can only occur where learning takes place. . . . It is not the purpose of this statement to trace the decline in our nation's schools, nor to dwell on past failures. Rather, our goal is to find new ways to provide all of our children with the opportunity to learn, to grow, and to become informed and productive adults."
• *Children in Need* (1987, p. 1)	Dramatic	"Our nation is defined by a vision—a dream which welcomes anyone who shares it. . . . But this vision is now becoming more distant for a growing underclass of Americans condemned by both discrimination and ignorance to only limited participation in the mainstream. . . . This year, more than one million babies will be born who will never complete their schooling. As they reach adolescence, many will be only marginally literate and virtually unemployable. Poverty and despair will be their constant companions. . . . The nation can ill afford such an egregious waste of human resources. Allowing this to continue will not only impoverish these children, it will impoverish our nation."

Note: *Dramatic*: rhetoric of crisis, transformation, revolution. Urgent need for reform to avert dire consequences. *Straightforward*: rhetoric of renewal, improvement, incremental change. Reforms build on current personnel and practice.

Any analysis of reform rhetoric is vexed by the problem of operationalization. In Table 5-4, we have attempted a simple, two-way classification of the language used in eleven reform reports, based on independent analyses of representative introductory paragraphs. We define "dramatic" language as language that fosters the perception of crisis in the present educational system, or that calls for urgent action to transform or redeem the system. "Straightforward" language addresses problems and proposes solutions without exaggeration, and calls for specific changes rooted in present educational practice.

The data in Table 5-4 do not provide much support for our hypothesis. Regardless of their place in the chronology of the school reform movement or of the composition of their membership, recent educational reform commissions have relied on the rhetoric of crisis to draw attention to themselves and to their policy proposals. Three of the five reports from the first wave, and four of the six from the second wave, made use of language that we have categorized as "dramatic"; two reports from the first wave and two from the second did not. The distribution of reform rhetoric is in fact not bimodal but continuous, and it could perhaps be argued that the rhetoric of *A Nation at Risk* and some other first-wave reports was *more* dramatic than that used by subsequent commissions. On the basis of the evidence presented here, however, we do not find any significant differences in the language of first- and second-wave reports.

THE POLITICAL VIABILITY OF REFORM PROPOSALS

The political viability of the proposals put forward by reform commissions from the first and second waves of the school reform movement remains difficult to assess. Each state has developed its own reform initiatives, and it is hard to draw confident generalizations about the translation of specific proposals from particular commissions into legislation. Nevertheless, the National Governors' Association, the Center for Policy Research in Education, and others have begun to produce data on the adoption and implementation of educational reforms at the state level since 1983, and these preliminary data allow some initial observations on the legislative outcomes of the commissions' efforts.

The flood of the state reforms that followed the publication of the 1983 reports shows that the first-wave commissions successfully won legislative approval for many of their reform proposals. All fifty states have adopted at least some of their recommendations, and many have approved comprehensive reform packages based on prescriptions from the commissions' reports (for data on state-level initiatives between 1983 and 1985 see *Education Week*, 11 February 1985).

In keeping with the nature of the first-wave commissions' proposals, however, almost none of the adopted reforms required structural changes in schools. Many states added resources or programs to the educational system, or established higher standards and increased regulations within the current structure, but most did not even try to change the way the system works. Moreover, the costs of the most significant changes were to a remarkable extent imposed on politically powerless groups, including high school students and prospective teachers, which made these reforms palatable to more influential constituencies (Plank, 1988). The recommendations of the first-wave commissions proved politically viable, but the extent to which their efforts will produce lasting changes in schools or better schooling for students remains to be seen.

The reform agenda and the time horizon of the second-wave commissions were quite different. The sense of urgency remains, but in contrast to the almost hysterical tone of *A Nation at Risk* and other first-wave reports the quest is not for immediate, visible changes but instead for permanent, structural improvements. The National Governors' Association acknowledges, for example, that *Time for Results* represents a "long-term education reform agenda," and that "neither the educational results [the governors] desire nor the state policy changes required to bring them about will be accomplished in short order" (National Governors' Association, 1987, p. 4).

In addition, the proposals for structural reform put forward by the second-wave commissions entail far more political controversy than do calls for less radical changes, as the members of the second-wave commissions recognize. On the publication of *Tomorrow's Teachers*, for example, a spokesperson for the Holmes Group stated that the members had "decided that we must work for the changes we believe to be right, rather than those we know can succeed" (Education Commission of the States, 1987, p. 17).

The available evidence suggests that the patience and realism counseled by the second-wave commissions are well-advised. Relatively few proposals for structural reform have yet been considered by state legislatures (National Governors' Association, 1987, pp. 14–19). Of those that have won approval, including "merit pay" plans for teachers in Florida and Tennessee and parental choice plans in Minnesota and Colorado, many were begun before the commissions made their recommendations, and some are now being scaled back or abandoned. Other initiatives that appear to promise structural change (such as career ladders for teachers) have been domesticated during implementation by constituencies within the educational system that distrust the consequences of reform (Malen & Hart, 1987). Fiscal problems in oil-producing and agricultural states have forced retreats on first-wave reforms, and make the adoption of expensive new initiatives unlikely (Montague, 1987; Viadero, 1987).

The prospects for structural reform are more promising at the local level.

New teachers' contracts in Rochester County (New York) and Dade County
(Florida), for example, offer the possibility of significant changes in the
distribution of power and authority within two local school systems, but the
Rochester contract has already faced one legal challenge (from system
administrators) and both confront important financial, political, and organizational obstacles as they are put into effect (Rodman, 1987b; Olson, 1987c).
Several states have initiated pilot projects to experiment with structural
reforms at the school level, but at least some schools participating in these
projects have encountered difficulties in gaining exemptions from prevailing
state regulations and union rules (Olson, 1987a).

CONCLUSIONS

In this chapter, we have shown that educational reform commissions in
the first wave of the reform movement included representatives from virtually all affected constituencies: teachers, state and local educational administrators, school board members, businesspeople, university and education
school faculty, governors, and state legislators. The breadth of these commissions had both positive and negative consequences. On the one hand, the
diversity of interests represented on the commissions served to blunt radical
initiatives and to limit reform proposals to those that offended no significant
interest, often because they were expressed in such general terms as to win
virtually universal assent. On the other hand, the inclusion of all affected
constituencies on the commissions ensured a high level of political support
for commission proposals, and thus helped to ensure that many of the
first-wave commissions' recommendations for reform would be approved.

In the second wave of the reform movement, in contrast, reform commissions were more narrowly based, sometimes comprising representatives from
a single constituency. Unconstrained by the need to win prior support from a
wide variety of interests, the more recent reform commissions have come
forward with more proposals for structural changes in the educational system
than did the first-wave commissions, though differences in the average
numbers of recommendations remain small. At the same time, however, their
failure to ensure broad support for specific policy initiatives calls into
question the ultimate political viability of the reforms they have proposed.

The data we have presented thus provide weak support for our first
hypothesis. Reform commissions from the first wave of the school reform
movement included representatives from a wide array of educational constituencies. Significantly, the composition of the array was almost invariant
across commissions. These commissions proposed reforms that almost uniformly required relatively minor changes in the organization and operation

of U.S. schools. Reform commissions in the second wave typically recruited their members from a much narrower set of constituencies, and the array of interests represented varied significantly across commissions. These commissions more often proposed structural changes in the educational system.

Significantly, the commissions that departed from the modal membership pattern of their respective waves diverged from the modal pattern in other respects as well. The Twentieth Century Fund Task Force on Federal Educational Policy focused its attention on a single aspect of the educational system, and was the only one of the first-wave commissions to report disagreements among its members. The National Commission on Excellence in Educational Administration resembled the first-wave commissions not only in its name and membership structure but also in its avoidance of specificity and potential controversy in nearly all its reform recommendations.

The available data provide somewhat stronger support for our second hypothesis. Assessing the political viability of specific commission proposals is difficult, because cause-and-effect relationships between reform proposals and eventual policy changes are nearly impossible to prove in U.S. politics. Nevertheless, a number of recent analyses of the school reform movement suggest that the first-wave reports (and especially *A Nation at Risk*) provided the catalyst for the adoption of a variety of educational reforms in each of the fifty states (see Murphy, Chapter 1 in this book). To date, however, relatively few of the policy recommendations of the second-wave commissions have been considered by state legislatures, and the structural changes in the U.S. educational system foreseen in their reports are barely on the horizon outside of a few school districts.

The data we examined did not support our third hypothesis. Our analysis of the rhetoric used in first- and second-wave commission reports suggested that the first-wave commissions made use of more dramatic language than those from the second wave (with *A Nation at Risk* as the limiting case), but virtually all the commissions from both waves of the reform movement relied on the rhetoric of crisis to build support for their policy recommendations. An atmosphere of high drama and momentous choices appears to be a nearly essential component of the rhetorical universe of reform commissions, no matter when or how they are constituted.

Taken together, these findings indicate some of the limitations of "blue-ribbon" commissions as agents for school reform. First, our analysis of the reform proposals put forward by panels from the first and second waves of the reform movement suggests that the commissions themselves played a relatively minor role in generating proposals for structural changes in the U.S. educational system, regardless of their composition. Instead, it appears that the commissions in both waves adopted their recommendations for structural reform from an array of choices that was fixed prior to and independently of their own discussions. The array was wider in the second wave than in the first, in large part because of the prior efforts of the first-wave commissions, but in both waves proposals for structural reform displayed a far greater similarity across commissions than did proposals for less sweeping changes. The relatively narrow constituency bases of second-wave panels may have made them more willing or able to recommend structural reforms than their first-wave counterparts, but it does not appear to have expanded the array of policy choices.

Second, our analysis of the language used in the first- and second-wave reports suggests that recourse to dramatic language and the rhetoric of crisis is nearly universal among reform commissions. Commissions are at best peripheral to the policymaking process, and whatever power they have derives from their success in fostering perceptions of their own importance among relevant audiences, including policymakers and the mass media. If they have nothing exciting to say, they are readily ignored, and so reform commissions almost invariably dress up their recommendations in lurid rhetoric in order to attract public attention. As the seminal importance retrospectively accorded to *A Nation at Risk* in the present school reform movement demonstrates, this strategy can yield great rewards. At the same time, however, it may represent an obstacle to the ultimate success of reform, both by raising unrealistic expectations about the efficacy of specific policy changes and by mobilizing dissent and opposition.

The arguments developed in this chapter and the available data provide few grounds for optimism concerning the likelihood of structural changes in the U.S. educational system. The system continues to be governed by a complex institutional consensus encompassing a large and diverse array of interests, and the fragmentation of authority and the existence of multiple vetoes within the system serve to block other than marginal reform initiatives. The first wave of the reform movement has operated for the most part within this institutional consensus, and has achieved some significant—if relatively small—successes. The second wave has attempted to move outside of the prevailing consensus, and has recommended a number of potentially exciting changes in the distribution of power and authority within the U.S. educational system. The failure of second-wave reformers to ensure the prior political support of key constituencies, however, makes it far less likely that any of these proposals will ever be enacted by legislatures or implemented in schools.

NOTES

1. Throughout this chapter we use the term *structural reform* to refer to changes that would alter the prevailing distribution of power and authority within the educational system. Such changes might include the professionalization of teaching or the establishment of merit pay for teachers, the decentralization of administrative control to the school site, or the introduction of educational vouchers, among other things. Other authors have variously referred to these kinds of changes as "system-changing reforms," "institutional reforms," and "second-order reforms," and also as issues of "institutional choice." See McDonnell and Elmore (1987); Adams, Cornbleth, and Plank (in press); Cuban (1987); and Clune (1987). Our usage of the term differs from that of Tyack, Kirst, and Hansot (1980) and Kirst and Meister (1985), who define structural reforms as those that add new layers or new units to existing organizational structures. In previous work, we have categorized such changes as "additive" reforms (Plank, 1988).

2. In his research on presidential commissions, Wolanin (1975) concluded that the work of such commissions often makes an important contribution to proposed or implemented federal policies.

3. For a comprehensive review of the recommendations put forward by commissions from the first and second waves, see the reports on the subject by the Education Commission of the States (1983, 1987).

4. It is worth noting that the additions and modifications to the reformers' menu in the second wave had entered the educational policy debate in part because of their inclusion in first-wave reports, including those by Boyer (1983) and Goodlad (1983).

REFERENCES

Adams, D., C. Cornbleth, & D. N. Plank. (In press). Between exhortation and reform: Recent educational changes in the United States. *Interchange*.

Boyd, W. L. (1987). Public education's last hurrah: Schizophrenia, amnesia, and ignorance in school politics. *Educational Evaluation and Policy Analysis, 9*, 85–100.

Boyer, E. L. (1983). *High school: Report on secondary education in America.* New York: Harper & Row.

Campbell, R. F., L. L. Cunningham, R. O. Nystrand, & M. D. Usdan. (1986). *Organization and control of American education.* Columbus, OH: Merill.

Carnegie Forum on Education and the Economy, Task Force on Teaching as a Profession. (1986). *A nation prepared: Teachers for the 21st century.* New York: Carnegie Forum on Education and the Economy.

Chance, W. (1986). *"The best of educations": Reforming America's public schools in the 1980s.* Chicago: MacArthur Foundation.

Clune, W. H. (1987). Institutional choice as a theoretical framework for research on educational policy. *Educational Evaluation and Policy Analysis, 9*, 117–132.

Commission on Precollege Education in Mathematics, Science, and Technology.

(1983). *Educating Americans for the 21st century.* Washington, DC: National Science Foundation.

Committee for Economic Development. (1985). *Investing in our children.* New York: Committee for Economic Development.

Committee for Economic Development. (1987). *Children in need.* New York: Committee for Economic Development.

Cuban, L. (1987, May). Constancy and change in schools (1880s to the present). Paper presented at the Inaugural Conference of the Benton Center for Curriculum and Instruction, University of Chicago.

Deal, T. E. (1985). National commissions: Blueprints for remodeling or ceremonies for revitalizing public schools? *Education and Urban Society, 17,* 145–156.

Education Commission of the States (1983). *A summary of major reports on education.* Denver: Education Commission of the States.

Education Commission of the States. (1987). *The next wave: A synopsis of recent education reform reports.* Denver: Education Commission of the States.

Education Commission of the States, Task Force on Education for Economic Growth. (1983). *Action for excellence.* Denver: Education Commission of the States.

Excellence: A fifty state survey. (1985, 11 February). *Education Week.*

Fullan, M. (1982). *The meaning of educational change.* New York: Teachers College Press.

Ginsberg, R., & R. K. Wimpelberg. (1987). Educational change by commission: Attempting 'trickle-down' reform. *Educational Evaluation and Policy Analysis, 9,* 344–360.

Goodlad, J. I. (1983). *A place called school.* New York: McGraw-Hill.

Guthrie, J. W. (1985). The educational policy consequences of economic instability: The emerging political economy of American education. *Educational Evaluation and Policy Analysis, 7,* 319–332.

Holmes Group. (1986). *Tomorrow's teachers.* East Lansing, MI: Holmes Group.

Kingdon, J. (1984). *Agendas, alternatives and public policies.* Boston: Little, Brown.

Kirst, M. W., and G. R. Meister. (1985). Turbulence in American secondary schools: What reforms last. *Curriculum Inquiry, 15,* 169–186.

Malen, B., & A. W. Hart. (1987). Career ladder reform: A multi-level analysis of initial efforts. *Educational Evaluation and Policy Analysis, 9,* 9–23.

McDonnell, L. M., & R. F. Elmore. (1987). Getting the job done: Alternative policy instruments. *Educational Evaluation and Policy Analysis, 9,* 133–152.

Meyer, J. W. (1983). Reform and change. *IFG [Institute for Finance and Governance] Policy Notes, 5,* 1–2.

Montague, W. (1987, 28 January). A critical crossroads. *Education Week,* pp. 1, 19.

National Commission on Excellence in Education. (1983). *A Nation at risk: The imperative for educational reform.* Washington, DC: U.S. Government Printing Office.

National Commission on Excellence in Educational Administration (1987). *Leaders for America's schools.* Tempe, AZ: University Council on Educational Administration.

National Governors' Association. (1986). *Time for results: The governors' 1991 report on education.* Washington, DC: National Governors' Association.

National Governors' Association. (1987). *Results in education: 1987.* Washington, DC: National Governors' Association.

Nienhuis, M. (1987, 4 February). Reformers neglect schools' cultures, author says. *Education Week*, p. 15.

Olson, L. (1987a, 18 February). Less is more: Coalition rethinking the basic design of schools. *Education Week*, pp. 1, 22–24.

Olson, L. (1987b, 16 September). Speech terms N.E.A. "most aggressive" foe of reform in nation. *Education Week*, pp. 1, 18.

Olson, L. (1987c, 2 December). "The sky's the limit:" Dade ventures self-governance. *Education Week*, pp. 1, 18–19.

Peterson, P. E. (1983). Did the education commissions say anything? *Brookings Review*, pp. 3–11.

Pfeffer, J. (1972). Size and composition of corporate boards of directors: The organization and its environment. *Administrative Science Quarterly*, *17*, 218–228.

Pfeffer, J. (1973). Size, composition, and function of hospital boards of directors: A study of organization-environment linkages. *Administrative Science Quarterly*, *18*, 349–364.

Plank, D. N. (1988). Why school reform doesn't change schools: Political and organizational perspectives. In William Lowe Boyd & Charles Kerchner, eds., *The politics of excellence and choice: The first annual politics of education yearbook*. Philadelphia: Taylor and Francis.

Polsby, N. W. (1984). *Political innovation in America: The politics of policy initiation*. New Haven, CT: Yale University Press.

Rodman, B. (1987a, 11 February). Futrell asks group to work with NCATE; broaden agenda, Shanker urges. *Education Week*, p. 16.

Rodman, B. (1987b, 30 September). Friendship and trust: Unusual keys to radical pact. *Education Week*, pp. 1, 20–21.

Snider, W. (1987, 22 April). Broader focus said key to next wave of reform drive. *Education Week*, p. 1.

Twentieth Century Fund Task Force on Federal Educational Policy. (1983). *Making the grade*. New York: Twentieth Century Fund.

Tyack, D. B., M. Kirst, & E. Hansot. (1980, Spring). Educational reform: Retrospect and prospect. *Teachers College Record*, *81*(3), 253–269.

Viadero, D. (1987, 30 September). Funding unlikely for Colorado reform goals. *Education Week*, p. 13.

Weick, K. E. (1976). Educational organization as loosely-coupled systems. *Administrative Science Quarterly*, *21*, 1–19.

Wirt. F., & M. Kirst. (1983). *Schools in conflict*. Berkeley: McCutchan.

Wolanin, T. R. (1975). *Presidential advisory commissions*. Madison: University of Wisconsin Press.

CHAPTER 6

Continuity and Incrementalism After All: State Responses to the Excellence Movement

William A. Firestone

Crisis is a constant in twentieth-century U.S. education. From the Committee of Ten in 1893 to the National Commission on Excellence in Education (*A Nation at Risk*) in 1983, reformers, critics, researchers, and policymakers have identified major problems and proposed what they portrayed as radical solutions (James & Tyack, 1983). Evoking a sense of crisis often galvanizes people to action. It creates a short spurt of optimism when much is attempted, but disappointment can follow if the expectations raised are not

Research reports are issued by CPRE to facilitate the exchange of ideas among policymakers and researchers who share an interest in educational policy. The views expressed in this report are those of individual authors, and are not necessarily shared by the U.S. Department of Education, CPRE, or its institutional partners. This publication was funded by the U.S. Department of Education, Office of Educational Research and Improvement, Grant Number G008690011.

met and proposed changes materialize only to a very limited degree (Cross, 1984).

This crisis mind-set fixed the expectations for assessing state educational reforms of the 1980s. These reforms are often seen as results of the educational excellence movement, with its host of commission reports (see Passow, 1984, for one review of these reports). The current reforms are often compared to other big periods of educational ferment in the postwar years, such as the *Sputnik* or the Great Society reforms (Boyer, 1984). This view would lead one to expect attempts at great change followed by either great success or substantial failure. Another view is that the state reforms were an outgrowth or acceleration of the gradual development of state government since 1960 (Murphy, 1982). This development substantially precedes and is independent of the recent reform reports. Viewing the reforms as part of this ongoing state-level evolution would lead one to expect policymakers to adopt modest incremental changes; such changes are more likely to persist.

This chapter argues for the second position: that what is most significant about the recent reform efforts is their continuity. The excellence movement may have provided a short-term acceleration of state activity and highlighted certain directions, but states did not make fundamental changes. Rather, they usually adopted incremental policies that extended current lines of development or slightly redesigned existing policies. Moreover, these changes often grew out of pre-1983 activities and have lasted longer than experienced observers expected (Guthrie, 1988). To place the current reforms in perspective, two interpretations of them are presented along with supporting arguments for each. Then, using data collected by the Center for Policy Research in Education (CPRE) on reform efforts in five states, three questions are raised. The first is, what is the magnitude of the reform measures that were actually passed? Larger reforms indicate a greater break with the past. The second and third are, how smooth was the transition from the period before 1983–1985 to the present, and what is the staying power of the reforms adopted?

CRISIS OR CONTINUITY?

How one interprets educational reform in the early 1980s depends in part on whether one takes a short- or long-term perspective. The shorter view emphasizes the educational excellence movement. This movement generated a substantial literature on education in a very short time. The document that has received greatest attention was *A Nation at Risk*, produced by the National Commission on Excellence in Education (1983). The reform literature created a crisis atmosphere, connecting U.S. economic decline with educational performance and suggesting that educational upgrading would lead to economic revitalization. It publicized a wide range of international comparison and trend data suggesting that students lacked both functional literacy and "higher-order skills." A major concern was clearly to develop skilled workers and managers for a high-technology future (National Commission on Excellence in Education, 1983).

The proposed reforms stressed a "get tough" approach with students, teachers, and administrators (Passow, 1984). Rejecting the "We want it all!" philosophy of the 1970s, most reports recommended something like the standard college preparatory curriculum with few electives and little curricular differentiation. The Twentieth Century Fund, for instance, stressed the importance of language, mathematics, and science (Graham, 1983), and *A Nation at Risk* recommended that states and local districts require students to take four years of English, three of mathematics, three of science, three of social studies, and half a year of computer science to graduate from high school (National Commission on Excellence in Education, 1983). That report also criticized minimum competency tests for setting a ceiling on what is taught, suggested more extensive use of standardized achievement tests as a promotion control, called for textbooks with more rigorous content, and recommended that students spend more time in school. Seven-hour school days and 200- to 220-day school years were advocated.

Proposals to reform teaching combined this get-tough approach with an effort to recruit better teachers. An important theme was that excellent teaching required high academic achievement by future teachers (Passow, 1984). Greater subject matter preparation and less training in teaching techniques were advocated, along with paper-and-pencil competency tests for initial teacher selection and "alternative routes" to allow into the field academically talented people without training in teaching. Salary increases for teachers were proposed. More revolutionary proposals included merit pay and career ladder schemes that would reward excellent teachers with increased income, higher status, and differentiated work (National Commission on Excellence in Education, 1983).

The excellence movement caught the country's eye. Support for improving—and financing—education grew (Boyer, 1984; Odden, 1984). Between 1983 and 1985, almost all states passed some of the recommended reforms. Forty-five initiated or increased graduation requirements, especially in mathematics and science. Several states imposed or expanded testing requirements for graduation or promotion. In addition, two-thirds of the states increased teacher testing. Teacher certification and recertification requirements were both tightened. A few states, such as Tennessee and Florida, experimented with merit pay and career ladder programs (Fuhrman, 1988).

Those taking a longer-term perspective would see the changes in the early

1980s as less monumental. It points to ninety years of commission reports in U.S. education and suggests that a great deal of symbolic activity is required for relatively modest change in educational practice. This "trickle-down" theory of commission behavior (Ginsberg & Wimpelberg, 1987) recognizes the cyclical nature of reform reports. The recommendations of a liberal period may become anathema to be stamped out in a conservative one (Passow, 1984). Moreover, it finds tenuous links between the goals set by the reform reports and their actual recommendations (Peterson, 1985) and even more tenuous links between the recommendations and changes in schools (Ginsberg & Wimpelberg, 1987).

This longer perspective also attends to less-publicized trends under way in the 1970s that set the stage for the 1980s reforms. Most specifically, state government developed considerably during the 1960s and 1970s (Murphy, 1982). In the 1960s, state departments of education were dull, understaffed places. The total number of state education employees grew from 641 in 1957 to 2,052 in 1986 (Bureau of the Census, 1988). State education staffs added more minorities and women and more professionals with training in social sciences, management, and other fields. Chief state school officers also became more policy oriented and aggressive in their approach to their jobs (Murphy, 1982).

Similar developments took place in state legislatures. Between 1968 and 1974, professional staff supporting legislatures grew by about 130 percent. By 1979, twenty-four states had over 100 professional staff members, with Michigan, Florida, New York, and California having over 500. A substantial portion of this development was in committee staff that could support the writing of legislation in specific areas (Rosenthal, 1981).

The growth of state government had important implications for how policy was formulated (Murphy, 1982). Perhaps more important, it helped states use the means at their disposal to influence schooling at the local level. Before the 1970s, the major contribution of state government was to fund local education. In the 1970s, reformers attempted to use this power of the purse to increase educational equity by equalizing spending across school districts in each state (Odden, 1984). These efforts involved considerable litigation and had only mixed success.

Meanwhile, with less fanfare, states developed new ways to shape district operations. Some of these reflected the improvement strategies of that time. For instance, a survey conducted by Odden and Dougherty (1982) just before the release of *A Nation at Risk* showed that twenty-eight states had programs to disseminate knowledge about new educational practices and encourage their adoption. The same number had programs that encouraged local planning for improvement, and fourteen had programs to increase parent involvement in education. Other state strategies anticipated the excellence movement to varying extents. For instance, twenty-three states had curriculum development efforts, thirteen had new types of teacher certification, and sixteen—mainly in the South—had already mandated teacher proficiency or competency tests. Perhaps the most popular state policy was student testing, an idea that had grown substantially during the 1970s (Madeus, 1984). By 1982, thirty-six states mandated some kind of student-testing program (Odden & Dougherty, 1982).

THE CPRE STUDY

Data to determine if the excellence reforms were a major break from past practice or simply continued ongoing development come from a longitudinal study of five states conducted by CPRE. The states were chosen to overrepresent those that actively embraced the excellence movement proposals (California, Florida, Georgia) as well as some that adopted current reform practices but less aggressively (Arizona, Pennsylvania).[1]

In the spring of 1986, CPRE researchers visited each state capital to learn about recent state policy initiatives. In addition to collecting voluminous documents, interviews were conducted with representatives of the governor; legislators; representatives of the chief state school officer; education department specialists on student standards policy, teacher policy, and monitoring practices; and people outside of government, often newspaper reporters. In the spring of 1987, visits were made to 19 school districts in these five states, at least two schools in each district, to learn about the implementation of the state reform initiatives. Interviews were conducted with people in a variety of positions, from the superintendent and school board members to teachers. Beginning in the fall of 1987, the evolution of state educational policy has been tracked by periodic telephone interviews with four or five key informants in each state capital and district who provided useful insights on developments in student standards and teacher policy and their relationships to the changing political context. In addition, newspaper articles and formal reports describing relevant state and local activities were collected. Information from all these sources allows us to assess the magnitude and continuity of state reform efforts.

THE MAGNITUDE OF THE REFORM POLICIES

Introducing small changes is usually easier for states and districts and maintains continuity from one time period to another. Large changes are often more difficult to handle; they create a greater break and can lead to (or result from) a sense of crisis. However, comparing reform policies is extremely difficult because there is no standard metric for examining the size of reforms. One step toward generating a metric for examining reforms is to create a set of dimensions for comparison.[2] Five such dimensions that facilitate at least rough comparison of reform policies are proposed here: the policy's breadth, cost, depth, complexity, and redistributive nature.

Dimensions for Comparing Policies

The first two dimensions, breadth and costs, are the most straightforward. The term *breadth* refers to the number of individuals or units (schools or districts) affected by a policy. A policy's breadth depends in part on the policy instrument used (McDonnell & Elmore, 1987). The major instruments are mandates and inducements. A mandate can affect all units within a jurisdiction, as when all schools are required to have safe fire exits. Inducements—for instance, competitive or categorical grants—are clearly selective in their impact. Individual schools or districts have the option of not taking the inducement and are thereby exempted from the conditions that go with it. However, such distinctions must be applied with caution. Some mandates apply to only a small set of units, such as districts with more than 30,000 students. These mandates might have less breadth than an inducement, such as Chapter I, made easily available to a larger number of districts. Moreover, when standards for mandates are set so low that most units already meet them, their breadth will be limited because most districts will not have to make changes.

Cost is a financial matter, involving both monies paid out and opportunities foregone. The reform commissions were repeatedly criticized for proposing changes that are quite expensive such as increasing the length of the school day and year (Odden, 1984; Peterson, 1985). Other changes seem to be much less costly. Although the gross costs of a reform can usually be assessed—especially at the state level—there are difficulties in making fine-grained determinations at the local level where personnel time is the major expenditure. Another difficulty is assessing opportunity costs: the value of those things that are *not* done *because* one is doing the reform in question.

A state reform can *expand* existing practice or *change* the way things are done. Expansions are assessed by their depth, changes by their complexity and redistributiveness. The term *depth* refers to the increase or decrease in the quantity of the thing required, the amount of difference from the existing condition. Some of the most frequently discussed reforms in *A Nation at Risk*—such as increases in courses required to graduate from high school, in the length of the school day, or the number of days in the school year—can be treated largely as depth issues. Comparing such increases is difficult, however, because the metrics involved are different. For example, it is not clear whether requiring high school students to take two more mathematics courses is a deeper change than adding ten more days to the school year.

The term *complexity* typically refers to the knowledge required for change (Hage & Aiken, 1969). In looking at classroom change, Fullan (1982, p. 58) suggests that complexity encompasses the "difficulty, skill required, and extent of alterations in beliefs, teaching strategies, and use of materials." Complexity can arise in other manners and at other levels. Applying a new technique, for instance, is often complex. Thus, policies that require developing new curricula, assessment systems, or software are more complex than those that do not. In addition, complexity can result from new interdependencies among positions, requiring people to learn new ways to work together. Team teaching or certain curriculum alignment systems that require administrators and teachers to work more closely with curriculum and testing specialists also increase complexity. Generally, it is useful to separate technological complexity, which requires applying new knowledge and skills, from administrative complexity. The latter has a knowledge component, because new roles and relationships must be learned, but it often includes adding staff and layers to the organization.

The final dimension rests on the distinction between *developmental* and *redistributive* policies. Looking at economic development, Peterson, Rabe, and Wong (1986) argue that developmental policies help the whole community, while redistributive policies benefit low-income or otherwise needy groups, potentially at the expense of others. Developmental programs are implemented with less conflict than are redistributive ones. This treatment of redistribution focuses on economic resources, but the allocation of authority is often equally important. Thus, career ladders that move responsibility for supervision and evaluation from principals to mentor teachers or choice programs that give parents more control over their children's schooling both redistribute authority away from administrators. Not all redistribution in the current wave of reforms is *from* those in authority *to* those without. Merit pay programs, for instance, redistribute financial rewards among teachers on the basis of performance rather than of seniority.

State Reform Policies

The five dimensions just described provide a useful way for comparing the reforms adopted by the five states in this study. Those reforms can be sorted into those that affect students and those that affect teachers.

Student Reforms. The most popular student reform has been the increase in high school graduation requirements. This change is potentially broad. All districts must comply, but standards are usually set at such a moderate level that most districts already comply. Costs, however, are low. Typically, states allocate no additional funds to help districts meet the requirements. Some districts have to add a few teachers to teach additional courses, but usually the existing staff can teach the new courses. The depth is also shallow. Most districts studied had to add only a few courses or sections, usually in mathematics or science. As a result of changed requirements in these states, roughly 27 percent of all students took an added mathematics class and 34 percent took an added science class. Social studies courses were also added (Clune, with White & Patterson, 1988). Complexity is at best a minor issue because there are no new role relationships, and staff often have a good idea of what should be taught, so very little effort is needed to add new courses. Finally, graduation requirements are more developmental than redistributive with regard to authority relationships and relative income to schools and districts.[3]

One exception to this general picture of graduation requirements as broad, easy change occurred in Florida, which required the most courses for graduation of all five states. This change was deeper than most. Beginning with the class of 1986, students were expected to complete 24 courses to graduate from high school. Previously, district requirements had ranged from 17 to 22 courses. In most districts, the number of required courses had fit comfortably into a six-period day, leaving a cushion for students who failed a course or wanted to take electives. The 24-course requirement eliminated that cushion. Moreover, policymakers wanted to lengthen the school day. As a result, they added provisions for a seven-period day.

Although *A Nation at Risk* called for lengthening the time students spend in school, Florida's seven-period day was one of the few such changes in the five states. (California provided inducements for districts to adopt a 180-day school year.) However, the policy probably shortened students' learning time. State support was to be given to schools with six 60-minute periods (360 instructional minutes) with greater incentives provided for those with seven 50-minute periods (350 instructional minutes). Because most schools went to a seven-period day, the amount of class time was actually reduced.

The seven-period day policy was originally built on a mandate with a small inducement, but the policy was so unpopular that after two years the mandate was revoked. The state funding formula was altered to give a higher reimbursement to high schools using the seven-period day. Because most Florida students already experience a seven-period day, this policy is of moderate to high breadth. It is also relatively expensive. State allocations for this policy increased from $27 million in 1983–84, to over $81 million in 1986–87, and some districts complained that the added subsidy did not cover the full costs they incurred.

Another popular change that preceded the reform reports was to increase·

student testing. Testing is a broad change, because it affects all schools. Cost, depth, and especially complexity depend on the number and designs of the tests, however. The addition of minimum competency graduation tests or "gate tests" for promotion, for instance, entail a certain amount of technical complexity for the state that must commission them and the districts that have to rearrange curricula to ensure that students pass. In this case, depth can also be increased by expanding the number of tests administered.

Minimum competency tests were decried in *A Nation at Risk*, however, as potentially setting a ceiling on the cognitive level of instruction. California was one of the few states to develop tests that measured higher-order cognitive skills—by revising its previously developed California Assessment Program (CAP) test. The technical complexity was considerably higher for this undertaking because the knowledge needed for developing such tests is much more limited than for developing tests of lower-order skills. Moreover, California state superintendent Bill Honig raised the complexity still more by coordinating testing with the state textbook approval procedures and by promulgating model curriculum standards. The intent was to coordinate the use of tests, curriculum, and texts to reinforce higher-order thinking.

Teacher Reforms. Most teacher reforms increased quality control over the profession, systematized inservice, or shifted the balance of incentives for educators. As suggested by *A Nation at Risk*, the quality control changes reduced the influence of education colleges over entry to the occupation. Some reforms required the testing of teachers. The breadth of such provisions varied. Pennsylvania tested only new teachers, while Georgia extended existing procedures to test both new and experienced teachers. Complexity also varied. Some of the tests examined only basic knowledge while others tested knowledge of subject matter (content) and teaching (pedagogy). The most technologically complex tests, like Georgia's Teacher Performance Assessment Instrument (TPAI), were in-class observations of teacher competence. This test predated *A Nation at Risk*, but the reform legislation expanded its use. Development costs and expenses to help current teachers who failed the test were high but rarely as high as reformers' proposals to lengthen time in school. Remediation costs in Georgia never went over $1 million. Moreover, these tests were developmental; they did not affect relationships among teachers or between teachers and administrators.

Another quality control reform, also foreshadowed in *A Nation at Risk*, was the development of alternative entry routes into teaching for people who had subject matter knowledge but who had not taken university education courses. This reform was narrow. In California, one very large urban district used it extensively, but most other districts did not. Its complexity and cost depended on the extent of training offered new teachers; but because training was often modest (Odden & Marsh, 1987), complexity and cost were usually low.

One training-oriented reform that was studied was Pennsylvania's continuing professional development program. All districts were required to develop plans for continuing development of teachers, but those with a master's degree were exempted from significant portions of the program, so it has a moderate-to-high breadth. The state, however, did not provide additional funds for these learning activities. Districts had to increase their own training expenditures. Sometimes this increase affected collective bargaining agreements, but apparently only modestly. The thrust of the program was to require districts to submit plans for staff training that could include coursework, master's degree programs, local inservice instruction, curriculum development, attendance at conferences, and/or supervised classroom observations of other professionals. Although the types of activity required were not new, the concept of coordinated planning was—especially planning with a team that featured teachers selected by other teachers as well as administrators. Thus, it increased complexity and was modestly redistributive.[4]

Two changes affected teacher incentives. The simplest was to increase teacher salaries. These policies (in Georgia, Pennsylvania, and California) were moderately expensive. However, they varied in their breadth. Only Pennsylvania mandated minimum salaries across the state. The increase was to $18,500, but even this revision was not as broad as it might seem, because the previous state minimum salary was $6,500, so most districts already exceeded the state standard. California, which provided incentives to help districts meet state minimum; and Georgia, with its market-sensitive salaries, developed procedures that did not require all districts to make changes.

The other modification of teacher incentives—career ladders and their variants—was potentially the most radical of all those enacted in the five states. Career ladders allow for professional advancement through a set of graduated steps such as beginning, regular teacher, and master teacher (Newcombe, 1983). The beginning teacher might have limited responsibilites and be frequently supervised and coached by a master teacher. Promotion comes when performance criteria are met. In some career ladder models, the master teachers as a group may essentially run the professional aspects of the school, hiring an administrator to handle more routine management tasks (such as Carnegie Forum, 1986). Because career ladders can reduce equity among teachers and can challenge the hierarchical teacher-administrator relationship, they are among the most redistributive reforms currently being considered.

In principle, career ladders are major reforms in other ways. First, they are expensive. Unless career ladders are funded through increases to existing salaries—that is, salary increments for master teachers—they will generate serious resentment (Newcombe, 1983). In addition, developing assessment procedures that are fair, reliable, and reasonable to teachers requires new technology. Moreover, the classroom observation required is often time consuming and strains existing administrative arrangements. Thus, these reforms are highly complex, both administratively and technologically.

Four states actively considered some form of teacher career ladder. Florida's plan was the most ambitious, although it was more of a merit teacher program than an actual career ladder. The program called for annual awards (not permanent salary increases) of $3,000 to teachers with four years of teaching experience, a superior score on a subject area test (or a master's degree), and superior performance on an in-class evaluation. Because all teachers could compete for the award but were not required to, the program's breadth was moderate. As much as $16 million per year was allocated for the program, so it was fairly expensive. The serious problems in developing and administering test procedures attest to the high complexity of this career ladder. Moreover, there were complaints that the program created an unhealthy level of competition among teachers. Still, because the awards were temporary and the master teachers did not take on new supervision, training, or administrative responsibilities, the program was only moderately redistributive. After three years, the program was terminated.

By developing proposals that were less extreme than Florida's, the three other states experienced less conflict with their programs. Georgia's program, which took three years to plan, is just being piloted in 1988–89. Teachers will not be selected until 1990–91. Arizona's career ladder rivals Florida's in redistributive impact, but is much narrower in breadth. It is a pilot effort implemented in 15 of the state's more than 200 districts. The requirement that districts develop a teacher compensation system that replaces conventional salary criteria with those based on quality (including evidence of increased student performance on achievement tests) or additional work ensures its redistributive nature and entails considerable complexity. Although the state is allocating only about $1.2 million for the program, participating districts report that they could not afford the salary increases involved without state assistance. Thus the cost is low for the state.

California's mentor teacher program gives incentives of $4,000 to teachers who develop special projects that are approved by a district committee consisting of administrators and teachers—the latter chosen by local teachers' associations. The temporary nature of the awards ensures that this program is only moderately redistributive. Because all districts can have mentor teachers, the program is moderately broad in scope. It cost the state $34.7 million in 1986 but was never fully funded. Selecting teachers on the basis of project proposals rather than good teaching reduces the complexity to a low-moderate level.

One other incentive program—Florida's merit schools program—gives a cash award to the entire staff of a school, not to individuals. The school-wide character of the award substantially alleviates the redistributive effect within schools.[5] Selection is based largely on school test scores so complexity has generally been in the low-moderate range. Since the program is administered through grants to school districts and twenty-nine of the state's sixty-seven districts participate, it is moderately broad. Over the years, funding for the program has been reduced from $30 million to $10 million annually.

Table 6-1 summarizes ratings on the five dimensions of reform magnitude and gives some sense of the overall pattern. Generally, the reforms are more modest than grand. Most strikingly, unlike the reform of the 1960s, most of the 1980s reforms are developmental rather than redistributive. The biggest exception is the career ladder programs. The reforms vary in complexity with the career ladders, the most complex being Georgia's teacher-testing program, and California's curriculum standards reform. Student-testing reforms affect the largest numbers of people. Very few reforms are challenging on several dimensions at once, with the career ladder reforms scoring highest on the greatest number of dimensions; even then, they score lower than the theoretical models that have been developed. By contrast, the most popular reform—increasing high school graduation requirements—is also among the easiest.

DEVELOPMENT IN FIVE STATES

Although most of the 1980s reforms were relatively modest, it is important to understand their implementation in historical context. Two of the five states, California and Florida, were among the first to introduce major reforms after the release of *A Nation at Risk* (Pipho, 1983). Georgia also initiated a comprehensive reform effort, but two years later. Arizona was another early initiator but on a less grand scale, and Pennsylvania followed shortly thereafter. Table 6-2 summarizes each state's history, which is presented in more detail in the next sections.

California

California has both a history of major educational reforms as well as more capacity than most states to put such initiatives into place. Work on the early 1980s reform package preceded the release of the major educational reports, and after the passage of the reform bill in 1983, implementation proceeded relatively smoothly.

A number of "big fix" reforms have been passed in California in recent years, including a compensatory education package in 1964, an early child-

Table 6-1

Comparison of the Magnitude of 1980s Reforms

Reform	State	Breadth	Cost	Depth	Complexity	Redistributive Impact
Student Standards						
Graduation requirements	All	Mod–High	Low	Low–Mod	NA	Low regarding authority and income. Mod among subjects and students.
Extended day	CA, FL	Mod	High	Neg–Low	NA	Low
Competency testing	AZ, FL GA, PA	High	Mod	NA	Mod	Low
Higher-order standards	CA	High	Mod	NA	High	Low
Teacher Reforms						
Teacher testing	PA	Low	Low–Mod	NA	Mod	Low
	GA	Mod	Low–Mod	NA	High	Low
Alternative route	CA	Low	Low	NA	Low	Low
Continuing professional development	PA	Mod–High	Low–Mod	NA	Mod	Mod
Salary increases	CA, GA	Mod	High	NA	NA	Low
	PA	High	High	NA	NA	Low
Career ladders	FL	Mod	High	NA	High	Mod
	AZ	Low	Mod	NA	High	High
	CA	Mod	High	NA	Mod	Mod
Merit schools	FL	Mod	Mod	NA	Mod	Low within schools

Note: Mod, *moderate;* NA, *not applicable.*

Table 6-2
The History of Reform Efforts

State	Prereform Activity	Postreform Activity
CA	History of big reform bills.	Reforms were institutionalized, and a new round is now being planned.
	Ideas on teacher reform and increasing student standards preceded the reform reports in the state legislature.	Mentor teacher shifted from curriculum development to helping teachers over time.
	Substantial reforms were already in place to build on.	Standards reform coordinated by superintendent to push for higher-order skills.
FL	Legislative activism in the 1970s. Previously established state graduation testing.	Repeal of master teacher plan. Merit schools plan developed but lost funding over time.
	Commission-generated reform proposals in 1982 before the reform reports.	Inducements replace mandate for seven-period day.
		Erosion of student standards.
GA	Two previous comprehensive reform bills had been passed but not funded.	Very few experienced teachers lost certification because of expanded teacher testing. Suit settled out of court. No change in testing.
	Previously established teacher- and student-testing systems.	Student testing expanded.
		Computer network way behind schedule.
AZ	Limited educational policy activity stressing accountability.	Pilot career ladder expanded very slowly.
		Competency requirements allowed department to require locally developed promotion tests. Testing expanded.
PA	History of departmental improvement initiatives, state board review of regulations, and appeals to legislature.	Continuing professional development requirements relaxed, then tightened. Minimum salary requirement added. Deadlines extended.
		TELLS data used comparatively. Plans to change system.
		Erosion of course requirements.

hood initiative in 1972, finance reforms in 1972 and 1977, and the school improvement program in 1979 (Fuhrman, 1988). In each case, small groups of legislative insiders developed ideas over two or three years before putting them together in a large omnibus bill. In 1983, SB 813 fit the same pattern.

It combined a number of themes that predated the commission reports, including State Senator Gary Hart's ideas about teacher development and new Superintendent Bill Honig's interest in increasing standards. These were integrated with such existing practices as a sophisticated statewide student-testing program—the California Assessment Program (CAP)—a school improvement program to promote local planning and implementation, and existing teacher inservice provisions. The resulting bill was a collection of some eighty loosely connected provisions, costing more than $800 million.

Five years later, most of the teacher policies are in place, although some are developing slowly. When the mentor teacher program was first initiated, most projects were funded to develop curriculum, not help new teachers. Moreover, in some districts, mentor teacher selection was highly influenced by teachers' association politics, so it was not clear that the better teachers were being selected. These situations have improved, and the legislation has been modified to encourage mentors to help new teachers. However, in some cases collaboration among teachers declined because of the competition the program created (Odden & Marsh, 1987). Although the mentor program is stronger now than it was, it has not been a major factor modifying the organization of teaching in California.

Assessment of the student standards policies is somewhat more complex. A point-by-point assessment of the reforms suggests that several have had limited impact. What is important, however, is how the state superintendent is orchestrating state-mandated CAP tests, model curriculum standards, and text selection to maintain the momentum for change and to address the issue of higher-order cognitive skills for students. High schools and junior high schools are especially sensitive to the CAP results and have been shown to modify their curriculum to ensure that they get high scores (Odden & Marsh, 1987). In the last two years, the CAP program has added grade levels that were previously untested and modified the existing twelfth-grade test to focus on more complex cognitive skills.

Recent discussions with school administrators in California suggest that the SB 813 reforms have been largely institutionalized. Whatever their impact, they no longer require a great deal of special attention. New policy initiatives have been considered but have not been developed because of constitutional limits on state spending.

Florida

Like California, Florida's reform efforts preceded much of the excellence movement literature. However, the state's reforms proved extremely ambitious and were substantially eroded in succeeding years.

The Florida legislature was quite active in the 1970s. Just a few examples are the passage of a new school-financing scheme in 1973 that equalized expenditures and weighted pupils according to their educational needs, an early childhood education reform bill in 1975, an act that established statewide assessment standards and a high school exit examination in 1976, and a bill in 1977 to provide remediation for students who could not meet the standards set the year before (Fuhrman, 1988).

The recent reform initiatives began in 1981, when the Florida Board of Education adopted the goal of moving into the top quartile of states on conventional achievement measures by 1986. In 1982 Governor Robert Graham established a special commission to examine the quality of education in the state. It reported that Florida high schools were performing dismally and introduced many ideas that were later included in the 1983 reform legislation. The national commission reports reinforced a number of ideas that were already gaining momentum in the state.

Still, achieving passage of the bill was extremely difficult. The final 1983 version combined the governor's master teacher proposal with the interests of the speaker of the House (technology education) and that of the president of the Senate (strengthening course requirements for graduation and lengthening the school day). Funding for the legislation was not worked out until after the governor vetoed the version passed during the regular legislative session because it was underfinanced. He called a special session of the legislature and stumped the state to get support for a better-funded package. The thirteenth-hour negotiations over the bill's contents and the governor's interest in obtaining a quick start-up limited the time available for developing regulations and procedures for implementing these complex initiatives.

Over the next four years, the State of Florida retreated from the great expectations of the original reform bill, especially in the area of teacher policies. The legislation created the Florida Quality Incentives Council to coordinate the master teacher and merit pay provisions of the bill and see to their smooth implementation. These tasks included the development of subject matter tests and in-class observation techniques for identifying exceptional teachers. The council issued its first report in March 1984. Even before then the governor began pushing for the implementation of the statewide incentive program. That spring the first master teachers were identified, but not without creating great opposition among teachers. They reported that the procedures for selection were poorly managed: applications and completed tests were lost; teachers were sent to the wrong test locations on the wrong days and at the wrong times; and peer evaluators who were involved with the in-class assessment component obtained inside-track information about how to get high evaluation marks. Only 3 percent of the state's teachers actually received master teacher awards. Complaints about early implementation of the program combined with teacher association opposition to make it a continuing political issue. Although better managed after the first year, it was repealed after the third.

Other reforms were also scaled back. Although the merit school program was relatively popular, support for it declined as the state's financial situation worsened. Within two years, erosion of the tough graduation standards began. The first step was changing the seven-period day from a mandate to an inducement. Currently, most students experience a seven-period day, but districts continue to complain that the incentive does not cover the costs incurred, and some threaten to return to six periods.

Three other, less drastic changes also took place. When the seven-period day became optional, the number of elective credits in remedial and compensatory programs that students could count toward high school graduation increased from two to nine. In addition, the substitution of vocational courses for some English, math, science, and elective courses was allowed under some conditions. Finally, implementing a requirement that students have a 1.5 grade-point average in order to graduate was delayed until 1989.

Georgia

Georgia's reform efforts began at about the time of the excellence reports and built on initiatives that were already under way in the state. For the most part, they remained intact three years later.

The state's 1980s reform package—the Quality Basic Education act (QBE)—had two precursors, the Minimum Educational Standards act of 1964 and the Adequate Program for Education act (APEG) of 1974. Both were governor's initiatives, but neither received adequate financial support after passage.

The current round of reforms began with the formation of the Education Review Commission in 1983 by newly elected Governor Joe Frank Harris. Although the excellence reports contributed to the deliberations of the commission, a more important stimulus was the concern of businesses about the quality of the state's work force. The QBE act was formulated to appeal to other interests as well. It was seen as a way to promote district consolidation and to limit the powers of the elected county superintendents, who were too politically entrenched to be removed. It also became a way to get additional funds to the poorest rural school districts with large black enrollments: districts that were often underfunded by the richer, white elements, who sent their children to private schools (Fuhrman, Clune, & Elmore, 1988). As with previous reform bills in Georgia, QBE was shepherded through the legislature by the governor. Once the final package was put together, it was passed unanimously (Fuhrman, 1988).

The QBE act's changes were modest but have generally been maintained. The expansion of existing testing programs to include experienced teachers without life certificates generated considerable opposition from the teachers' association. In 1987, 20,000 experienced teachers were required to take the new certification test (TCT), and only 327 failed. Although these teachers lost their certification, at least 139 were rehired as long-term substitutes, primarily in Atlanta. The Georgia State Department of Education took action to have them removed. Meanwhile, Georgia was one of three states where the NEA filed suits that teacher competency tests were discriminatory because a higher percentage of blacks than whites failed them. This suit was settled out of court in March 1988, with the legislation remaining intact.

In the standards area, the existing student-testing program was explained. New tests included a third-grade promotion test in 1986, a tenth-grade writing test in 1987, and a kindergarten promotion test in 1988. Although testing is one area where tightening of standards continues, there is no indication that the tests are pushing into the area of higher-order thinking.

The biggest setback for reform in Georgia was in the development of a statewide computer network to link all districts to the Georgia State Department of Education. This network was supposed to simplify reporting requirements, provide department personnel with data more quickly, and make the information more accessible to districts. A wide variety of data, including financial information and test scores, was to be included. By December 1987, development of the system was sixteen months behind schedule, primarily due to difficulties in developing software. It was being used in only a small number of pilot districts, and the reporting requirements for other districts were proving onerous.

Arizona

Arizona has kept up with some of the major national trends without relying on the large reform measures used in Florida, California, and Georgia. When Governor Bruce Babbitt proposed such a bill in 1982, it was defeated. Reforms came instead through a number of legislative and state board actions. More than other states in this sample, Arizona was influenced by the excellence reports. Although the changes enacted were relatively small, continuity has been maintained.

The most significant initiative in teacher standards was the pilot career ladder. This proposal was initiated by State Senator Anne Lindeman, who became aware of merit pay programs in other states through her connections with the Education Commission of the States and the National Council for State Legislators. Governor Babbitt originally was not interested in the career ladder proposal because he wanted larger and broader increases in teacher salaries than the bill would allow. However, as politicians concluded that their constituents would provide additional funds for education only if accountability was increased, he threw his support to the plan, and the bill passed in 1983.

In 1985 the first group of five pilot districts began implementing the new program. It expanded slowly with five additional districts added in 1986 and five more in 1987. The Arizona Education Association had originally opposed the career ladder plan, but in 1987 it began working more closely with the legislature by suggesting procedures for teacher evaluation that were then piloted by the districts starting the program in 1987. As long as Babbitt was governor, there was pressure to expand the program rapidly, because it provided the additional funds he sought for teacher salaries. However, when he was replaced by Evan Mecham, interest in immediate expansion waned.

In the standards area, the Arizona State Board of Education raised the state's high school graduation requirements in 1983 from sixteen to twenty courses. The change was actually quite small; only 4 of 83 districts surveyed by the Department of Education did not already meet that requirement. Since 1983, there have been only minor changes in graduation requirements, such as adding a half-year requirement in social studies that did not increase the total number of courses required and the creation of a loophole so special education students could receive a special certificate but be exempted from the requirements for regular students. The State Board considered raising the graduation requirements further in 1986 but declined to do so.

In 1983, the Arizona legislature also required that districts should list the competencies students needed to demonstrate to pass the eighth and twelfth grades. The Arizona Department of Education used this action to specify the competency areas that districts were mandated to cover, but the proficiency tests were to be locally developed criterion-reference instruments. Since then, the regulation has been expanded to require successful performance on a similar test for graduation from the third grade.

Pennsylvania

Rather than initiating reform, Pennsylvania's legislature generally acts as an appeals court for actions taken by the executive. In the 1970s, the state's education department established twelve educational goals, developed an assessment program to provide districts with test and survey data on how well schools met those goals, and mandated a planning process. In 1984 executive activism was influenced by the excellence agenda. That year, Pennsylvania Department of Education published *Turning the Tide*, its blueprint for educational reform. The report was published under the direction of Secretary of Education Robert Wilburn, who was a close ally of Governor Richard Thornburgh. It called for important changes in teacher and student policy.

New directions in teacher policies were incorporated in Chapter 49 of the state board regulations. The least controversial change was the introduction of a paper-and-pencil test for new teachers. A second initiative was the establishment of a teacher induction program. Originally, college graduates were to be given temporary teaching certificates, to be replaced with regular certificates after they had completed a one-year induction experience in a school district. Before the regulations became final, however, teacher association pressure ensured that novice teachers would be given regular certification on graduation from college. The most controversial teacher policy recommendation required that all teachers take six credits of continuing professional development coursework every five years. When this provision was successfully incorporated in the regulations, teachers' associations lobbied the legislature for redress because their experienced members had been granted permanent certificates. The legislature responded in 1986 with Act 178, which eliminated the continuing professional development requirement for teachers with master's degrees. It also removed an older provision that set standards for permanent certification. Instead, each district had to develop its own criteria with the advice of its teachers. All teachers without a master's degree were to participate in the district's continuing professional development program until these criteria were met.

When Robert Casey replaced Thornburgh as governor, the new Secretary of Education, Thomas Gilhool, tried to tighten teaching policies again. The new administration disapproved about fifty previously accepted teacher induction plans. In January 1988, it issued new, tougher continuing professional development guidelines. When educators again appealed to the legislature, the department responded by loosening some requirements and lengthening planning deadlines. In addition to these changes, the administration added one new initiative of its own. It successfully raised the minimum teacher salary to $18,500.

The *Turning the Tide* agenda included two student standards proposals. The first was an increase in graduation requirements. This increase put pressure on vocational programs because many students could not meet the requirements for vocational diplomas and high school graduation in four years. In response to pressure from vocational educators, graduation requirements were amended within two years to allow up to three vocational courses to count toward the "regular" graduation requirements.

The other standards innovation was the introduction of the legislation for

Testing for Essential Language and Literacy (TELLS) program (for additional information, see Chapter 10, by Wilson and Corbett, in this book). The TELLS program tested students in Grades 3, 5, and 8 to identify those who needed remedial reading and mathematics instruction. Districts were given remedial education funds on the basis of the number of students who failed the test; the more failures, the more money the district received. This creature of the Thornburgh administration was not popular with his successor, who developed plans to modify the program to give incentives to districts with high performance on the TELLS test, with increased post-secondary attendance, and with reduced dropout rates. Only a modest $5 million plan was passed in 1988.

CONCLUSION

The information on educational reform from the five states examined in this study includes both good and bad news. The bad news is that a substantial portion of the excellence movement's reform agenda has not been implemented. The school day and school year have not been extended. Although the amount of testing is increasing, only one state—California—is seriously attempting to move beyond minimum competency tests to assess higher-order thinking. Two states have increased teacher testing, and three have increased teacher salaries. Career ladders have been attempted only on a modest scale, and what might have been the most ambitious of these was repealed. The most notable success of the recent reforms has been the large number of states that raised graduation requirements. However, these increases were typically easy for districts to digest. When they were not, later modifications were made.

Although falling short of the expectations raised by the initial reform reports, the gains made are real. Moreover, they conform rather well with the trickle-down theory of reform reports: a large amount of rhetoric was required to get a modest amount of change. Thus, the current round of reforms parallels the pattern of past events.

Does the reform report rhetoric help generate some kinds of changes rather than others? This review suggests that the most costly reforms proposed in such reports—in this case, massive increases in the time students spend in school—are generally not adopted. The reform reports themselves are not sufficient to lead to a major redistribution in spending between sectors of government or to increase taxpayers' willingness to pay for education. However, where slack resources result from an improving economy or a willingness to modestly increase support for schooling, the reports reinforce that willingness and help target ideas about how funds should be spent. The less expensive ideas often do get supported. Similarly, the reform rhetoric can lend support to redistributive policies but will not overcome major resistance to shifts in resources and authority. Although small gains can be made on any one dimension, large changes on too many dimensions at one time will result in reform initiatives that will not last. Complex redistributive reforms such as career ladders will be attempted only by districts already inclined in that direction. Even then, outside financial assistance may be necessary for some of them to be successfully implemented. In sum, reform reports can contribute to modest increases on almost any of the five dimensions, but they do not lead to really major changes.

The good news is that *most* of the reforms that were adopted have been continued. Where something was ventured, something was gained. The only repealed policy was Florida's master teacher program, which was unusually expensive and redistributive. A few other policies—often in the area of graduation standards—have been softened. However, in most cases, states have stuck with their policies for the intermediate haul—that is, three to five years. In some cases, such as California, where the policy apparatus has moved on to other issues, the recent reforms have been largely institutionalized.

It is important to recognize, however, that the policies that stood the test of time were not simply reflections of the excellence movement. Some states were already moving into their reforms before the advent of the reports. In others, they were relatively logical developments from where the state had already been going, extensions or modest revisions of existing practice. In all cases, the course of development fit the pattern of policymaking in the state. Thus, state reform efforts in the 1980s reflect at least as much homegrown developments as they are replies to national calls for improvement.

NOTES

1. A sixth state, Minnesota, was also studied. However, since the major reforms in the state focus on expanding parental choice, a reform topic not prevalent in other state reform packages, it is not discussed here.

2. For a similar effort focusing more on extent of school and district implementation than on characteristics of policies, see Rosenblum and Louis (1981).

3. They are redistributive in two senses: first, some substantive areas like math and science are favored over others like vocational education and, second, they affect students in lower academic tracks rather than those in college preparation tracks (Clune, with White and Patterson, 1988).

4. Because plans are still being developed and have not yet been implemented, it is difficult to say what the actual level of complexity is.

5. Funds are redistributed among schools, but the award avoids the divisiveness among staff that is potentially problematic with career ladder proposals.

REFERENCES

Boyer, E. L. (1984). Reflections on the great debate of '83. *Phi Delta Kappan*, *65*(8), 525–530.

Bureau of Census. (1988). *Public employment in 1986*. Washington, DC: U.S. Government Printing Office.

Carnegie Forum for Education and the Economy. (1986). *A nation prepared: Teachers for the 21st century*. Hyattsville, MD: Carnegie Forum for Education and the Economy.

Clune, W. H., with P. White & J. Patterson. (1988). *The implementation and effects of high school graduation requirements: First step toward curriculum reform*. New Brunswick, NJ: Center for Policy Research in Education.

Cross, K. P. (1984). The rising tide of school reform reports. *Phi Delta Kappan*, *66*(3), 167–172.

Fuhrman, S. (1988). State politics and school reform. In R. Crowson & J. Hannaway, eds., *The politics of reform and school administration*. New York: Falmer.

Fuhrman, S., W. H. Clune, & R. F. Elmore. (1988). Research on education reform: Lessons on the implementation of policy. In D. Monk & J. Underwood, eds., *Micro-level school finance: Issues and implications for policy*. Cambridge, MA: Ballinger.

Fullan, M. (1982). *The meaning of educational change*. New York: Teachers College Press.

Ginsberg, R., & R. K. Wimpelberg. (1987). Educational change by commission: Attempting "trickle down" reform. *Educational Evaluation and Policy Analysis*, *9*(4), 344–360.

Graham, P. A. (1983). The Twentieth Century Fund task force report on federal elementary and secondary education policy. *Phi Delta Kappan*, *65*(1), 19–21.

Guthrie, J. W. (1988). Campaign '88 and education: A primer for presidential candidates. *Phi Delta Kappan*, *69*(7), 514–519.

Hage, J., & M. Aiken. (1969). *Social change in complex organizations*. New York: Random House.

James, T., & D. Tyack. (1983). Learning from past efforts to reform high schools. *Phi Delta Kappan*, *64*, 400–406.

Madeus, G. (1984). Test scores as administrative mechanisms in educational policy. *Phi Delta Kappan*, *66*(9), 611–617.

McDonnell, L. M., & R. F. Elmore. (1987). Getting the job done: Alternative policy instruments. *Educational Evaluation and Policy Analysis*, *9*(2), 133–152.

Murphy, J. T. (1982). Progress and problems: The paradox of state reform. In A. Lieberman and M. W. McLaughlin, eds., *Policy making in education*. Chicago: University of Chicago.

National Commission on Excellence in Education. (1983). *A nation at risk: The imperative for educational reform*. Washington, DC: U.S. Government Printing Office.

Newcombe, E. (1983). *Rewarding teachers: Issues and incentives*. Philadelphia: Research for Better Schools.

Odden, A. (1984). Financing educational excellence. *Phi Delta Kappan*, *65*(5), 311–319.

Odden, A., & V. Dougherty. (1982). *State programs of school improvement: A 50-state survey*. Denver: Education Commission of the States.

Odden, A., & D. Marsh. (1987). *How state education reform can improve secondary schools.* Berkeley: PACE (Policy Analysis for California Education).

Passow, A. H. (1984). Tackling the reform reports of the 1980s. *Phi Delta Kappan,* *65*(10), 674–683.

Pennsylvania Department of Education. (1984). *Turning the tide.* Harrisburg, PA: Pennsylvania Department of Education.

Peterson, P. E. (1985). Did the education commissions say anything? *Education and Urban Society, 17,* 126–144.

Peterson, P. E., B. G. Rabe, & K. K. Wong. (1986). *When federalism works.* Washington, DC: Brookings Institution.

Pipho, C. (1983). California and Florida set the pace for education reform. *Phi Delta Kappan, 65*(2), 85–86.

Rosenblum, S., & K. S. Louis. (1981). Stability and change. New York: Plenum.

Rosenthal, A. (1981). *Legislative life.* New York: Harper & Row.

CHAPTER 7

Local Response to the 1980s State Education Reforms: New Patterns of Local and State Interaction

Allan Odden and David Marsh

In the late 1960s, when researchers began to analyze local implementation of the newly created War on Poverty programs, the findings were sobering. Most studies found misuse of governmental funds, services provided to the wrong clients, and outright local resistance to, rather than acceptance of, these new governmental initiatives. In education, for example, early research showed that there was a lack of both capacity and will at all levels of government—the U.S. Office of Education, state departments of education, local district offices, and local schools—to develop and implement the newly created governmental programs, particularly Title I of ESEA (Elementary and Secondary Education Act), which were enacted to provide educational services to selected groups of students (Murphy, 1971). This research showed that most local educators did not want to implement such programs (the will was not there), and also that they did not know how to implement them (the capacity was not there). Subsequently, a large body of research emerged that essentially argued that state (or federally) initiated programs, for education or other social services, were doomed to failure on the shoals of local resistance to implementation, and that the priorities, orientations, and pressures of local governments (school districts in the case of education) were simply at odds with those of higher government levels (Pressman & Wildavsky, 1973; Derthick, 1976).

In addition, during the 1970s when regulatory structures were created to clarify the intent and acceptable operations of these new federal and state governmental programs, considerable analysis showed the weak impact these regulations had on local behavior and local priorities (Barro, 1978). Astute analysts realized that "street-level bureaucrats" (those local educators who had to implement admittedly grandiose state or federal programs, usually without sufficient resources) made the key policy decisions because what they did in the school and classroom constituted the program as implemented, despite the legislative intent or regulatory requirements (Weatherly & Lipsky, 1977). And in the early 1980s, seasoned implementation researchers concluded that it was difficult, if not impossible, for state or federal government programs to garner the interest, effort, and commitment of local educators to the higher-level government objectives (Elmore & McLaughlin, 1981).

A complementary line of research—on the local educational change process—concluded that it was difficult to get new programs (created or designed outside the local school district) fully implemented unless local educators could also tailor (adapt, change, and mold) the program to meet their unique, local needs and circumstances (McLaughlin, 1976). In short, early research on implementation, coupled with somewhat later research on local educational change, suggested that local response was inherently at odds with state (or federal) program initiative. If higher-level governments initiated policies, local educators would probably not implement those policies in compliance with either the spirit, expectations, rules, regulations, or program components created.

These tenets of "conventional wisdom" led to great skepticism about the efficacy of the state education reform movement that had begun in 1983 with publication of *A Nation at Risk* and large numbers of subsequent state commission reports calling for major overhauls in the country's elementary and secondary schools. Boyd (1987) provided one of the most elegant critiques of state education reform initiatives, invoking the early research on implementation and local educational change to argue that the top-down nature of state education reforms rendered them unlikely to improve local educational practice. Peterson (1983) criticized both the reform report rhetoric and the proposals themselves as largely lacking research support and thus doomed to failure.

Moreover, Cuban (1984) articulately voiced his skepticism that new state education standards and mandates would improve local school districts, schools, and classrooms. Through a series of local newspaper articles, Cuban took issue with California's chief state school officer, Bill Honig (a major designer of California's 1983 education reform and a rapidly rising state education leader) and strongly questioned the efficacy of that state's efforts to improve the quality of local districts, schools, and curriculum and instruction in classrooms.

Further, because state political leaders and the business community had designed education reforms with little input from the education community, there was concern that resistance would form simply because local educators had been denied participation in the education reform process. Finally, there was widespread concern that the new policy push for excellence and quality might "smother" and push aside the two-decade-old focus on improving equity in the nation's schools. In short, state education reformers appeared to face an army of skeptics and a concensus—at least among many educators and educational researchers—that state education reform "would not work."

But several other indicators at that time, largely ignored by critics, provided hope that state education reform initiatives might not be dashed on the shoals of local resistance to implementation. First, several state education policies initiated during the 1970s—school finance reform, collective bargaining, minimum competency testing—not only spread across the states faster than traditional political science predicted (McDonnell & Fuhrman, 1985) but also appeared to have at least some success (Odden, McGuire, & Belsches-Simmons, 1983). Second, although almost totally ignored by state education reformers, in the early 1980s several states had enacted a variety of school improvement programs (Dougherty & Odden, 1982), often based on the emerging effective teaching and schools research (Cohen, 1983). Studies have shown that several of these early state efforts had substantial impact on local school operations (Anderson et al., 1987). Third, indications from several other sources suggest that local educators were beginning, on their own initiative, to improve the regular curriculum and instruction program, so that new state programs in those same areas at least had a chance of reinforcing and strengthening local priorities rather than pushing them in directions not consistent with local priorities (which clearly was a major characteristic of governmental programs in the 1960s and 1970s).

The remainder of this chapter has three sections. The first section draws on several survey studies to describe local response to state education reform programs in a number of states. The section shows that local districts, by and large, implemented fully and quickly the major components of state education reform programs. The second section draws from in-depth Policy Analysis for California Education (PACE) studies in California and Center for Policy Research in Education (CPRE) investigations in six states to discuss the substantive elements of local response. The section argues that local implementation was typified more by proactive response that often went beyond state requirements, than by local resistance. The third section outlines how implementation research on education reform, thus, should be both conceptualized and designed differently from previous implementation studies of categorical programs.

LOCAL RESPONSE TO STATE EDUCATIONAL REFORM

Despite skepticism, there is now widespread evidence that response to education reform initiatives was swift. By the 1984–85 school year—that is, within two years after the *Nation at Risk* report—forty-one states had increased coursework requirements for high school graduation, twenty-two states had expanded or implemented student minimum competency-testing requirements, and several states had begun to test people who wanted to become teachers (Goertz, 1986). By 1986–87, further progress had been made. Forty-two states had increased high school graduation requirements, forty-four states required student testing for minimum academic competencies, and thirty-eight states required new teachers to pass a standardized state test before entering a teacher education program and/or before becoming certified to teach (Goertz, 1988). This response was greater even than the diffusion of the 1970s state education initiatives in school finance and collective bargaining, and far exceeded the conventional political science notions that it takes twenty-four years for a new innovation to be diffused across half the states, and upward of thirty-one years to affect 75 percent of the states. Several studies in specific states and on particular issues across several states provide additional evidence on the swift local response to the 1980s education reforms.

California

Numerous studies in California now document the rapid policy implementation of the key program components of California's 1983 education reform, Senate Bill 813. Just two years after passage, both the California Taxpayers' Association (Kaye, 1985) and the California State Department of Education surveyed local districts to determine policy response to the reform mandates and incentives. As PACE reported (1985), these studies found that

- Ninety-seven percent of all districts, which enrolled 99.7 percent of all students, were participating in the longer school day and longer school year incentives. Only 14 of the state's more than 1,000 districts, enrolling very few students, declined to participate.

- Eighty-four percent of all districts met the SB 813 new high school graduation requirements,[1] and 65 percent would meet the even stiffer state board of education high school graduation requirements.[2] Fully 90 percent of districts indicated they would meet the SB 813 requirements by 1988.
- Seventy-two percent of districts, enrolling more than 90 percent of all students, participated in the new Mentor Teacher Program.
- Almost 100 percent of districts participated in the tenth-grade counseling program, which required all sophomores to have their transcripts reviewed and a program of studies created that would lead to high school graduation.

More in-depth PACE analyses revealed additional details of these local responses. One study (Grossman, Kirst, Negash, and Schmidt-Posner, 1985) showed major changes in the primary reform goal of exposing students to more academic subjects. The study documented large rises in high school academic course sections offered between 1982–83 and 1984–85. Course sections increased 22 percent in science, 19 percent in mathematics, 12 percent in foreign language, 30 percent in world history, 21 percent in regular English, and 117 percent in advanced placement courses.[3] Enrollments in these academic courses continued to increase through the 1986–87 school year (PACE, 1988). A study by the Far West Laboratory showed widespread local participation in the Mentor Teacher Program and, after first-year difficulties, compliance with the rules and regulations of the program. Another PACE study (Swain, 1985) showed that the counseling program was providing the type of services expected, that sophomores were being counseled into programs that would lead to high school graduation, that students at risk of dropping out were receiving more intensive counseling services, and that there was greater school outreach to parents of these at-risk students. Although only 37 percent of districts participated in the California higher minimum teacher salary program, a PACE study showed that nonparticipating districts tended either already to have high beginning teacher salaries or not to have many beginning teachers (PACE, 1985). In sum, these studies showed that, at least in California, the local response was widespread, swift, and substantively "in line" with the new directions of the SB 813 policies and programs.[4]

South Carolina

Similar results on local district response to state-initiated education reform have been produced in South Carolina. A recent study (Carnegie

Foundation for the Advancement of Teaching, 1988) documents strong support for reform. After surveying teachers in all states, the Carnegie Foundation found the highest local support for state reforms in South Carolina. Six percent of teachers gave the reform an "A," and 46 percent gave it a "B," the highest percentages in the country for both grades. In addition, teachers rated the South Carolina reform the highest for several categories, including goal clarity, academic expectations for students, principal leadership, parental involvement, parental teacher support, teacher awards, and teacher morale.

Even more importantly, impact on students was substantial. For example, student attendance, a targeted goal of that state's reform program, improved from 94.6 percent in 1984 to 96 percent in 1987. More than 100,000 additional students, of a total enrollment of just over 600,000, met the minimum standards on the state's basic skills test. On a nationally norm-referenced test of basic skills, South Carolina students' scores increased from the forty-first percentile to the fifty-first percentile. SAT (Scholastic Aptitude Test) scores increased even more dramatically, rising from a combined verbal and mathematics score of 803 in 1984 to a combined score of 832 in 1987, which represented the largest statewide increase in the nation. This increase occurred even though more students took the SAT test, including a 250 percent increase in students enrolling in advanced placement examinations. Finally, average teacher salaries rose by nearly $6,000 from $17,384 in 1984, to $23,201 in 1987.

Although these figures obviously do not prove that state-created education reform is "working" in South Carolina or even "causing" these results, these indicators nevertheless suggest that the system is changing on several input and outcome measures—with many measures being key targets of the South Carolina education reform initiatives. The figures suggest that there has been substantial local positive response to South Carolina's reform initiatives, simultaneous with significantly improved student performance.

CPRE Six-State Study of High School Graduation Requirements

The Center for Policy Research in Education conducted an in-depth analysis of local implementation and impacts of increased high school graduation requirements in the six states of their core data base—Arizona, California, Florida, Georgia, Minnesota, and Pennsylvania (Clune, 1988). The results are similar to those just described. Within the two years after the states' reforms were enacted, all local districts had implemented the increased high school requirements. In the schools CPRE studied, about 27 percent of students ended up taking an extra mathematics course and 34 percent an extra science course. Many students also were taking new or added courses in history. The study concluded that the new courses were better than the previous courses students had been taking, but probably not as rigorous as they could possibly be. The study further found that the course changes probably increased average student academic achievement, and probably did not raise the dropout rate or hurt at-risk students. In short, implementation generally was prompt and complete, had the desired impacts, and satisfied the public about the value of educational reform. Although the study noted local difficulties accross several dimensions, lack of state technical assistance to implement the course changes, and many areas for improvements, the preceding results held nevertheless.

Curricular Change in Dade County, Florida

CPRE conducted a more detailed study of curricular and course enrollment changes these new high school graduation requirements caused in Dade County, Florida (Hanson, 1988). In 1983, the Florida legislature enacted, for the first time in history, state high school graduation requirements. The new law required 24 credits for graduation, whereas districts had been requiring only between 17 and 22 units. These high school requirements were bolstered by new requirements for entry to the Florida state universities system. For Dade County, the impact of these new requirements was mainly the addition of an extra science course for most students. The district already had been requiring most of the academic courses included in new state requirements. There were, however, changes in overall patterns of course taking.

More specifically, the study found the largest changes in science and foreign language. Enrollments in science increased by about 52 percent between 1982–83 and 1986–87 and by about 69 percent in foreign language. Enrollments in mathematics and social studies were stable, but there were changes within each area. Within mathematics, enrollments increased substantially in general mathematics and geometry; within social studies, enrollments increased in history and economics. As in the PACE study, enrollments declined in vocational education and physical education, 40 and 23 percent respectively.

In short, high school graduations, just as in California, seemed to substantially increase student enrollments in academic courses, a primary goal of both the Florida and California reform programs, as well as of most other state education reform programs.

Why These Results Should Not Be So Surprising

Despite previous implementation research, and acknowledging significant differences across the states, the preceding study findings of swift and positive local response to state education reform initiatives need not have been so surprising. First, as Yudof (1984) noted, the education system responds (swiftly) when there is a consensus for educational change on the part of political leaders outside the education system. This swift response is, in part, a result of the decentralized and lay control of schools in this country. And as McDonnell and Fuhrman (1985) argued, not only was there a consensus among the political elites for action, but there was also a consensus about the kinds of changes needed and a consensus to act "immediately."

Second, while taking many forms across the country, the general goals of state education reforms were to increase student achievement in academic subjects by improving the curriculum and instruction program in class-rooms, schools, and school districts. To greater or lesser degree, this focus on curriculum and instruction has always been the primary emphasis of local educators. Thus, to use Peterson, Rabe, and Wong's typology (1986), education reform was a developmental rather than redistributive program. Developmental programs are state or federal initiatives in areas in which local governments (school districts in the case of education) are already involved—curriculum and instruction for education. Thus, education re-form, while state-initiated, nevertheless reinforced and bolstered—in the main—substantive foci on which local educators were already working. Although there obviously were several differences between local foci on curriculum and instruction and state initiatives, the fact remains that both levels of government targeted the same issue for action. Further, Peterson, Rabe, and Wong (1986) show, from analysis of earlier federal programs, that developmental programs not only get implemented less contentiously, but also more quickly.

By contrast, redistributive programs—the bulk of education programs during the 1960s and 1970s—generally require local educators to focus on issues to which they had not been giving sufficient attention—desegregation, compensatory education, bilingual education, and so on. At least in part because of this redirective nature, redistributive programs have a much more contentious implementation process and take longer to "put into place." Because most of the "conventional wisdom" about education policy im-plementation was drawn from research on the early years of redistributive policy implementation, when local resistance was strongest, it was inappro-priate to apply this "wisdom" to the more developmental education reform initiatives.

Third and related, Murphy, Hallinger, and Mesa (1985) have noted that while the local school is the unit of organizational change, the local district together with the state are the units of system change. Systems can identify the substantive direction in which local units (such as schools) must move while allowing them to determine specifically how to move in those directions. State education reform is an example, they would argue, of these interactions.

THE SUBSTANTIVE NATURE OF LOCAL RESPONSE TO STATE EDUCATION REFORM

A criticism of the studies in the preceding section is that they are based largely on survey findings. Local response *could* be more symbolic than substantive. Both PACE (Odden & Marsh, 1987) and CPRE (Fuhrman, Clune, & Elmore, 1988), however, report on extensive field research in local schools and districts. This research was designed in part to push beyond the preceding more structural indicators of local response, to the meaning and substance behind those changes. This section reviews the findings of these studies. In general, the studies found that local response was not just symbolic; instead, it was substantive to a degree that was far beyond expectations.

The CPRE Six-State Study

The CPRE study findings are based on analysis of documents and interviews with state and local policymakers and educators in 59 schools in 24 districts in six states conducted between April 1986 and June 1987 (Fuhrman, Clune, & Elmore, 1988). To focus their study, they drew on earlier syntheses of implementation research (called the "conventional wisdom" in the preceding section) and made predictions about local implementation behaviors. CPRE *predicted* that

- Implementation success would be enhanced when the reform programs sent clear signals about policy intent.
- Local ownership would depend on the degree to which local educators were involved in the policymaking process. Low involvement would lead to little ownership. Little ownership would produce contentious implementation processes.
- Local response would vary, with some districts refusing to comply, others complying fully, and most "adapting" reforms to local goals and agendas.
- Local educators would more readily adopt policies that matched local capacity; that is, technical expertise.

- There would be little short-term response. It would take more time for local educators to transform reform programs into local practice.
- The reforms themselves and local response would be more symbolic than substantive and give more an appearance of change than meaningful change in students' experiences.

On nearly all these points, the study *found nearly the opposite*. The study concluded that

- Policy clarity was less crucial than predicted. Although some policies appeared more straightforward than others (increased student standards, for example), all policies had ambiguities and multiple meanings. Local districts coped nevertheless, responding to the spirit of nearly all policy elements. Local education leaders were able to take the various and disparate components of state education reform policies and weave them into an integrated local vision of new curriculum and instruction policy.
- Involvement in the policy development process was less crucial than predicted. In nearly all states and at both the state and local levels, educators were not involved in the reform development activities, but were active in designing policy responses to reform programs. The reforms themselves seemed to invigorate educator engagement in curriculum and instruction change. Widespread evidence showed that local and state educators, including teacher unions, were looking hard to make reforms "work." Educators saw the reform programs creating opportunities for them to accomplish many of their own objectives, especially the new funding that accompanied most reform programs.
- Local response was remarkably uniform, with little apparent local resistance. All districts and schools essentially implemented the key elements of the states' reform programs. There was little adaptation. Although increasing student standards (such as increasing high school graduation requirements and adding more traditional academic courses) matched local expertise more than did creating new roles for teachers under career ladder or mentor teacher programs (which experienced more initial implementation snags), all programs were quickly implemented in line with rules, regulations, and state intent.
- Local response was swift. The reform programs were implemented in the short term. It was not taking several years to transform reform programs into local practice.
- Local response was not symbolic but was substantive. Many districts had begun to revamp local curriculum and instruction programs before state education reform began; indeed, the study found a secular trend

for centralizing curriculum at the district level and aligning curriculum objectives, texts, tests, teacher evaluation, and other mechanisms.

Reform, thus, legitimated local initiative. Rather than resistance (predicted by the conventional wisdom), local response was characterized more by "strategic interaction" with state reform direction, both in responding to and affecting the content of state policy locally. Indeed, the study found that many districts had begun reform initiatives before state programs were enacted and went beyond several state standards and requirements.

The PACE Study of Secondary School Reform in California

In this study, researchers spent 11 days in each of seventeen local schools and their central district offices between October 1986 and May 1987, analyzing details of the schools' implementation of fourteen key programs of California's omnibus reform bill, SB 813. The study also examined characteristics of the local implementation processes themselves,[5] the outcomes on students, teachers, administrators, and the schools as organizations, and the treatment of special needs students. In short, the study analyzed the effect of both state education reform initiatives and local implementation porcesses on outcomes. Details of the study, methodology, data, research instruments and findings are provided in Odden and Marsh (1987). The study reached six major conclusions:

Finding 1. *Virtually all schools studied implemented key Senate Bill 813 education provisions in a manner consistent with state purposes.*

- In all the sample districts, SB 813's increased high school graduation requirements were implemented. In many locations, this change was already underway at the time SB 813 was enacted.
- SB 813's required model curriculum standards had been included in district guidelines at two-thirds of the high schools in the study sample and incorporated into actual subjects in half the schools.
- The combination of additional funds provided by SB 813 and new curriculum standards resulted in the selection and purchase of new, more rigorous texts in a majority of sample schools.
- The California Assessment Program (CAP) was receiving greater attention and use in most of the sample schools. It was used to assess educational progress, pinpoint problem areas, and modify curricula.
- All sample schools implemented the longer school day and year—this was started in many districts before the passage of SB 813.
- All sample schools implemented the tenth-grade counseling program.

Finding 2. *Senate Bill 813 reform provisions could be effective when woven into a cohesive school change strategy at the local level.*

- The study's sample schools showed that local education leaders wove the fragmented components of SB 813 and related state initiatives into a cohesive program of local schools change that, when implemented effectively, could improve schools.
- In many sample districts, both commitment to major reform and many concrete efforts to bring it about were underway through local initiation before SB 813. However, research teams concluded that SB 813's legislative force and fiscal resources were crucially important, and without them, many local reform efforts might have foundered.
- In sample schools and districts, SB 813 raised teachers' and administrators' commitment and efforts to improve the quality of education. In these schools generally, SB 813's combination of rigorous new standards and added resources produced a renewed determination to upgrade education, including a renewed emphasis on curriculum and instruction issues, education's core activities.
- Districts tended to centralize curriculum and instruction improvements and to move beyond formal state curriculum program implementation into broader curriculum upgrading. Many schools developed new emphases in reading and writing across curriculum content areas, and required more mathematics and science for the average student. New academic courses represented substantive academic rigor, not relabeled or watered-down versions of old courses.

Finding 3. *Successful local reform implementation showed the following key themes.*

- District leadership was important both in initiating local reform action and in supporting, over several years, full reform implementation.
- District leaders transformed disparate SB 813 elements into integrated district reform visions that retained the state's academic and intellectually demanding orientation and tailored them appropriately to local priorities.
- Schools added to this district vision a school focus on an improved learning environment, including heightened concern for all students and teacher collegiality.
- Teacher and site administrator participation in designing specific implementation activities balanced top-down district and state reform implementation. School and district "teaming" in ongoing reform implementation helped integrate school and district visions and activities.
- Staff development combined with follow-up assistance in schools and

classrooms produced the most improvements in teachers' and administrators' professional expertise.

Finding 4. *Attention to both the substance of curriculum and instruction and the process of school change were associated with higher test scores and better learning conditions for students.*

- Student CAP scores in the sample schools increased more than the statewide average. Further, CAP scores rose for all students, those at the bottom, those in the middle, and those at the top.
- Administrative expertise and practice in the sample schools improved. Administrators were more able to design and implement a strengthened program of instruction, manage a reform process, and supervise instruction.
- Teachers' sense of professional efficacy increased.
- Sample schools improved as institutions. They had plans and stronger norms of teacher collegiality.

Finding 5. *Students with special learning needs—the poor, remedial, limited-English-speaking, and at risk of dropping out—received services, but the services were of a type that has produced insufficient levels of academic achievement in the past. Equity was not overlooked in excellence implementation.*

Finding 6. *Sample schools wanted to move beyond the state agenda and engage in more complex school improvement, including a curriculum focused on problem-solving and higher-order skills, but were searching for more effective strategies and assistance to do so.*

State education reforms played a major role in improving these schools, but with the caveat that state initiatives interacted with local efforts that often were launched prior to SB 813. "SB 813 didn't cause the reform," said one local superintendent, "but it sure helped." In view of many local respondents, the state (1) increased the momentum and continuity of local reform; (2) provided useful direction and materials such as increased high school graduation requirements, new CAP tests, the mentor teacher program, model curriculum standards, and the new state curriculum frameworks. (3) provided critical technical assistance to districts and schools; and (4) monitored and reinforced successful performance.

In response, sample schools and districts did more than simply implement SB 813 curriculum initiatives. They used them as a springboard to engage in comprehensive curriculum upgrading. New district K–12 curriculum "scopes and sequences" were created; new academic courses were developed, particularly in mathematics and science for the average student; new cross-content emphases were begun, such as reading and writing across the curriculum; and new interest emerged for thinking and problem-solving skills.

Relationship of Implementation Process Variables to Outcomes

In addition to the substance and signals of state education reform, local implementation processes also affected outcomes. This section briefly discusses how two categories of outcomes—CAP score gains and increased organizational capacity to engage in substantive education reform—interrelated with local implementation processes.

CAP Score Improvements. California Assessment Program (CAP) gains between December 1983 and December 1986 were calculated for each high school and related to the strength of implementation processes. Although the average gain for all schools exceeded the statewide average, three patterns of CAP score gain were identified: (1) high-gain schools (4) with sizable gains in both reading and mathematics, (2) low-gain schools (4) with smaller gains in both reading and mathematics (but still about the same as the statewide average), and (3) mixed schools (4) for which either reading or mathematics gains, but not both, were sizable (see Odden & Marsh, 1987).

Patterns of high or low CAP gain were not related to district size or to the ethnic composition of a student body. Similarly, CAP score gains were not related to whether a school's 1983 CAP scores were high or low with respect to the overall statewide average. High-gain schools showed increases dramatically greater than the statewide average even though they were demographically typical of all schools in the state. Was there a pattern of CAP score gain?

Yes. High-CAP-gain schools had reform implementation processes that differed considerably from low-CAP-gain schools. High-gain schools were found in districts where the district vision of reform was clear and consistent. Districts with high-gain schools were more strongly committed to education reform, especially to improving basic skills, and were strong in communicating this commitment to schools.

High-gain schools displayed the following in comparison with low-gain schools:

- More active implementation reform management
- More active use of cross-role teams and implementation plans
- Stronger implementation coordination between schools and the district, and among departments within schools
- Greater use of initial training
- Greater ongoing assistance, from leaders at both the district and school

Curriculum development at high-gain schools was often extensive but was qualitatively not greatly different from the previous curriculum at the school. The pattern in low-gain schools was similar—neither type of school had already developed curriculum that was reflective of the new phases of reform. Both high- and low-gain schools, however, were active in aligning curriculum with texts, model curriculum standards, and CAP tests.

Ongoing administrative commitment and leadership were uniformly strong in high-gain schools. Conversely, low-gain schools had low commitment and leadership, except in the one special case of a one-school district in rural northern California. Administrative pressure and monitoring were high in all but one of the high-gain schools. In that school, administrative commitment and leadership were high, even though pressure and monitoring were not extensive. In low-gain schools, administrative pressure and monitoring were uniformly low. Further, high-gain schools were tightly aligned with their districts, and most change was initiated from the top.

Finally, teacher effort, skill mastery, and commitment at high-gain schools were dramatically different than at low-gain schools. Two of the four high-gain schools had consistently high ratings for teacher effort, skill mastery, and commitment. The two other schools had modest ratings in these areas but strong ratings for many other implementation variables, especially for site leadership and commitment. In turn, low-gain schools had consistently modest levels of teacher effort, skill mastery, and commitment.

Improved Organizational Capacity. Organizational capacity for continuing reform was defined as a combination of improvements in school climate and administrative practice. All the schools studied experienced an increased capacity to carry out quality improvements as a result of their involvement with the reform effort. But some schools gained more in organizational capacity—school climate and administrative practice—than others.

For this analysis, high schools were ranked by gains in school climate and administrative practices, clustered into high-, moderate-, and low-gain schools and analyzed with respect to the strength of implementation processes (see Odden & Marsh, 1987). Schools with higher organizational gains managed reform implementation more effectively. These schools were dramatically better at using cross-role terms and also had better implementation plans. The use of initial training at high-organizational-gain schools was not different from other schools. Teacher training in both content and pedagogy was not different in high- and low- organizational-gain schools, but administrative training was slightly higher in the high-gain schools. High-gain schools, however, received much more ongoing assistance from both inside and outside the district.

Schools that greatly increased their organizational capacity were similar to other schools in having a moderate amount of curriculum development, including only a minimal amount of qualitatively different curriculum. Like other schools, high-gain schools demonstrated considerable curriculum alignment. In terms of administrative leadership, however, high-organizational-gain schools differed substantially from other schools. High-gain schools showed considerable ongoing administrative commitment and leadership in implementing reform. Administrative pressure and monitoring were somewhat greater at high-gain schools but not intensive. High-gain schools also experienced more latitude in implementing reforms, with strong school-district alignment and a consistent direction of change.

Summary

In short, PACE and CPRE found significant differences in local response to state education reform than that which was predicted on the basis of conventional wisdom about local implementation. First, many local educators seemed to have the technical expertise to make the changes implied by state education reform—the competence was there. Second, districts tended to be proactive rather than reactive to state education reform initiative, seizing state policy components both to bolster local visions and to help with implementation difficulties—the will was there. If local response to new state (and federal) programs in the previous decades faltered on the lack of capacity and will, it seems those factors had been overcome for state education reform—at least in most districts studied by these two projects. In the 1980s, state initiatives in education reform appeared to coincide with the local will and required capacity to implement. Third, local implementation processes seemed to have a separate and independent impact on ultimate reform impacts. In short, implementation realities for education reform are different from what conventional wisdom suggests.

RESEARCH AND POLICY IMPLICATIONS

These findings suggest that state education reform programs are likely having a more substantial impact on local practice than most have predicted. Indeed, the preceding studies document substantial impact across several dimensions, with nearly all impact "in line" with reform objectives. The major implication is that "state education reform is working." The research implication is to focus more intensely on the nature of the impact.

We have described one approach for structuring such research (Odden & Marsh, 1989) where we suggest that education reform implementation research should

- Draw on the distinction between developmental and redistributive types of governmental programs, recognizing that education reforms are primarily developmental programs.

- Integrate analysis of the content of reform, the process of implementing it in the local setting, and its impacts.
- Focus on the influence of reform on the overall local education system as well as on implementing individual reform elements.
- Integrate a macro (state-level) with a micro (district- and school-level) focus for analyzing the preceding issues.
- Use recent research on the local education change process to analyze micro or local processes and relate the results to the macro context.
- Identify several types of outcomes, including impacts on the people within the local education systems (students, teachers, and administrators) and impacts on the local systems themselves (schools and districts).

Applying these design principles could help create a conceptual framework for education reform implementation research that would be quite different from frameworks typically used to study (redistributive) programs in the past. The framework would assume a degree of "strategic interaction" between state and local curriculum and instruction thrusts and would seek to identify the nature and impacts of those interactions.

Studies would need to capture the degree to which, and how, state education reform programs and policies become part of the local vision for educational excellence. Further, the vision at the district and school level would need to be analyzed separately from state education reform visions. Issues would include both the degree to which state programs help determine the substance of local visions, and how strong, *a priori*, local visions incorporate or weave into their fabric the substance of state initiatives.

Studies also would need to focus on the links between state policy initiatives and local implementation processes. For example, California's reform contained elements intended to shape implementation activities and assistance, such as incentives to establish mentor teacher programs or to establish other forms of staff development. In other cases, the state-mandated aspects of the local implementation process, such as the requirement that local administrators be certified by their local school board as being competent to evaluate teachers. The state also funded a set of regional curriculum centers that, in turn, were to provide implementation assistance to local districts on specific aspects of the reform. Further, state policy was designed to influence local accountability for the success of the reform process. Schools were provided with site-specific data on a set of state-defined "quality indicators" that included, for example, patterns of student enrollment in academically demanding courses, test results on the state achievement test and the national advanced placement tests, and dropout and attendance rates. The California Department of Education developed techniques for comparing schools having similar sociodemographic student characteristics and encouraged districts to develop more detailed school quality reports.

Studies would need (1) to draw on the local change literature to identify more specific elements of the local change process that facilitate or hinder education reform implementation, and (2) to distinguish clearly differences between initiatives, such as education reform, that are designed to improve the local education system, from past initiatives focused on specific groups of students. And since education reform in the early 1980s basically has required educators to restore traditional visions of effective schools, for which they had sufficient capacity and expertise, research would need to distinguish successful local implementation processes for that agenda, from implementation processes for more complex goals such as teacher professionalization, school restructuring, and curriculum reform emphasizing higher-level thinking skills, the latter three being prime goals for ongoing education reform.

Finally, future implementation research needs to document the impacts, including winners and losers, of education reform. Specifically, do all students benefit from more intensive exposure to academic courses? Does academic intensification increase the dropout rate? And does even successful education reform implementation teach a higher percentage of students the thinking, problem-solving, communication, and social interaction skills increasingly needed for successful participation in the work force?

In short, although local response to the "first wave" of state education reforms appears to differ from "conventional wisdom" predictions, and to be characterized more by "strategic interaction" than by resistance, the goals of education reform might not be ambitious enough for what the education system must now accomplish, and the nature of state and local interaction as well as implementation processes themselves might be very different for the "second and third waves of reform" that have evolved since the publication of *A Nation at Risk*. Put differently, although we need to expand and deepen understanding of the first wave of education reform, we also need to understand the nature and impact of evolving reform agenda as well, and be open to potentially substantial differences between the two.

NOTES

1. Three years of English, two of mathematics, two of science, three of social studies, and one of foreign language or fine arts.

2. Four years of English, three of mathematics, two of science, three of social studies, one-half of economics, and two of foreign language.

3. This study also showed substantial decreases in course sections for vocational education, in which course sections dropped 21 percent in home economics, 16 percent in industrial arts, and 11 percent in business education.

4. Impacts of the California reforms are discussed in the next section of this chapter.

5. The study analyzed seventeen implementation variables: new district goals and vision, initial central office commitment, district perception of program fit, site vision, initial site administration commitment, program adoption, implementation management including an implementation plan and cross-role implementation teams, initial content and skill training, curriculum and instruction vision after adoption, ongoing administrative commitment, pressure and monitoring, lattitude and fidelity, ongoing technical assistance, teacher effort, skills mastery, and teacher and administrator commitment.

REFERENCES

Anderson B., A. Odden, E. Farrar, S. Fuhrman, A. Davis, E. Huddle, J. Armstrong, & P. Flakus-Mosqueda. (1987). State strategies to support local school improvement. *Knowledge: Creation, Diffusion and Utilization, 9*(1), 42–86.

Barro, S. (1978). Federal education goals and policy instruments: An assessment of the "strings" attached to categorical grants in education. In M. Timpane, ed., *The federal interest in financing schools.* Santa Monica, CA: Rand Corporation.

Boyd W. (1987, Summer). Public education's last hurrah?: Schizophrenia, amnesia, and ignorance in school politics. *Educational Evaluation and Policy Analysis, 9*(2), 85–100.

Carnegie Foundation for the Advancement of Teaching. (1988). *Report card on national school reform: The teachers speak.* Princeton, NJ: Carnegie Foundation.

Clune, W. (1988). *The Implementation and effects of high school graduation requirements: First steps toward curricular reform.* New Brunswick, NJ: Center for Policy Research in Education, Rutgers University.

Cohen, M. (1983). Instructional, management and social conditions in effective schools. In A. Odden & L. D. Webb, eds., *School finance and school improvement: Linkages for the 1980s.* Cambridge, MA: Ballinger.

Cuban, L. (1984). School reform by remote control: S.B. 813 in California. *Phi Delta Kappan, 66*(3), 213–215.

Derthick, M. (1976). Washington: Angry citizens and an ambitious plan. In W. Williams & R. Elmore, eds., *Social program implementation.* New York: Academic Press.

Dougherty, V., & A. Odden. (1982). *State school improvement programs.* Denver: Education Commission of the States.

Elmore, R., & M. McLaughlin. (1981). Strategic choice in federal policy: The compliance-assistance trade-off. In A. Lieberman & M. McLaughlin, eds., *Policymaking in education.* Chicago: Chicago University Press.

Furhman, S., W. Clune, & R. Elmore. (1988, Winter). Research on education reform: Lessons on implementation of policy. *Teachers College Record, 90*(2), 237–258.

Goertz, M. E. (1986, January). *State educational standards: A 50 state survey.* Princeton, NJ: Educational Testing Service.

Goertz, M. E. (1988, March). *State educational standards in the 50 states: An update.* Princeton, NJ: Educational Testing Service.

Grossman, P., M. Kirst, W. Negash, & J. Schmidt-Posner. (1985). *Curriculum change in California comprehensive high schools: 1982–83 to 1984–85.* Berkeley: Policy Analysis for California Education (PACE), University of California.

Hanson, T. (1988). *Curriculum change in Dade County, 1982–83 to 1986–87: A replication of the PACE study.* Madison: Wisconsin Center for Education Research, School of Education, University of Wisconsin.

Kaye, L. (1985). *Making the grade? Assessing school district progress on SB 813.* Sacramento: California Tax Foundation.

McDonnell, L., & S. Furhman. (1985). The political context of reform. In V. Mueller & M. McKeown, eds., *The fiscal, legal, and political aspects of state reform of elementary and secondary education.* Cambridge, MA: Ballinger.

McLaughlin, M. (1976, February). Implementation as mutual adaptation: Change in classroom organization. *Teachers College Press, 77*(3), 339–351.

Murphy, J. (1971, February). Title I of ESEA: The politics of implementing federal education reform. *Harvard Educational Review, 41*(1), 35–63.

Murphy, J., P. Hallinger, & R. Mesa. (1985, Summer). School effectiveness: Checking progress and assumptions, and developing a role for state and federal government. *Teachers College Record, 86*(4) 615–641.

Odden, A., & D. Marsh. (1987). *How state education reform can improve secondary schools. Part II: Background and technical appendices.* Berkeley: Policy Analysis for California Education (PACE), University of California.

Odden, A., & D. Marsh. (1988, April). How comprehensive education reform can improve secondary schools. *Phi Delta Kappan, 69*(7).

Odden, A., & D. Marsh. (1989). State education reform implementation: A framework for analysis. In J. Hannaway & R. Crowson, eds., *The politics of reform and school administration.* Philadelphia: Falmer Press. Pp. 41–59.

Odden, A., C. K. McGuire, & G. Belsches-Simmons. (1983). *School finance reform in the states, 1983.* Denver: Educational Commission of the States.

Peterson, P. (1983). Did the education commissions say anything? *Brookings Review,* pp. 3–11.

Peterson, P., B. Rabe, & K. Wong. (1986). *When federalism works.* Washington, DC: Brookings Institution.

Pressman, J., & A. Wildavsky. (1973). *How great expectations in Washington are dashed in Oakland, or Why it's amazing that federal programs work at all.* Berkeley: University of California.

Policy Analysis for California Education (PACE). (1985). *Conditions of education in California, 1985.* Berkeley: PACE, School of Education, University of California.

Policy Analysis for California Education (PACE). (1988). *Conditions of education in California, 1988.* Berkeley: PACE, School of Education, University of California.

Swain, C. (1985). *SB 813 and tenth grade counseling: A report on implementation.* Berkeley: Policy Analysis for California Education, University of California.

Weatherly, R., & M. Lipsky. (1977, May). Street-level bureaucrats and institutional innovation: Implementing special education reform. *Harvard Educational Review, 47*(2), 171–197.

Yudof, M. (1984). Educational policy research and the new consensus in the 1980s. *Phi Delta Kappan, 65*(7), 456–459.

Reform Cases and Themes

CHAPTER 8

Teacher-Testing Programs

Martha M. McCarthy

The use of tests as a screening device for public educators is not a new phenomenon. In the early twentieth century, when college graduation was not required for teachers, competency tests of basic skills were administered to prospective teachers in most states. As educational requirements for teacher certification increased, the use of competency testing declined. Teacher education programs tended to assume the function of quality control in the teacher certification process. Thus, teacher testing became dormant for about fifty years (Sandefur, 1988).

Southern states were the first to reintroduce test requirements as a prerequisite to certification in the 1970s. Soon other states began following the southern lead as reports of declining student test scores and lack of public confidence in the schools focused attention on teacher competence.

This chapter builds in part on research conducted under the auspices of the Consortium on Educational Policy Studies at Indiana University: McCarthy, M., D. Turner, & G. Hall, (1987), *Competency testing for teachers: A status report* (Bloomington, IN: Consortium on Educational Policy Studies). I wish to thank Mark Buechler, research associate at Indiana University, who provided valuable assistance in conducting the 1988 survey of states, checking references, and reviewing numerous drafts of this chapter.

Policymakers became less sanguine about relying on university preparation programs, approved by state and regional accrediting agencies, to eliminate incompetent individuals from the teaching profession (Cole, 1979).

In 1980 the American Association of Colleges for Teacher Education was one of the first national groups to endorse teacher testing (Sandefur, 1987). Subsequently, the Council of Chief State School Officers' Ad Hoc Committee on Teacher Certification, Preparation and Accreditation (1984) recommended that every state implement a system of assessing and screening prospective teacher applicants. Although only ten states mandated testing of teachers prior to 1980, by 1988 almost all states had adopted test requirements for prospective teachers.

Without question, teacher testing has been a central component of education reform efforts in the 1980s. Petrie (1987, p. 175) has asserted that "it would not be too much of an exageration to say that evaluation and testing have become *the* engine for implementing education policy." Madaus (1985, p. 5) has called testing the "darling of policymakers across the country," and Pipho (1985, p. 19) has noted that "nearly every large education reform effort of the past few years has either mandated a new form of testing or expanded use of existing testing."

The purpose of this chapter is to provide an overview of teacher-testing mandates in state educational reform packages of the 1980s. Specific sections of the chapter deal with the rationale for teacher-testing programs, activity across states in implementing test requirements for educators, legal challenges to such requirements, and criticisms of testing programs. A concluding section addresses future directions of the testing movement and highlights some unresolved issues.

RATIONALE FOR TEACHER-TESTING PROGRAMS

Several developments have nurtured the renewed public interest in teacher testing in the 1980s. A series of national reports has underscored the need for educational reform, including programs to improve the quality of the teaching force. By far the most widely distributed report, *A Nation at Risk*, was issued by the National Commission on Excellence in Education in 1983. Within a year, several other reports were receiving national attention (Boyer, 1983; Education Commission of the States, 1983; Goodlad, 1984; Twentieth Century Fund, 1983). Although many of the educational reform efforts, including teacher-testing mandates, were initiated prior to 1983, the series of reform reports reformulated the education problems and focused public attention on seeking solutions. The reports noted deficiencies such as student illiteracy, declining Scholastic Aptitude Test scores, and the dismal showing of U.S. education in comparison with foreign competitors. They called for higher standards for students, an overhaul of teacher preparation, and improved working conditions for teachers. Responding in part to these reports, 700 pieces of legislation to upgrade the teaching force were introduced across states between 1983 and 1985 (Darling-Hammond & Berry, 1988).

A second wave of reform reports in the mid-1980s focused in part on improving teacher professionalism. For example, *Tomorrow's Teachers* (Holmes Group, 1986) and *A Nation Prepared: Teachers for the 21st Century*, prepared by the Carnegie Forum on Education and the Economy's Task Force on Teaching as a Profession (1986), both called for major reforms to improve the quality of the teaching force. Also, *Time for Results*, issued by the National Governors' Association (1986), demonstrated that governors' commitment to educational reform, including programs to address teachers' professionalism and school leadership. As discussed in the concluding section of this chapter, the Carnegie Foundation already has funded efforts to establish a National Standards Board to design a national teacher certification system. Petrie (1987, p. 176) has observed that this second wave of reform has shown more sophistication regarding what is needed to obtain lasting educational change, but still has retained "a major dependency on assessment, testing, and evaluation."

Although reform efforts of the 1960s and early 1970s focused on education access and programs to meet the needs of special groups of students who had been underserved in the past, (such as the handicapped, economically disadvantaged), the excellence movement of the 1980s addresses the basic core of education such as the components of the curriculum and standards of performance assessment (Guthrie & Koppich, 1988). Throughout the reform efforts of the 1980s, there has been an emphasis on quantifiable results, and this "outcome" focus has naturally led to the expansion of testing programs for both students and teachers. Nader (1987, p. 1) has asserted that "tests have proliferated partly because of the testing industries' promotional practices and partly because the people in charge find it easiest to judge people numerically and not qualitatively."

The public wants assurances that teachers will be at least minimally competent, and tests are viewed as a vehicle to screen unqualified individuals out of the profession. In the 1988 Gallup Poll of the Public's Attitudes Toward Public Schools, 86 percent of the respondents indicated that experienced teachers periodically should be required to pass a competency examination in their teaching area (Gallup & Elam, 1988). The general sentiment is that a competent teacher must know the subject she or he is teaching and should be able to pass a valid test measuring general subject matter and professional knowledge (Medley, 1984). Popham (1985, p. 24) has asserted that expecting certified teachers and administrators to "be able to read and write adequately does not seem to be an outlandish notion."

Advocates of testing programs consider them necessary, but certainly not sufficient, to ensure a competent teaching force. Tests do not assess classroom management skills, ability to establish rapport with parents or students, or ability to *apply* pedagogical knowledge. Instead, the current paper-and-pencil tests assess competence in basic skills and, in some cases, knowledge about teaching (Murray, 1986). Test scores are used to predict whether the individual does or does not have enough knowledge of content (or of content and pedagogic principles and techniques) to be minimally successful in the classroom (Madaus & Pullin, 1987). A test of knowledge cannot purport to measure teaching competence, but rather to identify incompetence in selected knowledge domains considered essential for teachers.

In other words, test proponents do not claim that the programs will assure excellence. Rather, they assert that testing programs will strengthen the profession by reducing the number of teachers who are not minimally competent in basic skill areas. Such efforts in turn may boost public confidence in education and attract better-qualified individuals into the profession (Rudner, 1987b). It is asserted that teacher quality may ultimately improve because testing programs will inspire brighter, more talented candidates to enter teaching, but a testing program per se will not identify superior teachers.

Another rationale for state-mandated teacher-testing programs is that they will make teacher education programs become more accountable for adequately preparing prospective teachers. Test advocates contend that testing programs will encourage institutions of higher education to strengthen requirements for admission into teacher education and that preparation programs will become more product-oriented (McCarthy, Turner, & Hall, 1987). In several southern states, this expectation has been made explicit. For example, in 1984 Tennessee enacted a law stipulating that teacher preparation programs would be placed on probation for one year if 30 percent or more of their students failed the state's basic skills test. Accreditation would be revoked if less than 70 percent passed the test for two years in a row. A Florida law requires 80 percent of a teacher preparation program's graduates to pass the teacher competency tests for the program to retain state approval. In 1986, eight programs lost state approval and twenty-four programs were placed on probation for failure to satisfy this standard ("Poor Test Scores," 1988).

ACTIVITY ACROSS STATES

This section presents a summary of data gathered from each state regarding test requirements for educators, career stages where tests are used, and the types of tests employed. Also addressed are efforts to validate tests for educators and costs associated with testing programs.

To gather data on the types of testing requirements being implemented or considered across states, a study was conducted under the auspices of the Consortium on Educational Policy Studies at Indiana University. Initially, a questionnaire was sent to each state education agency in the spring and summer of 1986 (McCarthy, Turner, & Hall, 1987). Follow-up telephone calls were made to states that did not respond to the questionnaire. State education agencies were contacted again in the summer of 1988 to ascertain developments since the initial survey. The data reported here depict activity across states as of August 1988.

Career Stages Where Tests Are Used

Tests for educators are used primarily at three career stages: (1) admission to teacher preparation programs, (2) initial certification, and (3) recertification. The states using test requirements at each of these career stages are displayed in Table 8-1.

Thirty-two states through legislation or state board of education policies prescribe tests for applicants to teacher preparation programs. Usually the admission decision is made after the candidate has completed two years of college. Tests used at this stage generally assess basic skills in reading, writing, and computation. Rudner (1987b) reported that the average pass rate is approximately 72 percent for admissions tests into teacher preparation programs. States and sometimes institutions of higher education within states vary as to the number of times applicants are allowed to take the admissions test and the availability of remediation opportunities for those who fail the test.

Forty-four states have adopted test requirements as a prerequisite to initial teacher certification; this is clearly the most popular career stage for testing programs. Some states condition graduation from teacher education programs on test passage, whereas others use test scores only for certification purposes. The central goal of certification testing programs is to identify candidates who are at least minimally competent to teach in the state. Thus, the tests usually assess basic communication and computation skills and knowledge about teaching that are felt to be essential for beginning teachers regardless of grade level. In some states, certification applicants also must pass subject matter tests within their area of teaching specialization. The average pass rate on certification tests was 83 percent in 1986 (Rudner, 1987b). As with admissions testing, states vary regarding policies on retaking the test (that is, number of retakes allowed, and the time that must elapse between testings).

Table 8-1
Teacher Competency Testing Programs—1988

Entrance Requirement for Teacher Education Programs	Exit Requirement from Teacher Education Programs or Prerequisite to Certification[a]		Requirement for Recertification[b]
Alabama	Alabama	Ohio	Arkansas
Arizona	Arizona	Oklahoma	Georgia
Arkansas	Arkansas	Pennsylvania	Texas
California	California	Rhode Island	
Colorado	Colorado	South Carolina	
Connecticut	Connecticut	Tennessee	
Florida	Delaware	Texas	
Georgia	Florida	Virginia	
Kansas	Georgia	Washington (1993)	
Kentucky	Hawaii	West Virginia	
Louisiana	Idaho	Wisconsin[f]	
Massachusetts	Illinois		
Michigan (1991)	Indiana		
Minnesota	Kansas		
Mississippi	Kentucky		
Missouri	Louisiana		
Nebraska	Maine		
Nevada	Maryland		
New Mexico[c]	Massachussetts		
North Carolina	Michigan (1991)		
North Dakota	Minnesota		
Ohio	Mississippi		
Oklahoma (1989)	Missouri (1990)		
Oregon	Montana		
South Carolina	Nebraska (1989)[d]		
Tennessee	Nevada (1989)		
Texas	New Hampshire[e]		
Utah[c]	New Jersey		
Washington	New Mexico		
West Virginia	New York		
Wisconsin	North Carolina		
Wyoming	North Dakota		

[a] Most of the states that test for initial certification also require practicing teachers to take subject area tests when seeking certification endorsements in additional subject areas.

[b] Once teachers pass the initial certification or recertification test, they are not subject to the test requirement for subsequent certificate renewals.

[c] The state requires each institution of higher education to establish a process to screen teacher education applicants for basic skill mastery.

[d] Only applicants who have not graduated from Nebraska teacher prepration programs are subject to the test requirement at this career stage.

[e] The state requires graduates of teacher education programs to have demonstrated competence in basic skills. Some institutions of higher education use an exit examination, while others test applicants for admission to teacher education programs.

[f] The law requires applicants for certification to take subject area examinations, but the legislature has not yet funded implementation of the law.

Three states (Texas, Arkansas, and Georgia) have adopted test requirements that apply (one time only) to practicing educators. Testing programs at this career stage have been by far the most controversial and, as discussed later, have sparked litigation in each state where such mandates have been adopted.

In Texas, administrators as well as teachers who received certification prior to 1 February 1986 were required to pass the Texas Examination of Current Administrators and Teachers (TECAT) to be eligible for continued certification after 30 June 1986. After two administrations of the TECAT, the pass rate was 99 percent (Shepard & Kreitzer, 1987).

Arkansas also imposed a temporary test requirement; all certified educators in the state were required to pass the Functional Academic Skills Test (FAST) between 1985 and 1987.[1] About 3.5 percent of the certified personnel in Arkansas did not pass the FAST by the 1987 cutoff date; however, some of these people will retain their teaching positions for a number of years until their current ten-year certificates expire.

In Georgia, educators seeking renewal of their five-year certificates who did not pass the teacher certification test (TCT) when initially certified, must pass the TCT to become recertified. Once individuals pass the TCT, they do not have to take it again for subsequent certificate renewals. State officials estimate that by 1990 all teachers in Georgia will have taken the test, with the exception of those who earned lifetime certificates prior to adoption of the test requirement.

In addition to these three basic career stages, tests also can be part of career ladder, merit pay, or beginning teacher internship programs. For example, Tennessee's career ladder program includes a testing component for teachers who have not been tested at the precertification stage (Murray, 1986). South Carolina for several years used scores on the National Teachers Examination (NTE) to determine certification grades, which in turn determined where teachers were placed on the salary scale. A number of states include performance assessments in their beginning teacher assistance programs, but these assessments usually entail observations and performance inventories rather than paper-and-pencil tests.

Types of Tests

The most commonly used tests are those produced by the Educational Testing Service (ETS). Specifically, the NTE[2] and the Pre-Professional Skills Test (PPST) are the most popular. Thirty states use one or both of these tests as a requirement for admission to or graduation from teacher education programs or as a prerequisite to initial state certification. The ETS and the NTE Policy Council have refused to allow the NTE Core Battery to be used to assess the competence of practicing teachers, because it was not designed for this purpose (Anrig, 1986).

The most popular test used for admission to teacher education programs is the PPST, which covers basic communication and computation skills. Twelve of the states requiring test passage for teacher education admissions use this test. Other tests used at this stage in at least two states each are the California Basic Education Skills Test (CBEST), the California Achievement Test (CAT), the American College Test (ACT), and the Scholastic Aptitude Test (SAT).

The NTE, available since 1939, is clearly the most popular certification test; it is used in twenty-three states at this career stage. The ETS estimates that about 200,000 people take the NTE each year ("Educational Testing Service," 1988). The NTE includes a Core Battery that covers basic skill areas (communications, mathematics, and general knowledge of social studies, literature, fine arts, and science) and a component that addresses professional knowledge of teaching. The NTE also contains subject matter tests in twenty-six fields. Some states use other standardized tests, such as the PPST or the CBEST, at the certification stage.

The National Evaluation Systems (NES) provides customized testing services to states. Fifteen states use customized tests for admission to teacher education or for certification. Some states use a customized test in conjunction with a test developed by the ETS as a prerequisite to certification. All three states that have implemented test requirements for recertification have used customized tests. An ad hoc committee of the Council of Chief State School Officers (1984, p. 22) reported that many state education executive officers believe that "a locally developed test wins acceptance more easily because it emphasizes competencies that are valued locally, it is validated with local teachers, and it is developed with the participation of important local organizations." However, primarily because of their costs, most states have not implemented customized testing programs.

Validation Studies

Whether using a customized test or a national test, each state must validate its test instrument. For certification tests, usually the relationship between the test and the curriculum of teacher preparation programs is assessed. Also, the test's content validity is determined by assessing the relationship between the test and knowledge needed to perform the tasks required of teachers. The ETS has required that a content validity study be conducted in each state that uses the NTE, and the ETS has conducted 60 percent of the state studies (Gifford, 1987).

In 1978 the Equal Employment Opportunity Commission (EEOC) issued *Uniform Guidelines on Employee Selection Procedures* designed to assure that employment practices with an adverse impact on a group protected by Title VII are justified by a business necessity. Under the *Guidelines*, employment tests are expected to be reliable (in that the measurement instrument is accurate and provides dependable data) and valid (in that the instrument actually measures what it purports to measure). The EEOC will allow criterion-related validation (data indicating that the test predicts job performance), content-related validation (data showing that the test is representative of important aspects of job performance), construct-related validation (data indicating that the test measures the degree to which candidates have characteristics determined to be important in successful job performance), or other types of validation studies that meet recognized standards of the American Psychological Association and of basic textbooks and journals in the field of personnel selection. The *Guidelines* emphasize the importance of the test being validated for its intended purpose (such as initial screening or performance evaluation).

By far the most popular validation procedure for teacher-testing programs uses expert panels. Judges (teachers, administrators, teacher educators) are asked to rate the test items in terms of their coverage of knowledge a minimally qualified teacher should possess, irrespective of teaching field or grade level (Madaus & Pullin, 1987). Panel members initially are asked to assess the similarity between the tests and the teacher preparation program; that is, whether students enrolled in a standard teacher preparation program would have been exposed to the material covered on the examination. In most validation studies, test questions are classified as appropriate if more than half of the panel members indicate that at least 90 percent of the teacher education students would have had an opportunity to learn the specific item (Rudner, 1987a). Experts also are asked to assess the appropriateness of the test's emphasis (that is, does the test appropriately emphasize specific topics) and to identify important topics in the teacher preparation curriculum that are not covered on the test. Finally, the panel is usually asked if the skills covered on the test are relevant to effective teaching (Elliot & Nelson, 1984; Elliot & Patterson, 1984).

A more costly and little used content validation strategy is to conduct a job analysis of teaching to ascertain if the test covers work behaviors that are critical to successful job performance. Such an analysis may involve surveys of practitioners to determine the need for particular skills and knowledge on the job and the frequency that such skills and knowledge are required by teachers. Murray (1986, p. 24) has noted that a job analysis can also involve "direct observations, interviews, and analysis of records." In 1986 the ETS conducted a job analysis study to validate the "job relatedness" of the NTE by identifying important teaching tasks that cut across grade levels and content area (Rosenfeld, Thornton, & Skurnik, 1986). The study employed literature reviews, interviews with teachers and administrators in sample school districts in three states, and consultation with advisory committees. The findings supported that the content domain of the NTE Core Battery is related to important teaching functions.

The NTE Policy Council has recommended that tests be validated by establishing the empirical relationship between test scores and teaching performance. This type of validation necessitates gathering longitudinal data. Test scores would be obtained for a pool of individuals who would then be assessed using other measures (such as supervisor ratings) while on the job. The relationship between test score and teaching performance would be analyzed to determine how well the scores predict teaching success (Madaus & Pullin, 1987). Although this type of validation may be preferable to assure job relatedness of the test, given the time and expense involved, this strategy is not likely to be widely used to validate teacher-testing programs.

Fiscal Issues

Teacher-testing programs, particularly customized testing programs, are expensive. Rudner (1987b) estimated that it costs $50,000 to $100,000 to develop a customized test and between $5,000 and $50,000 to validate the test. Costs can approach $1 million if a state uses a customized basic skills test and twenty-five subject area tests (Flippo, 1986). In addition, costs for the administration and scoring of tests average over $100 per examinee (Rudner, 1987b). A spokesperson for the NES, which provides the majority of customized services to states, has indicated that costs can be reduced substantially by adapting customized tests that have already been developed for use in other states (Michael Chernoff, personal communication, 7 January 1987).

Although less expensive, using an existing test—such as the NTE—is still costly. Alan (1985) has estimated that a validity study of the content area tests for the NTE could cost a state as much as $50,000. After the test is developed (or purchased) and validated, some of the costs of administration can be passed on to those taking the test.

Costs of preparing applicants to take initial certification tests are borne by teacher preparation programs, and the state usually does not pay for people to take the test. But where tests are used with practicing educators, state and local education agencies incur significant expenses associated with training sessions and test administration. In Texas, for example, implementing the TECAT cost many times over the anticipated amount (Shepard & Kreitzer, 1987). The contracted cost to develop, administer, and score the TECAT in 1986 was $4,833,000, but the state's expenditures far exceeded this amount. The state paid $26,260,000 for an inservice day for educators to take the test, and local school districts also incurred costs for test sites ($138,500) and workshops ($4,150,000) at which about 90,000 educators were prepared to take the test (Shepard & Kreitzer, 1987). The Texas Education Agency also subsidized the state appropriation by assigning regular assessment staff to the TECAT project at an estimated cost of $232,500. Shepard and Kreitzer reported that the total tax-supported cost of TECAT in 1986 was $35,500,000.

Fiscal concerns often have determined the type of test chosen and the nature of the validity study. Also, fiscal considerations, such as the costs of remediating teachers and filling vacancies in selected fields, have played a role in determining passing scores on examinations. In addition, the costs of recertification testing programs may be deterring a number of state legislatures from implementing such test requirements for practicing educators.

LEGAL STATUS OF TEACHER-TESTING PROGRAMS

The wave of state-level activity to assure competent teaching staffs has been accompanied by legal challenges to employment decisions that are based on examination results. This section provides a brief overview of litigation involving claims that teacher-testing programs violate rights protected by the U.S. Constitution or by civil rights laws.

The most frequent allegation is that employment tests are discriminatory in that minorities disproportionately score poorly. Some claims have been grounded in the equal protection clause of the Fourteenth Amendment that prohibits states from denying citizens equal protection of the laws. The U.S. Supreme Court has rejected equal protection challenges to testing programs if substantiated that the use of a test is rationally related to a legitimate employment objective and not accompanied by discriminatory motives. In the leading constitutional case, the Supreme Court in 1976 reasoned that a written skills test used as an entrance requirement for the Washington, D.C., police-training program was directly related to requirements of the training program and was not administered for discriminatory reasons, even though the test disqualified a disproportionate number of black applicants (*Washington v. Davis*, 1976).

Two years later the Supreme Court affirmed a lower court's conclusion that South Carolina's use of NTE scores to screen certification applicants and to determine teachers' initial placement on the salary scale satisfied Fourteenth Amendment equal protection guarantees (*United States v. South Carolina*, 1978). The trial court reasoned that the test was valid in that it measured knowledge of course content in teacher preparation programs. The court also recognized that the test was used for the nondiscriminatory and legitimate purpose of encouraging teachers to upgrade their skills.

Although a few employment-testing programs have been invalidated under the equal protection clause (for examples, *Baker v. Columbus Municipal Separate School District*, 1972; *United States v. North Carolina*, 1975; *Walston v. County School Board of Nansemond County*, 1974), individuals generally have not prevailed in attacking prerequisites to employment under the U.S. Constitution. For example, in 1986 the Fifth Circuit Court of Appeals upheld use of a basic skills test as a prerequisite to enrollment in teacher education programs in Texas (*United States v. Lulac*, 1986). The court reasoned that a state is not obligated to educate or certify teachers who cannot pass a valid test of basic skills necessary for professional training. Only with evidence of intentional discrimination would the state be prevented from implementing the testing program.

However, plaintiffs have been more successful in proving violations of Title VII of the Civil Rights Act of 1964 in connection with employment-testing programs. Where facially neutral requirements (such as tests) have a disparate impact on a group protected by Title VII (such as minorities), the employer must produce evidence of a *business necessity* for the challenged practice. In 1971 the Supreme Court found that the use of a test of general intelligence as a prerequisite to employment violated Title VII because the requirement disproportionately eliminated minority applicants and was not shown to be job related (*Griggs v. Duke Power Company*, 1971). In a subsequent case, the Court elaborated on the business necessity standard, recognizing that Title VII requires an employment test to be validated for the specific jobs for which it is used (*Albemarle Paper Company v. Moody*, 1975). In 1982 the Court held that an employment-testing program could violate Title VII if the tests have a disparate impact on minorities and are not substantiated as job related even though the "bottom line" of the hiring or promotion process is an appropriate racial balance (*Connecticut v. Teal*, 1982). The Court held that for employees to establish an inference of discrimination, they must show that the statistical disparities are the result of the specific practices being challenged. The Court also clarified that while the employer has the burden of producing evidence of a legitimate business justification for a practice with a disparate impact, the ultimate burden of persuasion remains with those challenging the practice (*Wards Cove Packing Company v. Frank Atonio*, 1989).

In 1984, the Golden Rule Insurance Company, the Educational Testing Service, and the state of Illinois reached a settlement that has implications for teacher-testing programs (*Golden Rule Insurance Company v. Washburn*, 1984). Two of the four licensing tests used by the Illinois Department of Insurance were challenged as abridging Title VII, and the state agreed in an out-of-court settlement to review the tests in a systematic fashion to reduce racial bias. The procedure entails identifying the rate of correct responses to each item for minorities and nonminorities. The test publisher agreed to select items from a pool of equally difficult items that display the least difference in correct answer rates between majority and minority test-takers (less than 15 percent difference where possible). Legislation requiring a similar review of test items in public employment-testing programs has been introduced in a number of states ("Golden Rule in the States," 1987), and this "Golden Rule" strategy, as it has come to be known, has been sought as a remedy in recent cases involving challenges to teacher-testing programs (*Allen v. Alabama State Board of Education*, 1986). Although some test developers contend that the Golden Rule strategy reduces the reliability and validity of tests as indicators of the abilities tested (Faggen, 1987; Linn & Drasgow, 1987; Walden & Deaton, 1988), this strategy has influenced employment-testing programs.

As discussed previously, in 1978 the EEOC issued *Uniform Guidelines on Employee Selection Procedures* to ensure that prerequisites to employment are properly validated and nondiscriminatory. The *Guidelines* stipulate that evidence of adverse impact of the prerequisite to employment will be established if a selection rate of any racial or ethnic group or either gender is less than 80 percent of the rate for the group with the highest selection rate. In several school cases, courts have relied on Title VII and the EEOC *Guidelines* in concluding that specific tests with an adverse racial impact cannot be used in making employment decisions without proof that they have been adequately validated (*Chance v. Board of Examiners*, 1972; *York v. Alabama State Board of Education*, 1983; *York v. Alabama State Board of Education*, 1986).

The statewide certification testing program in Alabama has been the subject of a seven-year court case. In a 1985 consent agreement, the Alabama Board of Education agreed to pay damages to black applicants who were denied certification because they failed the test, which had not been properly validated. The board also agreed to change the scoring system and to design a new examination giving special attention to the elimination of racial and cultural bias. A modified version of the Golden Rule strategy was to be used to evaluate test items for bias. In addition, test failure alone no longer would result in the denial of certification; for those who failed the test, grade-point averages were to be considered on a sliding scale (lower test scores would require higher grades). Reacting to substantial public criticism of the settlement, the state board attempted to renege on the agreement, but the Eleventh Circuit Court of Appeals ruled in 1986 that the agreement was binding (*Allen v. Alabama State Board of Education*, 1986). In 1988, however, the Alabama Board of Education announced that efforts to design a new certification examination were being abandoned ("Poor Test Scores," 1988).

Although employment-testing programs are more vulnerable to a successful legal challenge under Title VII than under the equal protection clause, it is not impossible for an employer to establish a business necessity for policies with a disparate racial impact. For example, in the South Carolina case discussed previously, the U.S. Supreme Court affirmed the trial court's holding that Title VII as well as the equal protection clause did not preclude the use of the NTE for certification and salary purposes to further the legitimate objective of assuring minimally competent teachers (*United States v. South Carolina*, 1978). The Fourth Circuit Court of Appeals similarly found no constitutional or Title VII violation in connection with a school district's use of certification levels based on scores on the NTE to determine teachers' salaries (*Newman v. Crews*, 1981). The court reasoned that the practice was justified by the business necessity of attracting the best qualified teachers and encouraging improvement among marginal teachers.

Testing mandates, particularly the required passage of examinations by practicing teachers to determine whether they will retain their jobs, seem destined to generate future legal challenges. Litigation has resulted in each state that has implemented a test requirement for recertification. State courts in Texas and Arkansas have rejected challenges to the testing programs, finding no impairment of due process, equal protection, or contractual rights (*Stanfield v. Turnbow*, 1985; *State v. Project Principle*, 1987; *Texas State Teachers' Association v. Texas*, 1986). However, the EEOC ruled in 1988 that the TECAT used in Texas discriminates against blacks and people over 40 years of age ("Agency Cites Texas Competency Tests," 1988). The EEOC has agreed to reconsider its decision based on additional data being submitted by the Texas Education Agency.

Litigation in Georgia was recently settled in a consent decree in which the state has agreed to revise all subject area tests by the 1991–92 school year (*Georgia Association of Educators v. Georgia*, 1988). Also, free study courses will be provided to teachers who have not yet passed the tests; a $6,000 study grant will be awarded to each teacher who lost certification because of test failure; and provisional teachers who have not yet passed the test will be awarded $2,000 for enrolling in the two-week test preparation course. An advisory committee will monitor test administration and scoring (LaMorte, 1988).

Although several teacher-testing programs have withstood legal challenges, the recent trend appears to be for parties to settle the controversies through consent decrees. No settlement to date has barred the use of a properly validated test to make decisions regarding admission to teacher education programs, certification, or recertification, but modifications in the test instruments, validation process, and scoring procedures have been required. Thus, both sides have claimed partial victories in the consent decrees.

CRITICISMS OF TESTING PROGRAMS

Competency-testing programs for teachers have been faulted for many of the same reasons that student-testing programs have been attacked. For example, concerns have been raised over the low passing rate for minorities, the validity of the instruments, and the effectiveness of the programs in attaining their asserted purpose. This section presents an overview of the central criticisms that have been voiced in connection with testing programs for educators.

Impact on Minorities

One of the central concerns is the well-documented disproportionate failure rate of minorities, particularly Blacks and Hispanics (Gifford, 1986; Goertz & Pitcher, 1985; Irving, 1983; "Poor Test Scores," 1988; Rudner, 1987b). A nineteen-state study released in 1988 documented passing rates for first-time test takers of 71 to 96 percent for Caucasians, 37 to 77 percent for Asian-Americans, 39 to 65 percent for Hispanics, and 15 to 50 percent for Blacks (Wells, 1988). Passing rates of under half of minority candidates compared with over three-fourths for nonminority candidates have been common. For example, between 1978 and 1984 only 10 percent of the students graduating from predominantly Black colleges in Louisiana passed teacher certification tests (Rudner, 1987b). Thirty-six percent of the Black candidates and 49 percent of the Hispanics compared with 88 percent of the Caucasians passed the Florida Teacher Certification Examination in 1987 ("Poor Test Scores," 1988).

Several researchers project that minority representation in the teaching force nationwide could be reduced from over 12 percent in 1980 to less than 5 percent by 1990 if trends in passing rates on teacher tests are maintained (Gifford, 1987; "Poor Test Scores," 1988; Smith, 1984). Gifford (1987, p. 19) has cautioned that "the combination of high minority failure rates on teacher examinations and high minority pupil enrollment rates, if unchecked by dramatic interventions, could result in a high degree of tension between minority parents and a largely nonminority teaching staff."

Test Validity

In addition to the disparate impact of testing programs on minorities, concerns have been raised about the validity of the test instruments. For example, the use of expert panels to validate competency tests for teachers has been questioned because of the asserted lack of consensus among practitioners and researchers as to the knowledge that beginning teachers should possess (Gifford, 1987). Murray (1986) has argued that a weakness in validation by expert panels is that the test items themselves rather than a defined content domain of essential skills or knowledge set the parameters for the validation study. There is some concern that the NTE validity studies focus more on the test's relationship to the content of teacher-training programs than to competencies required for teachers (Owen, 1985).

Criticizing the use of content-related evidence gathered from panels of experts, Madaus and Pullin (1987) have questioned whether the objectives, skills, and competencies purportedly measured by the test are necessary for minimal success in the classroom and whether the test items actually measure those objectives, skills, and competencies. Arguing that construct- and criterion-related evidence is also needed to be able to judge minimum competence, they have contended that policymakers want a relatively cheap testing program and are therefore not willing "to allocate necessary funds for serious validation studies" (p. 33).

Darling-Hammond (1986) also has questioned the validity of paper-and-pencil tests to make decisions regarding teaching competence. After analyzing each item on the professional knowledge tests of the NTE, she concluded that the tests "are limited in their measurement by the scarcity of important teaching questions answerable in multiple-choice formats: the questions with clear, correct answers are not very important or profound" (pp. 21, 46).

In a study released in 1988, the New York Public Interest Research Group (NYPIRG) reported that the NTE is poorly validated and tainted by gender and racial bias ("Teacher Test Flunks," 1988). Shortly after the NYPIRG study was released, the New York State Education Department announced plans to conduct a major study of occupational licensing tests under its control, including the NTE.

Even if there is an adequate match between a given test and the content of teacher preparation programs, questions remain regarding the validity of such tests to predict success or failure as a teacher. Critics have cited studies indicating that there is little correlation between test scores and actual teaching performance (Andrews, 1984; Darling-Hammond & Wise, 1983; Hyman, 1984; Medley, 1984; Pugach & Raths, 1983). For example, Quirk, Witten, and Weinberg (1973) reviewed forty studies conducted on the NTE Common Examinations covering general education questions; they found an adequate correlation between teachers' scores and their college grade-point averages, but test scores were not good predictors of the ratings teachers received during student teaching or subsequent on-the-job assessments by their supervisors. Medley, Coker, and Soar (1984, p. 31) subsequently concluded that there is no evidence that NTE scores "predict success in teaching whether estimated from ratings or from gain scores of pupils." The Southern Regional Education Board reported the results of a Georgia validity study of the NTE area tests, indicating practically no relationship between test scores and supervisors' ratings of teachers' ability to "put content over" in the classroom (Andrews, 1984). Critics have argued that most tests do not assess teachers' abilities to implement learned skills, to apply learned knowledge, or to nurture a positive learning environment (Hyman, 1984; Brophy, 1979).

Impact on Teacher Preparation Programs

There is some evidence that certification tests, once implemented, drive the curriculum of teacher education programs. Having a test guide the curriculum is not necessarily detrimental if the test covers competencies that exemplary teachers should possess. However, if a test of minimum basic skills determines the curriculum, teacher educators may ignore some of the complexities involved in effective teaching (Melnick & Pullin, 1987). Shepard and Kreitzer (1987) have further cautioned that the emphasis on students becoming "test wise" can overshadow content mastery.

Successful teaching requires far more than minimum competency in basic academic skill areas. Although such skill mastery is necessary, it is not sufficient to make someone a master teacher. Given the pressure being placed on colleges and universities for their graduates to do well on certification tests, if teacher preparation programs deviate substantially from the test content their graduates may be disadvantaged. Madaus and Pullin (1987, p. 33) have observed that the content of tests can "freeze the curriculum of teacher preparation programs without anyone's ever paying serious attention to the question of whether or not the material covered in that curriculum actually relates to eventual teaching performance." Nader (1987) also has argued that if standardized tests are allowed to drive the teacher education curriculum, significant domains such as strategic reasoning, creativity, and writing will be ignored.

Low Passing Scores and Safety Nets

States have to grapple with determining the level of test performance that is considered acceptable. Decisions must be made in setting cutoff scores whether to reduce the chance of false positives (those who pass the test actually do not possess the knowledge tested) or false negatives (those who fail the test actually possess the knowledge). Usually there has been an effort to reduce chances of false negatives by setting the qualifying scores at one or two standard errors of measurement below the initially recommended qualifying score (Goodison, 1985). Because most states have made adjustments to reduce the probability of failing marginally qualified candidates (for example, across states, individuals are required to answer correctly between 35 and 55 percent of the items to pass the professional component of the NTE), the likelihood of passing someone who is marginally unqualified has been increased (Rudner, 1987a, 1987b). In essence, if the cutoff score is placed low to guard against eliminating those who have mastery of the skills, many who do *not* have mastery will be declared competent because of measurement error (Shepard & Kreitzer, 1987). Ellwein, Glass, and Smith (1988, p. 6) have concluded that standards are not based on "how much must be known," but rather on "how many should pass and how many should not." Thus, pass rates are determined by political and economic acceptance rather than by an analysis of essential teaching skills and competencies.

There is some evidence that even when standards are raised, safety nets (such as multiple attempts to pass the test, exemptions, tutoring for retests) are used to catch those who fail (Ellwein, Glass, & Smith, 1988; Glass & Ellwein, 1986). Thus, most of those who initially fail the test eventually pass. Shepard and Kreitzer (1987) have observed that the high pass rate on the Texas recertification test could be attributed in part to the tutoring programs that emphasized test-taking skills. Ellwein et al. (1988, p. 7) have asserted that safety nets constitute an adaptive response so that school districts can avoid "the havoc certain to be created by rigid adherence to uniform standards of competence."

Researchers also have noted the irony in mandating certification tests while forty-six states still allow emergency teacher certification and eighteen states allow alternative routes to certification (Adelman, 1987; Darling-Hammond & Berry, 1988). Thus, even if passing scores are made more stringent on tests required for initial certification, as long as people are allowed to teach without satisfying certification requirements, a teaching force that exhibits minimum competence in basic skills will not be assured.

As noted previously, some individuals who have demonstrated adequate mastery of the knowledge domain tested still may be substandard teachers. School boards traditionally have been reluctant to dismiss incompetent teachers, relying instead on screening devices that may be inadequate to assure a minimally competent teaching force.

FUTURE DIRECTIONS

There are no signs that teacher-testing programs are diminishing in popularity among policymakers or the general public. Politically, testing programs are more palatable than many other proposed educational reforms (McCarthy, Turners, & Hall, 1987). Ellwein, Glass, and Smith (1988, p. 8) have concluded that the actual impact of tests on the quality of the teaching force may be incidental; competency tests function as "symbolic and political gestures, not as instrumental reforms." In essence, the public's perception of the standard is more important than is the impact of the testing program.

Although the emphasis on testing is not likely to dissipate, changes are already evident in the nature of the tests and the levels where tests are used. For example, there has been some movement to implement testing requirements for prospective administrators. Hazi (1986) has referred to the testing of administrators as the "third wave" in the testing movement, following the legislative mandates pertaining to students and teachers. A 1984 study reported that seven states required prospective administrators to take a test as a prerequisite to certification (Gousha, Jones, & LoPresti, 1986). By 1987, twelve states had such requirements, and three additional states had adopted mandates for future implementation (Egginton, Jeffries, & Kidd-Knights, 1988). As with teacher-testing programs, the southeastern states have taken a lead in requiring tests for administrators. The most popular standardized test is the ETS Test for Educational Administration and Supervision (EAS), but over half the states implementing tests for administrative certification are using customized tests. In addition to the states with tests specifically designed for administrators, nineteen states require a general knowledge test as a prerequisite to certification for all educators.

In contrast to the increase in testing programs for administrators, teacher testing for recertification purposes has lost momentum in the past few years. Although the National Education Association (NEA) and the American Federation of Teachers (AFT) have endorsed testing programs for initial teacher certification, they oppose the use of tests in determining whether practicing educators will retain their positions. Both the NEA and the AFT have devoted substantial energy and financial resources to attacking such programs; each of the states that have adopted mandates requiring practicing educators to be tested have been involved in costly litigation. Also, such recertification testing programs have proven to be more expensive to implement than anticipated (Shepard & Kreitzer, 1987). Given these developments, lawmakers in other states have moved cautiously in considering test requirements as a prerequisite to recertification or continued employment for educators.

Responding to criticisms directed toward paper-and-pencil multiple-choice tests, alternative types of assessments are receiving consideration.

Increasingly popular are state-mandated beginning teacher internship programs that condition renewable certification on passage of an internship. The American Association of Colleges for Teacher Education reported in 1986 that thirty-nine states had adopted or were considering adoption of some type of beginning teacher internship program (Darling-Hammond & Berry, 1988), and several of these programs have elaborate lists of competencies that beginning teachers are expected to master. As currently designed, most internship programs do not include a paper-and-pencil testing component to assess performance. Generally, beginning teachers are provided assistance from a team of experienced teachers, administrators, and university faculty members. These people observe beginning teachers and help them develop self-improvement plans. The teams, or designated members, complete assessment forms and recommend at the end of the year whether the beginning teacher should receive a renewable certificate. Such personnel assessments, however, are expensive, require skilled observers, and lack the objectivity associated with paper-and-pencil tests. Thus, while internship programs may improve the quality of the teaching force, they are not likely to replace certification testing programs as a screening device.

Because of the narrow focus of most current test instruments, some attention is being directed toward developing instruments that can assess classroom management techniques, motivational strategies, and other teaching skills. One strategy is to use case scenarios with candidates asked to choose various responses. Based on a study of teacher licensure, Wise and Darling-Hammond (with Berry & Klein, 1987) concluded that the optimum test would include both written and oral tasks to assess whether teaching skills have been acquired. They offered examples of possible written tasks such as preparing a lesson or unit plan and grading student essay responses. They suggested that appropriate oral tasks might include a short lecture on a specified subject or a case evaluation in a consultation session.

The Carnegie Foundation has funded Stanford University's Teacher Assessment Project to develop a series of exercises that differ from multiple-choice tests currently used as a prerequisite to certification. These exercises are being designed for the national teacher certification program, proposed by the Carnegie Forum on Education and the Economy. Lee Shulman, the project director at Stanford, has suggested that the "national board may want to certify teachers based on some combination of education, experience, paper-and-pencil tests, assessment center exercises, and documentation at the school site" ("Exercises," 1988, p. 21). He has asserted that assessments involving a teacher's performance in the classroom, rather than reliance solely on a multiple-choice test, should help reduce minority failure rates. According to Gary Sykes, a project associate, existing tests have "tended to trivialize and reduce teaching to a few measurable but 'scientifically validated' kinds of skills. . . . Everybody is recognizing that a lot of that just sells teaching terribly short" ("Teacher Assessment Assessed," 1987, p. 7).

The ETS has also announced plans to develop a new generation of tests for teacher certification that will replace the current form of the NTE by 1992 ("Teachers," 1988). According to ETS President Greg Anrig, the replacement test will include new features such as interactive video segments and computer simulations ("Educational Testing Service," 1988; Wells, 1988). Various components of the package will be designed to screen applicants for entrance into teacher education programs and for initial certification and to assess teaching performance after individuals have gained some classroom experience.

CONCLUSION

Unrealistic expectations should not be attached to testing programs. Paper-and-pencil tests of basic skills cannot guarantee that those who pass will be effective teachers. If a policy's goal is to ensure excellence in the teaching force, a test of minimal competence in selected knowledge domains is the wrong strategy to attain that goal. Basic skills tests may eliminate some of those who are not minimally competent, but a test alone will not assure excellence.

Tests can serve a screening function, and the implementation of teacher-testing programs has served notice that state legislatures and state education agencies are sensitive to public concerns about teacher competence. However, even if the goal is to screen incompetent teachers out of the profession, a basic skills test will not necessarily assure that this goal is achieved. A test of academic skills can only screen out people who are incompetent in one domain, and depending on the passing score selected, some academically incompetent people will still pass the test.

Although it has been politically popular for states to jump on the teacher-testing bandwagon, policymakers need to weigh the costs and benefits of testing programs in light of the desired goals of the reform efforts. Are there other ways to spend this amount of money that would better advance the objective of improving the quality of public schools (such as incentives for talented people to enter the teaching profession, or rewards for exemplary teachers to remain in the classroom)? Can the money being spent on remediation to bring teachers' skills to a minimally acceptable level be justified, or should school districts become more assertive in dismissing incompetent teachers? Should staff development programs focus on improving classroom experiences rather than on passing a test? These are just a few of the questions that have not yet received sufficient attention from state policymakers.

There is a crucial need for empirical data regarding the impact of teacher-testing programs and the relationship between test items and teaching performance. Ellwein, Glass, and Smith (1988) have called for comprehensive assessments of the impact of testing programs on schools and society as a whole. Without such data, we cannot determine whether the teacher-testing movement is simply a symbolic, rather than substantive, reform. Petrie's (1987) caution seems particularly pertinent to teacher-testing programs. He has warned that unless we move judiciously, "we may create the illusion of reform, but at best we will change nothing. At worst, we will radically distort our educational system as we try harder and harder to appear better and better on inadequate and inappropriate measures" (p. 176).

NOTES

1. In addition, applicants for recertification in Arkansas were required to pass the NTE subject area test or earn six credit hours of graduate coursework.

2. Formerly called the National Teachers Examination, *NTE* is currently the official name of this test according to the Educational Testing Service.

REFERENCES

Adelman, N. E. (1987). An examination of teacher alternative certification programs. In L. M. Rudner, ed., *What's happening in teacher testing: An analysis of state teacher testing practices*, pp. 131–134. Washington, DC: Office of Educational Research and Improvement, U.S. Department of Education.

Agency cites Texas competency tests as unfair for minority, older teachers. (1988, 21 September). *Education Week*, p. 12.

Alan, R. (1985, February). National evaluation systems. Presentation to the Superintendent's Advisory Committee on Teacher Testing, Madison, WI.

Albemarle Paper Company v. Moody, 422 U.S. 405 (1975).

Allen v. Alabama State Board of Education, 612 F. Supp. 1046 (M.D. Ala. 1985), *rehearing*, 636 F. Supp. 64 (M.D. Ala. 1985), *rev'd*, 804 F.2d 1228 (11th Cir. 1986).

Andrews, T. E. (1984). *Teacher competency testing: 1984.* Olympia: Superintendent of Public Instruction, State of Washington.

Anrig, G. (1986). Teacher education and teacher testing: The rush to mandate. *Phi Delta Kappan, 67,* 447–451.

Baker v. Columbus Municipal Separate School District, 329 F. Supp. 706 (N.D. Miss. 1971), *aff'd*, 462 F.2d 1112 (5th Cir. 1972).

Boyer, E. L. (1983). *High school: A report on secondary education in America.* New York: Harper & Row.

Brophy, J. E. (1979). Teacher behavior and its effects. *Journal of Educational Psychology*, *71*, 733–750.

Carnegie Forum on Education and the Economy, Task Force on Teaching as a Profession. (1986). *A nation prepared: Teachers for the 21st century*. New York: Carnegie Forum on Education and the Economy, Task Force on Teaching as a Profession.

Chance v. Board of Examiners, 458 F.2d 1167 (2d Cir. 1972).

Civil Rights Act of 1964, Title VII, 42, U.S.C. § 2000e et. seq. (1964).

Cole, R. W. (1979). Minimum competency tests for teachers: Confusion compounded. *Phi Delta Kappan*, *61*, 233.

Connecticut v. Teal, 457 U.S. 440 (1982).

Council of Chief State School Officers, Ad Hoc Committee on Teacher Certification, Preparation, and Accreditation. (1984). *Staffing of the nation's schools: A national emergency*. Washington, DC: Council of Chief State School Officers, Ad Hoc Committee on Teacher Certification, Preparation, and Accreditation.

Darling-Hammond, L. (1986). Teaching knowledge: How do we test it? *American Educator*, *10*(3), 18–21, 46.

Darling-Hammond, L., & B. Berry. (1988). *The evolution of teacher policy*. Santa Monica, CA: Rand Corporation.

Darling-Hammond, L., & A. Wise. (1983). Teaching standards or standardized teachings? *Educational Leadership*, *41*(2), 66–69.

Education Commission of the States, Task Force on Education for Economic Growth. (1983). *Action for excellence: A comprehensive plan to improve our nation's schools*. Denver: Education Commission of the States, Task Force on Education for Economic Growth.

Educational Testing Service unveils new, high-tech teacher licensing tests. (1988, 28 October). *Education Daily*, pp. 1–2.

Egginton, W. M., T. S. Jeffries, & D. Kidd-Knights. (1988). State-mandated tests for principals—a growing trend? *NASSP Bulletin*, *72*(507), 62–71.

Elliot, S. M., & J. Nelson. (1984, April). Blueprinting teacher licensing tests: Developing domain specifications from job analysis results. Paper presented at the annual meeting of the American Educational Research Association, New Orleans.

Elliot, S. M., & S. Patterson. (1984, April). Establishing standards for licensing and certification tests: Theory versus practice. Paper presented at the annual meeting of the American Educational Research Association, New Orleans.

Ellwein, M. C., G. V. Glass, & M. L. Smith. (1988). Standards of competence: Propositions on the nature of testing reforms. *Educational Researcher*, *17*(8), 4–9.

Exercises offer different approach to teacher tests. (1988, 8 June). *Education Week*, p. 21.

Faggen, J. (1987). Golden rule revisited: Introduction. *Educational Measurement: Issues and Practice*, *6*(2), 5–8.

Flippo, R. (1986). Teacher certification testing: Perspective and issues. *Journal of Teacher Education*, *37*(2), 2–9.

Gallup, A., & S. Elam. (1988). The twentieth annual Gallup poll of the public's attitudes toward public schools. *Phi Delta Kappan*, *70*(1), 33–46.

Georgia Association of Educators v. Georgia, No. C86–2234A (N.D. Ga. 1988).

Gifford, B. R. (1986). Excellence and equity in teacher competency testing: A policy perspective. *Journal of Negro Education*, *55*, 251–271.

Gifford, B. R. (1987). Excellence and equity. In L. M. Rudner, ed., *What's happening in teacher testing: An analysis of state teacher testing practices*, pp. 19–26. Washington, DC: Office of Educational Research and Improvement, U.S. Department of Education.

Glass, G. V., & M. C. Ellwein. (1986, December). Reform by raising test standards. *Evaluation Comment* [newsletter of the Center for the Study of Evaluation, UCLA], pp. 1–6.

Goertz, M. E., & B. Pitcher. (1985). *The impact of NTE use by states on teacher selection.* Princeton, NJ: Educational Testing Service.

Golden rule in the states. (1987). *FairTest Examiner, 1*(1), 1, 3.

Golden Rule Insurance Company v. Washburn, No. 419–76 (Ill. Cir. Ct. 1984).

Goodison, Marlene. (1985, June). Pros and cons of paper and pencil tests for teacher assessment. Paper presented at the Annual Assessment and Policy Conference of the Education Commission of the States, Boulder, CO. (ERIC Document Reproduction Service No. ED 276 747)

Goodlad, J. (1984). *A place called school: Prospects for the future.* New York: McGraw-Hill.

Gousha, R. P., A. H. Jones, & P. L. LoPresti. (1986, April). Where are we and where are we going in school administrator preparation in the United States? Paper presented at the annual meeting of the American Educational Research Association, San Francisco.

Griggs v. Duke Power Company, 401 U.S. 424 (1971).

Guthrie, J., & J. Koppich. (1988). Exploring the political economy of national educational reform. In W. L. Boyd & C. T. Kerchner, eds., *The politics of excellence and choice in education*, pp. 37–48. New York: Falmer Press.

Hazi, H. M. (1986). *The third wave: Competency tests for administrators.* ECS working paper No. E1–85–1. Denver: Education Commission of the States.

Holmes Group. (1986). *Tomorrow's teachers: A report of the Holmes Group.* East Lansing, MI: Holmes Group.

Hyman, R. T. (1984). Testing for teacher competence: The logic, the law, the implications. *Journal of Teacher Education, 35*(2), 14–18.

Irving, C. (1983, 31 July). Little improvement in state teacher scores. *San Francisco Examiner*, Section A, p. 20.

LaMorte, M. W. (1988, April). The law and competency testing for teachers. Paper presented at the annual meeting of the American Educational Research Association, New Orleans.

Linn, R. L., & F. Drasgow. (1987). Implications of the golden rule settlement for test construction. *Educational Measurement: Issues and Practice, 6*(2), 13–17.

Madaus, G. F. (1985). Public policy and the testing profession—you've never had it so good. *Educational Measurement: Issues and Practice, 4*(4), 5–11.

Madaus, G. F., & D. Pullin. (1987). Teacher certification tests: Do they really measure what we need to know? *Phi Delta Kappan, 69*, 31–38.

McCarthy, M., D. Turner, & G. Hall. (1987). *Competency testing for teachers: A status report.* Bloomington, IN: Consortium on Educational Policy Studies.

Medley, D. (1984). A valid teacher competency test: Is such a thing possible? *Journal of Human Behavior and Learning, 1*(2), 1–5.

Medley, D., H. Coker, & R. Soar. (1984). *Measurement-based evaluation of teacher performance: An empirical approach.* New York: Longmans.

Melnick, S. L., & D. Pullin. (1987). Testing teachers' professional knowledge: Legal and educational policy implications. *Educational Policy, 1,* 215–228.

Murray, S. L. (1986). *Considering policy options for testing teachers.* Contract No. 400–86–0006. Portland, OR: Northwest Regional Educational Laboratory. (ERIC Document Reproduction Service No. ED 276 721)

Nader, R. (1987). 60 years of idiocy is enough. *FairTest Examiner, 1*(1), 1, 3.

National Commission on Excellence in Education. (1983). *A nation at risk: The imperative for educational reform.* Washington, DC: U.S. Government Printing Office.

National Governors' Association. (1986). *Time for results: The governors' 1991 report on education.* Washington, DC: National Governors' Association.

Newman v. Crews, 651 F.2d 222 (4th Cir. 1981).

Owen, D. (1985). *None of the above: Behind the myth of scholastic aptitude.* Boston: Houghton Mifflin.

Petrie, H. G. (1987). Introduction to "evaluation and testing." *Educational Policy, 1,* 175–180.

Pipho, C. (1985, 22 May). Testing—can it measure the success of the reform movement? *Education Week,* p. 19.

Poor test scores bar many minority students from teacher training. (1988, 10 November). *Chronicle of Higher Education,* pp. 1, 32.

Popham, W. J. (1985). Recertification tests for teachers. *Educational Measurement: Issues and Practice, 4*(3), 23–25.

Pugach, M., & J. D. Raths. (1983). Testing teachers: Analysis and recommendations. *Journal of Teacher Education, 34*(1), 37–44.

Quirk, T. J., B. J. Witten, & S. F. Weinberg. (1973). Review of studies of the concurrent and predictive validity of the national teachers' examinations. *Review of Educational Research, 43,* 89–113.

Rosenfeld, M., R. F. Thornton, & L. S. Skurnik. (1986). *Analysis of the professional functions of teachers: Relationships between job functions and the NTE core battery.* Research Report No. 86–8. Princeton, NJ: Educational Testing Service.

Rudner, L. M. (1987a). Content and difficulty of a teacher certification examination. In L. M. Rudner, ed., *What's happening in teacher testing: An analysis of state teacher testing practices,* pp. 33–38. Washington, DC: U.S. Department of Education, Office of Educational Research and Improvement.

Rudner, L. M. (1987b). Questions and answers concerning teacher testing. In L. M. Rudner, ed., *What's happening in teacher testing: An analysis of state teacher testing practices,* pp. 3–8. Washington, DC: U.S. Department of Education, Office of Educational Research and Improvement.

Sandefur, J. T. (1987). Historical perspective. In L. M. Rudner, ed., *What's happening in teacher testing: An analysis of state teacher testing practices,* pp. 11–14. Washington, DC: U.S. Department of Education, Office of Educational Research and Improvement.

Sandefur, J. T. (1988, April). Teacher competency testing: Historical perspective. Paper presented at the annual meeting of the American Educational Research Association, New Orleans.

Shepard, L. A., & A. E. Kreitzer. (1987). The Texas teacher test. *Educational Researcher, 16*(6), 22–31.

Smith, G. P. (1984). The critical issue of excellence and equity in competency testing. *Journal of Teacher Education, 35*(2), 6–9.

Stanfield v. Turnbow, Chancery Ct., Pulaski County, Arkansas, (22 March 1985).

State v. Project Principle, 724 S.W.2d 387 (Tex. 1987).

Teacher assessment assessed. (1987). *FairTest Examiner, 1*(2), 7.

Teacher test flunks New York study: Movement to overhaul exams grows. (1988). *FairTest Examiner, 2*(1), 1, 7.

Teachers. (1988, 2 February). *Education Week*, p. 5.

Texas State Teachers' Association v. Texas, 711 S.W.2d 421 (Tex. App. 1986).

Twentieth Century Fund, Task Force on Federal Elementary and Secondary Education Policy. (1983). *Making the grade*. New York: Twentieth Century Fund, Task Force on Federal Elementary and Secondary Education Policy.

Uniform Guidelines on Employee Selection Procedures, 29 CFR §§ 1607 et seq. (1978).

United States v. Lulac, 628 F. Supp. 304 (E.D. Tex. 1985), *rev'd*, 793 F.2d 636 (5th Cir. 1986).

United States v. North Carolina, 400 F. Supp. 343 (E.D.N.C. 1975).

United States v. South Carolina, 445 F. Supp. 1094 (D.S.C. 1977), *aff'd*, 434 U.S. 1026 (1978).

Walden, J. C., & W. L. Deaton. (1988). Alabama's teacher certification test fails. *Education Law Reporter, 42*, 1–17.

Walston v. County School Board of Nansemond County, Virginia, 492 F.2d 919 (4th Cir. 1974).

Wards Cove Packing Company v. Frank Antonio, 57 U.S.L.W. 4583 (1989).

Washington v. Davis, 426 U.S. 229 (1976).

Wells, A. S. (1988, 16 March). Teacher tests assailed as biased and vague. *New York Times*, Section B, p. 7.

Wise, A., & L. Darling-Hammond, with B. Berry, & S. Klein. (1987). *Licensing teachers: Design for a teaching profession*. Report No. R-3576-LSTP. Santa Monica, CA: Rand Corporation.

York v. Alabama State Board of Education, 581 F. Supp. 779 (M.D. Ala. 1983).

York v. Alabama State Board of Education, 631 F. Supp. 78 (M.D. Ala. 1986).

CHAPTER 9

Career Ladders and Work in Schools

Ann Weaver Hart and
Michael J. Murphy

New structures for schools and teacher work that will help teachers become more proficient, reward and retain the best teachers, and attract an increased share of academically able students to a teaching career are being widely explored. Proponents of restructuring and work redesign reason that teaching lacks appeal for a sufficient number of talented and motivated people and increasing this appeal will create a better work force and improve schooling (Carnegie Forum on Education and the Economy, 1986; Holmes Group, 1986; Rosenholtz, 1987; Rosenholtz & Smylie, 1984). A number of reform plans have been proposed that include merit pay, job enlargement and enrichment, job redesign, schools of choice, school site management, career development, and multiple combinations of these structures. Initially, most of these efforts to redesign teaching were based on traditional beliefs about work and the quality of work life offered by a teaching career (Bacharach, Conley, & Shedd, 1986; Bacharach & Conley, 1986; Malen & Hart, 1987; Mitchell, 1986). Empirical studies of the effects of these reforms are limited. This chapter, an examination of the interaction of schools as a social unit with a teacher career ladder, contributes empirical evidence to the consideration of teacher work redesign reforms.

Studies of the kind reported here provide important data about the potential of career ladder reforms. Career ladders have been enacted with three primary goals in mind: (1) to achieve pay efficiencies, (2) to improve teaching and learning, and (3) to professionalize teaching (Carnegie Forum on Education and the Economy, 1986; Hart, 1987). They were early and popular reforms. By 1985, over three-quarters of the states had adopted or were studying career advancement plans. The diversity of these plans has increased since then, although their numbers have declined slightly, largely because of funding decisions (Cornett, 1988). Although they come in many forms, career ladders tend to include three major features: (1) performance-based pay, (2) increased teacher involvement in school-wide tasks, and (3) new roles and the reconfiguration of work and authority among teachers and administrators. Pay efficiencies can be studied using actuarial data. Improvements in teaching and learning and changes in teaching that professionalize the work must be studied at the work site.

Consequently, we studied the operation of one career ladder plan in five schools, focusing our attention on perceptions of the organizational health and effectiveness of the schools and subsequent adaptations of the new work structure. We accepted the assumption that the social unit of the workplace in which these teacher work changes take place will interact with the new structures, affecting in turn their operation and the behavior of teachers holding new roles (Bosworth & Kreps, 1986; Schlechty, 1976). Because this interaction between work site and work structure is a powerful moderator of attitudes toward and outcomes of work redesign, an examination of it is an important aspect of our overall understanding of the impacts of school restructuring reforms where they affect teachers and students—at the school.

If the interaction of the teachers and principals and career ladder is productive, we reasoned, school organizational health and effectiveness should be enhanced. Consequently, we took as our framework for this inquiry a classical model of healthy organizations and more recent research on effective schools in order to assess the functional interaction of the new structure and schools. Combining Miles's (1969) model of organizational health with elements of effective schools (Bossert, Dwyer, Rowan, & Lee, 1982), we sought to assess the interaction of a career ladder with the school, resulting in teachers' perceptions of their increased capacity to teach, career professionalization, and work behaviors. This synthesis of organizational theory and effective schools research provided three main issues of effective work redesign implementation in schools on which to focus: (1) accomplishing goals, (2) maintaining quality, and (3) ongoing adaptation.

Accomplishing Goals. All schools exist to educate students, and competence toward this end is an important ingredient in accomplishing goals. To be competent, schools should have clear, attainable, and common goals; good internal communication, including performance monitoring and feedback mechanisms; and strong programmatic leadership. Goal focus, communication adequacy, and optimal power equalization (Miles, 1969) in concert with clear instructional objectives, monitoring of performance, a strong programmatic leader in the principalship, school-wide staff development related to instruction, and positive expectations for student achievement (Bossert et al., 1982) should enhance the accomplishment of goals in schools.

Maintaining Quality. Quality must also be maintained. Schools must not only be able to accomplish goals initially, but they must be able to sustain programs and the capacity to perform over time. Maintaining quality, Miles (1969) argues, requires using human and fiscal resources, nurturing cohesiveness and collegiality, optimal power equalization and staff development, and sustained morale—conditions that also enhance the collegiality, planning, and school learning climate necessary for effective schools.

Ongoing Adaptation. The final major focus of interest in our study was the sustained ability to innovate and adapt. This element encompasses general innovativeness (including the further development of new roles) and problem-solving adequacy combined with school site autonomy. Good schools must be flexible; they must adapt to external demands and create solutions to internal problems as they arise.

These three dimensions became our organizing framework for the analysis of work redesign in schools we report in this chapter. We examined teachers' perceptions of the impact of the new structure on these aspects of school health and effectiveness. Further, we examined how people's perceptions and subsequent actions in the context of the schools affected the design and function of the new structure.

METHODOLOGY

The research followed established procedures of qualitative methods. The setting, data collection, and data analysis are briefly described as follows.

The Setting

The 1984 Utah career ladder legislation allowed each district to plan a career ladder for teachers and provided funds to support the system.[1] Each year for the next three years, the legislature appropriated additional funds. In 1986–87, it appropriated nearly $35 million, or about $1,900 for each of the state's teachers and other instructional personnel. This amount represented a major investment for the state in new configurations of work and reward for teachers.

The career ladder we investigated is in place in a large metropolitan school district in Utah. The ladder has two promotional levels (teacher specialist and teacher leader), an extended contract year, and a performance bonus. Specialist and leader positions are allocated to schools by a formula based on the number of teachers in the school—one teacher leader position and three teacher specialist positions for every ten faculty members. Job descriptions for career ladder teachers were developed by teachers and administrators at each school. Teachers applied and competed for appointment to the positions, which were open to all tenured faculty at the school. The appointments had a fixed term of one or two years, and competition for ladder appointments was limited to each school's current faculty.

The study was conducted in five schools in the district—one senior high school, one intermediate school, and three elementary schools. After permission to conduct the study was obtained from the superintendent, the principals in each school volunteered to be part of the study. Schools were selected to represent each level of instruction, were geographically distributed across the district, and represented a broad socioeconomic and cultural spectrum.

Data Collection

Teachers were recruited in four of the schools to act as participant observers. Several of these observers were working on master's degrees at the University of Utah at the same time. In one school, a participant observer was not available. A graduate student in the Department of Educational Administration at the university conducted interviews in that school.

Three types of data were collected from the five schools—interview, document, and critical incident. Each is described in detail, as follows.

Nine people were selected to be interviewed in each school by the participant observer or researcher. They included the principal, career ladder teachers, nonparticipants who were eligible for career ladder positions but either chose not to apply or who applied but were not appointed, and ineligible teachers. During the winter and spring of 1986, four interviews were conducted with each individual in the sample. The interview guides, which were nine or ten questions long, focused on the three elements of healthy organizations and effective schools. Other questions were added to interview guides as they arose from preceding interviews, from critical incidents, or from document analysis. Each interview took forty-five minutes to one hour. The participant observers recorded responses during the interviews and then elaborated their field notes, clarifying and fleshing out comments within 36 hours after the interview. Using this method, thirty-six interviews were conducted in each of the five schools for a total of one-hundred-eighty interviews. At an average of forty-five minutes per interview, data included at least 135 hours of formal interviews.

In addition to interviews, participant observers gathered all pertinent career ladder documents. These included memoranda and instructions from the district office and all school messages, guidelines, and job descriptions.

The final source of data was a collection of critical incidents. Each of the participant observers was asked to keep a log containing critical incidents that related to the career ladder. The incidents were summarized weekly and were sometimes focused on specific themes. Incidents included events occurring whenever teachers formally or informally discussed or experienced the career ladder.

Data Analysis

The critical incidents, recorded as field notes, and documents were used mainly as supporting data; analysis focused on the 135 hours of interviews. Two approaches were used to analyze interview data: inductive coding and a comparison of responses across items on each interview. For inductive coding, site researchers made two passes through the data. First, codes were developed from one reading of the data for issues appearing in each of the four interview sets. Coding was completed by site researchers within a week of the completion of the interviews. When all interviews were completed, the codes were collapsed by the five site investigators and the research team. Each interview was then recoded by the original investigator using these categories. Site investigators audited one another's coding of the interviews. A research team member also read interviews in each set to audit coding across interviews. When a coding disagreement occurred, the site investigator, auditor, and a research team member re-examined the field notes and reached a consensus on the interpretation of the data.

Once interview coding was completed, case studies describing the career ladder experience in the schools were prepared by each investigator. The cases were then used to examine the intensity and representativeness of factors coded during the inductive coding process across schools.

For the analysis across items, all interview responses were compared by question across respondents both within and across schools. To assess the full range of perceptions, responses from all forty-five respondents were compared. The codes and questions were then regrouped into the three elements of organizational health and effective schools with which we began—accomplishing goals, maintaining quality, and ongoing adaptation—and the analysis of responses across items compared for conceptual consistency and relevance.

SCHOOL EFFECTIVENESS AND THE CAREER LADDER

As we noted, the impacts of externally introduced structural reforms are determined in large part by how jobholders interpret and adapt the reform. Individual and group differences as well as information cues in the social environment cause different workers and work groups to implement structural reforms differently (Hart, in press-a). In the case of the career ladder reform under study, we found that the schools differed considerably on all three dimensions of our research framework. First, differences among teachers and school social interactions modified fundamental concepts of the purpose of the career ladder as it related to the work of schools. Principals differed in their reaction to the ladder, and their leadership during the implementation altered interaction patterns. Career ladder jobs were shaped by local interpretations.

Second, these differences in interpretation and enactment of goals influenced the usefulness of the new tasks and roles to maintain the overall quality of the schools. The way the career ladder work redesign was processed and adapted at the schools influenced perceptions of the career ladder's contribution to ongoing organizational health and effectiveness. In schools where participants saw their experience as successful, teachers said the career ladder contributed to skill development and instructional problem solving. In schools where perceptions of its usefulness were less, teachers saw the ladder as unnecessary extra work.

Finally, in schools where the new structure was interpreted as a vehicle for improved goal accomplishment and quality maintenance, teachers and principals actively affected the ongoing adaptation of the new roles through a continuing process of role innovation, altering the actual structure of tasks without much concern for extant job descriptions or bureaucratic control. They used the ladder to do their work better. They interpreted it as a contribution to the effectiveness of their schools. In schools where the ladder broke down, structure received little or no adaptation in response to emerging problems and tasks and roles were, at varying levels, ignored once designed. They remained, during the study period, superfluous to the central work of the schools. In different schools, career ladder tasks ostensibly identical (in their formal descriptions) emerged quite altered in composition and function.

These conclusions emerged from our examination of how teachers processed the career ladder reform, adapted it to fit local perceptions and preferences, and interpreted its contribution to organizational health and effectiveness. Pictorially this flow may be seen as follows:

Implementation—Work Unit Dynamic

Externally ⟶ Work unit processes ⟷ Work unit members'
mandated   and adaptations   assessments of
structural   during   structural reform's
reform   implementation   contribution to
                                       organizationl health
                                       and effectiveness

This flowchart illustrates the crucial fact that an externally introduced structural reform is judged and modified at the work site. These implementing and assessing functions are interactive and eventually affect the tasks and functions of the new structure. Further, the utility of the interaction between implementation and assessment can be usefully viewed in terms of goal accomplishment, quality maintenance, and ongoing adaptations, categories that reflect the natural thinking of teachers and are conceptually integrated with the goals of structural reform. In the discussion that follows, we illustrate this process with data from the five study sites as they relate to the three dimensions of our framework of organizational health and school effectiveness.

Accomplishing Goals

Because accomplishing goals is an important component of healthy and effective school organizations, the relationship of the new structure to goal accomplishment was a crucial aspect of our study. The bifurcation of school goals from career ladder goals, far more pronounced in the schools where perceptions were negative, isolated the career ladder from the core function of the school and left people speculating about other, perhaps dysfunctional, goals the new program might promote.

The three schools where cautious or negative perceptions about the career ladder's contribution to organization health and effectiveness dominated shared several characteristics that relate to goal accomplishment. Expressed uncertainty about the goals of the career ladder were common; the relation-

ship of the career ladder to core school functions was ephemeral; communication relevant to the career ladder was procedural and structural in focus,
and an articulate advocate of the new structure's usefulness in accomplishing
school goals was absent; and oversight and feedback about the new roles'
functioning in the school was scarce. In the two schools in which teachers
perceived that the new structure was successfully marshaled as a resource for
goal accomplishment, less uncertainty about career ladder goals was present;
the career ladder roles were tied to teaching and learning—core school
functions; communication about the career ladder structure was adequate,
and communication by articulate advocates emphasized the new structure's
usefulness as a resource for accomplishing valued goals; and feedback
mechanisms focused on goal accomplishment were developed.

Uncertainty about the purposes of the career ladder or refusal to consider
it a resource for professional or school improvement characterized the sites
dominated by negative perceptions. At best, only a vague sense that it was
intended to improve instruction and curriculum permeated these staffs.
When pressed, many staff members could not articulate how the career
ladder would improve instruction, and some thought it would detract from
teaching by distracting and exhausting teachers. Teachers and principals
within these schools were unsure of specific career ladder goals or named
widely divergent objectives ancillary to teaching and learning. They also
disagreed about whether the career ladder was capable of promoting the
accomplishment of any productive goal. In the school in which teachers held
the most negative views about the career ladder, the respondents were
unable to identify any such goals, arguing that the program was just a
state-mandated gimmick to convince voters that Utah was responding to
A Nation at Risk (National Commission on Excellence in Education, 1983). As
one teacher said, "I don't know [what the goals are]. No one has explained
the goals of the program in this school."

This confusion left many teachers with no idea what they should be
accomplishing with the new roles and resources. Most unsettling of all, they
were by no means certain that the career ladder could contribute to the
improvement of instructional quality. Disagreements over the usefulness of
the career ladder seemed partly due to means and ends conflicts. Most
teachers believed that teachers ought to work together, to share, to jointly
solve problems in the school, and to have greater say in school decisions. Yet
doubts about the career ladder contribution toward these ends persisted.

Although positive perceptions dominated at two schools and negative or
cautious perceptions at three, the majority of teachers at all schools were
ambivalent about the career ladder's overall potential to improve goal
accomplishment. They recognized benefits and advantages but found some
features of the program objectionable or dysfunctional and found adjusting
to the new work configurations difficult. These teachers experienced a

discomfort common in all major work redesign endeavors: even those enthusiastically in favor of a new design and active in its creation experience adjustment problems during implementation (Hackman & Oldham, 1980).

However, teachers and principals in schools dominated by positive perceptions of the career ladder were able to identify goals for the career ladder structure consonant with overall school goals. These included the identification and rewarding of good teachers, placing the best teachers in positions where they could help other teachers, increased professionalism and career opportunities for teachers, providing incentives to encourage teachers to work harder, and moving teaching toward become a "full-time profession."

This ability to identify career ladder goals and their relationship to school goals was a second major difference between the schools dominated by negative or positive perceptions. At schools where the prevailing perceptions were positive, a consensus developed that career ladder roles and tasks contributed to the central work and core functions of the school. In these two schools, career ladder goals were linked in people's minds to specific programmatic and instructional endeavors either currently under way or on teachers' and principals' agendas or "wish lists." Teachers said they used the career ladder to "accomplish many things they had always wanted to do." The two principals often pointed out that activities central to the career ladder (clinical supervision, assistance for new teachers, curriculum development) enhanced ongoing efforts and met many unmet needs for mentors, evaluation, professional development, and curriculum development. They described how the new roles and resources could be used to accomplish the central mission of the school—the education of students through improved teaching and learning. We found perceptions of career ladder effect on student achievement, quality of instruction, curriculum, goal subscription, clarification of school goals, and the principal's instructional leadership role in the school. Teachers who felt the career ladder contributed to student achievement based their belief on a linear argument: the career ladder was being used to promote instructional effectiveness; improved instruction helps students learn better; student learning is reflected in educational achievement. One respondent said, "Student achievement is probably increased by improving lesson design. If teachers are teaching better, probably there is more learning, but we have to wait for test results." As one teacher put it, "It has increased enthusiasm for teachers about their jobs and themselves."

Communication about goals and a working consensus about core goals is another major component of goal accomplishment. Communication and its contribution toward a developing perceptual consensus also distinguished the schools in the study.

Although many teachers remained unclear about the goals of the career ladder, the plan's structure and requirements for participation were well understood by the staffs in the five schools. Most communication about the career ladder was directed toward even greater procedural and structural understanding. A dominance of communication directed toward procedural compliance was most apparent in the three schools characterized by the least positive perceptions. This finding is somewhat problematic. The formal plan, the structure, was simple enough to understand, but the fundamental purposes for the structure—its goals and relationship to teaching and learning—remained difficult to interpret and communicate. Simple understanding of formal rules and procedures appeared to change few behaviors, yet formal communication about the career ladder focused on procedural issues rather than on central purposes and the relationship of the new structure to these purposes. Memoranda and handouts, both from the district and school administration, literally bombarded teachers. Meetings and meetings to plan meetings consumed a great deal of time. One teachers said, "I'm bored to death when they talk about career ladders. It has been the main focus of almost all faculty meetings. It's not that I don't think it's a good idea. It's just that I'm bored to death with it."

Because communication remained at the procedural level, the relationship of new roles to goals and of new structures to established structures remained ephemeral in these schools. Because the time left by the state in 1984 between planning and implementation was limited, job descriptions often were modeled after pre-existing special projects and unrecognizable from conventional practice (Malen & Hart, 1987). In addition, the new positions were added without adjustments to existing roles (including site-based school improvement councils and department or grade-level leadership positions) with which they might conflict. Although some tolerance for ambiguity was thus required to sustain participation, teachers and principals argued that unclear jurisdictions eventually would have to be resolved to avoid an escalation of turf conflicts.

The two schools that most effectively integrated the career ladder structure into their core functions and goals had regular communication systems set up to provide information and coordinate career ladder activities. The work of the career ladder teachers was discussed in team meetings, providing a system of informal accountability. In these schools, general knowledge about career ladder roles was widespread. Teachers talked about frequent observations and instructional talk, changes in school programs, and modifications they were making in their teaching work as a result of their interactions with the career ladder teachers. Career ladder teachers altered tasks, met and talked about inappropriate or overlapping responsibilities, and publicized their work. Tasks evolved in response to school needs, and role development was common. Principals, teacher leaders, and teacher specialists were the main advocates of the career ladder, but other teachers also talked about career ladder benefits to the school.

In contrast, where negative perceptions dominated, people felt a leadership void. Faculty members argued that there were no advocates for the career ladder at their schools. At two schools, this view was held by only a few teachers, but at one it was the dominant perception of the faculty. In only one school did the faculty as a whole identify with and promote the career ladder.

Principals were key players in communicating the connections between goals and career ladder tasks. Most people said they depended on the principal for information about the career ladder and for explanations when misunderstandings developed. Principals actively shaped sensemaking processes in all schools. The principals regularly disseminated structural and procedural information in faculty meetings, in memoranda, in bulletins, and in personal conversations. But implicit as well as explicit messages were conveyed about the career ladder by principals. Although all principals in the schools we studied said they favored the career ladder, the messages they communicated about it varied. Only the two who presided over the development of positive perceptions about the career ladder invested their energies in trying to make sense of it as a positive contribution to teachers' work, talking about instruction, school activities, and student outcomes in concert with the new roles.

The other principals complained about the extra administrative responsibilities associated with the career ladder. One openly maintained that its success or failure had no connection to her; it was the responsibility of the teachers. In this school, queries about career ladder leadership elicited the following response: "That question assumes somebody is [providing leadership]." The five principals had five very different responses to the challenges posed to their authority relationships by the career ladder, ranging from active participation in instructional leadership and chief executive style oversight, to total abdication (Murphy & Hart, 1988).

Although principals were free to lead in communication articulating and promoting the career ladder, a split in most schools between those in favor and those opposing the career ladder made pro-career ladder leadership on the part of teachers problematic. Career ladder teachers feared their peers would believe they advocated the program primarily in pursuit of their own interests, to set themselves above the teachers. Consequently, many career ladder teachers reported that they devalued their own hard work and contribution to the school in conversations with other faculty members much as good students sometimes refuse to acknowledge their good grades to their peers. A teacher in one school said, "We don't preach the career ladder or things get testy and vitriolic." Teachers felt constrained by social pressure from advocating or praising the career ladder. Consequently, communication often diverted attention from people's real attitudes and, in some schools, a communication vacuum developed. Respondents and participant observers both reported that faculty members were unaware of the true feelings of colleagues about the career ladder, and teachers deliberately withheld their feelings from each other and the principal. In one school, teachers asked the researcher if their responses matched what other teachers were saying. In some cases, teachers said they deliberately misrepresented their opinions about the career ladder to the principal. They felt that to criticize the career ladder would be risky.

This social pressure exerted on teachers made articulation by principals of the connection between goal accomplishment and career ladder even more crucial. Although teacher leadership and empowerment were expressed goals of the reform, in the early stages—when the traditional school norms against differentiation were first assailed by the new structure—articulation by principals had a noticeable impact on teachers' positive attitudes. They held formal and legitimate authority and were invulnerable to accusations of betrayal of fellow teachers.

A final aspect of goal accomplishment, feedback, played an important role in attitudes about the career ladder. The amount and relevance of feedback provided to career ladder teachers based on monitoring of their work varied, but, in the midst of a procedural information blitz, little systematic monitoring of the actual career ladder work accomplished occurred and little feedback was provided to program participants. This was true in all schools. No catalog of accomplishments or failures for future reference and adjustment was kept where the career ladder experience was least successful. As several of our respondents noted, "We assume people are doing the work." An assumption that the program was largely self-executing within schools predominated; once individuals were selected and given their job descriptions they would complete their jobs or tasks and develop career ladder roles for the future. Outcomes thus faded farther into the background as procedures continued to take center stage. Because no good way of describing career ladder accomplishements was available and principals in these same schools also abdicated the articulation role, information circulating on the underground rumor network dominated interpretations. These rumors often promoted the belief that some career ladder teachers "never did a thing." Only in the two schools where regular communication channels were set up and knowledge about the work being accomplished by career ladder teachers was widespread, was there a consensus that feedback was available. Even there, however, formal performance monitoring of the teachers in new roles was not implemented. This failure to monitor performance in the new roles and provide feedback to career ladder teachers hampered the potential of nascent connections between the new structure and goal accomplishment in all the schools.

Maintaining Quality

Like the accomplishment of goals, quality maintenance is an important part of organizational health and effectiveness. To achieve this outcome, schools must use fiscal and human resources effectively and efficiently, nurture cohesiveness and collegiality, sustain morale, and establish optimal power equalization and staff development (Miles, 1969). In schools where faculty members expressed the most positive perceptions of their experience with the career ladder, teachers described a high but sustainable level of effort, effective use of the pool of professional talent, distribution of power, appropriate training opportunities, and highly visible career ladder tasks. In addition, teachers and principals were concerned about maintaining the professional growth of teachers, the overall quality of their school, teacher plans for future participation in the ladder, and teacher and administrator working relationships.

A consensus that some people were working much harder as a result of the career ladder emerged. All the principals said they were devoting considerable time to the career ladder. One said he spent about half of his time on career ladder matters. But perceptions about the principal's level of effort seemed to influence attitudes only in one school—where teachers judged their career ladder experience almost without redeeming value and their principal's effort low. The hard work of career ladder teachers predicted positive attitudes more accurately.

In general, teacher leaders and teacher specialists were perceived by their faculty colleagues as working hard. In fact, one teacher said of the career ladder teachers, "It has changed many of them to the point that I don't know them. They are strained and pressured." Another said, "It seems a great effort is required by the teacher leaders and principal. There is a great burden placed on them. It seems the career ladder would die on the vine if they weren't working their tails off." Where negative perceptions about the career ladder were strong, however, stories continued to circulate that this effort was uneven, that some career ladder teachers were doing little or nothing. Where hard work was most visible, assessments were most positive.

This praise for the effort expended by teachers had its dark side as well. Many teachers had serious doubts whether the effort required to keep the career ladder going was worth the return. Throughout the interviews, teachers in all five schools argued that the money provided by the ladder was not enough to compensate for the amount of time and pressure involved in the job.

Although the issue of sustainability emerged in all five schools, few resources were devoted to helping people overcome the professional and personal challenge of redesigned work and role transition. The resulting strain was apparent. In addition, principals found themselves in a state of authority and role transition of their own while they simultaneously were expected to facilitate the transitions experienced by teachers (Murphy & Hart, 1988). Career ladder contributions to the instructional program, more apparent as the stress of implementation declined, made some teachers more sanguine about their ability and willingness to continue working at such high levels of effort, but the lack of specific provisions for helping people cope with initially high expenditures of energy was felt keenly.

The potentially unmanageable impact of this pressure and the lack of organizational support for the teachers experiencing it may have contributed to a somewhat ironic outcome—teachers were backing away from career ladder participation in two schools where the program seemed to enjoy the greatest support. Everyone expended so much effort that teachers talked of "burnout" in those schools; many teacher leaders and specialists said they would not reapply for their positions. Although some of these people did reapply, it remains to be seen what the level of participation will be in subsequent years. Many of our respondents said that they were not going to get very concerned about long-range participation in the career ladder simply because they did not think it would last very long. Three opinions led to this perception: (1) it was experimental, (2) considerable opposition to it remained, and (3) the legislature would probably cut off funding.

Hard-working career ladder teachers did not alone create positive perceptions about the impact of the plan on the quality of the schools. The wise use of professional talent in the school by the career ladder program also distinguished schools. Teachers' judgments of their career ladder peers' qualifications and the quality of the work varied with the same mix between schools. In these same two schools, perceptions of promoted teachers' quality and qualifications were all positive; in the others, assessment ranged the full gamut from praise to condemnation. In the school where teachers' perceptions were most negative, a widespread belief persisted that career ladder participants were far from the most qualified teachers in the school. "They're not the teachers everyone admires," one teacher reported. Another teacher said that "*in most areas*" [emphasis his], they were well qualified. "In a couple of areas we had no one interested. But all are hardworking—some better than others—the best are the ones who won from the hardest competition." Many teachers said they felt almost any of their colleagues could have done the job. They described career ladder participants by saying, "They were as qualified as anyone else in the building."

Descriptions of the power distribution promoted by the career ladder provided a third differentiation factor among the schools important for quality maintenance and often coincided with principals' own successful transitions into new authority relationships with the promoted teachers (Murphy & Hart, 1988). In three schools, teachers praised the increased influence of their professional group over decisions. Some teachers criticized the career ladder for creating an oligarchy consisting of principals and career ladder teachers, but (particularly in the schools where the principal dominated decision making before the career ladder) people said, "At least some teachers are involved in important decisions." Teacher leaders and specialists had considerable influence in the decision-making process, and some nonparticipants felt they had more input into decisions, a development they attributed to the career ladder. One teacher said, "I think teachers are more influential in improving instruction in the classroom."

Where teachers failed to sense any change in decision and power distribution, the principal either had abdicated leadership of the career ladder program or had proceeded in a "business as usual" manner (Murphy & Hart, 1988). Tension and contention between the regular and career ladder teachers sometimes surfaced in these two schools. One teacher said, "Decisions seem to come down from those in career ladder positions. It appears the influence has been removed from those not in such a position."

This new power distribution affected perceptions about the quality of decisions. Decisions were judged not on their outcome but on the process people observed. For example, the selection process focused judgments about the fairness of career ladder decisions in general, and the less the principal dominated this process the more positive the perceptions. A telling difference of opinions about this aspect of the career ladder was apparent in the data. Unlike other perceptions about the merit of power distribution among teachers and principals, judgments about principal domination over the career ladder selection process differed more within than between schools. Some teachers said the process was open, fair, and characterized by the right amount of competition among teachers. Others in the same schools said the process was dominated by the principal, arguing that appointments were virtually foreordained. They reported that "the principal got the ones [he or she] wanted." The power and authority issue remained relevant on largely a personal rather than a school level.

Interpretations of the form of principals' domination over selection fell into three categories. First, the principal was accused of openly selecting the candidates, essentially daring teachers on the committee to protest. In one school, teachers on the selection committee said they felt forced to appoint teachers of the principal's choosing. Second, principals let it be known through verbal and other clues which candidates they preferred and, because of that formal authority, teachers did not feel free to differ with those choices. The third interpretation was more subtle. Principals possessing charisma, expertise, powers of persuasion, and strong personalities argued the cases of candidates of their choice so well that they convinced the teachers on the selection committee. Even though the principals felt the selection process had been followed stringently, many teachers felt that their principals had dominated the selection of career ladder participants. Teachers acknowledged that, over time, they should become more accustomed to wielding power in the selection committees and in the schools, but for the time being the formal change in power distribution was hard to realize in practice.

Training oppotunities—for teacher leaders and specialists and for all faculty members because these career ladder teachers shared their new expertise—provided additional benefit to school quality in curriculum and lesson design. Comments about the training and professional development opportunities provided by the career ladder were usually positive in all schools. But teachers cautioned against a growing enthusiasm for mandatory workshops organized by career ladder teachers. One said, "I don't want to attend meetings I don't need or sit through presentations I've already heard, so they can say they've done their jobs." Fear of criticism from their peers that they were not earning their money sometimes spurred the proliferation of mandatory inservice, placing career ladder teachers in a Catch-22 trap. Career ladder participants felt obligated to give presentations, so they could say they had done their jobs.

The training provided by this new resource had some uneven impacts on teachers' skill development. Varying degrees of benefit from the training were apparent, faculty members pointed out, through substantially different degrees of skill in classroom observations conducted by teacher leaders. Several instances were reported in which less experienced teacher leaders seriously offended veteran teachers they observed although it was unclear whether the offense resulted from poor observation and feedback or from a legitimately substandard teaching performance. Widespread observation and feedback skills among a pool of teacher leaders were just developing.

The professional development opportunities presented by this increase in training and in the flow of ideas may have influenced teachers' willingness to apply for positions even when they were cautious about the potential of the career ladder over the long run. No paucity of applicants for career ladder positions developed, even in the one school where criticism raged. When teachers were asked why people applied for career ladder positions (as an indication of what opportunities they saw in the ladder), they reported that it presented opportunities to earn extra money, pursue personal development, and exercise influence. For some, it was a personal challenge. Duty and professional responsibility also motivated participation. One teacher said, "I had mixed feelings about the career ladder. It could be positive. I wanted an active role in it." Another said that the career ladder provided "an opportunity to work on a favorite project and fill a need for the school as well as get some money and status." Consequently, the pairing of resources and opportunity in the minds of teachers created a generally positive impression. Whenever these connections were strong, the use of the ladder and positive attitudes about the ladder were strong. One teacher said, "The career ladder has emphasized that we are professionals. We have requirements we need to meet. It's helped improved instruction a bit." Those most involved in ladder activities—those who experienced most directly the resource and opportunity dimensions of the plan—found them most useful.

Limited versus broad access to this enlarged pool of resources and opportunities for teachers remained a point of considerable debate among teachers. Although career ladder teachers often were praised as a professional resource in the schools, the opportunities for professional growth were perceived as the monopoly of career ladder teachers. Opportunity has been praised by some organizational researchers who promote the design of career development structures as a career incentive (Bacharach, Conley, & Shedd, 1986), but the limited scope of this ladder, providing no horizontal growth opportunities and a limited number and short path of vertical opportunities, moderated enthusiasm. One teacher summed up feelings about the scarcity of opportunities on the ladder. He reported that the career ladder provided "more leadership opportunities for a few teachers, more money but not enough really, and specialized training for career ladder people." But the opposite point of view was also expressed. Others criticized the time-definite appointments designed to spread the limited opportunities around, calling the plan "a step ladder. You step on and you step off." But when pressed, these teachers were unwilling to advocate permanent promotion, fearing the appearance of elitism and limited access.

Appropriate and useful feedback about the career ladder was an additional challenge to ongoing quality maintenance. As we pointed out in our discussion of feedback and monitoring, not only did career ladder teachers lack appropriate levels of feedback on their performance in new roles, but also teachers were only sporadically informed about what their career ladder colleagues did. Consequently, information processing affected perceptions. Teachers were selective in their listening and reading, and "show and tell" at faculty meetings had little effect on staff members' perceptions of career ladder teachers' work. Instead, the visibility of the work played a key role in teacher assessments of the worth of the program. When new tasks were integrated with daily teaching and learning activities and when interactions among teachers clarified the contribution of the new roles to the basic work of the school, judgments were positive. Principals played an important part in this process, calling attention to career ladder activities, interpreting and explaining the contributions of the new roles. Just as it enhanced perceptions of the impact of the career ladder on goal accomplishment, this articulation role of principals influenced perceptions about the career ladder's utility as a means for enhancing school quality. Silence about the work had a deadening effect.

Our data also suggest that teachers' concern for overall school quality was growing. They saw individual teachers' improvement as the most appropriate route to this goal in all five schools. One teacher said, "The self-awareness is important. We haven't looked at it before. The efforts to improve instruction have made us grow." This heightened awareness existed even in schools where teachers and principals expressed a negative or neutral attitude toward the program. But school quality remained a sum of individual performances in people's minds. A group sense of each school's combined instructional effectiveness was undiscernible.

Another quality maintenance issue raised by respondents related to the effects of the program on the career plans of teachers. By the end of the study year (the second year of the program), the career ladder had not yet had a major impact on teachers' plans for their careers in any of the schools. Although some teachers not holding career ladder positions said they would seek positions in subsequent years or apply for the merit bonus because "it's easier," participation appeared to stem from motives unrelated to long-range career plans. Teachers expressed a desire to get a piece of the pie, to participate in "the only game in town" or to exercise their professional responsibility to join and contribute, rather than conviction that their careers would fundamentally change.

A lack of future orientation toward the career ladder appeared in several ways. Many teachers concealed their plans. As one said, "You don't want to advertise it in case you don't get it. You know, people wonder why." In the one school where opposition ran high, teachers who were very negative in the attitudes still applied for career ladder positions. Ambivalence and some uncertainty about the status and prominence of career ladder teachers were widespread. Some teachers resented the implications that career ladder teachers were better teachers. (Television advertisements aired by the teachers' union and the State Board of Education designed to marshall public support for the program did draw this inference.) Others found publicity for teachers flattering. As one teacher put it, "A lot of people have pride in what they do. They may not want to participate in the career ladder, but they want the status. It's like a club now. If you have career ladder status, you are one of the best teachers in the building."

Time pressures also moderated the influence of the ladder on teachers' career plans. A number of teachers chose not to apply for career ladder positions simply because of the time involved and conflict with other commitments. Frequently elementary career ladder teachers complained about the amount of classroom instructional time that they missed. They felt their students were shortchanged. This feeling stemmed in part from a lack of careful planning for times when the teacher was absent for career ladder duties. Only a few teacher leaders could explicitly describe the instructional activities they designed for their permanent substitutes. They lacked a concept of differentiated staffing and continued to feel personally responsible for each and every teaching task. Other time pressures and entanglements also limited interest in the ladder. One teacher told us, "Many of us have other commitments." Outside jobs, family obligations, and other activities (obligations teachers accepted before career ladders) limited available time and energy.

Finally, the career ladder affected quality maintenance through its influence on teacher-teacher and teacher-administrator working relationships. In one school, the principal spent much more time in teachers' classrooms observing their work. Teachers and administrators shared decision-making responsibilities. The teachers in that school were overwhelmingly positive about this change. In another, teachers and administrators seldom interacted, and the teachers said competition and secretiveness increased. School-level data suggest some reasons for these divergent effects on working relationships. Our data reveal that the career ladder can pressure principals and faculties. When there was a low level of trust, or decision-making structures were not appropriate, or the school administration was authoritarian or paternalistic, or the faculty resented or had doubts about the quality of their principal's leadership, then the added pressures accompanying the ladder led to a further deterioration in those relationships. The demands of this innovation highlighted existing climate and school culture deficiencies in one school in particular. Where relationships were positive, and where the faculty respected one another and the principal, the career ladder provided opportunities that allowed for increased collaboration and a sense of pride in their accomplishments. This effect was most apparent in two schools.

Ongoing Adaptation

The last of the three dimensions of healthy and effective school organizations that we examined yielded far less data than did the first two features. Respondents simply were less concerned and informed about ongoing adaptation than they were about school goals and quality. The career ladder was in the early stages of implementation. As many teachers pointed out, the "bugs" were still being worked out. So much effort had gone into implementing the career ladder that relatively little energy was devoted during the period of time encompassed by the study to modify or change the plan as flaws were discovered. In all five schools, only the principals, career ladder teachers, and Career Ladder Task Force members were aware of planned adaptations to the career ladder program. Others were aware of the existence of a district task force and, in three of the schools, most could identify their elected task force representative. They were not able to describe any specific ways in which this person functioned to bring about changes in the program.

The lack of monitoring of career ladder teachers' work amplified the negative impact of this ignorance about the continuing work of the district's task force on the career ladder. As we pointed out earlier, once the new roles were designed, many ignored them. And role innovation was not monitored or assessed on a district or school basis, a major deficiency identified by all participants. Respondents raised several issues when talking about ongoing adaptation of the career ladder and of their school organization. They said that the revision and adaptation of the program in each school was needed on an ongoing basis, autonomy at the school level was necessary in order to adapt the program to school needs, career ladder resources should continually be refocused on effective teaching and overall instructional quality, and teachers' participation in leadership positions and decision making should increase.

When the tasks and functions of the career ladder at the school level were monitored, that contributed to teachers' ability to make small, minor revisions and adaptations of the program as needed. In the one school where a regular weekly meeting of teacher leaders and administrators was held, all were well informed about new roles and activities in the school. The new roles were more frequently altered to accomplish intended outcomes than in other schools. The extreme opposite of careful monitoring and adaptation was also reported; at one school, the career ladder teachers never met, either with the administrators or alone. Alienation was a theme of respondents' comments at this school. Even at the second school where perceptions of the career ladder were quite positive, the major criticism offered by career ladder teachers was that the principal expected it to proceed on its own. They felt they needed more leadership attention to potential adjustments in the new roles. Teachers often suggested ongoing re-evaluation to adjust the level of effort required in the new roles, to make expectations more comparable across roles (specialist to specialist), and so people could respond more swiftly to evolving school needs.

Although they called for increased monitoring and adaptation, respondents praised one major feature of the ladder—site-developed job descriptions—as an asset promoting appropriate adaptation. However, the district career ladder structure was, in the perception of most respondents, not something from which they could deviate with impunity. Little thought had been given to providing autonomy to alter the formal job descriptions at the school level once they were written and approved to adjust to unique contexts and emerging needs. The demands of collective bargaining and pressures for all teachers to be treated equally mitigated against this flexibility, as did the fear that variability would lead to accusations of favoritism or loss of control.

One positive adaptation that developed in four of the five schools was stimulated by teachers' commitment to quality teaching and learning and their conviction that they needed to solve their unique instructional problems with varying approaches. Career ladder teachers concentrated their time primarily on instructional supervision, the development of new instructional strategies, and curriculum. They provided helpful suggestions and ideas for others. The major focus of career ladder teachers, identified by all respondents, was effective teaching and lesson design, and the formal structure made possible by the ladder facilitated district and school efforts to support adaptations in instructional methods and the improvement of individual teachers' work.

Finally, a contribution of the plan to the overall ability of the schools to innovate and adopt was apparent in the participation of teachers in decision making and leadership roles. At all but one of the study sites, career ladder teachers were more involved in problem-solving sessions and formal decision making than teachers had been in the past. Our respondents praised this development without exception and expressed a desire to see this trend gain momentum. They argued that it facilitated a quickened pace for the communication of problems and improved the overall understanding of teachers' perceptions of school needs. Yet only at one school was the new structure leading to a strong collegial leadership team in which the faculty at large felt a sense of involvement and empowerment.

IMPLICATIONS AND CONCLUSIONS

Our data provide evidence that a work redesign structure can provide resources and processes for enhancing the goal accomplishment, quality maintenance, and ongoing adaptation conducive to healthy and effective school organizations. Further, they support the contention that, regardless of the potential of the new structure, the social work unit shapes the application of this potential to the core functions and activities of the school. Whatever the intrinsic appeal of new structures for schools or the ideological commitment to staged career opportunities for teachers, the ultimate arbiter of their usefulness should be the outcomes in each school and their effects on the central mission of teaching and learning (Hart, in press-b; Pierpont, 1989). Because school reforms are site implemented, teachers and principals are on the forefront of the reform effort. They will shape these outcomes through the social power of the sensemaking process and the individual behaviors with which it interacts.

Calls for the restructuring and redesign of work in schools are grounded in the assumption that more appealing and more effective structures of work can be developed for schools. Our data from five different schools implementing the same basic career ladder structure revealed common themes related to goal accomplishment, quality maintenance, and ongoing adaptation that point to the crucial role of the school social unit in shaping the usefulness of new work structures. Our data further support the notion that teachers judge a reform on the basis of its contribution to goal accomplishment, quality maintenance and, to a lesser degree, capacity to innovate. Thus they think of schools in terms of health, as Miles (1969) describes it, or effectiveness, as the term is used in the education literature. The effective use of this career ladder to promote the accomplishment of goals was tied by our respondents to the integration of clear and common career ladder goals with the core activities of instruction and curriculum aimed at improved student outcomes. Although they talked about goal clarity, commonality, and feedback, teachers returned with striking regularity to core functions of the school and the contribution of the new structure to those core functions. Teachers also associated quality maintenance and ongoing adaptation with teaching and learning functions and with the effective use of the human and material resources provided by the new structure.

The wide variability of implementation success in the five schools we observed sparked fundamental questions about work restructuring in schools. How do those at the work site take structural reforms and recast them into action and belief systems that contribute to the elements of healthy organizations and effective schools? How do teachers think about their work under new structures? How do they use them to accomplish their educational goals?

The data reveal the role of the school social unit in the search for answers to these questions. Teachers' perceptions of this plan's utility in their pursuit of work and personal goals related to goal quality through a close tie between the purposes of the career ladder and their teaching and learning goals, leadership that articulated this close relationship, and monitoring and feedback that helped them keep new roles and tasks focused on this goal. The data suggest that positive perceptions also are tied to the relationship between work quality and the hard work of people who are filling the roles, a belief that the best talent available is being used, improved distribution of professional power, increased training and growth opportunities for all teachers, communication facilitating the flow of necessary information, an emphasis on the group's (school's) quality as well as improved individual performance and more positive teacher career plans, and better working relationships among the professionals in the school. Finally, the necessary school-level autonomy must exist to accomplish important revisions and adaptations in tasks and roles that enhance the tie between the redesigned work and the core functions of the school.

Further, the data reveal important factors in transforming a structural reform at the work site level into an action-and-belief system contributing to successful and healthy school organizations that begin to answer these questions. Within all three elements of healthy organizations and effective schools, respondents pointed to the importance of the core function of the school—teaching and learning—and the role of leadership in interpreting the new structure as a resource in performing this core function. Teachers cared very much about teaching and learning. They varied widely, however, in their understanding and use of the new structure toward these ends. When teachers exhibited a belief in the effect of the new structure on their teaching and of teaching on student outcomes, they were most positive about the career ladder. This belief—that their effort could spark improvement in student learning—is an integral part of teacher efficacy, which has been tied to student performance (Ashton & Webb, 1986). This tie between the career ladder and efficacy is receiving some support in research on new structures in other educational settings. Rhodes (1988) found that positive responses to two other career ladder structures in Utah are stronger in teachers with high professional and personal efficacy. However, longitudinal studies of instructional development and student performance using a variety of measures will be required to bear out these beliefs. Our findings also support conclusions from widely disparate research on organizations pointing to the importance of sensemaking and thinking about work in translating structures into behaviors and using behavior to alter the functions of a structure (Lipsky, 1980; Pfeffer, 1981).

Our study of a work redesign career ladder emphasizes a crucial element of work restructuring currently receiving far too little attention in the reform environment—the role of sensemaking within the social unit (and of leadership in sense making) in creating the behaviors leading to the outcomes of a structural reform. This sensemaking process, identified in organizational and leadership research as a central function of management, operated in the five schools we studied in three central ways (Pfeffer & Lawler, 1980). First, the new structure's relationship to the core function and central norms of schooling was crucial to a useful experience, and teachers and principals made sense of new roles and relationships according to perceived congruence with core functions. Second, the new structures were interpreted either as parallel and competing or as reinforcing and enhancing elements of the existing work structures, and their utility was judged accordingly. Finally, principals and influential leaders among teachers influenced sensemaking by facilitating the integration of new roles and tasks into core functions and structures and by helping to modify norms and expectations and the sensemaking process itself. The primary link between a successful use of new work structures and core school functions through the sensemaking process in our data cannot be overemphasized. As David Cohen (1988, p. 55) points out,

> Teaching is a practice of human improvement . . . similar to psychotherapy, organizational consulting, some parts of social work, and sex therapy. . . . Practitioners try to produce states of mind and feeling in other people or groups, by direct work on and with those they seek to improve.

Although their perceptions of the ultimate usefulness of the career ladder differed, our respondents raised similar themes as they described the process through which they judged and then chose to use or resist the new structure. They emphasized goal clarity, commonality, feedback, and monitoring. They raised questions about the sustainability of the reform, its usefulness as a professional resource, and the appropriate distribution of training opportunities and power and influence in schools. They called our attention to the time and energy available and the contribution (or distraction) of the new structure to these critical resources. But their experiences continually highlighted the importance of information processing, or sensemaking, in translating a structure into an integrated contribution to the core work in schools. Otherwise, it became another regulation with which to comply, a parallel and competing addition to their already heavy workloads.

The objective features of the structure had little or nothing to do with this outcome. What did affect it was the articulation of the principal and respected and highly visible leaders among teachers who highlighted the utility of the new structure for promoting goal accomplishment, quality maintenance, and ongoing adaptation to emerging needs. They used their power and knowledge to help people understand how to make use of the new structure and manipulated their autonomy at the school level to redefine and refine tasks and roles as a school-level resource, useful to all and focused on the central ends of schooling. They accomplished these goals by using, not dismantling, the reform. The teachers were constrained in this early stage of the reform from a too zealous participation in this vital function because they feared and experienced peer censure, which made the role of the principals even more crucial.

These observations have important implications for the distribution of resources toward successfully implementing promising new work structures for schools. First, the spotty participation of principals in the process of making sense of and integrating the career ladder into the central work of the schools points out the need to help school-level leaders make better sense of these structures themselves. Tremendous effort had gone into designing the career ladder, yet staff development activities for principals and career ladder teachers in the new roles were directed primarily toward the formal structure, rules, and processes of the new program, not toward the effective use of this new resource for the creation of healthy and effective school organizations. Although a few days before the beginning of the school year had been devoted to some inservice training and preparation for principals designed to help them with power sharing and role assessment, no follow-up contacts and in-school assistance were provided. Second and closely related, those who design new structures will need to carefully articulate for themselves ways in which the new tasks, roles, and rewards promote teaching and learning. They can then help people who work in schools make use of the roles and tasks created to enhance their work.

These changes in the manner with which we approach restructuring will alter the emphasis of many of the reforms. New structures, to be resilient and long range, must be a means to an end, and must focus on the core functions and outcomes of schools. Restructuring is a necessary but not a sufficient first step in work redesign in all kinds of organizations (Hart, in press-b). Currently in Utah, legislation forbids the use of money appropriated for the career ladder for training and development activities. A recent experiment begun in Utah in 1988 with block grants could alleviate this oversight if the districts so choose, but no clear movement in this direction is currently observable. Our data affirm the importance of the sensemaking process in the use of the new resources, preventing a retreat into *pro forma* and procedure compliance with a new set of administrative regulations (Amsler et al., 1988). They also highlight the role of leadership at each school in creating an implementation environment in which people are able to reinterpret and redefine new roles and structures of work toward desired ends.

Education reformers sometimes make facile assertions about the utility and desirability of fundamental change in the organization of work in schools. As Cohen (1988) points out, current practices reflect views with deep cultural roots imbedded in the values of teachers, parents, and students. People need help in understanding and then marshaling the new structure to accomplish valued goals. They also need help in developing the skills and orientation necessary to influence this crucial organizational process. These skills and processes do not come automatically to principals and teacher leaders simply because these people are appointed to formal roles. Such skills and processes require personal and group development activities designed specifically to enhance the success of the human system that must take action to implement new structures and perform new tasks successfully in unfamiliar and initially awkward work arrangements.

Indeed, sensemaking, or information processing, may be a central function of management during both work redesign and maintenance. As Pfeffer and Lawler (1980, p. 54) point out,

> The implication is that organizing involves not only the structuring of behaviors, a process that must be continually reaccomplished (Weick, 1969), but also the structuring of information and meaning, a process that must also be continually reaccomplished. Indeed, what the social psychological experimenter does in the laboratory may be one of the more important tasks of management—making certain information salient and pointing out connections between behaviors and subsequent attitudes . . . creating meaning systems and consensually shared interpretations of events for participants.

Our data revealed that the sensemaking link was weak in the restructuring process in school reform. Only two of our five school principals successfully used this important management function to promote the use of the new tasks and roles in schools. Only these two were able on their own to interpret the new roles in terms congruent with goal accomplishment, quality maintenance, and adaptation and, thus, use them to improve the work of teachers in their schools. The other three principals either interpreted the reform as an imposition—an add-on to their work that used up time without contributing to the core function of the school—or as an unmanageable burden to be foisted on the teachers. The new structure consequently competed with existing structures rather than contributing to them. We assume that reform is mounted with the intent to succeed. Our findings support the contention that the success of new configurations of work in schools requires thoughtful and deliberate attention to the work site variables in human systems at every school in which they are implemented.

NOTE

1. Our discussion is limited to one plan in five different schools. A number of policy reports and evaluations generalizing across district career ladder plans in Utah are available (Hart, in press-b; Malen, Murphy, & Hart, 1988; Amsler, Mitchell, Nelson, & Timar, 1987). Consequently, we chose to focus this chapter on the school site effects of a particular career ladder plan in order to obtain a better understanding of the impacts of work reform on those who work and study in schools.

REFERENCES

Amsler, M., D. Mitchell, L. Nelson, & T. Timar. (1988). *An evaluation of the Utah career ladder system.* San Fransisco, CA: Far West Laboratory for Education Research.

Ashton, P., & R. Webb. (1986). *Making a difference: Teachers' sense of efficacy and student achievement.* New York: Longman.

Bacharach, S. B., & S. C. Conley. (1986, April). *Educational reform: A managerial agenda.* A paper presented at the annual meeting of the American Educational Research Association, San Fransisco.

Bacharach, S., S. Conley, & J. Shedd. (1986). Beyond career ladders: Structuring teacher career development systems. *Teachers College Record, 87,* 653–674.

Bossert, S., D. Dwyer, B. Rowan, & G. Lee. (1982). The instructional management role of the principal. *Educational Administration Quarterly, 18,* 34–64.

Bosworth, S. L., & G. A. Kreps. (1986). Structure as process: Organization and role. *American Sociological Review, 51,* 699–716.

Carnegie Forum on Education and the Economy. (1986). *A nation prepared: Teachers for the 21st century.* Hyattsville, MD: Carnegie Forum on Education and the Economy.

Cohen, D. (1988). Teaching practice: Plus que ça change. In P. W. Jackson, ed., *Contributing to educational change: Perspectives on research and practice,* pp. 27–84. Berkeley, CA: McCutchan.

Cornett, L. (1988, December). Is "paying for performance" changing schools? The SREB career ladder clearinghouse report 1988. Atlanta, GA: Southern Regional Educational Board.

Hackman, J. R., & G. R. Oldham. (1980). *Work redesign.* Reading, MA: Addison-Wesley.

Hart, A. W. (1987). A career ladder's effect on teacher career and work attitudes. *American Educational Research Journal, 24*(4), 479–504.

Hart, A. W. (In press-a). Work redesign: A review of literature for education reform. In S. B. Bacharach, ed., *Advances in research in school management.* Greenwich, CT: JAI Press.

Hart, A. W. (In press-b). A work redesign view of Utah career ladders. In L. Frase, ed., *Teacher compensation systems and motivation.* Lancaster, PA: Technomic Publishing.

Holmes Group. (1986). *Tomorrow's teachers.* East Lansing, MI: Holmes Group.

Lipsky, M. (1980). *Street-level bureaucracy: Dilemmas of the individual in public services.* New York: Sage Foundation.

Malen, B., & A. W. Hart. (1987). Career ladder reform: A multi-level analysis of initial efforts. *Educational Evaluation and Policy Analysis, 9*(1), 9–24.

Malen, B., M. J. Murphy, & A. W. Hart. (1988). Restructuring teacher compensation systems: An analysis of three incentive strategies. In K. Alexander, ed., *American Education Finance Association Yearbook,* pp. 91–142. Cambridge, MA: Ballinger.

Miles, M. B. (1969). Planned change and organizational health: Figure and ground. In F. D. Sergiovanni, & T. J. Carver, eds., *Organizational and human behavior: Focus on schools,* pp. 375–391. New York: McGraw-Hill.

Mitchell, S. M. (1986, April). Negotiating the design of professional jobs. A paper presented at the annual meeting of the American Educational Research Association, San Fransisco.

Murphy, M. J., & A. W. Hart. (1988, October). Preparing principals to lead in restructured schools. A paper presented at the annual meeting of the University Council for Educational Administration, Cincinnati, Ohio.

National Commission on Excellence in Education. (1983). *A nation at risk: The imperative of educational reform.* Washington, DC: National Commission on Excellence in Education.

Pfeffer, J. (1981). *Power in organizations.* Marshfield, MA: Pitman.

Pfeffer, J., & J. Lawler. (1980). Effects of job alternatives, extrinsic rewards, and behavioral commitment on attitude toward the organization: A field test of the insufficient justification paradigm. *Administrative Science Quarterly, 25,* 38–56.

Pierpont, B. (1989, 22 January). The price of excellence. *CBS Sunday Morning.*

Rhodes, M. (1988). Work alienation, teacher efficacy, and career ladder reform. Unpublished doctoral dissertation, University of Utah, Salt Lake City, Utah.

Rosenholtz, S. J. (1987). Education reform strategies: Will they increase teacher commitment? *American Journal of Education, 95,* 534–562.

Rosenholtz, S. J., & M. A. Smylie. (1984). Teacher compensation and career ladders. *Elementary School Journal, 85,* 149–166.

Schlechty, P. C. (1976). *Teaching and social behavior: Toward an organizational theory of instruction.* Boston, MA: Allyn & Bacon.

Weick, K. E. (1969). *The social psychology of organizing.* Reading, MA: Addison-Wesley.

CHAPTER 10

Statewide Testing and Local Improvement: An Oxymoron?

Bruce L. Wilson and
H. Dickson Corbett

During the early part of this decade, state departments of education, state legislatures, and governors have initiated a series of reforms designed to improve the quality of education. As an example, close to 60 percent of the states have mandated some form of standardized testing for local school systems (Marshall, 1987). Yet the effects of implementing such testing programs on the daily lives of school staff and students and how differences in state programs magnify or minimize these effects have not been well documented by empirical research despite this flurry of effort (Airasian, 1987; Rosenholtz, 1987; Stake, Bettridge, Metzer, & Switzer, 1987).

The work on which this chapter is based was funded by the Office of Educational Research and Improvement, U.S. Department of Education. The opinions expressed do not necessarily reflect the position or policy of the department, and no official endorsement should be inferred.

A Carnegie Foundation for the Advancement of Teaching (1988, p. 1) survey reported teachers to be very critical of the reform movement in general and statewide testing in particular, pointing out that "The relationship between the teacher and the student is at the heart of education, and only when improvements reach the classroom will excellence be achieved." Carnegie's survey of 13,500 teachers, published in *Report Card on School Reform: The Teachers Speak*, found that teachers do not believe the majority of the reforms have done much positively for the classroom and are troubled by the potential for negative impacts. Concerning standardized testing, teachers noted a dramatic increase in their use over the past five years, and practitioners' comments on this development led Carnegie (1988, pp. 5–6) to conclude that "there is something troubling—even paradoxical about these findings. We are disturbed that testing instruments are crude and often measure that which matters least"; and, compounding the problem, "In the end, what we test is what we teach." Nevertheless, the tests have been implemented with scant attention to their daily impact, positive or negative, on teachers and students.

This chapter is based on a study we conducted that addressed this imbalance by documenting the impact of state-mandated testing programs on the work lives of teachers and students. The chapter contrasts two states' testing programs, one with "low-stakes" consequences attached to student performance and the other representing a "high-stakes" situation. After comparing the programs and describing the research design, we detail teachers' perceptions of the tests' effects on their work lives and their students. Then we document differences in impacts between the low- and high-stakes conditions. During the research, the tests' stakes increased (dramatically, in the low-stakes situation), and the effects of those changes are presented next. The chapter concludes with a discussion of the value of state minimum competency testing for improvement of practice in local districts.

THE TESTING PROGRAMS IN TWO STATES

Educators from Pennsylvania and Maryland participated in the study. The states represented "low-stakes" (Pennsylvania) and "high-stakes" (Maryland) situations. The level of the stakes associated with a test is the extent to which students, teachers, administrators, and/or parents perceive test performance to be "used to make important decisions that immediately and directly affect them" (Madaus, 1988). Relatively minor consequences attended student performance on Pennsylvania's minimum competency tests (MCT) in language and math. The purpose of both tests was to identify

Table 10-1

Summary of Two Mandatory, Minimum-Competency, State Testing Programs in Pennsylvania and Maryland

Areas of Difference	Pennsylvania	Maryland
Test content	Reading, math	Reading, math, writing, citizenship
Grades tested	3, 5, 8	8, (practice) 9, 10–12 retests
Participation	Mandatory	Mandatory
State focus	Use of test results to identify students in need of additional instruction	Identification of failing students to aid districts in curriculum planning
Local consequences	Additional state funds for low-scoring students	Students must pass test to graduate; districts required to provide appropriate assistance to failing students; no additional state funds
Stimulus	Legislative response to reform based on critiques of early 1980s	State department curriculum improvement initiative begun in late 1970s

students needing additional classroom instruction who may have been overlooked by other means. Maryland's "high-stakes" strategy required students to pass reading, writing, math, and citizenship MCTs in order to receive a high school diploma. The tests were being phased in as graduation requirements; at the time of the survey phase of the research, only the reading and math tests "counted."

The two states' MCT programs had several important differences (see Table 10-1). The first difference concerned the purposes just detailed. Second, Pennsylvania students were tested in the third, fifth, and eighth grades. Maryland tested students beginning in ninth grade, with a practice instrument administered in the eighth grade. Third, Pennsylvania students took tests in reading and math, whereas Maryland students also were examined in writing and citizenship. Fourth, the Pennsylvania legislature appropriated funds for remediation; Maryland offered no special financial assistance. Fifth, Pennsylvania's legislated program responded to calls for educational reform in the early 1980s and, after soliciting educators' input on appropriate test objectives, invited commercial test publishers to bid on a contract to develop the state's instrument. Maryland initiated a statewide curriculum improvement program several years prior to beginning the testing program, with the expressed purpose of anticipating the instructional quality necessary to perform well on the tests. Educators from around the state were used by the state department to provide input into the content and form of the tests.

The programs' stakes changed during the study. In Pennsylvania, the chief state school officer (CSSO) released district rankings based on the test scores prior to the 1987–88 school year and touted the test as an appropriate indicator of school effectiveness. Study interviews conducted subsequent to this event revealed considerable concern on the part of local educators that the tests were being used in ways for which they were not originally intended, even though the rankings were quickly withdrawn due to the furor surrounding them. Regardless, the importance of the tests increased for both educators and the public. Maryland had no similar dramatic event; instead, its districts had to reconcile themselves to the inevitable day when all four tests would affect whether students graduated, with the writing and citizenship tests generating much controversy and calls for revision. In fact, administrators and teachers reported that students had difficulty passing these two tests and that this difficulty increased the pressure on teachers and administrators.

Madaus (1988) and Airasian (1987) argue that such differences in the purposes of statewide testing programs should have different impacts on their respective school districts. Because high-stakes tests are used for important decisions such as promotion or graduation, they can influence system behavior—even direct it (Madaus, 1988). In low-stakes situations, no important sanctions follow test performance and thus the tests likely have little effect on the system. Airasian (1987) claims that standardized testing once served general purposes, namely to identify areas where instruction needed improvement and to gauge how well the educational system as a whole was functioning. More recently, the success of these traditional uses of the tests has led to acceptance of a new purpose:

> This second use is most aptly termed state-mandated certification testing. In this approach, testing is not used to guide classroom instruction or to monitor educational policy. Rather, state-mandated certification testing has made testing and test results a crucial aspect of educational policy itself. (Airasian, 1987, p. 403)

In other words, states have begun to use tests as a policy to try to spur improvements. These tests, of which MCT is one form, often have characteristics in common: they are mandated for most students in selected grades; they eliminate local discretion by using one instrument to be administered and scored similarly across all systems; and they usually measure performance on a pass-fail basis. The consequences of such a testing policy are that test information becomes of interest to a wide population, and not just a few professionals and concerned parents; local control over the curriculum may be eroded; and tension is created between quality of education and equality of educational opportunity.

The two states examined in this chapter were selected with this potential for differences in impact in mind. Pennsylvania's approach was much more in line with Airasian's (1987) assessment of the traditional use of standardized testing and contained low stakes for the system as a whole, although remediation money was given to districts on the basis of how many students fell below the cutoff point—a potential negative incentive for improving scores. Maryland, however, designed the test as a specific policy tool and tied student performance to high school graduation. Thus, the administrators, teachers, and students in this state faced a high-stakes situation.

The available literature offers little guidance as to what precisely the differential impacts of such programs might be. Stake et al. (1987) provide an initial review of research on the effects of state assessment initiatives, examining the topic across six categories of effects: achievement standards; public attitude toward schools; the morale and motivation of those tested; the utility of test information for school administration; the reactions of teachers to standardized test results; and the curriculum. The review notes that few studies have been conducted to compare the local system consequences of statewide standardized (and/or maximum competency) testing programs.

In a review of testing research, Airasian (1987, p. 408) suggests, "The crucial issues of testing are not technical. Issues of testing today are social, economic, and value-laden, involving the distribution and redistribution of resources and prerogatives." Research on minimum competency testing, defined in policy terms as "a device for conditioning student promotion or graduation on test achievement" (Darling-Hammond & Wise, 1985, p. 318), has not yet caught up with this argument.

There are several reasons why higher-stakes situations can be expected to have greater local impacts. First, mandatory tests are likely to force adjustments in a system by creating expectations for what the outcomes of schooling should be. According to Mintzberg (1983), stipulating outcomes is one means used widely in organizations to affect operations. Some standard—no matter how narrowly defined—has to be met, regardless of what else staff members may want to accomplish. In situations where the standard is easily attained, its importance as a criterion of success may remain no more pre-eminent than any of a myriad of indicators. However, in situations where the standard is less readily reached, its importance looms larger and perhaps more directly defines what happens in the schools.

Second, one of the schools' primary tasks is to move students smoothly through a series of grades to graduation (Schlechty, 1976). In most communities, staff size, the number of classrooms needed, and the availability of sufficient materials are all predicated on the assumption that essentially all first-graders will become second-graders and that most seniors will graduate on time. A few exceptions cause no problems, but testing programs change the assumptions by inserting a checkpoint for determining the progress of all students, based on something other than student age, credits obtained, or time spent in school. Obviously, some checkpoints are more formidable than others, as in the case where successful completion of the test determines whether or not students graduate. But even relatively innocuous checkpoints may force some remediation and thereby affect subsequent progress.

Third, establishing a standard all students must meet as a visible indicator of effectiveness runs counter to the ethos of many educators (Rosenholtz, 1987). In spite of enormous standardization, a tone of individualism permeates U.S. education (Lortie, 1975). Teachers are allowed considerable autonomy in deciding what and how to teach, and they expect to handle their classrooms themselves. Testing programs challenge this ethos. Test items highlight critical content to cover; test administration dates determine the deadline for teaching the content; item formats affect how the information will be accessed; and the standards add a quality of sameness to what students should achieve. The tests, therefore, have major effects on school culture. Wilson (1971) defines culture as "definitions of what is and what ought to be." Deal (1985) describes it as "the way we do things around here." Testing programs are likely to require serious examination of definitions of what being a student or teacher is and should be. The literature on educational change is replete—although this is not always recognized—with descriptions of the clash between (1) values implicit in an innovation and (2) the values implicit in the way people who are expected to innovate were accustomed to behaving (Sarason, 1971; Gordon, 1984; Rossman, Corbett, & Firestone, 1988).

Of course, greater impact is not tantamount to improvement. After describing the study design, the remainder of this chapter is devoted to detailing the type of impacts that local systems felt with respect to teachers' and students' work lives.

STUDY DESIGN

The preceding discussion simplifies a complex situation. Introducing and operating a mandatory statewide MCT program involves a wide range of potential challenges to a district. Although some of these challenges can be anticipated by theoretical understanding or past research, using an inductive approach in which the present research can take advantage of unexpected developments can be equally valuable (Miles & Huberman, 1984). For this reason, the study was designed to include both (1) in-depth, open-ended qualitative fieldwork in a small number of sites and (2) large-scale structured questionnaires.

The study had three phases. First, researchers conducted a preliminary round of qualitative fieldwork wherein they visited six school districts in each of the two states for several days to interview a wide variety of staff members. Second, the results from the interviews were used to design a questionnaire to be administered throughout districts in the states studied. Third, the survey results were used to structure a final round of feedback and interviews in the original sites. These latter interviews were conducted with mostly administrators during half-day visits in eleven of the twelve districts.

Phase One: Fieldwork in Twelve Sites

Six sites in each of the two states were visited. Site selection was made on the basis of district size and type of community served, primarily because these characteristics were assumed to determine the kind of staff resource demands providing test-related follow-up instruction would take. Equally important was the willingness of the district to participate because the purpose of this phase was to explore issues in depth, not to generalize to a larger population. Selection was carried out with the input and assistance of key state department staff members in each state.

Six experienced field researchers conducted the site visits. One researcher spent two or three days in each site, depending on district size. The first day was spent in the central office, interviewing the superintendent (if available), the person(s) responsible for handling the testing program, and other district staff members who dealt with the test. Also, pertinent documents were examined where available. On Days 2 and 3, school interviews were conducted with administrators, guidance counselors, teachers, and students. When all appropriate schools in a district could not be visited, selection was made in collaboration with district personnel. Sampling a variety of schools in the district was the foremost criterion. Over 250 local educators and students participated in the interviews.

Interview Questions. Field researchers operated from interview guides with broad categories of questions. For further documentation of interview protocols and data summaries, see Corbett and Wilson (1988). Specific phrasing of questions and the particular probes used were determined by the researcher on site. In training sessions conducted prior to the site visit, researchers had an opportunity to generate and discuss potential questions and follow-up probes, but fieldwork of this type demands that the researcher have considerable flexibility in determining to whom to talk, what to ask, and when to ask it. The goal was to obtain data on each question from multiple sources but not necessarily from every source.

Data Management. A multiple-case, multiple-researcher, open-ended interview study places a heavy burden on the data management system. Finding a systematic way of determining data gaps, locating overlooked sources, making data accessible to other researchers, and being able to retrieve parts of the data was imperative. To accomplish this goal, resources were allocated more to developing data summaries than to making handwritten field notes presentable or to typing transcripts from tape recordings. When researchers returned from a site visit, they completed a series of data summary charts: (1) a summary of information sources and the question categories for which each source supplied information; (2) a description of source-identified effects, coupled with the researcher's designation of which and how many staff members listed each effect; (3) a summary of data on the district's instructional, organizational, and cultural contexts as well as its relationship with the surrounding community and the state; and (4) a listing of residual incidents and data worthy of note that did not fit cleanly in the structured charts.

We used these data summary charts to conduct the cross-site analysis. They were the stimulus for determining whether additional information needed to be gathered from particular sites.

Data Analysis. The analysis activities consisted of reviewing the data summary charts to identify implementation themes that cut across the twelve sites. The specific goal of the analysis was to develop items for the questionnaire to be used in the second phase of the study.

We returned to the original field notes to review the terminology local educators used in discussing the tests. Using the list of themes, the data summary chart information, and this review of responses, we constructed individual questionnaire items. A questionnaire with 83 items was produced from this synthesis. The items fell into five categories: (1) local internal and external operating contexts, (2) the administration of the tests in the local setting, (3) the strategies used to maximize student performance, (4) the purposes the tests were used for in the local setting, and (5) the impact of the tests on instruction, organization, and culture.

Phase Two: Survey Design

The second phase of the study involved a quantitative assessment of the local ramifications of mandatory statewide testing programs. Four major activities—instrumentation, sampling, data collection, and analysis—were conducted during this phase.

A first draft of the questionnaire was designed so that it could be self-administered in twenty to thirty minutes. A pilot test of the draft instrument was administered in several districts to ensure that the questionnaire was clear, communicated the intent of the project, and could be completed within time constraints. Changes to the questionnaire were made on the basis of the criticism that was offered.

All districts in both states were invited to participate in the study (Pennsylvania = 501, Maryland = 24). Three different role groups familiar with the testing program were targeted from each district: central office administrators, principals, and teachers. A separate questionnaire was completed by each group member. In Maryland, where there were fewer but larger school districts, three respondents from each role group within the district were asked to complete the survey. Only one person from each role group within the district completed the survey in Pennsylvania. The participating staff members in each system were selected by the superintendent or a designee.

In Pennsylvania, 277 of the 501 districts responded with one respondent from each of three role groups (central office, principal, and teacher). In Maryland, 23 of the 24 districts returned usable questionnaires with three respondents from each of three role groups. An analysis of the participating and nonparticipating districts in Pennsylvania showed no significant differences between the two groups in terms of basic demographic characteristics (such as size, wealth, and location).

The analysis had two foci. The first was to identify educators' responses concerning the adjustments they had made. Frequency distributions for questionnaire items were used to display these responses. The second focus was to examine cross-state differences for instructional adjustments. Analyses of variance were conducted to compare responses in the two states.

Phase Three: Follow-up Fieldwork

In the fall of 1987, field researchers returned to 11 of the original 12 sites visited in Phase One, with one Maryland district declining to participate. The purposes of these visits were to trace subsequent developments in the operation of the state testing program and to get help in interpreting the results of the survey. Over eighty local educators participated in this activity. The interviews concentrated on the findings contained in the section on within-state district variations. The findings were presented to participants, and they then reacted to specific numbers, interpretations, and implications. These reactions then were incorporated into the quantitative results section of this chapter.

FINDINGS REGARDING EDUCATORS' REACTIONS
TO STATEWIDE TESTS

This section gives a flavor of how educators felt about their respective state's program and hints at important differences between the two states. The specific focus for this chapter is on items addressing teacher work lives and the lives of students. In each case, sample items representing the general theme of teacher work life and student life were included in the survey.

The "student life" items were not intended to comprise an all-encompassing category. The items included in this group offered a glimpse of how the character of student life fared under the testing program in terms of the extent of change in each of the following areas:

- Students are more serious about their classes.
- Teachers have more empathy for students who are achieving poorly.
- Staff members know more about students who have serious learning problems.

Respondents were asked to indicate the extent of impact on a five-point scale (0–4) from "No change" to "Total change" as a result of the testing program. A higher score meant a more positive impact on student lives.

Similarly, the "teacher work life" category sampled six items focusing on the extent of change in important conditions that define the working conditions for teachers, such as

- There is a decreased emphasis on using educators' professional judgment in instructional matters.
- Time demands on staff have increased.
- Staff members have been reassigned.
- Staff members are under pressure to improve student performance.
- Paperwork has increased for staff.
- Staff members are more worried about the potential of a lawsuit.

This measure was not intended to include all aspects of work generally discussed in the working conditions literature, but at least the items provided an indication of whether teachers' work lives were affected by the new testing programs. Like the previous items, the respondent choices were on a five-point scale (0–4) from no change to total change. In this case, the higher the score, the more stressful the work environment for teachers.

Frequency distributions for the respondents in each state are presented in Table 10-2. Teacher responses were used rather than responses from the other two role groups surveyed (building principals and central office ad-

Table 10-2
Percent of Respondents, in Two States, for Student Life and Teacher Work Life Items

Student life	No Change		Minor Change		Moderate Change		Major Change		Total Change		Mean Score	
	PA	MD	PA	MD	PA	MD	PA	MD	PA	MD	PA	MD
1. Students more serious	37	26	32	34	25	28	5	12	0	0	1.00	1.26
2. Increased empathy for poor achievers	38	12	27	35	30	38	5	13	0	0	1.02	1.58
3. More known about learning problems	18	15	27	35	42	33	13	16	1	2	1.54	1.56

Teacher work life	No Change		Minor Change		Moderate Change		Major Change		Total Change		Mean Score	
	PA	MD	PA	MD	PA	MD	PA	MD	PA	MD	PA	MD
1. Decrease in professional judgment over instructional matters	63	26	22	16	12	34	4	20	0	4	0.56	1.60
2. Increased time demands	39	3	25	0	25	27	9	52	2	18	1.10	2.81
3. Staff reassignment	58	15	23	31	14	37	3	12	3	6	0.70	1.61
4. Increased pressure for student performance	36	3	26	8	24	25	12	46	2	18	1.17	2.67
5. Increased paperwork	41	2	29	2	21	31	6	43	3	23	1.01	2.84
6. More worry about lawsuits	74	19	13	37	9	22	4	15	0	7	0.43	1.56

Note: The number of respondents varies from the number reported in the discussion of the research design because a few districts did not provide teacher respondents and because some respondents did not answer all the items. The average number of valid responses in Pennsylvania was 250 and 57 in Maryland.

ministrators) because it was felt that teachers were in a better position to be informants about their own work lives and student lives than other role groups. In each district, the teachers(s) were nominated by the superintendent because of their knowledge of and experience with the state testing program. The numbers in the table represent the percentage of teachers responding to each category.

The findings from the three items focusing on the quality of student life indicate that teachers, on average, were reporting only minimal impact as a result of the test. Approximately half of the teachers from both states reported "No change" or only "Minor change" on students as a result of the test. As interviewees commented,

> The students are not impacted. The test identifies the same kids with the same problems [as other diagnostic instruments]. No one had to tell us who was having problems. They had already been identified.

> The student impact is low because there is nothing obtrusive to affect students.

The mean scores for the three items demonstrate further the minimal impact but also reveal some differences between the two states. On average, the impact is "Minor" in Pennsylvania and between "Minor" and "Moderate" in Maryland. Although differences are present, there are no substantial added benefits for students, particularly in whether teachers know more about students than before. This finding is interesting in that improving this knowledge is a common justification for beginning the testing program in the first place. Apparently teachers feel confident that they do not need additional tests to show them who needs help.

Another explanation for the low positive impact on students may be the counterbalancing negative impact that teachers mentioned during interviews:

> Testing adds a negative image for kids who fail. It's another way of telling someone "I'm dumb." It makes it difficult for kids to get up in the morning.

> Those who fail are second class citizens . . . we take them out of regular instruction for remediation.

> We don't get the mileage out of better kids that we used to. We are teaching to the middle.

The findings from the six items sampling the quality of teacher work life reveal a greater relative impact in Maryland, the high-stakes site. For three of the six items—time demands, pressure for performance, and paperwork—

over half the respondents in Maryland indicated the change was "Major" or "Total." Comments in the interviews reinforced the negative impact on teachers' lives:

> Teacher self-esteem goes down another notch each time something like this happens.

> The paperwork is horrible and getting worse.

> Professionals aren't trusted—the tests carry the aura of respectability.

> It takes too much time . . . too much of that time has to be taken from other stuff I used to do.

> Teachers feel jerked around. The test tells them what to teach.

On average, Pennsylvania teachers reported only "minor" change ($x = 1.0$) while Maryland teachers reported the impact to be between moderate ($x = 2.0$) and major ($x = 3.0$). Clearly, the differences in high- and low-stakes conditions accentuated the impact of testing on teachers' work lives.

The findings reported in Table 10-2 offer a snapshot of teachers' reactions to the initiation of statewide mandatory minimum competency tests. The survey findings suggest that, regardless of stakes, teachers believe relatively minor benefits flow to students. The evidence is stronger when considering teacher work lives. Teachers perceive the tests as placing more negative demands on their already overcrowded schedule: "The test is just one more add-on activity."

STATE COMPARISONS

Clearly, for the reasons discussed earlier, Maryland's MCT program should have had a greater impact on its local systems than Pennsylvania's program, primarily because Maryland's policy insinuated itself into an important orgranizational event—graduation—and because preceding state-wide improvement and actual test development activities engendered a cumulative anticipation of the day the tests would be put into place. Pennsylvania's program, however, arose from dialogue limited mostly to state-level legislators and officials. Limited local knowledge about the program plus its lack of implications for school operations seemed to ensure that the test would have little impact beyond its stated purpose of identifying students in need of additional instruction.

Table 10-3
**Analysis of Variance Comparison of Student Life and Teacher Work Life
Scores by State**

Cluster	Mean PA	Mean MD	F
Student life	1.29	1.48	6.3[a]
Teacher work life	0.81	2.17	152.2[b]

Note: The number of respondents varies from the number reported in the discussion of the research design because a few districts did not provide teacher respondents and because some respondents did not answer all the items. The average number of valid responses was 250 in Pennsylvania and 57 in Maryland.
[a] $P \leq 0.01$
[b] $P \leq 0.001$

The results in Table 10-3 assess the differences between teacher respondents in the two states. A mean score for each respondent was computed by combining the three student life items into one scale and the six teacher work life items into another. An analysis of variance was conducted on the two scales. Before combining these items to create a scale, statistical tests were conducted to ensure the appropriateness of such a step. First, correlation matrices were examined to ensure that there was at least a moderate correlation among the combined items and that there were not any excessively high correlations. Second, an analysis of reliability (internal consistency) was conducted to test coherence among items. The results of those calculations produced a reliability coefficient of 0.70 for student life and 0.83 for teacher work life, suggesting high internal consistency.

The findings were striking and consistent. For both measures, statistically significant differences between the states were found. Staff in Maryland school districts reported more impact on students and their own work lives than did their Pennsylvania colleagues.

Essentially, the two states had different intentions in mind when the testing programs were initiated, and the study data indicate that both were being met. The data reflect the differences in the modest versus the more ambitious approaches.

Recent Developments in the Two States: Raising the Stakes

The preceding quantitative comparisons present a snapshot of the differences in teachers' reactions to the testing programs. The picture was taken in the late fall of 1986 and the early winter of 1987. Events in both states subsequent to the survey administration seemed to increase the level of the stakes associated with the tests and had an effect on staff sufficient to alter their perceptions of the effects of the testing programs. In both states, an increase in the impacts on students and teachers was noted. A detailed account of these changes is available in Corbett and Wilson (1988).

The key event in Pennsylvania was the publication of the results from the spring 1987 test administration. Rather than the customary low-key sending of the scores to districts for each to handle as it saw fit, the release of the data was orchestrated by the chief state school officer (CSSO). In a pubic media briefing, the CSSO provided documents that ranked districts in the state from top to bottom in terms of the percentage of students who passed the cut-off point on the MCT. In addition, schools that had achieved 100 percent passing rates despite having "high-risk" student populations were singled out as being "poised on the brink of excellence." And to cap off the presentation, the CSSO touted the tests as the best measure available to assess the effectiveness of Pennsylvania's schools. An immediate protest over this use of the scores arose from educators across the state and resulted in the withdrawal of the documents containing the rankings.

The withdrawal of the rankings did not strike the event from either educators' or their communities' emotional record. Administrators in three of the six Pennsylvania districts visited in Phase Three argued that the "game" had now changed in their systems. Reflecting on the impact on students and teachers, they commented,

> The purpose of the test changed in September. It is no longer for remediation but to rank order schools.

> The results should be between the state and the school district if the test is to help. When they release scores and say 58 kids need help, we can say we've already identified 40 of them. But the negativism starts; it starts [phone] calls and there is no question I now have pressure on me.

> The test was not all that important. . . . But we might as well face up to it; with the publication of school by school results. . . . One of the goals will be to raise the percentage above the cut score.

What really seemed to be changing for three districts in Pennsylvania were the stakes; they got higher, primarily through the increased visibility of score comparisons and the subsequent increased, albeit reluctant, acceptance of the scores as a benchmark—that is, as a widely recognized point of reference when discussing the performance of schools in the district and in surrounding districts. Staff in the three districts reported that they did not believe the tests to be particularly important educationally and did not embrace the tests as valid indicators of achievement. They nevertheless acknowledged that they already were, or would soon be, treating the scores more seriously than in previous years.

This shift is best illustrated by a district whose surrounding districts performed similarly on the MCT, even though the district felt that its carefully and systematically developed curriculum far surpassed the offerings of their neighbors. The superintendent responded,

> We don't believe in the tests that strongly but we will be forced to see all material is covered before the tests. We definitely are going to do it. We won't be caught in the newspapers again.

The brunt of not "getting caught" again was to be borne by the reading program—a recently revised, developmental curriculum. The timing of the test administration required shifting the sequence of topics to be covered. An outraged reading coordinator responded,

> You have to alter a curriculum that is already working well and so we can't follow the developmental process. Kids are already growing in a structured program; but it [pressure to change] comes from the board, community, and adverse publicity.

The superintendent empathized with the coordinator,

> I don't have much faith in the tests. I don't want to change the curriculum, and it's not a major revision, but we've got to do better. Still, it's not the right thing to do to anyone. I don't want to over-react but I'm also going to have to spend time on things I shouldn't have to do as well: public relations, testing meetings—just to make the board feel comfortable. It'll never happen again when we see a worse district doing better than us.

The interviews suggest that these districts were planning expedient strategies to improve the test scores and just as clearly that there was resentment to do so and a concern that what they were doing was compromising some standard of good professional practice. The message they were giving was that their test scores were becoming benchmarks for political reasons, namely to appease school boards and community members who had the opportunity to see their school systems compared to neighboring districts and did not like what they saw.

No single event dramatically heightened the impact of the tests in Maryland. Instead, the stimulus was the approach of the time when students had to pass all four of the tests in order to receive a diploma. The four tests were not regarded equally. Phase Three interviews revealed that educators discriminated between the reading and math tests on one hand and the writing and citizenship ones on the other. The reading and math tests, in Maryland educators' minds, were adequate measures of basic competence in the respective content areas and covered objectives already well entrenched in the curriculum. The curriculum development aspect of the state initiative began in the late 1970s, and these two tests were the first to be developed, trial-tested, and implemented. Actual local curriculum and instruction changes had been in place for seven to nine years in some settings. By 1987, these alterations had become institutionalized to the point that interview subjects in 4 of the 5 Phase Three districts argued that the impact scores may have been too low because staff had forgotten that what was now routine was once novel. The result was that the two tests were no longer intrusive.

Such was not the case for the writing and citizenship tests. Both generated considerable controversy. The writing test did so primarily because staff viewed it as demanding a performance level well beyond that necessary to be minimally competent in writing. The citizenship test was controversial because it required students to memorize information about local, state, and federal governments—information that even the teachers said they did not possess without special study. Fueling educators' concerns were the facts that students had much more difficulty succeeding in trial administrations of these two tests and that the time when the first cohort of students would have to pass all four tests to receive a diploma was inexorably approaching. For special education teachers and teachers with responsibilities in the grades tested and for affected content areas, the pressure to achieve passing scores was building and the impact on their work lives was great. According to two administrators,

> We've changed the whole social studies curriculum. We had to expand the 7th and 8th grade American Studies to include more history (to make up for content not being taught later) and now teach government in the last term of 7th and 8th grades which we did not teach at all as a separate entity in the past. And we have structured in key points in the language arts scope and sequence.

> It depends on who the teacher is and what the teacher teaches. You can't have a bigger impact than on sequence or inserting a new course. We now offer courses not included before and content that changed from 10th to the 9th grades. With government, the impact is overwhelming.

As illustrated in the preceding quote, there was a "differentiated" impact of implementing the tests. Some parts of the system were affected little, while others felt considerable ramifications. Such a situation caused statistical measures of central tendency, such as the mean scores just presented, to disguise this important impact of the tests.

The "discomfort" of subgroups of staff involved with the two controversial tests focused their attention more and more on the percentage of students passing the tests and on adopting expedient methods of improving scores. This "concentrated" approach was apparent in all five systems where Phase Three interviews were conducted.

Reading teacher:
"We are concentrating more on basics. We are now spending from September to November on basic skills rather than on our developmental program."

Teacher:
"I'm not opposed to the idea of testing. But I'm not so sure we haven't gone overboard; the tail is wagging the dog. The original idea was that there were to be certain standards the *student* would have to meet, but if the student doesn't pass, people will ask what's wrong within the school and teachers."

Central office administrator:
"When the scores are low, it takes me into the school for the names of the kids who failed. There is no stroking in schools where scores have dropped. Everyone is sitting around with bated breath waiting for the test scores."

Building administrator:
"We realize a kid is taken out of science every other day for citizenship and will fail science to maybe pass the citizenship test."

These very targeted means for getting students to pass were acknowledged as a necessary evil:

Central office administrator:
"We've had to do things we didn't want to do."

Teacher:
"We have materials provided by the county as 'quick help.' We were told 'here's how to get kids to pass the test fast.' They were good ideas but specifically on the test. For example, if the area in a rectangle is shaded, you multiply; if not, you add."

And in response to the preceding stream of comments, a teacher summarized, "Talk about games and game-playing!"

It is important to note that the stakes were raised in the two states for two different reasons: (1) public pressure to improve test scores that resulted from readily available comparisons of performance in Pennsylvania, and (2) the proximity of both the yearly test administration day and the day when the two troublesome tests would actually serve as an obstacle to graduation in Maryland. Interestingly, the stakes increased in what were originally both low- and high-stakes situations. As they did so, educators' concern shifted almost completely to influencing test performance. Put differently, the manifestations of the seriousness with which the test was taken shifted. The change can best be described as one from a long-term focus to a short-term one, from using the tests as one indicator among many to treating the next set of test results as the most important outcome of schooling.

CONCLUSION

Under either the low- or high-stakes condition, teachers perceived that the statewide testing programs offered relatively few benefits for students, particularly in terms of providing additional information that schools did not already possess to determine which students could be better served. There seemed to be little justification in educators' minds for adding another test to the set of existing instruments being administered at the local level simply to identify several more students in need of special instruction.

However, in high-stakes situations, great attention was paid to this admittedly uninforming information. An important question is "Was this increased attention to test scores for the better?" The qualitative data from Phase Three of the study suggested that as the perception of the importance of the test increased, there was a point at which district responses took on the flavor of a single-minded devotion to specific, almost "gamelike" ways to increase the test scores. Pennsylvania districts, in particular, that began to take tests more seriously reported that they did so for political reasons, not because they believed that they were actually improving the lives of students or teachers. Before this point, the strategies emphasized more systematic changes in the curriculum. Beyond this point, staff began to respond to questions about effects with the phrase "Some good things have happened as a result of the tests, *but* . . ." Staff members' reservations about the practices they were engaging in to improve the scores followed the "but." When the stakes but not the quality of the information contained in the tests changed, so did local attention to improving scores. But a turning point was reached, and the modest positive effects associated with having additional diagnostic information available was overwhelmed by perversion of local practice, with the primary goal becoming to improve test scores. Many of the negative behaviors associated with "teaching to the test" thus emerged. The exact turning point likely varied from district to district; but it was clear that the test scores were beginning to govern activity more directly, as Mintzberg (1983) predicted could be the case when an organizational outcome increases in importance.

Concomitant with increased attention to improving test results was greater disruption to teachers' work lives. Although teachers acknowledged that a narrowed curriculum could also be an improved one (Wilson and Corbett, in press), few indicated in interviews that their actual teaching had improved. On the contrary, they reported that they occasionally strayed from sound instructional practices in order to get students to pass. They also reported that, under high-stakes conditions, there was a decreased reliance on their professional judgment in instructional matters, increased time demands, more staff reassignments, greater pressure, more paperwork, and heightened concern about liability.

If a statewide testing program engenders little additional benefit for students and greater disruption for teachers without improving practice, then it would seem the program has little educational value. So why the popularity? Statewide tests are primarily a political device; they are easily legislated and—when results are reported in the form of passing grades— easily interpreted. These results can be effective rallying points to mobilize pressure on almost any school or system to "improve," depending on what level of success is deemed appropriate by a particular community. Thus, the presence of publicly available and understood results affords the opportunity for greater state and local community involvement in determining what goes on in the schools.

It is interesting that both state policymakers and community members define improvement as greater standardization across schools and as achievable within a yearly testing cycle. The press for more uniformity and quick success, however, contradicts everything that is known about the process of improving schools. School improvement succeeds when the idiosyncracies of school demographics, culture, and organization are taken into account in a process that incorporates generous dollops of technical assistance and staff interaction within a three- to five-year time span. It takes considerable time to plan what to improve, to try out means of attaining that goal, to assess which means are effective, and to take steps to ensure that the effective means become part of the operational routine. The testing cycle, on the other hand, forces the compression of this process into a single year and increases reliance on the lifeline of a common set of testing objectives (regardless of the student population) to avoid drowning in a sea of public criticism. The only available escape is to focus directly on those objectives, a strategy that definitely can raise test results in the short term but accomplishes little systematic improvement in the long term.

REFERENCES

Airasian, P. W. (1987). State mandated testing and educational reform: Context and consequences. *American Journal of Education*, *95*(3), 393–412.

Carnegie Foundation for the Advancement of Teaching. (1988). *Report card on school reform: The teachers speak*. Princeton, NJ: Carnegie Foundation for the Advancement of Teaching.

Corbett, H. D., & B. L. Wilson. (1988). Raising the stakes on statewide mandatory testing programs. In R. Crowson & J. Hannaway, eds., The *politics of reforming school administration*. Philadelphia: Falmer Press.

Darling-Hammond, L., & A. Wise. (1985). Beyond standardization: State standards and school improvement. *Elementary School Journal*, 85(3), 315–336.

Deal, T. E. (1985). The symbolism of effective schools. *Elementary School Journal*, 85(3), 600–620.

Gordon, D. (1984). *The myths of school self-renewal*. New York: Teachers College Press.

Lortie, D. (1975). *Schoolteacher: A sociological study*. Chicago: University of Chicago Press.

Madaus, G. F. (1988). The influence of testing on the curriculum. In L. Tanner, ed., *Critical issues in curriculum: 87th yearbook of the NSSE, Part I*. Chicago: University of Chicago Press.

Marshall, J. C. (1987). *State initiatives in minimum competency testing for students*. Policy Issue Series No. 3. Bloomington, IN: Consortium on Educational Policy Studies.

Miles, M. B., & A. M. Huberman. (1984) *Qualitative data analysis: A sourcebook for new methods*. Beverly Hills, CA: Sage.

Mintzberg, H. (1983). *Structure in fives: Designing effective organizations*. Englewood Cliffs, NJ: Prentice-Hall.

Rosenholtz, S. J. (1987). Education reform strategies: Will they increase teacher commitment? *American Journal of Education*, 95(4), 534–562.

Rossman, G. B., H. D. Corbett, & W. A. Firestone. (1988). *Change and effectiveness: A cultural perspective*. Albany, NY: SUNY Press.

Sarason, S. B. (1971). *The culture of the school and the problem of change*. Boston: Allyn & Bacon.

Schlechty, P. C. (1976). *Teaching and social behavior*. Boston: Allyn & Bacon.

Stake, R. E., J. Bettridge, D. Metzer, & D. Switzer. (1987). *Review of literature on effects of achievement testing*. Champaign, IL: Center for Instructional Research and Curriculum Evaluation.

Wilson, E. K. (1971). *Sociology: Rules, roles, and relationships*. Homewood, IL: Dorsey.

Wilson, B. L, & H. D. Corbett. (In press). Two state minimum competency testing programs and their effects on curriculum and instruction. In R. E. Stake, ed., *Advances in program evaluation: Effects of changes in assessment policy, vol. 1*. Greenwich, CT: JAI Press.

CHAPTER 11

Changes in Course Selection by High School Students: The Impact of National Educational Reform

Ted Bartell and Julie Noble

Publication of *A Nation at Risk* in April 1983 focused national attention on the academic preparation of U.S. secondary students. Since then, at least thirty-nine states have passed legislation increasing high school graduation requirements, and at least sixteen states have either proposed or adopted increased college entrance requirements.

Little research has been done on how curricular reform has changed the course-taking patterns of various population subgroups. Although the U.S. Department of Education's Center for Statistics plans to collect high school transcript data in 1991, people need to know earlier than that what the overall impact of the reform movement on student course selection has been.

In analyzing data from High School and Beyond (a database held by the

Department of Education), Rock, Ekstrom, Goertz, and Pollack (1985) noted that schools with predominantly low-SES (socioeconomic status) students typically offered fewer advanced academic courses in mathematics, natural science, and foreign language than schools with high-SES students and, in fact, also required their college preparatory students to take fewer academic courses. Blacks and other minority students were nearly four times as likely to attend low-SES schools as were white students. Similarly, a study of the academic preparation of college-bound student athletes (Bartell, Keesling, LeBlanc, & Tombaugh, 1984) found substantial differences in high school course-taking patterns between black and white students.

The purpose of this study was to examine recent changes in course-taking patterns within a large national population of high school students. In addition to overall changes in course taking, trends were evaluated in the context of several sociodemographic variables (size of high school graduating class, gender, community size, family income, and race and/or ethnicity) and changes in state policies regarding the number of units required for high school graduation. The latter variable was categorized to reflect three levels of change during the period 1980–1984: (1) an increase of more than two units required for high school graduation, (2) an increase of two units or less, and (3) no change or decrease in units required.

The data used for this study were taken from the ACT Assessment files for the high school graduating classes of 1978, 1982, and 1988. These years were selected for two reasons: (1) to establish baseline trends prior to 1983, when The National Committee on Excellence in Education issued *A Nation at Risk*, and (2) to examine the impact of curricular reform up to and including 1988. Seniors graduating in 1988 would have enrolled as ninth-graders in 1984, and thus represent the first postreform student cohort to enter and complete high school.

The ACT Assessment Program is a comprehensive evaluative, guidance, and placement service used by over one million college-bound students each year. The Student Profile section of the ACT Assessment requests information on the background characteristics, self-reported grades in the high school core curriculum, out-of-class accomplishments, and college plans of these students. Students are also asked about the number of years of coursework they have taken (or plan to take) in high school English, mathematics, social studies, natural science, and foreign languages, and whether they received advanced placement in these subject areas. The large samples for each year allow subclass comparisons within a single year, as well as trend analyses across years within individual subclasses.

DATA FOR THE STUDY

For the years 1978, 1982, and 1988, the data files consisted of 10 percent samples of the ACT-tested national graduating class for each year ($N = 73,876$, $N = 79,171$, and $N = 83,984$, respectively). The files were formed so that, for example, the 1978 graduating class included juniors from 1976–77 and seniors from 1977–78. For all the files, only the most recent data record was retained for students testing more than once.

The dependent variables were the number of years of courses taken in English, mathematics, social studies, natural science, and foreign languages; the total number of years of core academic courses; and the total number of areas of advanced placement. The independent variables were state policy change, size of graduating class, gender, community size, family income, and race and/or ethnicity.

The overall composition of the tested population remained relatively stable during the entire period from 1978 to 1988 (see Table 11-1), thus minimizing the likelihood that compositional changes could explain any aggregate shifts in course selection observed across years. Therefore, findings for the 1978, 1982, and 1988 files are directly compared in the remainder of this chapter.

It should be noted that the samples for this study included only ACT-tested, college-bound students. Although the ACT Assessment is the predominant college admissions test employed in twenty-eight states, the students in the samples are not representative of all high school students or all college-bound students.

In order to make the files as comparable as possible, and to maximize sample sizes for minorities, two sets of transformations were performed:

- The family income ranges established by ACT had been adjusted each year to reflect societal income trends; therefore, the income ranges for 1978, 1982, and 1988 were not directly comparable. As a result, frequency distributions were used to determine cutoff points for low, middle, and high incomes so as to retain similar proportions of students in the three groups. The resulting percentage distribution was approximately 20 percent low, 25 percent middle, and 55 percent high for each year.
- The racial and ethnic group item included categories from American-Indian/Alaskan Native, Puerto Rican/Cuban/Other Hispanic, and Other. Due to the relatively small sizes of the first two groups, they were combined with the Other category.

Table 11-1

Percentages of Students Having Specific Background Characteristics by Year of Graduation

Background Characteristic	Year of Graduation		
	1978	1982	1988
Size of graduating class less than 200	39%	41%	43%
Community size less than 10,000	41	43	42
Family income less than $12,000	19	21	12
Female	55	55	54
Black	8	8	9
White	83	85	83
Mexican-American	2	2	2
Asian-American	1	1	2
Other minority	6	4	4

METHOD

For the examination of percentage differences in course taking, cutoffs were established for the years of courses taken in each subject area, the total years of core academic courses, and the total number of areas of advanced placement. Where possible, these cutoff points were based on the numbers of years recommended in *A Nation at Risk*: four or more years of English, and three or more years of mathematics, social studies, and natural science. A cutoff of two or more years was used for foreign language (all languages combined), and thirteen or more years for total years of core courses. These dichotomized variables were analyzed for each year by all the independent variables and for the total group of students; the numbers and percentages of students falling above and below each cutoff were computed.

The multiple-regression analyses consisted of full model equations using all the sociodemographic characteristics to explain the years of courses taken in each subject area, the total years of core courses taken, and the total number of areas of advanced placement. For race and ethnicity, effect coding was used in place of the original values. When effect coding is used, each value of race and ethnicity is converted to a separate variable, except for the last value. Within each new variable (such as White), the value of 1 is given if the student fits the variable, 0 (zero) if the student fits any other value except the last (for example, Black, Mexican-American/Chicano, or Asian-American), and −1 if the student was in the final group (that is, Other). This

Table 11-2

Percentages of Students Taking Specific Numbers of Years of Core Courses, by Year of Graduation, and Percent Change by Period

Core Courses	Year of Graduation			Percent Change	
	1978	1982	1988	1978–1982	1982–1988
4 or more years English	77%	78%	89%	1%	11%
3 or more years mathematics	64	71	86	7	15
3 or more years social studies	65	64	77	−1	13
3 or more years natural science	45	47	63	2	16
2 or more years foreign language	44	42	62	−2	20
13 or more years academic courses	43	47	68	4	21
One or more areas of advanced placement	43	47	50	4	3

type of coding allows for direct comparison of resultant coefficients of one racial and ethnic group with all other groups. Standard dummy variable coding (1, 0) allows direct comparisons of the coefficients of each racial and ethnic group with the final group.

RESULTS

Table 11-2 reports the changes in course taking for all dependent variables using the total group. The percentages of students meeting the cutoffs for the numbers of years of courses taken are reported for the years 1978, 1982, and 1988. In addition, the changes in these percentages from 1978 to 1982, and from 1982 to 1988 are reported.

As the results show, there was a substantial increase in the number of students meeting the specified cutoffs between 1978 and 1988. This increase, however, was not consistent across subject areas. For example, students' course taking in mathematics increased by 7 percent between 1978 and 1982, and by 15 percent between 1982 and 1988. For the other subject areas, however, minimal gains, or even decreases in percentages occurred from 1978 to 1982; course taking in social studies and foreign languages declined by 1 and 2 percent, respectively. The decline for foreign languages was reversed dramatically during the 1982–1988 period, with an additional 20 percent of the students reporting two more years in 1988 than in 1982. For English and natural sciences, the trends indicated relatively small increases between 1978 and 1982 in percentages of students taking a high number of

Table 11-3

Percentage of Students Taking Three or More Years of Mathematics or Natural Science, by Gender and Year of Graduation, and Percent Change by Period

Subject Area	Gender	Year of Graduation			Percent Change	
		1978	1982	1988	1978–1982	1982–1988
Mathematics	Female	57%	66%	84%	9%	18%
	Male	73	77	87	4	10
Natural science	Female	39	42	61	3	19
	Male	53	53	67	0	14

courses, followed by increased percentages between 1982 and 1988 equivalent to those found for mathematics. The thirteen percentage-point increase in social studies course taking between 1982–1988 reversed the 1 percent decline noted earlier for the period 1978 to 1982.

Changes in course taking were then examined with regard to the sociodemographic characteristics of the students tested. The intent was to examine differential course taking over time based on these characteristics. The results of the analysis indicated that changes in course taking did vary on the basis of student characteristics, though contingent on the dependent variable under consideration. The background characteristics most consistently related to changes in course taking were (1) gender and (2) race or ethnicity.

From 1978 to 1982 the number of women taking three or more years of mathematics and natural science increased by 9 percent and 3 percent, respectively, whereas men increased by 4 percent and 0 percent for the same time period (see Table 11-3). This differential gain continued into the 1982–1988 period, with women increasing by 18 and 19 percent, and men by 10 and 14 percent. By 1988, the percentage of women taking three or more years of mathematics was almost equivalent to that of men (84 percent versus 87 percent).

With regard to race and ethnicity, the percentage increases for Black and Mexican-American students taking mathematics and natural science courses were relatively large, when compared to Whites, Asian-Americans, and other minorities, as shown in Table 11-4. The percentage of Black students taking three or more years of mathematics increased by 10 percent between 1978 and 1982, and by 18 percent between 1982 and 1988, compared to 6 and 14 percent for Whites. Although large percentage differences in mathematics

Table 11-4

Percentage of Students Taking Three or More Years of Mathematics or Natural Science, by Race and Ethnicity and Year of Graduation, and Percent Change by Period

Subject Area	Race and Ethnicity	Year of Graduation			Percent Change	
		1978	1982	1988	1978–1982	1982–1988
Mathematics	Black	55%	65%	83%	10%	18%
	White	66	72	86	6	14
	Mexican-American	56	64	87	8	23
	Asian-American	73	86	91	13	5
	Other minority	57	68	82	11	14
Natural science	Black	31	33	55	2	22
	White	48	49	65	1	16
	Mexican-American	32	33	53	1	20
	Asian-American	54	66	74	12	8
	Other minority	38	42	59	4	17

course taking existed between Blacks and Whites in 1978, by 1988 almost the same proportions of Blacks and Whites (83 versus 86 percent) had taken three or more years of mathematics. For natural science, the percentage of Black students increased by 2 percent between 1978 and 1982, and by 22 percent between 1982 and 1988, compared to 1 percent and 16 percent for Whites. The increases between 1982 and 1988 in mathematics and natural science course taking for Mexican-Americans exceeded those of Whites (23 versus 14 percent; 20 versus 16 percent). These students also evidenced a relatively large increase in English courses taken during this period (12 percent increase), as shown in Table 11-5.

The results showed that the gains in mathematics during the 1982–1988 period may have been somewhat greater for students from lower-income families, and those from smaller high schools and communities. As shown in Table 11-6, mathematics course taking increased by 18 percent between 1982 and 1988 among students from lower-income families (compared to 12 percent among students from higher-income families).[1] Differential gains were not observed in English, social studies, and natural science.

The final stage of the analysis consisted of establishing linear multiple-regression equations for each year, using all the sociodemographic variables to explain students' course taking. The independent variables were entered into the equation simultaneously. Comparisons of the standardized regression coefficients across years provided an indication of the extent to which

Table 11-5

Percentage of Students Taking Four or More Years of English, by Race and Ethnicity and Year of Graduation, and Percent Change by Period

Race and Ethnicity	Year of Graduation			Percent Change	
	1978	1982	1988	1978– 1982	1982– 1988
Black	76%	77%	85%	1%	8%
White	78	78	89	0	11
Mexican-American	73	77	89	4	12
Asian-American	76	79	89	3	10
Other minority	72	74	85	2	11

Table 11-6

Percentage of Students Taking Three or More Years of Mathematics, by Family Income and Year of Graduation, and Percent Change by Period

Family Income	Year of Graduation			Percent Change	
	1978	1982	1988	1978– 1982	1982– 1988
Low	54	62	80	8	18
Medium	61	69	82	8	13
High	70	76	88	6	12

any observed relationship persisted over time when all other variables were controlled. For these analyses, the state policy variable was also used so as to allow assessment of the direct influence, if any, of changed high school graduation requirements on course selection.

Table 11-7 shows the results of the regression analysis for mathematics and natural science course taking. The R^2 values obtained for these subject areas were quite small, accounting for 3 to 7 percent of the variability in course taking. A positive relationship was shown between mathematics and natural science course taking and size of graduating class, community size (mathematics only), family income, and gender for each of the three years. Note, however, the decline in magnitude of the coefficients for family income and gender from 1982 to 1988 in mathematics. This decline was also found in the gender coefficients for natural science. These findings reflect the larger relative gains since 1982 in both mathematics and natural science course

Table 11-7

Standardized Regression Coefficients, by Year of Graduation for Years of Mathematics and Natural Science Course Taking by Sociodemographic Characteristics and State Policy

Predictors	Mathematics			Natural Science		
	1978	1982	1988	1978	1982	1988
State policy	.00	−.01	.00	−.01	−.02	−.01
Size of graduating class	.03	.05	.04	.00	.00	.01
Community size	.07	.07	.06	−.01	.00	.02
Family income	.11	.12	.09	.10	.11	.10
Gender	.19	.14	.08	.14	.12	.07
Black	−.02	−.03	−.04	−.06	−.07	−.06
White	.03	−.01	.00	.06	.02	.03
Mexican-American	−.02	−.04	−.02	−.03	−.04	−.03
Asian-American	.05	.07	.07	.06	.08	.07
R^2	.07	.06	.03	.05	.04	.03

taking for female students, and in mathematics for students with lower family incomes.

Likewise, the negative regression coefficients for Mexican-American students moderated slightly from 1982 to 1988, indicating a slight reduction in their disadvantage relative to all other racial and ethnic groups. The negative coefficients for Black students moderated slightly in natural science but declined in mathematics, relative to other groups. In contrast, Asian-American students increased their taking of mathematics and natural science courses relative to other racial and ethnic groups between 1978 and 1988.[2] These findings were supported by the changes in percentages of students enrolled in high numbers of courses mentioned earlier; the percentage differences between Blacks, Mexican-Americans, and Whites were substantially reduced in these subject areas between 1978 and 1988. Of particular importance, the overall variance (R^2) explained by this entire set of variables related to social class declined during the decade between 1978 and 1988, indicating a lessening of class-related differences over this ten-year period.

The slight moderation in negative coefficients for the state policy variable in both the mathematics and natural science regression equations suggests that states with the lowest levels of course taking in 1982 gained most during the period 1982 to 1988. This is in fact the case, as shown in Tables 11-8 and 11-9. On average, it was the states with the lower levels of mathematics, science, and foreign language course taking in 1982 that increased their graduation requirements and, in turn, benefited from relatively larger gains in these subject areas.

Table 11-8

Percentage of Students Taking Three or More Years of Mathematics or Natural Science, by Change in Units Required for Graduation, and Percent Change by Period

Subject Area	Change in Units required	Year of Graduation			Percent Change	
		1978	1982	1988	1978– 1982	1982– 1988
Mathematics	No change or decrease	64%	72%	84%	8%	12%
	Increase of 2 units or less	64	71	87	7	16
	Increase of more than 2 units	65	70	86	5	16
Natural science	No change or decrease	47	49	63	2	14
	Increase of 2 units or less	46	47	64	1	17
	Increase of more than 2 units	43	45	63	2	18

Table 11-9

Percentage of Students Taking Two or More Years of Foreign Language by Change in Units Required for Graduation, and Percent Change by Period

Change in Units Required	Year of Graduation			Percent Change	
	1978	1982	1988	1978– 1982	1982– 1988
No change or decrease	47%	46%	61%	−1%	15%
Increase of 2 units or less	48	45	68	−3	23
Increase of more than 2 units	36	33	56	−3	23

DISCUSSION

The shifts in course taking described in this chapter parallel the recommendations of the Excellence Commission and the types of reform initiatives that were occurring in many parts of the country around 1983. The sheer magnitude of the change in course selection is quite remarkable, particularly given the small increases (and even declines) experienced in most academic subject areas during the four years immediately preceding 1983.

The contrasts presented between states that enacted increased graduation requirements between 1980–1984, versus states that did not, lend additional credence to the interpretation that the changes in course taking observed since 1982 have in fact been produced by specific reform efforts in individual states.

No evidence was found in these data for partial or lagged implementation of educational reform among disadvantaged groups. In fact, the opposite appeared to be the case. Among college-bound students, those responding to curricular reforms were more often the very groups that previously had lower levels of exposure to core academic courses: women, students for lower-income families, and minorities. Although no direct evidence shows that these findings extend to the universe of all high school students (rather than just the college bound), there is also no reason to believe they do not.

NOTES

We wish to thank Merine Farmer, Scott Van Fossen, and Jeff Zear for their substantial assistance in preparing the data files and implementing the analysis procedures used in this chapter.

1. A corresponding relationship was observed between changes in mathematics course taking between 1982–1988 and size of community, with students from smaller towns and cities reporting roughly 1½ times the amount of increased mathematics course taking as those from large metropolitan areas.

2. No consistent patterns emerged from the regression analysis of years of English and social studies taken, perhaps owing to the smaller aggregate change evidenced by students in these subject areas between 1978 and 1988. The regression equations for years of foreign language indicated positive relationships (and increased coefficients over time) for size of graduating class, community size, family income, and female gender. The same relationships were evident for the regression of number of advanced placement courses on the set of independent variables.

REFERENCES

Bartell, T., J. W. Keesling, L. A. LeBlanc, & R. Tombaugh, (1984). *Study of freshman eligibility standards: Technical report.* Reston, VA: Advanced Technology.

Rock, D. A., R. B. Ekstrom, M. E. Goertz, & J. M. Pollack. (1985). *Determinants of achievement gain in high school.* Princeton, NJ: Educational Testing Service.

CHAPTER 12

The Reform of School Administration: Pressures and Calls for Change

Joseph Murphy

I am thoroughly and completely convinced that, unless a radical reform movement gets underway—and is successful—most of us in this room will live to see the end of educational administration as a profession. (Griffiths, 1988, p. 1)

Visions for improving student learning have found life in the policies advocated by governors and adopted by state legislatures, but these same leaders share my conviction that any reform strategy failing to recognize the need for new, sustained leadership in the schools will not endure. (Clinton, 1987, p. 3)

Although decision makers at all levels of government were slow to turn their attention to the reform of school administration (National Governors' Association, 1987; Nunnery, 1982; Peterson & Finn, 1985), it was inconceivable that issues of leadership and management could long be ignored as the educational reform movement of the 1980s continued to gather speed and momentum. Problems in programs for the preparation of aspiring administrators and for the training of those already employed were simply too obvious to be overlooked. Questions about the proper role of management in a reformed educational system were too crucial to be left on the back burner. Issues of leadership and vision were becoming too enmeshed in the larger management environment in which schools operate to pass over administrators of schools. A deep, if not widely practiced, self-examination of the gains made in the practice of educational administration since the adoption of the social science paradigm was too thoroughly underway and too critical of our progress to allow school administration to continue unaltered on its current course. And lurking behind all the pressures for change was the growing belief that a reform movement that did not address issues of management and leadership was unlikely to have a lasting impact.

In this chapter, we examine the reform of school management in the 1980s. Because reform initiatives in administration have lagged behind changes in other areas—curriculum, testing, teacher preparation—we know less about the effects of these efforts than we would like. However, we can thoroughly document the forces that have led to demands for improvements in the preparation and functioning of principals and superintendents, and we can chart how states have begun to respond to these pressures. The first part of the chapter provides this documentation. The pressures considered in this section can be viewed as contextual or macro-level influences on the reform of school administration. Next we turn to an analysis of micro-level pressures. The latter are endemic to the process of recruiting, preparing, and placing principals and superintendents. The discussion in this section is drawn from two sources—(1) critical analyses of educational administration and (2) reform reports of diverse types. The next chapter examines state-initiated responses to calls for the reform of school management. We cull information from secondary sources and look directly at activity in one state, Illinois. We also review some issues concerning the topic of school administration reform that deserve further attention.

PRESSURES FOR REFORMING SCHOOL ADMINISTRATION: MACRO-LEVEL ISSUES[1]

In a later section, we discuss difficulties with preparation programs in educational administration. Here we are more concerned with the larger environment surrounding school management and how it has contributed to demands for improvements in the profession. We review six of the influences in the following sections.

Re-emergence of the School Administrator as a Key to School and District Improvement

> In study after study, it has been shown that one key determinant of excellence in public schooling is the leadership of the individual school principal. (Education Commission of the States, 1983, p. 29)

For much of the last quarter-century, a general belief in the professional impotence of administrators has prevailed. The picture of the school superintendent or principal as the beleaguered professional who can exercise little influence over his or her organization, and who is only distally connected to important educational processes and outcomes, has been widely accepted in educational administration circles. The development of this mind-set coincided with a number of events that threw education in general into a tailspin (Campbell, 1981). In addition, the frameworks and models used to describe educational administrators within organizations, especially open systems and political decision-making models, have contributed to the emerging characterization of school administrators as little more than caretakers.

Three conditions are currently unfolding, however, that show principals and superintendents can exert considerable influence over their schools and districts. First, there is a growing understanding that the very real conditions in schools captured by open systems and political decision-making theories render the administrator's job difficult, but not impossible. A general feeling of resignation is being replaced by analyses of ways in which administrators can work more effectively within the reality of schools as complex organizations.

In addition, the dark cloud that has hung over education in general in the recent past is gradually dispersing. Education is once again at the forefront of the public agenda. Increases are being observed in highly visible measures of school outcomes, such as SAT scores. There has been a leveling off and even a small turnabout in the decline of public confidence in schools. The devastating effects caused by declining student enrollments have largely played out in most places. Schools have a stronger sense of direction and a more unified purpose than they have had for some time. In a similar vein, some of the unrealistic expectations with which schools have been saddled have been somewhat tempered. There is a growing sense of confidence in the technology of schools, a belief that we are better able to implement factors that will result in student learning outcomes. Anguish over the breakup of the educational coalition has been replaced with the knowledge that pluralistic bargaining actually works fairly well in the service of education's broader goals. And finally, the upheaval caused by the onslaught of collective bargaining has receded somewhat as the catastrophic predictions of widespread teacher-administator hostility and rampant loss of administrator influence have failed to materialize.

An array of information is also emerging that shows more directly that school administrators are generally a key factor in change and improvement in schools and districts. Support for this position is derived from five related literature sources: school change; school improvement; staff development; administrator as instructional leader; and school effectiveness and district effectiveness (see Murphy, 1989, for a review). Common to all this literature is a sense of the power of the administrator to be a significant force for improving organizational conditions and processes and student outcomes.

An Emerging Belief That New Models of School Organization, Governance, and Management Are Needed

> Efforts to improve the performance of schools without changing the way they are organized or the controls they respond to will therefore probably meet with no more than modest success; they are even more likely to be undone. (Chubb, 1988, p. 29)

The incompatibility of the traditional bureaucratic model of organization and governance of schools with the type of educational systems many scholars believe will be needed in the future is a central tenet of recent reform reports (Boyer, 1983; Carnegie Forum on Education and the Economy, 1986; Carnegie Foundation for the Advancement of Teaching, 1988; Green, 1987; Holmes Group, 1986; Sedlak, Wheeler, Pullin, & Cusick, 1986; see also Frymier, 1987). Reformers have turned their attention to the development of models of school organizations that offer more potential for school improvement than do bureaucracies. Most of these newer perspectives share common characteristics. One of these is decentralization of authority to the site level (Goodlad, 1984; National Commission on Excellence in Educational Administration [NCEEA], 1987; National Governors' Association, 1986). Recent attention in the literature to such topics as site-based management and shared governance (see Caldwell & Spinks, 1988; Duttweiler & Hord, 1988) reflects this theme. A second important aspect of these newer models is a restructuring of the roles and functions of teachers and principals (see Carnegie Forum on Education and the Economy, 1986; Clark, 1987). Discussions of team approaches to school management (Glatthorn & Newberg, 1984; Lieberman, 1988), self-managing teams (Hackman, 1986; Manz & Sims, 1987), and lead teachers (Carnegie Forum on Education and the Economy, 1986; Goodlad, 1984) address this issue. New views about appropriate bases of administrative authority comprise a third component of organizational models being developed to shed the yoke of bureaucratic constraints (Angus, 1988; Kearns, 1988). In these emerging perspectives, administrators rely less on formal authority and control mechanisms and more on expertise (American Association of Colleges for Teacher Education [AACTE], 1988). They manage as stewards rather than as autocrats. They empower professionals rather than control employees. Buttressing these new views of organizational governance, control, and management in schools are descriptions of leadership in successful noneducational settings (Deal & Kennedy, 1982; Peters & Waterman, 1982) and trends toward the evolution of business organizations that encompass decentralization, new forms of leadership, and empowerment (Association for Supervision and Curriculum Development, 1986; Kearns, 1988).

Embedded in these newer forms of organization are views about the role of management that are quite different from those emphasized in many university departments of school administration. Rossmiller (1986, p. 3) reminds us that as these newer principles take hold in schools, there are clear implications for "the way we prepare administrators, [and] the focus we give programs." Not only will new skills need to be emphasized in preparation programs, but considerable attention will need to be devoted to the underlying fabric—the values, beliefs, and assumptions—to which school administrators are exposed (National Commission on Excellence in Educational Administration, 1987).

The Growing Realization That Administrators Are Often Inept Managers of Technical Core Operations

> The technical tasks associated with producing student learning are not supervised, managed, or coordinated in any serious sense across managerial levels in school districts. (Hannaway & Sproull, 1978–79, p. 4)

Campbell (1981, p. 7) has noted that "the sub-areas of curriculum and instruction have particular significance for educational administration since administration is, after all, designed to enhance teaching and learning." However, most training programs provide little exposure to these crucial areas. Miklos (1983), Boyan (1981), and Culbertson (1981) describe how, over the last quarter-century, preparation programs have come to be dominated by the social sciences. Khleif (1979) presents a particularly cogent example of how one elite training program for superintendents socializes prospective administrators away from educational issues and concerns for students and toward management and organizational issues. Sergiovanni and his colleagues (1987) and Marshall and Greenfield (1987) show how these socialization pressures actually *de*-skill principals in curricular and instructional areas. Although some scholars (such as Erickson, 1977) have suggested refocusing theory on issues of curriculum and instruction in administrative preparation programs, their calls have generally gone unheeded. After analyzing the content of superintendent-training programs, Champagne and his colleagues (1984) reached the following conclusions:

> Our investigation indicates that the training of our most powerful educational leaders, our superintendents, is directed mainly to concerns other than those of the learning of students. In fact, a great many superintendent training programs appear to exclude *any* in-depth study of curriculum, instruction or supervision. (p. 14)

> Thus we are saying that principals do not study any of these areas in any depth either. (p. 16)

Gerritz, Koppich, and Guthrie (1984) concluded that a major problem with university training programs, according to California school administrators, is their failure to provide skills in the technical areas of observation and evaluation of classroom behavior. Sarthory (1974), Snyder and Johnson (1985), and Peterson and Finn (1985) reached similar conclusions.

Research at every level of educational management consistently uncovers administrators who believe they should devote more time to instructional issues (Casey, 1980; McLeary & Thompson, 1979; Willower & Fraser, 1980). Yet the instructional management role is one that most administrators perform neither well nor often. Studies at the district office level have determined that superintendents neither spend much time on curricular and instructional matters at the central office nor coordinate and monitor these areas at the school level (Duignan, 1980; Hannaway & Sproull, 1978–79; Willower & Fraser, 1980). Investigations of the principalship at both the secondary (Blank, 1986; Blumberg & Greenfield, 1980; California State Department of Education, 1984; Little & Bird, 1984; Martin & Willower, 1981; Willis, 1980) and elementary (Howell, 1981; Morris, Crowson, Porter-Gehrie, & Hurwitz, 1984; Peterson, 1977–1978) levels also find that instructionally informed administrators are a rare commodity. As I have reported elsewhere,

> Taken together, these studies present a picture of administrators whose time is heavily devoted to matters other than curriculum and instruction, to issues of student discipline, parent relations, plant operations and school finance. Most principals do not formally supervise and evaluate teachers, plan and coordinate curriculum, actively monitor the technology of the school or the progress of students, or spend much time in classrooms. In short, most principals do not act as instructional leaders. Rather, in most districts and schools, curriculum and instruction are managed by default. (Murphy, 1989)

This judgment is not surprising given the lack of consideration accorded to technical core issues in formal administrative training programs and inservice activities (Aplin & Daresh, 1984; Champagne et al., 1984; Daresh & LaPlant, 1984; Gousha, Jones, & LoPresti, 1986; Kowalski, 1986; Pellicer, 1982). Absence of instructional leadership is often attributed to the multiple demands and time pressures inherent in administrative roles. Although this factor clearly contributes, an even more powerful explanation is administrators' lack of knowledge about how to manage technical core operations. As our understanding of the correlation between active instructional management and student learning has grown (see Murphy, 1989, for a review), so has pressure to change training content to provide superintendents and principals with the technical skills needed to successfully manage curriculum and instruction in their districts and schools.

Growing Disenchantment with the Theory Movement

> Some might say it [the behavioral science theory engine] was yanked off front and center stage because it did not yield descriptions, explanations, and predictions that were judged sufficiently useful to warrant its continuance as the driving force in the study of educational administration. (Carver, 1988, p. 1)

One major force contributing to calls for reform in educational administration is an increasing disillusionment with the theory movement and the social science frameworks that have shaped preparation programs over the last thirty years (Boyan, 1981; Campbell, 1981; Cooper & Boyd, 1987; Crowson & McPherson, 1987). Elsewhere we have observed that

> Trying to adequately grasp the role of the school principal with reference solely to normative theories and models is like turning on one's high beams to see more clearly in the fog; the area of illumination is increased, yet clarity of vision is reduced. (Murphy, 1986, p. 126)

Culbertson (1981, p. 41) made the same point when he observed that the "mission, stance, and approaches of the theory movement have offered insufficient guides for the study of educational administration."

Although it is beyond the scope of this chapter to develop all the critiques that have been leveled against the theory movement, and although it is important to remember that behavioral science theory has made important contributions to educational administration (Willower, 1987), we will discuss three problems identified by these analyses that are contributing heavily to the demands for the reform of school administration. All three concern the practical applications of the theory movement. First of all, Campbell (1981, p. 13) has declared that "educational phenomena have served the disciplines instead öf the disciplines being brought to bear upon educational problems." Translating theory into strategies to improve schools is difficult enough when serious attempts to do so are undertaken. In the absence of such efforts, theory is likely to be of little use to school personnel.

Second, there is an inherent assumption in the theory movement that scholars adept at developing models and frameworks are also skilled in translating them into practice and that universities can effectively develop bridges between research and practice. Mann (1975) and Campbell (1981) have both commented on the inaccuracy of this assumption. As a consequence, theory has often remained untranslated and has provided little guidance to administrators in the day-to-day operation of schools (Goldhammer, 1983; Griffiths, 1988).

Third, the theory perspective has failed to adhere to its own core ideas and subsequently has become, to some extent, a movement conducted more for its own sake than for improving schools. Culbertson (1981) identifies the four core characteristics of the theory movement as (1) research originating from and guided by theory; (2) reliance on social and behavioral science concepts and methods of investigation; (3) almost exclusive reliance on hypothetico-deductive systems; and (4) an emphasis on description of practice rather than prescriptions for administrative behavior. It is our position that the theory movement has become tarnished because it is perceived to have only marginal practical value to school personnel. However, unlike some, we do not believe that this is due primarily to emphasis on theory or reliance on the social sciences. Rather, the general disillusionment with the usefulness of the theory movement stems from overemphasis on the hypothetico-deductive approach and the concomitant failure to stress inductive approaches and to use qualitative lenses to examine organizational phenomena. As a result, the "upward seepage of empirical juice" (Culbertson, 1981, p. 34) that was expected to refine theory to the conditions of the workplace has failed to materialize. In time, the theory movement has begun to look less and less descriptive and more and more normative (see Morris et al., 1984). The theory movement's failure to adhere to its own philosophical underpinning of "reality checking" has caused it to be viewed by many practitioners as worse than useless. This perceived lack of usefulness and inability to accurately describe organizational conditions have contributed to the demands for the reform of school administration, especially of preparation programs.

Increasing Disgruntlement with the Prevailing University Training Model

The attempt by professional educators to develop a pseudo arts and science degree has been met with scorn in most universities. (Griffiths, 1988, p. 18)

Evidence suggest[s] that the training-and-certification sequence leaves something to be desired. Survey after survey of practicing school administrators reveals that most judge their university training to have been easy, boring, and only intermittently useful to them in their work. (Peterson & Finn, 1985, p. 49)

It is not surprising that a model of training that promulgates ideas often judged to be impractical and unconnected to the realities of the workplace, that neglects to provide guidance in managing technical core operations, and that often fosters the perception of professional impotence should be subject to demands for reform. Daresh and LaPlant (1984, p. 5) reviewed the university training model for adherence to the principles of quality staff development and found numerous deficiencies. In their judgment,

University courses are excellent ways for participants to earn degrees, satisfy scholarly curiosity, or meet state certification requirements, but as long-term solutions to the need for more effective administrator inservice, they are limited.

In addition, both Mann (1975) and Bridges (1977) have written provocative essays in which they describe how the processes and procedures stressed in university programs are often diametrically opposed to conditions that characterize the workplace milieu of schools (see Peterson & Finn, 1985, for a review). For example, as Bridges (1977) has observed, while within the school context a premium is placed on verbal skills, the ability to make quick decisions, and activeness, we train our administration students to be passive, to use rational decision-making models, and to develop their written skills to the near exclusion of oral ones. Practitioners have become disillusioned by the failure of university programs to ground training procedures in the realities of the workplace and by their reluctance to treat content viewed as useful by administrators. This disenchantment, in turn, is partially fueling the demand for changes in methods of preparing school administrators (Nunnery, 1982).

Growing Perception of Little Improvement in Administrative Practice

> The organizational changes in schools that had been generated by the old paradigm had extremely disappointing results. (Reynolds, 1988, p. 7)

There is an emerging belief that, for a number of reasons, including those just noted, all the labors of the past thirty years have produced few real improvements in administrative practice and school organization. After his review of the research on school administration between 1967 and 1980, Bridges (1982, p. 25) reported that

> The research seemed to have little or no practical utility. In short, there is no compelling evidence to suggest that a major theoretical issue or practical problem relating to school administrators has been resolved by those toiling in the intellectual vineyards since 1967.

Blumberg (1984, p. 27) in his essay on school administration as a craft, goes even further:

> My bets are that one cannot point to a single administrative practice that has been influenced in any significant degree by research on the behavior of administrators.

Although these critiques might be viewed as disenchantment with the theory movement or with university training programs, we note them separately because they reflect a more global dissatisfaction with the status quo in educational administration. They not only reflect the new era of turmoil (Griffiths, 1979), but also feed demands for the reform of educational administration in general, and of administrative training programs in particular.

CALLS FOR REFORM: PROBLEMS WITH THE PREPARATION OF SCHOOL ADMINISTRATORS

There is then, pressure either to get rid of administrators as we now know them, or to take people untarnished by departments of educational administration. While this is the rumbling, the criticisms of present-day administrators and their preparation are loud and clear and the demand for reform is heard on all sides. While some of the criticism is overstated, and certainly all does not apply to everyone, I find the central thrust to be accurate, and, in fact, to coincide with what so many in the profession have been saying in private for years. (Griffiths, 1988, p. 8)

Calls for the reform of school administration are based primarily on analyses of problems with the ways principals and superintendents are recruited into preparation programs, trained once they are there, and certified and selected for positions once they complete coursework. There is a widespread belief that preparation programs lack coherence, rigor, and standards and that administrators are ill prepared to effectively assume their duties once they leave these programs. Reformers in the 1980s tend to approach administrators from one of the following two distinct perspectives (Slater, 1988). One group (for example, see Chubb, 1988) tends to see principals and superintendents as "the problem" and therefore as a target of reform, and proposes reform strategies to neutralize or eliminate their influence (for example, see Holmes Group, 1986). A second group maintains that educational administrators are an important cog in the reform machine and that lasting educational improvement is unlikely to occur without their commitment, assistance, and leadership (National Commission on Excellence in Educational Administration [NCEEA], 1987; National Governors' Association, 1986).

In the rest of this section, we analyze the messages conveyed by both groups, and thereby develop a fairly comprehensive picture of the problems in school administration. In compiling this review, we relied on a cross section of influential reform reports and studies as well as reviews and critiques from the general literature. We attempted to extend the information presented in the thoughtful analyses that have already been undertaken in this area (for example, see Gerritz, Koppich, & Guthrie, 1984; Griffiths, 1988; Murphy & Hallinger, 1987; Peterson & Finn, 1985; Pitner, 1982).

Recruitment and Selection

The lack of sound recruitment programs may be the most serious problem of all. (American Association of Colleges for Teacher Education [AACTE], 1988, p. 12)

We are aggressively non-selective. It is as if we felt that all teachers have an inalienable right to study to become administrators, akin to our support of a free, open, public elementary and secondary school. (Clark, 1988, p. 3)

Analysts of the recruitment and selection processes used by educational administration programs have generally found them to be wanting (Gerritz, Koppich, & Guthrie, 1984). Procedures are often informal, haphazard, and casual (Clark, 1988; Goodlad, 1984). Prospective administrators are often self-selected, and there are few leader recruitment programs (Achilles, 1984; AACTE, 1988; NCEAA, 1987). Standards for admission are often conspicuous by their absence (Gerritz, Koppich, & Guthrie, 1984), and, not surprisingly, the quality of applicants is quite low (Rossmiller, 1986). For example, Griffiths (1988, p. 12) reported that "of the 94 intended majors listed in [the] *Guide to the Use of the Graduate Record Examination Program 1985–86* . . . educational administration is fourth from the bottom"; only students entering the fields of physical education, social work, and home economics scored lower. Many prospective administrators not only are of low ability, but also tend to be politically conservative and adverse to taking risks (Achilles, 1984). Finally, ample evidence shows that the current procedures have not produced the quantity of minority administrators needed to lead our racially diverse schools (Griffiths, 1988; NCEEA, 1987).

Calls for reform in the area of recruitment usually begin with recommendations that standards for admission be raised (Educational Commission of the States, 1983). The institutionalization of district programs, sometimes in cooperation with universities, to identify employees with leadership potential and to provide incentives for them to enter preparation programs has also been suggested (AACTE, 1988; Goodlad, 1984; NCEEA, 1987). It has also been proposed that programs be established specifically for recruiting minorities and women (NCEEA, 1987). In conjunction with this equity objective, some reform reports have called for the creation of fellowship programs to be funded by the federal government (NCEEA, 1987). Other reports have drawn attention to the need to establish fellowships for the general pool of potential recruits to preparation programs.

Training Content

> Moreover, the knowledge and skills needed to become an effective educational leader and school manager are generally not those provided by current Administrative Service Credential Programs. (Gerritz, Koppich, & Guthrie, 1984, p. 1)

> In fact, they [Gross and Herriott] found a negative correlation between number of courses taken in Educational Administration and their indicators of success. (Erlandson, 1979, p. 151)

A number of significant problems afflict the knowledge base undergirding programs in educational administration. To begin with, most programs do not provide job candidates with a good general education. Within these programs, "course content is frequently banal and outdated" (Clark, 1988,

p. 5). There is a profound lack of agreement about what the content of preparation programs should be (Griffiths, 1988) and a pervasive unwillingness to act as if such information were useful (Goldhammer, 1983). "Preparation programs are essentially diverse collections of formal courses that, taken together, do not reveal consistent purposes or a systematic design" (National Association of Secondary School Principals [NASSP], 1985, p. 2; see also Achilles, 1984; Peterson & Finn, 1985). There is a general absence of a "continuum of knowledge and skills that become more sophisticated as one progresses" (Peterson & Finn, 1985, pp. 51, 52; see also Pitner, 1982).

One of the most serious problems with the knowledge base in educational administration preparation programs is that it does not reflect the realities of the workplace (March, 1978; Murphy & Hallinger, 1987; NASSP, 1985; Nunnery, 1982; Pitner, 1982). The problem, as Griffiths (1988, p. 19) correctly concluded, is that the theory and research that we have borrowed from the social sciences have "never evolved into a unique knowledge base informing the practice of school administration" (see also Culbertson, 1981; Goldhammer, 1983). Better methods are needed to get at what Carver (1988, p. 1) labeled the central issue in the study of educational administration—"our ability to understand practice." Most initial efforts in this direction are moving us toward developing a professional and clinical knowledge base similar to that emphasized in other professions, such as law and medicine (see especially the work of Silver, 1986, 1987). In order to more fully develop a professional knowledge base for educational administration, we must shift focus from deductive to inductive research strategies and devote increased attention to grounded theories and ecologically valid research (AACTE, 1988; Murphy & Hallinger, 1987). The development of much needed collaborative relationships between schools and universities may be a potential by-product of using a professional knowledge base in preparation programs (Griffiths, 1988).

In addition to reflecting more appropriately the world of practice, the new content of training programs must address a number of other important problems. To begin with, despite some very well-reasoned pleas (see especially Erickson, 1979), remarkably little content in preparation programs is based on administrator effects on organizational outcomes. Boyd and Immegart (cited in Boyan, 1981, p. 11) elegantly laid out the solution path for this problem when they reported that "The task before us, then, is to redirect research and practice in educational administration toward a primary (but obviously not exclusive) concern for student outcomes."

As already reported, most administrative programs do not provide prospective administrators with the foundation that they need in the areas of curriculum and instruction. Yet it is clear that technological acumen often distinguishes more effective from less effective principals and superintendents (see Murphy, 1989; Murphy & Hallinger, 1986)—"leadership in high-performance schools is more pedagogical and less managerial than in low-performance ones" (Chubb, 1988, p. 33). In order to offset this deficiency in the current knowledge base, the new package of content in preparation programs must be more student oriented and should be more focused on issues of curriculum and instruction. A more logical and appropriate knowledge base will also need to be based more on the principles of effective change and school improvement. A number of authors have pointed out that newly minted administrators are poorly prepared to successfully promote change in their organizations, "especially at the level of practical decisions" (Fullan & Newton, 1986, p. 11; see also Greenfield, Marshall, & Reed, 1986; Hall & Rutherford, 1983).

Although important problems may accompany an overemphasis on skill-based instruction, the pervasive antirecipe philosophy that characterizes many programs of educational administration has resulted in significant gaps in the prevailing knowledge base (Murphy & Hallinger, 1987), an almost complete absence of performance-based program components (NASSP, 1985), and a truncated conception of expertise (see Kennedy, 1987). Administrators consistently report that the best way to improve training in preparation programs is to improve instruction of job-related skills (Erlandson & Witters-Churchill, 1988; Notar, 1988–89; Weindling & Earley, 1987). Griffiths (1988, p. 17; see also Erlandson, 1979) has chronicled the costs that accompany this knowledge gap in our training programs and our consistent unwillingness to address the problem:

> Probably more school administrators fail because of poor skills than any other single reason, yet program and faculty in educational administration fail to do anything about it. It's as though a baseball team in spring training gave the player books to read and lectures on the theory of baseball and did not have the player practice hitting and fielding. Administrators have to perform, and in order to perform well they must have the basic skills of administration.

The solution consists of greater attention to developing practical skills (in a variety of different formats) in administrative preparation programs (Gerritz, Koppich, & Guthrie, 1984; Weindling & Earley, 1987).

Finally, it is clear that the newer paradigms of school organization and governance reviewed earlier—site-based management, shared governance, self-managing teams—hold implications for the knowledge base in educational administration programs (AACTE, 1988). As the NCEEA (1987, p. 5) has concluded, school-based models of governance lead to "awesome and exciting differences . . . in the responsibilities of school administrators and in the skills they would need." Analyses of these new responsibilities and skills must be made and the information gained thereby should be integrated into program content.

The Delivery System

> The program should be conceived in the framework of the professional school model, not the arts and science model, meaning that the program should prepare students to act, not merely think about administration. Clinical training should be stressed, without neglecting the intellectual aspects of preparation. (Griffiths, 1988, p. 14)

The current arts and science model used to train administrators has neither furnished professors with the status for which they had hoped (Griffiths, 1988) nor provided graduates with the tools they need in order to be successful practitioners (Peterson & Finn, 1985). In addition, it has driven a wedge between professors and practitioners, creating what Goldhammer (1983, p. 265) has labeled the "university-field gap." For these reasons, it has become clear to many professors and administrators that a fundamental change is required in the basic delivery system employed in preparation programs. A consensus seems to be emerging about the need for a professional model of preparation—a program that is clearly separate from the Ph.D. training sequence and that focuses on the problems of practice and on the clinical aspects of the administrator's role (AACTE, 1988; NCEEA, 1987).

Not only has the basic delivery system been subject to severe criticism, but considerable problems have also been uncovered with the training processes employed within preparation programs. Specifically, methods of delivery are incongruent with the conditions administrators face on the job. Thus, both program content *and* the procedures used to convey it are decoupled from the realities of the workplace. In our earlier review of the works of Mann (1975) and Bridges (1977), we reviewed some of the most startling discrepancies between the methods employed in the training of administrators and those that they need to use on the job. It is clear that fundamental changes in the delivery model will need to be accompanied by significant shifts in delivery procedures if the worlds of the university classroom and the school are to be bridged effectively.

A professionally-based delivery system offers hope of addressing another problem with current preparation programs—the lack of shared responsibilities between universities and schools (Griffiths, 1988). In a particularly insightful essay, Carver (1988, p. 6) pointed out that "the absence of any meaningful coupling between the training arm and the employing agents" is the point in the fabric of educational administration where the threads are the weakest. Delivery procedures are much needed to help create bridging mechanisms and allow the various partners to do what each does best. The work of the National Association of Secondary School Principals (1985) in the area of performance-based preparation is particularly instructive on this point.

Finally, it is important that the format of any delivery system reflect commitment on the part of the students and provide them with richer opportunities to become socialized to their chosen profession than is now the case. Current programs have drifted far afield from the traditional residency model; as many as 95 percent of all students are now part-timers (Griffiths, 1988), and "many students complete their training . . . without forming a professional relationship with a professor or student colleague" (Clark, 1988, p. 5). There is a need for a delivery system in which students go through their program as a cohort and which makes "administrator preparation full-time academic and clinical work" (Griffiths, 1988, p. 21).

Instructional Approaches

Overall quality of teaching in educational administration training programs should be improved. A good deal of what occurs in these programs is labeled as teaching solely because it involves an instructor and students. Little of it is of quality. (Murphy & Hallinger, 1987, p. 256)

It is probably not surprising, although it is disheartening, that inappropriate content ineffectively packaged should also be poorly delivered in many preparation programs. Next to the general absence of effective teaching techniques, the most serious problem is the lack of variety of approaches used to provide instruction (AACTE, 1988; Nunnery, 1982). For example, in the Texas NASSP study (Erlandson & Witters-Churchill, 1988), principals reported "lecture and discussion" to be the primary instructional mode used for eight of nine skill areas examined—and it was a close second for the ninth skill, written communication! In communicating the appropriate knowledge base, greater emphasis should be placed on reality-oriented instructional situations and materials (AACTE, 1988; Hoyle, 1987; Miklos, 1983), recent technological advances (Griffiths, 1988), models of instruction employed in other professional schools (NASSP, 1985), and experiential learning methods (Weindling & Earley, 1987). In addition, preparation programs need to ground instructional approaches more heavily on the principles of adult learning (AACTE, 1988; Levine, Barth, & Haskins, 1987; Pitner, 1987).

The clinical aspects of most preparation programs in educational administration are notoriously weak. Despite an entrenched belief that supervised practice "could be the most critical phase of the administrator's preparation" (Griffiths, 1988, p. 17) and a long history of efforts to make field-based learning an integral part of preparation programs (see Daresh, 1987, for a review), little progress has been made in this area. The field-based component continues to be plagued by problems: (1) inadequate attention to clinical experiences; (2) activities arranged on the basis of convenience; (3)

poor planning, supervision, and follow-up; (4) absence of integration between classroom and field-based experiences; and (5) overemphasis on low-level (orientation-type) activities (Clark, 1988; Erlandson, 1979; Peterson & Finn, 1985).

Clinical experiences (AACTE, 1988; Clark, 1988; Daresh, 1987; Erlandson, 1979; Hughes, 1987; NASSP, 1985) need to

1. Become a more important component of each student's program
2. Be well-planned and carefully supervised
3. Begin early and be spread across the entire preparation program
4. Be based on a series of planned experiences rather than designed to fit. around the student's job
5. Involve significantly more contact with and observation of practicing administrators
6. Be more fully integrated with other graduate coursework
7. Be arranged in a "continuing interactive two-way process of action learning" (Hughes, 1987, p. 138)
8. Allow students to work together in learning teams
9. Rely much more heavily on practicing school administrators in the planning, implementation, and evaluation phases.

Standards of Performance

Most schools of education are embarrassed by the academic performance of the doctoral students in educational administration. The model grade given to students is an "A"; not because we have criterion referenced performance standards that all could ultimately meet but because we have given up on holding tired, end-of-the-day students to graduate level performance. (Clark, 1988, p. 4)

The lack of rigorous standards is a serious problem that touches almost every aspect of educational administration. Previously, we noted the general absence of standards at the point of entry into preparation programs—"if entrance requirements exist at all, they are not very competitive and most applicants are accepted" (Peterson & Finn, 1985, p. 51; see also Gerritz, Koppich, & Guthrie, 1984). Once students enter preparation programs, the situation does not improve. They are not exposed to rigorous coursework: "Students move through the program without ever seeing a current research study (other than a local dissertation), without ever having read an article in *ASQ* or *EAQ* or *AJS* (*Administrative Science Quarterly*, *Educational Administration Quarterly*, and *American Journal of Sociology*, respectively). They are functionally illiterate in the basic knowledge of our field" (Clark, 1988, pp. 4–5; see also AACTE, 1988). Because performance criteria are ill defined, there is also very little monitoring of student progress (Hawley, 1988). Not surprisingly, very few entrants to certification programs fail to complete their programs for academic reasons (Gerritz, Koppich, & Guthrie, 1984). The delivery system most commonly employed—part-time study in the evening or on weekends—contributes to the evolution and acceptance of low standards (Clark, 1988; Hawley, 1988; Mann, 1975). Exit requirements in turn are often "slack and unrelated to the work of the profession" (Peterson & Finn, 1985, p. 54). Compounding the lack of standards at almost every phase of preparation programs are university faculty who, because they are only marginally more knowledgeable than the administration students, are unable or unwilling to improve the situation (Hawley, 1988; McCarthy, 1987). An even greater obstacle to improving standards are the bargains, compromises, and treaties that operate in preparation programs—the exchange of standards for high enrollments and compliant student behavior:

> The solution is often to conclude a treaty of mutual non-aggression with one's students. The terms of the treaty are usually that the professor won't plague the students with "irrelevant" ideas if the students will keep quiet about that professorial non-performance. The glue on the agreement is high grades based on low or no performance, which is traded for silence. (Mann, 1975, p. 144; see also Cusick, 1983; Oakes, 1985, Page, 1984; Powell, Farrar, & Cohen, 1985; Sedlak et al., 1986; and Sizer, 1984 for descriptions of these compromises between teachers and students at the elementary and secondary levels.)

Peterson and Finn (1985) have concluded that the time has come to markedly elevate standards in school administration. Throughout this part of the review, we discuss potential avenues for raising standards and in the next chapter analyze specific actions states have taken along these lines.

Certification

> But whether few or many, these requirements are nearly always stated in terms of paper credentials supplied by colleges of education—transcripts and credit hours that must parallel those on a list maintained by the certification bureau or the state education department. License-seekers rarely have to pass any sort of test or examination analogous to a bar exam or to medicine's "national boards," nor does the education profession enforce any substantial standards for those seeking administrative certification. (Peterson & Finn, 1985, p. 144)

Suggestions for the reform of educational administration extend beyond preparation programs to address problems with the certification and employment of principals and superintendents. The major criticisms of certification and accreditation processes are that they are unduly costly and cumbersome

(Goodlad, 1984); focus on requirements and skills different from those that administrators need to be successful on the job (Clinton, 1987); reduce the pool of potential leaders to applicants who have worked in public schools (Bennett, 1986); operate at only one period of time, such as at the completion of preparation programs (NCEEA, 1987); and, in total, do not promote excellence in the profession (NCEEA, 1987).

Advocates for reform have proposed a number of solutions for these problems. Perhaps the most controversial are those that establish alternative routes to certification, thus allowing prospective administrators to maneuver around educational administration programs altogether. Such proposals are designed "to encourage service in the public schools by qualified persons from business, industry, the scientific and technical communities and institutions of higher learning" (Education Commission of the States, 1983, p. 39; see also Clinton, 1987; Bennett, 1986). Other proposals call for bringing greater coherence to the licensing process by eliminating the piecemeal methods by which certification can be gained (Peterson & Finn, 1985) and by establishing a tighter coupling between certification requirements and the skills prospective administrators need in order to be effective (National Governors' Association, 1986). A few influential reports have suggested the use of multiple levels of licensure. For example, the National Governors' Association (Clinton, 1987) and the NCEEA (1987) both have called for provisional or entry-level certification of new administrators to be followed by full certification after the documentation of successful performance. Coupled with these suggestions are proposals for recertification every few years "on the basis of successful performance and continuing professional development" (NCEEA, 1987, p. 27). At least one report has been farsighted enough to draw the connection between licensure and successful performance on a posttraining examination (Gerritz, Koppich, & Guthrie, 1984).

Employment

> How a principal gets a job is strikingly quixotic. Most principals are judged by a set of local and custom-bound criteria that may be as cloudy as anything existing in the contemporary job market. (Boyer, 1983, p. 221)

> In particular these individual experiences illuminate a central finding about common practices in principal selection: the process itself *cannot* be characterized as merit-based or equity-centered. (Baltzell & Dentler, 1983, p. 19)

The first major problem in the area of employment deals with the processes used to select new administrators. Although "remarkably little is known about just how these critical educational leaders are chosen" (Baltzell

& Dentler, 1983, p. 1), tentative evidence suggests that selection procedures are quixotic (Boyer, 1983), random (Achilles, 1984), and chance-ridden (Baltzell & Dentler, 1983). There is little evidence that educational leadership is either demanded of or sought in candidates. In general, there is a lack of criterial specificity that

> opens the way for widespread reliance on localistic notions of "fit" or "image" which emerged as centrally important. . . . However, time and time again, this "fit" seemed to rest on interpersonal perceptions of a candidate's physical presence, projection of a certain self-confidence and assertiveness, and embodiment of community values and methods of operation. (Baltzell & Dentler, 1983, p. 7)

The most clearly developed proposal for reform in this area has been articulated by Baltzell and Dentler (1983, pp. 42–44). They suggest, among other things, the use of more highly focused selection criteria with better linkage to merit standards, a layered screening process, greater reliance on data and less on interpersonal judgments, and more direct attention to equity issues. On this last matter of equity, Clark (1988, p. 8) has examined the role that departments of educational administration have played in the selection process and has found that they "are part of the problem, not the solution, in increasing the placement of women and minority groups in positions of educational leadership." He suggests renewed attention to equity issues in colleges of education. Finally, relevant reform reports consistently recommend that selection criteria be more heavily weighted in favor of educational leadership skills (Clinton, 1987).

A second important employment topic that has been targeted for reform is the changing nature of authority in schools. Criticisms of the status quo in this area come from two separate but related sources—discussions of the supposed failure of bureaucratic school structures (Frymier, 1987; Holmes Group, 1986; Sedlak et al., 1986; Sizer, 1984) and reanalyses of the proper distribution of influence across levels in professional organizations such as schools (Boyer, 1983; Goodlad, 1984; Kearns, 1988). Both groups of critics generally conclude that there is insufficient authority at the site level for the principal and teachers to effectively manage the school. Calls for change follow one of two avenues. Most reformers see the need for additional authority for principals, especially in the areas of finance and personnel (Adler, 1982; Kearns, 1988). Many proponents of change argue for the devolution of authority to the school as a unit—"a genuine decentralization of authority and responsibility to the local school" (Goodlad, 1984, p. 275)—to the principal plus the teachers and parents (Boyer, 1983; Sizer, 1984; National Governors' Association, 1986).

A final employment problem noted in recent reform reports is the lack of postemployment training opportunities for principals and superintendents. Three facets of the problem have been revealed. To begin with, there is a virtual absence of induction programs for newly appointed administrators (Peterson & Finn, 1985). Neither are experiences in the assistant principalship being deliberately structured to nurture administrators for the principalship (Weindling & Early, 1987); if anything, the experience may be providing dysfunctional training (Greenfield, Marshall, & Reed, 1986). In addition, the pool of continued professional growth opportunities for administrators is limited, and these experiences often accumulate in an unsystematic manner (Daresh & LaPlant, 1984; NCEEA, 1987). Reform proposals have called for increased attention to ongoing professional development for administrators. Mentorships and enhanced peer interactions are often emphasized in these proposals (U.S. Department of Education, 1987). The content foci are both educational and managerial skills, and the preferred delivery structures are networks and centers outside of the control of colleges of education and educational administration faculty (Boyer, 1983; Education Commission of the States, 1983).

NOTE

1. Section based on material from Joseph Murphy and Philip Hallinger, eds., *Approaches to Administrative Training in Education*, pp. 247–253 (Albany: State University of New York Press, 1987), and included by permission of the publisher. © 1987 State University of New York. All rights reserved.

REFERENCES

Achilles, C. M. (1984, Fall). Forecast: Stormy weather ahead in educational administration. *Issues in Education, 2*(2), 127–135.

Adler, M. J. (1982). *The Paideia proposal*. New York: Macmillan.

American Association of Colleges for Teacher Education (AACTE). (1988). *School leadership preparation: A preface for action*. Washington, DC: American Association of Colleges for Teacher Education.

Angus, L. (1988, April). School leadership and educational reform. Paper presented at the annual meeting of the American Educational Research Association, New Orleans.

Aplin, N. O., & J. C. Daresh. (1984, Winter). The superintendent as an educational leader. *Planning and Changing, 15*(4), 209–218.

Association for Supervision and Curriculum Development (ASCD). (1986, September). *School reform policy: A call for reason*. Alexandria, VA: Association for Supervision and Curriculum Development.

Baltzell, D. C., & R. A. Dentler. (1983, January). *Selecting American school principals: A sourcebook for educators.* Washington, DC: U.S. Department of Education/National Institute of Education.

Bennett, W. J. (1986). *First lessons: A report on elementary education in America.* Washington, DC: U.S. Department of Education.

Blank, R. K. (1986, April). Principal leadership in urban high schools: Analysis of variation in leadership characteristics. Paper presented at the annual meeting of the American Educational Research Association, San Francisco.

Blumberg, A. (1984, Fall). The craft of school administration and some other rambling thoughts. *Educational Administration Quarterly, 20*(4), 24–40.

Blumberg, A., & W. Greenfield. (1980). *The effective principal: Perspectives on school leadership.* Boston: Allyn & Bacon.

Boyan, N. J. (1981, February). Follow the leader: Commentary on research in educational administration. *Educational Research, 10*(2), 6–13, 21.

Boyer, E. L. (1983). *High school: A report on secondary education in America.* New York: Harper & Row.

Bridges, E. M. (1977). The nature of leadership. In L. L. Cunningham, W. Hack, & R. O. Nystrand, eds., *Educational administration: The developing decades.* Berkeley: McCutchan.

Bridges, E. M. (1982, Summer). Research on the school administrator: The state of the art, 1967–1980. *Educational Administration Quarterly, 18*(3), 12–33.

Caldwell, B. J., & J. M. Spinks. (1988). *The self-managing school.* New York: Falmer Press.

California State Department of Education. (1984, January). *California high school curriculum study: Paths through high school.* Sacramento: California State Department of Education.

Campbell, R. F. (1981, Winter). The professorship in educational administration: A personal view. *Educational Administration Quarterly, 17*(1), 124.

Carnegie Forum on Education and the Economy. (1986, May). *A nation prepared: Teachers for the 21si century.* Carnegie Forum on Education and the Economy.

Carnegie Foundation for the Advancement of Teaching. (1988). *Report card on school reform: The teachers speak.* Princeton, NJ: Carnegie Foundation for the Advancement of Teaching.

Carver, F. D. (1988, June). The evaluation of the study of educational administration. Paper presented at the Educational Administration Alumni Association (EAAA) Allerton House Conference, University of Illinois at Urbana-Champaign.

Casey, H. (1980). Managerial behavior of principals. Unpublished doctoral dissertation, Stanford University.

Champagne, D. W., J. L. Morgan, M. B. R. Rawlings, & D. Swany. (1984, April). Analysis of the content of training programs for chief school administrators in the areas of instructional methodology, curriculum, and instructional supervision. Paper presented at the annual meeting of the American Educational Research Association, New Orleans.

Chubb, J. E. (1988, Winter). Why the current wave of school reform will fail. *Public Interest* No. 90, pp. 28–49.

Clark, D. L. (1987, August). Thinking about leaders and followers: Restructuring the roles of principals and teachers. Paper presented at a conference on Restructuring Schooling for Quality Education, Trinity University, San Antonio, Texas.

Clark, D. L. (1988). Charge to the study group of the National Policy Board of Educational Administration. Unpublished manuscript, College of Education, University of Virginia.

Clinton, B. (1987, July). *Speaking of leadership*. Denver: Education Commission of the States.

Cooper, B. S., & W. L. Boyd. (1987). The evolution of training for school administrators. In J. Murphy & P. Hallinger, eds., *Approaches to administrative training*. Albany: State University of New York Press.

Crowson, R. L., & R. B. McPherson. (1987). The legacy of the theory movement: Learning from the new tradition. In J. Murphy & P. Hallinger, eds., *Approaches to administrative training*. Albany: State University of New York Press.

Culbertson, J. A. (1981, Winter). Antecedents of the theory movement. *Educational Administration Quarterly, 17*(1), 25–47.

Cusick, P. (1983). *The egalitarian ideal and the American high school*. New York: Longman.

Daresh, J. C. (1987, February). The practicum in preparing educational administrators: A status report. Paper presented at the annual meeting of the Eastern Educational Research Association, Boston.

Daresh, J. C., & J. C. LaPlant. (1984, April). Inservice for school administrators: A status report. Paper presented at the annual meeting of the American Educational Research Association, New Orleans.

Deal, T. E., & A. A. Kennedy. (1982). *Corporate cultures*. Reading, MA: Addison-Wesley.

Duignan, P. (1980, July). Administrative behavior of school superintendents: A descriptive study. *Journal of Educational Administration, 18*(1), 5–26.

Duttweiler, P., & S. Hord. (1988). *Dimensions of effective leadership*. Austin, TX: Southwest Educational Development Laboratory.

Education Commission of the States. (1983). *Action for excellence*. Denver: Education Commission of the States.

Erickson, D. A. (1977). An overdue paradigm shift in educational administration, or how can we get that idiot off the freeway? In L. L. Cunningham, W. G. Hack, & R. O. Nystrand, eds., *Educational administration: The developing decades*. Berkeley: McCutchan.

Erickson, D. A. (1979, March). Research on educational administration: The state-of-the-art. *Educational Researcher, 8*, 9–14.

Erlandson, D. A. (1979, Fall). Language, experience, and administrator preparation. *Planning and Changing, 10*(3), 150–156.

Erlandson, D. A., & L. Witters-Churchill. (1988, March). The Texas NASSP study. Paper presented at the annual meeting of the National Association of Secondary School Principals.

Frymier, J. (1987, September). Bureaucracy and the neutering of teachers. *Phi Delta Kappan, 69*(1), 9–14.

Fullan, M., & E. Newton. (1986, April). Principals as leaders of instructional change in large high schools: The perspective of external researchers. Paper presented at the annual meeting of the American Educational Research Association, San Francisco.

Gerritz, W., J. Koppich, & J. Guthrie. (1984, November). *Preparing California school leaders: An analysis of supply, demand, and training.* Berkeley: Policy Analysis for California Education, University of California.

Glatthorn, A. A., & N. A. Newberg. (1984, February). A team approach to instructional leadership. *Educational Leadership, 41*(5), 60–63.

Goldhammer, K. (1983, Summer). Evolution in the profession. *Educational Administration Quarterly, 19*(3), 249–272.

Goodlad, J. I. (1984). *A place called school: Prospects for the future.* New York: McGraw-Hill.

Gousha, R. P., A. H. Jones, & P. L. LoPresti. (1986, March). Where are we and where are we going in school administration preparation in the United States? Paper presented at the annual meeting of the American Educational Research Association, San Francisco.

Green, J. (1987). *The next wave: A synopsis of recent education reform reports.* Denver: Education Commission of the States.

Greenfield, W. B., C. Marshall, & D. B. Reed. (1986, Winter). Experience in the vice-principalship: Preparation for leading schools? *Journal of Educational Administration, 22*(1), 107–121.

Griffiths, D. E. (1979, Fall). Intellectual turmoil in educational administration. *Educational Administration Quarterly, 15*(3), 43–65.

Griffiths, D. E. (1988). *Educational administration: Reform PDQ or RIP.* Tempe, AZ: University Council for Educational Administration. (Occasional Paper No. 8312).

Hackman, J. R. (1986). The psychology of self-management in organizations. In M. S. Pallak & R. O. Perloff, eds., *Psychology and work: Productivity, change, and employment.* Washington, DC: American Psychological Association.

Hall, G. E., & W. L. Rutherford. (1983, April). Three change facilitator styles: How principals affect improvement efforts. Paper presented at the annual meeting of the American Educational Research Association, Montreal.

Hannaway, J., & L. S. Sproull. (1978–79). Who's running the show? Coordination and control in educational organizations. *Administrator's Notebook, 27*(9), 1–4.

Hawley, W. D. (1988). Universities and improvement of school management. In D. E. Griffiths, R. T. Stout, & P. B. Forsyth, eds., *Leaders for America's schools.* Berkeley: McCutchan.

Holmes Group. (1986, April). *Tomorrow's teachers.* East Lansing, MI: Holmes Group.

Howell, B. (1981, January). Profile of the principalship. *Educational Leadership, 38*(4), 333–336.

Hoyle, J. (1987). The AASA model for preparing school leaders. In J. Murphy & P. Hallinger, eds., *Approaches to administrative training.* Albany: State University of New York Press.

Hughes, M. G. (1987). Trends and issues in educational management development in England and Wales. *Journal of Educational Administration, 25*(1), 126–142.

Kearns, D. L. (1988, 20 April). A business perspective on American schooling. *Education Week, 7*(30), 32, 24.

Kennedy, M. M. (1987). Inexact sciences: Professional education and the development of expertise. In E. Z. Rothkoph, ed., *Review of research in education.* Washington, DC: American Educational Research Association.

Khleif, B. B. (1979). Professionalization of school superintendents: A sociological study of an elite program. In R. Barnhardt, J. Chilcott, & H. Wolcott, eds., *Anthropology and educational administration.* Tucson: Impresora Sahuaro.

Kowalski, T. J. (1986, Fall). Barriers to preparing effective principals. *Illinois School Research and Development, 23*(1), 1–7.

Levine, S. L., R. S. Barth, & K. W. Haskins. (1987). The Harvard principals' center: School leaders as adult learners. In J. Murphy & P. Hallinger, eds., *Approaches to administrative training.* Albany: State University of New York Press.

Lieberman, A. (1988, May). Teachers and principals: Turf, tension, and new tasks. *Phi Delta Kappan, 69*(9), 648–653.

Little, J. W., & T. D. Bird. (1984, April). Is there instructional leadership in high schools? First findings from a study of secondary school administrators and their influence on teachers' professional norms. Paper presented at the annual meeting of the American Educational Research Association, New Orleans.

Mann, D. (1975, May). What pecularities in educational administration make it difficult to profess: An essay. *Journal of Educational Administration, 13*(1), 139–147.

Manz, C. C., & H. P. Sims. (1987, March). Leading workers to lead themselves: The external leadership of self-managing work teams. *Administrative Science Quarterly, 32*(1), 106–128.

March, J. G. (1978, February). American public school administration: A short analysis. *School Review, 86*(2), 217–250.

Marshall, C., & W. Greenfield. (1987, April). The dynamics in the enculturation and the work in the assistant principalship. *Urban Education, 22*(1), 36–52.

Martin, W. J., & D. J. Willower. (1981, Winter). The managerial behavior of high school principals. *Educational Administration Quarterly, 17*(1), 69–90.

McCarthy, M. M. (1987, Winter). The professoriate in educational administration: Current status and challenges ahead. *UCEA Review, 28*(2), 2–6.

McLeary, L. E., & S. D. Thompson. (1979). *The senior high school principalship.* Vol. 3: *Summary report.* Reston, VA: National Association of Secondary School Principals.

Miklos, E. (1983, Summer). Evolution in administrator preparation programs. *Educational Administration Quarterly, 19*(3), 153–177.

Morris, V. C., R. L. Crowson, C. Porter-Gehrie, & E. Hurwitz, Jr. (1984). *Principals in action: The reality of managing schools.* Columbus, OH: Merrill.

Murphy, J. (1986, Winter). Essay review of "Principals in action: The reality of managing schools." *Educational Administration Quarterly, 22*(1), 125–128.

Murphy, J. (1989). Principal instructional leadership. In L. S. Lotto & P. W. Thurston, eds., *Recent advances in educational administration,* vol. 1B. Greenwich, CT: JAI Press.

Murphy, J., & P. Hallinger. (1986, Summer). The superintendent as instructional leader: Findings from effective school districts. *Journal of Educational Administration, 24*(2), 213–236.

Murphy, J., & P. Hallinger, eds. (1987). *Approaches to administrative training.* Albany: State University of New York Press.

National Association of Secondary School Principals (NASSP). (1985). *Performance-*

based preparation of principals: A framework for improvement. Reston, VA: NASSP.

National Commission on Excellence in Educational Administration (NCEEA). (1987). *Leaders for America's schools.* Tempe, AZ: University Council for Educational Administration.

National Governors' Association. (1986). *Time for results: The governors' 1991 report on education, chairman's summary.* Washington, DC: National Governors' Association.

National Governors' Association. (1987). *The governors' 1991 report on education—time for results: 1987.* Washington, DC: National Governors' Association.

Notar, E. E. (1988–89). What do new principals say about their university training and its relationship to their jobs? *National Forum of Applied Educational Research Journal, 1*(2), 14–18.

Nunnery, M. Y. (1982). Reform of K–12 educational administrator preparation: Some basic questions. *Journal of Research and Development in Education, 15*(2), 44–52.

Oakes, J. (1985). *Keeping track: How schools structure inequality.* New Haven, CT: Yale University Press.

Page, R. N. (1984, April). Lower-track classes at a college-preparatory high school: A caricature of educational encounters. Paper presented at the annual meeting of the American Educational Research Association, New Orleans.

Pellicer, L. O. (1982, October). Providing instructional leadership: A principal challenge. *NASSP [National Association of Secondary School Principals] Bulletin, 66*(458), 61–70.

Peters, T. J., & R. H. Waterman. (1982). *In search of excellence.* New York: Harper & Row.

Peterson, K. D. (1977–78). The principal's task. *Administrator's Notebook, 26*(8), 1–4.

Peterson, K. D., & C. E. Finn. (1985, Spring). Principals, superintendents, and the administrator's art. *Public Interest, 79,* 42–62.

Pitner, N. J. (1982, February). Training of the school administrator: State of the art. Occasional paper. Eugene: Center for Educational Policy and Management, Collenge of Education, University of Oregon.

Pitner, N. J. (1987). Principles of quality staff development: Lessons for administrative training. In J. Murphy & P. Hallinger, eds., *Approaches to administrative training.* Albany: State University of New York Press.

Powell, A. G., E. Farrar, & D. K. Cohen. (1985). *The shopping mall high school: Winners and losers in the educational marketplace.* Boston: Houghton Mifflin.

Reynolds, D. (1988, April–June). British school improvement research: The contribution of qualitative studies. *Qualitative Studies in Education, 1*(2), 143–154.

Rossmiller, R. A. (1986, Winter). Some contemporary trends and their implications for the preparation of educational administrators. *UCEA [University Council for Educational Administration] Review, 27*(1), 2–3.

Sarthory, J. A. (1974). Educational renewal: An inclusive process-oriented model of leadership development. In J. A. Sarthory, ed., *Educational leadership, renewal, and planning.* New York: MSS Information Corporation.

Sedlak, M. W., C. W. Wheeler, D. C. Pullin, & P. A. Cusick. (1986). *Selling students short: Classroom bargains and academic reform in the American high school.* New York: Teachers College Press.

Sergiovanni, T., M. Burlingame, F. Combs, & P. W. Thurston. (1987). *Educational governance and administration.* 2nd ed. Englewood Cliffs, NJ: Prentice-Hall.

Silver, P. F. (1986, Summer). Case records: A reflective practice approach to administrator development. *Theory into Practice, 25*(3), 161–167.

Silver, P. F. (1987). In J. Murphy & P. Hallinger, eds., *Approaches to administrative training.* Albany: State University of New York Press.

Sizer, T. R. (1984). *Horace's compromise: The dilemma of the American high school.* Boston: Houghton Mifflin.

Slater, R. (1988, March). How does leadership affect teaching and learning? *School Administrator, 45*(3), 13–15, 20.

Snyder, K. J., & W. L. Johnson. (1985) Retraining principals for productive school management. *Educational Research Quarterly, 9*(3), 19–28.

U.S. Department of Education. (1987) *Principal selection guide.* Washington, DC: U.S. Department of Education.

Weindling, D., & P. Earley. (1987, November). The first years of headship—toward better practice. *Educational Research, 29*(3), 202–212.

Willis, Q. (1980, July). The work activity of school principals: An observational study. *Journal of Educational Administration, 18*(1), 27–54.

Willower, D. J. (1987, Winter). Inquiry into educational administration: The last twenty-five years and the next. *Journal of Educational Administration, 25*(1), 12–28.

Willower, D. J., & H. W. Fraser. (1980). School superintendents on their work. *Administrator's Notebook, 28*(5), 1–4.

CHAPTER 13

School Administration Responds to Pressures for Change

Joseph Murphy

State action on school leadership and management has proceeded more slowly than on teaching—improving the teaching profession continues to dominate the state education reform agenda. However, leadership and management issues are finally receiving, appropriately, attention by state policy makers as new roles for teachers, principals, and superintendents are debated. (National Governors' Association, 1987, p. 14)

Consistent with the larger reform movement (see Boyd, 1987; Coombs, 1987; Kirst, 1984; Guthrie & Kirst, 1988), efforts to make improvements in school administration have emanated primarily from state governments. Because reformers did not turn their attention to issues of leadership and management until quite recently, our understanding of the effects of implemented reform measures is still rather limited. However, some preliminary information is available, and in this chapter we review these findings. We begin by developing a picture of what is known about reform efforts nationwide. We outline the scope and areas of change and, when possible, the effects of those efforts. The second part of the chapter examines administrative reform efforts in one state, Illinois.

ADMINISTRATIVE REFORMS: THE NATIONAL PERSPECTIVE

Although teachers bore the brunt of accountability demands, administrators did not get off scot-free. If students were not achieving enough, teachers must not be teaching well enough, and logically, administrators must not be doing enough either. (Association for Supervision and Curriculum Development [ASCD], 1986, p. 32)

By and large, state reform initiatives to improve school administration have been directed at the certification-selection-employment loop rather than at preparation programs themselves. Neither the recruitment of potential administrators nor the content[1] and delivery of preservice training programs has received much attention to date. There are a number of explanations for this reform pattern. Universities have historically enjoyed a good deal of autonomy from legislative action outside of the budget arena; technical core issues such as program content have been particularly well buffered from environmental influences. Thus, it was easier for policymakers to direct their energies at targets other than preparation programs. Coupled with this historical pattern of legislative restraint was the type of already existing policy tools—from earlier state initiatives on teacher reform and administrative improvements from other stakeholders (for example, the National Association of Secondary School Principals assessment centers)—that state-level reformers could use in their efforts to improve school administration (see ASCD, 1986). In general, these existing tools did not focus on preparation programs. Concomitant with these trends was a demonstrated predilection by state policymakers for accountability mechanisms as the instruments of reform. For all these reasons, the reform of school administration has not focused primarily on preservice training programs.[2]

The remainder of this section is a brief review of action in the areas related to administration where state initiatives have been most prevalent since 1979.

Certification. Eighteen states legislatively amended their certification requirements between 1983 and 1986 (Underwood, 1989). Consistent with the preceding discussion, however, they did not concentrate on delineating more specific competencies (Gousha, Jones, & LoPresti, 1986). Five states mandated testing for certification (Underwood, 1989), and three states increased their classroom teaching experience requirements (Gousha, Jones, & Lo-Presti, 1986).

Selection. Twelve states developed assessment çenters to evaluate the skills of prospective administrators (National Governors' Association, 1987). Data from these evaluations often become a component of the procedures used by districts to select administrators.

Postemployment Training. The topic in the area of school management and leadership that has received the most attention during the current reform movement is continued professional development for principals and superintendents (Education Commission of the States, 1984; National Governors' Association, 1987). Between 1983 and 1986, twenty-four states enacted legislation focusing on postemployment training for school administrators (Underwood, 1989). Most of these legislative acts were designed to establish leadership academies and administrative training centers (ASCD, 1986). Some of these states have also established professional development requirements for recertification.

School-based Management. Twelve states have enacted programs to facilitate the development of site-level management (National Governors' Association, 1987). The key component of all but one of these programs is regulations allowing schools to petition to waive existing laws that interfere with school-level decision making. However, the major aspects of school-based management discussed in the preceding chapter (such as redistribution of control and authority among teachers, parents, and administrators) are not directly addressed in this structural approach to developing models of school-level governance.

Principal Evaluation.[3] Between 1979 and 1987, fifteen states instituted or expanded administrator assessment programs (National Governors' Association, 1987), thus bringing to thirty-one the number of states with mandated principal evaluation systems (Peters & Bagenstos, 1988).

Rewards and Sanctions for Administrators and schools. From 1979 to 1987, twenty-six states initiated programs to provide performance-based rewards and sanctions to principals and schools. Ten states had multiple programs (National Governors' Association, 1987). Although the majority of these programs focused on the provision of incentives for improvement and the recognition of success, some were distinctly punitive; for example, the academic bankruptcy programs in Kentucky and Georgia.

ADMINISTRATIVE REFORM IN ILLINOIS[4]

Like most of the other states, Illinois has been actively involved in the educational reform movement of the 1980s. In 1985 the legislature passed SB 730, which contains 169 discrete items directed at the reform of elementary and secondary education in Illinois. Of these, six substantive pieces deal specifically with school administration: (1) administrative certification and recertification; (2) proficiency examination for initial certification; (3) scholarships for women and members of minorities in administration; (4) administrative internships for women and minority members; (5) redefinition of the principal's role; and (6) the creation of the Illinois Administrators' Academy. This section of the chapter is a detailed examination of these components of the Illinois package reform. However, first let's review what is known about administrators' responses to the 1985 reform initiatives.

Administrator Perceptions of Educational Reform in Illinois

The data here are disheartening for those who believe that administrative support and commitment are required to ensure the successful institutionalization of change initiatives. For a number of reasons, but principally because of the failure of the legislative and executive branches to live up to their pledges to fund the reform package adequately, Illinois administrators have become increasingly disgruntled with the reform movement. In a survey conducted by the Illinois Association of School Administrators (Glass, 1988), over 60 percent of the responding superintendents reported that SB 730 had little or no effect (41 percent) or a negative effect (21 percent) on their districts. Only 6 percent reported that very positive effects had accrued to their districts as a result of the reform package.[5]

As part of a study conducted among the eighteen university departments of educational administration in Illinois (Murphy, 1989b), department chairs were asked to provide their perceptions, based on their work with practitioners, about the effects of SB 730 on principals and superintendents. Specifically, they were asked to furnish their assessments about how school administrators viewed this reform. Analyses of this open-ended question revealed that half of the department chairs cast practitioner views in a negative light, 36 percent provided mixed judgments about administrators' perceptions, and only 14 percent concluded that principals and superintendents considered the reform package to be a positive force. The evidence suggests that administrators in Illinois are, at best, unenthusiastic about the recent reform package.

Administrative Certification and Recertification

One major piece of administrative reform in Illinois concerns a change in emphasis in administrative certification—a focus not found in our national review of the reform of school administration. The following four areas of emphasis were added to certification requirements: (1) "establishing productive parent-school relationships," (2) "establishing a high-quality school climate," (3) "promoting good classroom organization and management," and (4) "providing instructional leadership." Illinois certification requirements, as expressed in experiences to be engaged in during coursework, were then altered (see Tables 13-1, 13-2, and 13-3).

In general, the new requirements for the *general supervisory endorsement* look somewhat different from the old mandates (see Table 13-1). There are no changes in areas of study that comprise approximately 40 percent of the program—A (Curriculum), B (Educational Research), or E (Clinical Experience). Nor are there any changes in the total (minimum) number of hours of study required or the general headings for the areas of study. The new requirements under areas C (Supervision and Staff Development) and D (Schools and Public Policy) are both more specific and more reflective of the reform emphasis than the older guidelines. Specifically, somewhat vague references to "general staff development" and "interpersonal communication" in Area C have been replaced by a call for work that provides knowledge of "instructional leadership" and "program and staff development/evaluation." Here, the new guidelines appear to represent an improvement over the old ones. This is less clear, however, in Area D (Schools and Public Policy). The previous requirements mandated coursework "in the social, psychological, and political context of schools, educational policy analysis and educational thought"—a comprehensive foundation for understanding schools and schooling. The new requirements dictate coursework that develops knowledge in "parent-teacher communication and parent involvement in schools." Although these latter areas of study are quite consistent with the reform act, the change does not represent an improvement. The new areas of emphasis represent a very limited and narrow conception of schools and public policy.

The most significant differences in certification requirements are found in the *general administrative endorsement*. Three changes stand out: (1) Instructional Leadership (Area A) is new, (2) the Instructional Leadership area has been given prominence both in its placement within the various areas of study and in the amount of coursework required, and (3) three semester hours have been shifted from studies in support areas (that is, from Area B, Management of Public Schools) to work in topics related to the technical core (that is, to Area A, Instructional Leadership). Although these revisions are hardly radical in nature, they represent an important change in emphasis

Table 13-1
General Supervisory Endorsement

Pre-1986 Requirements	Post-1986 Requirements
This endorsement is required for supervisors, curriculum directors, and other similar or related positions as indicated in 23 Ill. Adm. Code Part 1 Appendix B.	This endorsement is required for supervisors and other similar or related positions.

Minimum Requirements of Graduate-Level Study:		Minimum Requirements of Graduate-Level Study:	
1. Areas of Study	Semester Hours	1. Areas of Study	Semester Hours
A. *Curriculum*	3	A. *Curriculum*	3
B. *Educational Research*	3	B. *Educational Research*	3
Work in Areas A and B combined must total (8) semester hours		Work in Areas A and B combined must total (8) semester hours	8
C. *Supervision and Staff Development*	8–9	C. *Supervision and Staff Development*	8–9
Must be general in nature, applicable to all educational staff and include interpersonal communication		Must include work that provides knowledge of i. Instructional leadership ii. Program and staff evaluation iii. Program and staff development	
D. *Schools and Public Policy*	8–9	D. *Schools and Public Policy*	8–9
Must include work in the social, psychological and political context of schools, educational policy analysis and educational thought		Must include work that provides knowledge of i. Parent-teacher communication ii. Parent involvement in schools	
E. *Clinical Experience* appropriate to the endorsement or prior experience in a role requiring this endorsement while holding a certificate of comparable validity		E. *Clinical Experience* appropriate to the endorsement or prior experience in a role requiring this endorsement while holding a certificate of comparable validity	
2. Two years of full-time teaching experience or school service personnel experience		2. Two years of full-time teaching experience or school service personnel experience	

Table 13-2
General Administrative Endorsement

Pre-1986 Requirements		Post-1986 Requirements	
This endorsement is required for the following positions: principal, assistant principal, assistant or associate superintendent, and other similar or related positions.		This endorsement is required for the following positions: principal, assistant principal, assistant or associate superintendent, and other similar or related positions.	

Pre-1986		Post-1986	
Minimum Requirements of Graduate-Level Study:		Minimum Requirements of Graduate-Level Study:	
1. Areas of Study	Semester Hours	1. Areas of Study	Semester Hours
A. *Management of Public Schools* Must include work in school law, school finance, school governance, personnel management and interpersonal communication	12	A. *Instructional Leadership* i) Promoting academic achievement ii) Implementing school improvement iii) Long-range planning iv) Program evaluation v) Personnel evaluation	12
B. *Program Development and Operation* Must include curriculum, research, supervision, and staff development.	8–9	B. *Management of Public Schools* Must include work that provides skills in i) Personnel management ii) School governance iii) School law iv) School finance v) Interpersonal communication	9
C. *Schools and Public Policy* Must include work in the social and political context of schools, educational policy analysis, and educational thought	4–6	C. *Schools and Public Policy* Must include work that provides skills in i. Establishing effective school-community communication and involvement ii. Analysis of political and social context of schools	4–6
D. *Clinical Experience* appropriate to the		D. *Clinical Experience* appropriate to the	

(*continued*)

Table 13-2 *(continued)*
General Administrative Endorsement

endorsement or prior experience in a role requiring this endorsement while holding a certificate of comparable validity 2. Two years of full-time teaching experience or school service personnel experience	endorsement or prior experience in a role requiring this endorsement while holding a certificate of comparable validity 2. Two years of full-time teaching experience or school service personnel experience

Table 13-3
Superintendent Endorsement

Pre-1986 Requirements		**Post-1986 Requirements**	
This endorsement is required for superintendents of school districts.		This endorsement is required for superintendents of school districts.	
Minimum Requirements of Graduate-Level Study:		Minimum Requirements of Graduate-Level Study:	
1. Areas of Study	Semester Hours	1. Areas of Study	Semester Hours
A. *Governance of Public Schools* Must include work in intergovernmental relationships in education and school-community relationships	6	A. *Governance of Public Schools* Must include work in intergovernmental relationships in education and school-community relationships	6
B. *Management of Public Schools* Must include work in school business and interpersonal communication in addition to that required for the general administrative endorsement	6	B. *Management of Public Schools* Must include work in school improvement; that is, the modification of curriculum and practice based on research in effective teaching and learning in addition to that required for the general administrative endorsement	6

Table 13-3 (*continued*)
Superintendent Endorsement

C. *Educational Planning*	6	C. *Educational Planning* Must include work in organizational development	6
D. Additional graduate credit	12	D. Additional graduate credit	12
E. *Clinical Experience* appropriate to the endorsement or prior experience in a role requiring this endorsement while holding a certificate of comparable validity		E. *Clinical Experience* appropriate to the endorsement or prior experience in a role requiring this endorsement while holding a certificate of comparable validity	
2. Two years' school supervisory or administrative experience and possession of the general supervisory or general administrative certificate or comparable out-of-state certificate		2. Two years' school supervisory or administrative experience and possession of the general supervisory or general administrative certificate or comparable out-of-state certificate	

and begin to address a deficiency in preparation programs that was reviewed in the preceding chapter—their failure to provide prospective administrators with needed knowledge and skills in the areas of curriculum and instruction (see Murphy, 1989a, for a review). The shift of the one course (3 hours) from management to leadership is significant, representing about a 10 percent change in the total requirement package. Of particular significance in this new emphasis on instructional leadership are the direct references to work that builds skills in "promoting academic achievement," "implementing school improvement," and "personnel evaluation." Also, under Area C (Schools and Public Policy), coursework that provides skills in "establishing effective school-community communication and involvement" has been added, while—unlike requirements for the general supervisory endorsement—the emphasis on the political and social context of schools has not been eliminated.

Revisions in requirements for the *superintendent's endorsement* are more modest than those for the general administrative endorsement. There are, however, two noteworthy changes. Most importantly, Area B (Management of Public Schools) has been redefined. Although the previous focus was on management, the new emphasis is on instructional leadership. Particularly significant are the emphases on "school improvement," "curricular modification," and "effective teaching and learning." In addition, Area C (Educational Planning) has been altered to include "work in organizational development."

Overall, a number of conclusions can be made about these changes in certification requirements. First, on the whole, the revisions are not especially dramatic. Much of what was included in guidelines before the reform package remains unaltered. Additional coursework has not been added. Neither are there many additions to the various areas of study. The critical area of clinical experiences (see preceding chapter) has been left untouched. Second, the changes undertaken generally reflect well the four topics of reform emphasis noted earlier. This is most true for parent-school relations and intructional leadership. Required experiences on the topics of school climate and classroom organization and management are more difficult to locate. Third, the changes provide the structure for graduate schools of education to bring their preparation programs more in line with calls for expanded experiences in the technical core areas of curriculum, instruction, and supervision. For example, while none of the coursework for the superintendent's endorsement dealt with technical core issues before 1986 (see also Champagne, Morgan, Rawlings, & Swany, 1984), fully one-third of it has the potential to do so now.[6]

This first piece of administrative reform also contains provisions to revise the way supervisors, principals, and superintendents are recertified. The legislative intent was to substitute a more rigorous set of recertification requirements "based on a broad portfolio of assessment sources, including input from subordinates, pupil performance, peer review, continued professional education, and examinations" (Illinois School Code, Chapter 122) for automatic certificate renewal (with annual registration). Language dealing with remediation and loss of certification for failure to "successfully demonstrate administrative competence" (Illinois School Code, Chapter 122) is also contained in the legislation. To date, very little action has occurred in the area of recertification. Illinois State Board of Education (ISBE) personnel believe that recertification reform, as defined in the school code, is inappropriate and unworkable. Therefore, they have not devoted their efforts to implementing the law, but have rather been actively engaged in efforts to change the original legislation before the first group of administrators will need to be recertified in June 1991. ISBE personnel are developing a plan that will tie recertification to accumulated hours of professional educational experiences.

Table 13-4
Results on the Examination for Initial Certification in School
Administration

Certification Area	Taken (Number)		Passed			
			(Number)		(Percent)	
	July 1988	October 1988	July 1988	October 1988	July 1988	October 1988
General supervisory	18	19	14	16	78%	84%
General administrative	140	172	135	169	96	98
Superintendents	24	19	24	19	100	100
Total	182	210	173	204	95%	97%

Proficiency Examination for Initial Certification

SB 730 requires students completing administrative preparation pro-grams after June 1988 to pass a proficiency examination before they can receive their certification. The test is composed of two parts, one on basic skills and the other on subject matter specific to school administration. The original test was developed and piloted during the 1986–87 school year. To date, the test has been administered twice, in July and October 1988. Because results on the basic skills component of the test were not disaggre-gated by type of certification sought, information on how examinees seeking administrative certification performed on this part of the test is not available. Results on the subject matter specific section of the test are contained in Table 13-4. Unfortunately, because construction of the school administration test was comingled with the development of other tests for certification, no information on the cost of developing this examination is available. Cost-effectiveness studies (see Levin, 1988) cannot be completed.[7]

Scholarships for Women and Minorities in Administration

One part of the Illinois educational reform package "enacted a plan to encourage women and minorities into school administration" (Underwood, 1989). The central feature of that plan is a scholarship program. Funds are distributed to applicants on a first-come, first-serve basis, although current grantholders have first priority. Once the needs of all students already in the pool have been met each semester, requests from new applicants are consid-ered. Membership in one of the two targeted groups is the only criterion used to determine eligibility. Grants are provided to cover all tuition and fees at any public or private university in the state. Information in Table 13-5 shows how monies have been distributed during the early phases of the program. During each of the first two full years of the program, 1986–87 and 1987–88, approximately 400 awards for $650 each were made to 170 individuals, 40 percent of whom were minorities.

The data clearly show that the scholarship program is channeling funds to women and minorities in administration preparation programs. It is less clear, however, whether the program is sufficient. There are approximately 10,500 school administrators in Illinois. Sixty-five minority recipients of awards represent about one-half of one percent of this total. It is also becoming increasingly apparent that the needs of women and minority members, as they relate to school administration, are different. The number of women in many preparation programs is quite high, approaching or surpassing 50 percent (Gerritz, Koppich, & Guthrie, 1984). The problem for women is not entry to preparation programs, but access to jobs. The number of minority students in departments of educational administration, however, remains woefully inadequate (Griffiths, 1988). In order to make a more concerted effort to increase minority representation among principals and superintendents, it may be appropriate to earmark the entire pool of scholarship funds for them and to devise other approaches to place more women in administrative roles.

There are also nagging questions about the effectiveness of the scholarship program. For example, it is unclear whether the scholarships are fulfilling their goal of attracting women and minorities into school administration, or whether they are simply providing resources to those already enrolled. Because we lack both documentation about additions to the credentials pool and knowledge about postcertification employment trends for scholarship recipients, it is difficult to assess this policy tool. Possibly other strategies might overcome problems inherent in self-selection, expand the pool of minorities in administration programs, do a better job of ensuring employment after credentialing, and be more cost-effective. For example, an argument could be made that state-funded, district-controlled programs to identify and place minority candidates in administrative positions would be more effective than the current scholarship system.

Administrative Internships for Women and Minorities

The ISBE was provided with $5,000 to develop plans for administrative internships for women and minorities during the 1985–86 academic year. No funds to implement the internship program were ever provided.

Table 13-5
Women and Minority Scholarships in Administration

	Winter 1985–86	Summer 1986	Fall, Winter, Summer 1986–87	Fall, Winter, Summer 1987–88
	Number (percent)		Number (percent)	Number (percent)
Number of Awards				
Female	203 (88.6)		371 (90.3)	333 (89.5)
Male	26 (11.4)		40 (9.7)	39 (10.5)
	229 (100.0)	97	411 (100.0)	372 (100.0)
Number of Individuals				
Female	203 (88.6)		163 (90.1)	147 (91.3)
Male	26 (11.4)		18 (9.9)	14 (8.7)
	229 (100.0)		181 (100.0)	161 (100.0)
Total Award Amount	$131,500		$263,000	$252,700
Per award	574		640	679
Minority Awards (Individuals)				
Black	55 (24.0)		55 (30.4)	49 (30.4)
Hispanic	5 (2.2)		4 (2.2)	7 (4.4)
Asian-American	8 (3.5)		6 (3.3)	5 (3.1)
Alaskan Native	0 (0)		1 (0.6)	1 (0.6)
Native American	2 (0.8)		1 (0.5)	1 (0.6)
	70 (30.5)		67 (37.0)	63 (39.1)
Certification Sought				
General supervisory	0 (0)		4 (2.2)	6 (0.4)
General administrative	193 (84.3)		141 (77.9)	132 (76.8)
Chief school business official	1 (0.4)		1 (0.6)	0 (0)
Superintendent	35 (15.3)		35 (19.3)	34 (19.8)
	229 (100.0)		181 (100.0)	172[a](100.0)

[a] Eleven individuals went to more than one college.

Redefinition of the Principal's Role

SB 730 requires local boards of education "to specify in their formal job descriptions for principals that their primary responsibility is the improvement of instruction and that a majority of their time shall be spent on curriculum and staff development" (Illinois State Board of Education, 1986, Item 62). The so-called 51 percent law represented a rather radical change in the definition of the principal's role. Theretofore trained, hired, and promoted on the basis of their management and political acumen (see Murphy, Hallinger, Lotto, & Miller, 1987; Murphy, 1989a), principals were suddenly expected to assume the unaccustomed role of instructional leadership.

Revising job descriptions was relatively easy. Getting boards and superintendents to understand and accept the fundamental nature of this change, and principals to act differently, has proven to be more difficult. The ISBE has undertaken these complex tasks through a series of related initiatives. As we discussed earlier, revisions in certification requirements were designed to underscore the importance of instructional leadership. To date, however, these alterations have led to only modest changes in the content of administrator preparation programs in Illinois (Murphy, 1989b). A second strategy to develop more instructionally informed administrators has been to offer professional development opportunities to principals through the newly constituted Illinois Administrators' Academy. Since the establishment of this training institute was itself a major item in the Illinois educational reform package, it is handled separately, later. A third approach has been the development of programs to increase superintendents' and board members' knowledge of the instructional leadership activities of principals. ISBE has focused its initial energies in this area on training superintendents as leaders of boards. All superintendents in the state are required to participate in a workshop designed to expand their understanding of the dimensions of instructional leadership and to help them evaluate the instructional functions of the principalship. Between its development in 1986 and October 1988, 1,854 superintendents and assistant superintendents participated in this Level One training module. During this same time period, an advanced-level training program entitled "A Research-Based Model for Evaluation of Instructional Leaders" attracted 585 participants. The goals of this advanced workshop were to help districts develop job descriptions for principals based on the instructional leadership functions and establish standards and criteria for assessing these indicators. Two additional training programs in this area are currently being developed. Both are designed for board-administrator teams. The first module will provide instruction on the components of effective schools; the second will prepare administrators and board members to work together more productively.

In a preliminary study of the redefinition of the role of the principalship, Ward and Hildebrand (in press, p. 10) reached the following conclusion:

> The Illinois instructional leadership mandate does not provide enough incentive for school building principals to change their own behavior to comply with the legal mandates of the Illinois General Assembly, even though they have a professed desire to do so. One of the reasons is that the state policy directive has not been supported by the necessary resources and incentives to compel compliance. Unless appropriate incentives for compliance are designed and implemented, it is likely that the initiative for instructional leadership on the part of school principals will lose momentum and fall far short of desired goals.

The reasons for this pessimistic conclusion are not difficult to discern. The path between state educational policy directives and the behavior of individuals in schools is long and highly segmented. A successful navigation of the road requires considerable planning, including the packaging of materials to develop new path segments as the trip unfolds. Evidence of this planning around the redefined role of the principal is difficult to find. Reform legislation does not provide details about how the mandate is to be implemented; few incentives or sanctions are employed; conditions creating the status quo—that is, the management focus in the principalship—have been completely overlooked; and school-based resources to help principals alter their behaviors are conspicuous by their absence. Efforts to develop more instructionally informed principals by altering curricular content in preparation programs in educational administration, through changes in certification requirements, have produced only modest results (Murphy, 1989b). The strategy of encouraging more pedagogically focused leadership at the school site by changing district norms has also been less than fully successful. For example, Ward and Hildebrand (in press) reported that only 35 percent of the principals in their study felt pressure from the district office to meet the "51 percent mandate."

There is a positive side to the redefinition ledger, however. The Illinois reform mandate does set a clear expectation for how principals should allocate their time. Illinois Administators' Academy programs are providing school leaders with important knowledge and skills in the area of instructional leadership. And a modest change in the content of preparation programs may be all that is required to shift the focus from management to leadership. It is also important to remember that the state's move to increase instructional expertise within its administrative core is not occurring in isolation. Some departments of educational administration, a number of the professional associations, and many of the burgeoning principals' centers are reinforcing the importance of expertise in technical core areas. The larger discussion of restructuring schools, with the concomitant shift in the base of administrative authority, are also contributing to the evaluation of principals who lead through instructional expertise, rather than through line authority. Indeed, there is evidence that teachers are beginning to see principals increasing the leadership dimensions of their jobs. For example, the Carnegie Foundation (1988) found that over half (56 percent) of the 13,500 teachers in its nationwide study reported that their principals were taking more of a leadership role.

Administrators' Academy

The most important and visible school administration component of SB 730 is the Illinois Administrators' Academy, which was established to meet the postemployment professional development needs of principals and superintendents throughout the state. Program development is under auspices of the Department of School Improvement of the ISBE. Training experiences are designed around the training-of-trainers model and delivered through eighteen geographically dispersed Educational Service Centers. The academy operates on a budget of approximately $1 million per year.

The academy is designed to provide participants with flexibility in meeting their professional development needs, although, as noted earlier, some training experiences are mandated for all school administrators. Currently, four separate strands of training are offered:

The Required Strand consists of evaluation training appropriate for meeting requirements of Section 24A-3 of *The School Code* requiring administrators to attend training in evaluation of certified staff on a schedule to be developed by SBE;

The Selective Strand consists of training designed to assist administrators in developing or improving specific skills in a short length of time;

The Designation Strand consists of intensive, long-term training and provides opportunities for administrators to earn professional recognition; and

The Clinical Strand consists of opportunities for administrators to receive individualized assessments of their instructional leadership skills and/or to request assessment of a school's climate as it impacts on instructional leadership. (Illinois State Board of Education, internal memo, no date)

The first two strands were activated in 1986, the Designation Strand in 1987, and the Clinical Strand in 1988.

Information about the academy's impact is limited to data about number of programs developed and number of participants served, and to assess-

Table 13-6
**Participation in Statewide Illinois Administrator Academy Programs
(through September 1988)**

Program	Length	Date Approved	Number of Participants
Teacher observation	3 days	4/01/86	9,755
Improving teacher performance: Formative evaluation	2 days	10/01/86	811
Evaluation of principals as instructional leaders	2 days	4/01/86	1,916
Research-based model for evaluation of instructional leaders	2 days	9/28/86	821
Evaluation of ancillary school personnel	1 1/2 days	9/18/86	926
Linking teacher observation to staff development	2 1/2 days	2/13/88	162
Individualized assessment of instructional leadership and school climate	7 days	8/88	45 (in process)

ments of the quality of the delivery of selected programs. Follow-up studies that examine the effects of training modules on administrative behavior, school structures and activities, and student outcomes have not yet been conducted. Through September 1988, the ISBE had developed seven programs for statewide dissemination. Information on attendance at these workshops is contained in Table 13-6. In addition to these statewide programs, individual Educational Service Centers have developed a variety of training programs specifically for the administrators in their regions. To date, the approximately forty such programs have been attended by more than 6,200 school principals and superintendents.

NOTES

1. It is important to point out, however, that in addition to serving other functions, changes in certification requirements can be designed to improve the content of preparation programs.

2. We do not mean to imply that no state initiatives were directed at improving university-based preparation programs. For example, between 1983 and 1986 three states added internship requirements to their preservice training programs.

3. For a comprehensive treatment of recent state activity in this area, see Peters and Bagenstos (1988).

4. The information reported in this section, unless otherwise noted, has been compiled from interviews with Illinois State Board of Education administrators and reviews of source documents they provided. I am particularly grateful to Dianne Ashby, Sue Bentz, and Ray Schaljo for their assistance.

5. These results are consistent with teachers' assessment of the reform movement nationwide. In its 1988 study, the Carnegie Foundation reported that teachers graded the reform movement as follows: A (2 percent); B (29 percent); C (50 percent); D (13 percent); and F (6 percent).

6. It is interesting to compare changes in certification requirements with changes made in course content at the colleges and universities that have programs to prepare students in the coursework needed for licensure in Illinois. Department chairpersons report some, but not a great deal of, change in the content of their programs. On a scale of 1 to 5 (1 = very little, 3 = some, 5 = a great deal), department leaders rate change in course content at 2.6. The changes they do report, however, are consistent with the intent of the reform legislation.

7. For cost-effectiveness information on the teacher certification test in Texas, see Shepard and Kreitzer (1987).

REFERENCES

Association for Supervision and Curriculum Development (ASCD). (1986, September). *School reform policy: A call for reason.* Alexandria, VA: ASCD.

Boyd, W. L. (1987, Summer). Public education's last hurrah?: Schizophrenia, amnesia, and ignorance in school politics. *Educational Evaluation and Policy Analysis, 9*(2), 85–100.

Carnegie Foundation for the Advancement of Teaching. (1988). *Report card on school reform: The teachers speak.* Princeton, NJ: Carnegie Foundation for the Advancement of Teaching.

Champagne, D. W., J. L. Morgan, M. B. R. Rawlings, & D. Swany. (1984, April). Analysis of the content of training programs for chief school administrators in the areas of instructional methodology, curriculum, and instructional supervision. Paper presented at the annual meeting of the American Educational Research Association, New Orleans.

Coombs, F. S. (1987, April). The effects of increased state control on local school district governance. Paper presented at the annual meeting of the American Educational Research Association, Washington, D.C.

Education Commission of the States. (1984). Action in the states: Progress toward education renewal. Denver: Education Commission of the States.

Gerritz, W., J. Koppich, & J. Guthrie. (1984, November). *Preparing California school leaders: An analysis of supply, demand, and training.* Berkeley: Policy Analysis for California Education, University of California.

Glass, T. (1988, 5 May). *1988 IASA superintendents survey results*. News release. Springfield: Illinois Association of School Administrators.

Gousha, R. P., A. H. Jones, & P. L. LoPresti. (1986, March). Where are we and where are we going in school administration preparation in the United States? Paper presented at the annual meeting of the American Educational Research Association, San Francisco.

Griffiths, D. E. (1988). *Educational administration: Reform PDQ or RIP*. Occasional Paper No. 8312. Tempe, AZ: University Council for Educational Administration.

Guthrie, J. W., & M. W. Kirst, (1988). *Conditions of education in California 1988*. Berkeley: Policy Analysis for California Education.

Illinois School Code. (1988). Springfield: Illinois State Legislature.

Illinois State Board of Education. (1986). *Summary of Illinois reform package of 1985*. Springfield: Illinois State Board of Education.

Illinois State Board of Education. (No date). Internal memo. Springfield: Illinois State Board of Education.

Kirst, M. W. (1984). State policy in an era of transition. *Education and Urban Society*, *16*(2), 225–237.

Levin, H. M. (1988, Spring). Cost-effectiveness and educational policy. *Educational Evaluation and Policy Analysis*, *10*(1), 51–69.

Murphy, J. (1989a). Principal instructional leadership. In L. S. Lotto and P. W. Thurston, eds., *Recent advances in educational administration*, vol. 1B. Greenwich, CT: JAI Press.

Murphy, J. (1989b). The responses of departments of school administration in Illinois to educational administration reform initiatives. *Administrator's Notebook*, *33*(3).

Murphy, J., P. Hallinger, L. S. Lotto, & S. K. Miller. (1987, December). Barriers to implementing the instructional leadership role. *Canadian Administrator*, *27*(3), 1–9.

National Governors' Association. (1987). *Results in education 1987*. Washington, DC: National Governors' Association.

Peters, S., & N. T. Bagenstos. (1988, April). State-mandated principal evaluation: A report on current practice. Paper presented at the annual meeting of the American Educational Research Association, April 1988.

Shepard, L. A., & A. E. Kreitzer. (1987, August–September). *The Texas teacher test*. *Educational Researcher*, *16*(6), 22–31.

Underwood, J. (1989). State legislative responses to educational reform literature. In L. S. Lotto and P. W. Thurston, eds., *Recent advances in educational administration*, vol. 1. Greenwich, CT: JAI Press.

Ward, J. G., & A. Hildebrand. (In press). Developing incentives for instructional leadership: An inquiry into the political economy of school change. *NASSP [National Association of Secondary School Principals] Bulletin*.

CHAPTER 14

Consolidation Reform in Illinois

Allan D. Walker

School district reorganization and consolidation have long been contentious, highly sensitive political issues in Illinois. For more than a hundred years, as other states have moved steadily toward greater centralization, a strong, historically inbred tradition of local control has slowed the initiatives of would-be consolidationists in Illinois, whether they be politically, educationally, or financially motivated (Evenson, 1969; Governor's Commission on Schools, 1973; Grant & Snyder, 1986). The last major legislative assault involving school district consolidation in Illinois began in 1945 and, over the next twenty years, did result in a considerable reduction in the number of school districts (Evenson, 1969; McLure & Stone, 1955). However, the rate of consolidation showed a marked decline by the early 1960s, and by the mid-1970s little progress was being made toward reducing the number of districts (Geske & Hoke, 1985). By 1985–86, there were still 997 independent school districts in Illinois, placing the state third in the nation for such complexity, behind only California and Texas (Cullen, 1985).

The early 1980s saw a revitalized interest in district consolidation in Illinois. Renewed concern was fueled in part by increased public and business dissatisfaction with schools and the concomitant demand for increased accountability and efficiency. Falling enrollments, the farm crisis, and a shrinking tax base all fueled this constantly smoldering issue. These factors were accentuated by the renewed interest in education and the accompanying thrust toward educational reform that was surfacing throughout the United States. It was within this environment that the issue of school district reorganization was to re-emerge in Illinois, and, for a relatively short time, dominate reform discussions and a gubernatorial election.

On 18 July 1985, the Illinois General Assembly almost unanimously passed PA84-126 into law. The legislation, commonly referred to as Senate Bill 730 (SB 730), was a concoction of reform bills poured into the one, comprehensive, history-making package. A small section of the bill included some fairly permissive legislation regarding the reorganization of school districts. Within less than a year, however, the same legislators and governor repealed the requirements, leaving them almost worthless (Walker, 1987).

The purpose of this chapter is to explicate the events, actors, and processes that initiated and promoted consolidation legislation in Illinois within the educational reform movement of the 1980s, and subsequently repealed the infant legislation (for greater detail, see Walker, 1987). Following a brief description of the key actors who influenced this issue, and an overview of the study design, the story of the school consolidation "battle" unfolds in four phases. Phase 1 overviews the political origins and background of consolidation reform. Phase 2 focuses on the reactive politics of consolidation reform. Phase 3 analyzes the impact that the specter of a statewide election had on consolidation reform. Finally, Phase 4 treats the aftermath of a failed reform. For the purposes of this chapter, the terms *consolidation* and *reorganization* are regarded as synonymous. They both refer to the amalgamation of two or more independently operating school districts to form one new district (Geske & Hoke, 1985).

STUDY

The study reported in this chapter attempted to investigate the range, causes, and sources of the factors that initially prompted state-level policymakers to implement a controversial policy change, as part of an overall education reform movement, and then abandon it before it could be fully implemented.

The research design used document analysis and in-depth interviews. Data were gathered from both semistructured interviews and primary and secondary documents to allow triangulation between the two techniques. Respondents were selected using an iterative method, with the final list of respondents being validated by a team of experts. Respondent categories included elected officials, interest groups, state agency officials, and others. Data were analyzed to identify common themes, concepts, and propositions. The results of the analysis were presented in the form of a historical, descriptive case study.

KEY ACTORS

The following actors, although not the only people who affected the consolidation issue, were the major players in terms of influence:

- *Gov. James R. Thompson* (Republican): Governor Thompson had previously been elected governor of Illinois on three occasions (1976, 1978, 1982). Although he had never been considered an education-oriented governor, when Thompson decided to run for an unprecedented fourth term, he believed he needed a strong educational platform. Thompson set out to put Illinois on the reform map, and, at the same time, to enhance his state and national reputation in the area of education. His soon-to-be-unveiled interest in school district consolidation was only part of a broader, new set of educational interests.
- *Rep. Gene Hoffman* (Republican, Elmhurst): Hoffman had been heavily involved in state educational policymaking for almost twenty years. He was widely regarded as "Mr. Consolidation" in Illinois and had been the major force behind almost every major piece of consolidation legislation since 1973. He was determined to have a school district reorganization section included in the Illinois educational reform package.
- *Sen. John Maitland* (Republican, Bloomington): Senator Maitland was a relative newcomer to the consolidation issue. He represented a rural constituency and believed that many students in small rural districts were being denied an adequate education.
- *Ted Sanders* (Illinois State Superintendent of Education, ISBE): Sanders became state superintendent in the midst of the reform movement of the 1980s. He had been the state superintendent in Nevada and was an acknowledged Republican who supported school district consolidation.
- *Adlai Stevenson III* (Democratic gubernatorial challenger): Stevenson was a former U.S. Senator who had run for governor against Thompson in 1982, only to be defeated by a meager 5,000 votes (Barone & Ujifusa, 1987). He was not noted for being particularly strong on educational issues.
- *Douglas Whitley* (President, Taxpayer Federation of Illinois, TFI): Whitley was an outspoken proponent of consolidation on the grounds of

efficiency. He demanded the cooperation of politicians on this issue in exchange for his organization's political support.

- *Small District Superintendents and School Board Members*: These individuals comprised the backbone of the anticonsolidation movement. They believed that any move toward reorganization should be voluntary.

PHASE 1: THE POLITICAL ORIGINS OF CONSOLIDATION REFORM

With educational reform discussions dominating the political climate in Illinois in the mid-1980s, Governor Thompson instructed his staff in March 1984 to develop an educational platform that was both educationally sound and politically acceptable. The resulting reports laid out three major issues on which Thompson's staff believed that he needed to take a stand: merit pay for teachers, accountability measures for schools, and school district reorganization. After a period of refinement and testing, the governor decided on a position that was considered reasonable as well as politically safe. The inclusion of a reorganization plank in this reform platform was not solely a product of the aforementioned process, however. Thompson had long been encouraged by the director of the Bureau of the Budget and by Douglas Whitley to unify districts on the grounds of economic efficiency. He had shown his support for reorganization by cooperating with Representative Hoffman on consolidation proposals in the 1983–84 legislative session.

Although Thompson decided to include a reorganization section in his reform proposals, he was too politically astute to openly support mandated consolidation. He believed that districts should not be forcibly combined but, rather, that a combination of incentives and mandates should be employed to encourage districts to unify (Ross, 1985). So when Thompson released his public position, he was sure that it was predominantly permissive, politically reasonable, and unlikely to elicit strong opposition. His platform was loudly applauded by efficiency-minded noneducation interests and was undergirded by his unstated desire to score some political points.

At the same time that Governor Thompson was developing his educational reform proposals, a number of other organizations were also developing recommendations (League of Women Voters of Illinois, 1985). The most influential of these groups was the legislature's own committee, the Illinois Commission on the Improvement of Elementary and Secondary Education. The commission held hearings throughout the state during 1983–84 to solicit reform recommendations (see Illinois Commission on the Improvement of Elementary and Secondary Education, 1984). House Speaker Madigan conducted an invitational statewide conference on educational issues, encouraging citizens to comment on their educational concerns. Former State Superintendent Michael Bakalis, in an attempt to revive his political visibility, chaired the Illinois Project for School Reform. The major educational pressure groups, interest groups concerned with educational matters, and the Illinois State Board of Education (ISBE) met collectively and individually to develop positions on various issues.

The years of 1983 and 1984 were devoted to discussions of educational reform as major educational, business, and political interests strove to determine what legislation would be included in the Illinois educational reform package. During this period, Hoffman, encouraged by Thompson's support, began planning to introduce some form of consolidation initiatives into the legislature. Two key actors in the reorganization issue had thus begun to move; (1) Thompson, developing educational proposals designed as part of his overall strategy for re-election in 1986; and (2) Hoffman, working toward what he had seen for years as an essential ingredient in improving the overall quality of education in Illinois.

At the same time that Hoffman and Thompson were laying the groundwork for reorganization legislation, Hoffman was involved in a more immediate quest. For the second time, he was actively campaigning for the position of state superintendent of education, an appointed position he desperately wanted. In a somewhat surprising and confusing set of circumstances, Hoffman was passed over in favor of Ted Sanders, the state superintendent of public instruction in Nevada. With him, Sanders brought a dedication to consolidation and, many claimed, an ignorance and unwillingness to learn the "local district ethos" in Illinois.

Sanders was immediately exposed to the governor's feelings on reorganization when he was present at a meeting in which Thompson told a group of influential superintendents and school board members that he would not sign school reform legislation unless it included a district consolidation component. Thompson reiterated this pledge a number of times during the reform formation stage. It must have been obvious to Sanders that the governor would require that a reorganization initiative be included in the overall reform package. He was also undoubtedly aware that the politician he had defeated for the superintendency (Hoffman) strongly supported reorganization and was an extremely potent force in state educational policymaking. These two influences, combined with Sanders's own proconsolidation philosophy, appeared to have convinced him that ISBE should actively support reorganization as an integral component of reform.

During 1985, the designated "year of reform in Illinois," the various commissions and interest groups issued their final reports. The recommendations pertinent to consolidation covered the entire spectrum, from no action to mandated unifications. The most influential recommendations were, not surprisingly, those emanating from the General Assembly's own commission.

After discussing reorganization at considerable length, both privately and at public hearings, the commission decided to avoid the issue altogether. It was not convinced that adequate evidence tied district size to educational quality. It also perceived the following political reality: including strong recommendations on consolidation would be so divisive that they could detract from other reform measures and perhaps neutralize the entire reform package.

Hoffman, however, who was a member of the commission, decided to pursue consolidation through his own bill, House Bill 935 (HB 935). He was still encouraged by Thompson's support. When HB 935 was introduced in April 1985, it became one of 370 separate education bills introduced in the General Assembly that year ("Education reform," 1985). Hoffman's bill mandated that consolidation feasibility studies be conducted and that plans be developed, and granted the ISBE the power to review and revise district-developed plans. It also mandated minimum enrollment criteria for districts: 1,500 students for unit districts, 1,000 for elementary districts, and 500 for high school districts. These criteria were to form the basis of the strongest opposition to Hoffman's proposal.

Business-based interest groups supported the bill, traditional education-based interest groups were surprisingly silent, and grassroots anticonsolidation groups began to sit up and take note. HB 935 was also somewhat reluctantly supported by the ISBE, although the ISBE had played no part in its formation. Its earlier active support had become tempered by its disgruntlement with the numerical criteria for elementary districts. Sanders had requested that Hoffman delete them, but he refused to budge. Some claimed Hoffman's intransigeance was due to his failure to secure the state superintendent's job. This failure, and the effect it had on the way he framed his consolidation legislation, continued to haunt him for the remainder of the legislative session (for a rebuttal, see Hoffman, 1985).

Despite Sanders' disagreement with the enrollment criteria for elementary schools, he personally backed the bill because it still reflected much of his own thinking about reorganization, it continued to enjoy the support of the governor, and the ISBE maintained some enthusiasm for the measure. ISBE support stemmed from the fact that Hoffman's bill reinforced some ISBE policies, and was the most viable avenue available in the legislature for pursuing reorganization reform, which continued to be one of ISBE's goals.

The Issue Becomes Public: New Forces Impact Consolidation

The ISBE support for district consolidation was reinforced in May 1985 when Sanders released the report *School District Consolidation in Illinois* (Illinois State Board of Education, 1985). The report, and subsequent reactions to it, served to rocket the consolidation issue into the public limelight. The central arguments for encouraging consolidation were based on positive relationships between high school size and the number of course offerings and student achievement (Thurston & Clauss, 1985).

The release of the report affected the reorganization issue in a number of ways. It certainly instilled fear and anger in anti-consolidationists, conditions that were accentuated when the report elicited severe criticism on both methodological and philosophical grounds. (Glaub, 1985; Humphreys, 1985; Nowland, 1986; Phipo, 1985; Pierman, 1985). When school superintendents also began to openly criticize the report, the press latched onto the issue (Armstrong, 1985; Weber, 1985).

There has been much speculation as to why Sanders released the report when he did. The most obvious conclusion is that he wanted to show his support for the governor and at the same time offer Hoffman an "olive branch." His move may also have been designed to encourage legislators to support reorganization by providing them with some empirical evidence that consolidation was desirable. Whatever the reasons, it was believed that releasing the report would build support for consolidation legislation. In reality, as the issue progressed, the report actually hurt Hoffman's cause more than it helped. Another effect of Sanders's move was that the publicity surrounding the study caused the focus of the media and anticonsolidation groups to shift from Thompson and Hoffman to Sanders. The press began to refer to Sanders as the main architect of mandated consolidation when, in large part, he had become involved to support Hoffman and the governor (Armstrong, 1985; Mabry, 1985; Weber, 1985).

Regardless of the growing public concern, Hoffman, with Thompson and Sanders squarely in his corner, managed to have HB 935 passed in the Illinois House of Representatives. Evidence suggests that the bill slipped through the House of Representatives largely unnoticed because it got lost in the myriad of educational reform proposals being floated at the same time. However, by the time the bill reached the Senate, many school leaders realized what was happening and began pressuring their legislators. As small districts saw their independence threatened, the consolidation issue became increasingly emotion-laden, and many senators began to express their concerns with HB 935, especially Senator Maitland.

Even though Maitland favored consolidation, he disagreed with HB 935's dictatorial approach, especially the minimum-enrollment criteria. He and a number of his colleagues, therefore, moved to amend the bill and delete much of the mandatory language. Not surprisingly, Hoffman did not agree with these proposed changes and the bill reached the Senate without significant modifications (State of Illinois 84th General Assembly, House of Representatives, 1985). Under increasing public pressure, the Senate narrowly defeated HB 935, and it was subsequently scheduled for reconsideration at a later date. Rather than try to pass the bill again, Hoffman decided to include it in the overall educational reform package that was being crafted.

Hoffman remained optimistic. He believed HB 935 was defeated for reasons other than those touching directly on the consolidation issue. He knew that he retained the support of the governor, the ISBE, the influential Maitland (as long as he was willing to show flexibility on the enrollment criteria issue), and a number of powerful business-based interest groups. However, as noted by a Republican staff analyst, he was opposed by a "cast of thousands" (Holmes, 1985). The ramifications of the original HB 935, with its mandatory language, continued to haunt the reorganization issue even after the consolidation proposal was substantially amended and softened, and slotted into PA84-126 (SB 730).

During the struggle for HB 935, most of the traditional educational interest groups adopted a fairly low profile on reorganization, while the major noneducational interests that became involved in the issue actively supported reorganization. The most vocal of these was the powerful TFI, who, under the direction of President Whitley, made it quite clear that its support for any reform funding was contingent on the passage of some type of consolidation legislation.

Consolidation in a Broader Educational Reform Environment

It is important to understand that the consolidation issue was only one, albeit large, component of the overall education reform discussions occurring during the first half of 1985. Following the release of the myriad reform proposals, everybody even remotely connected with education began lobbying, bargaining, and pushing for his or her preferences to become law. As expected, the Legislative Commission's recommendations formed the heart of the reform legislation. It was decided, at the commission's suggestion, that all reform measures would be included in the one omnibus bill. The philosophy behind this strategic move was twofold: it was believed that by packaging the bills together, real strides could be made toward reform; it was also felt that an omnibus bill would limit the power of special-interest groups to defeat specific pieces of the reform package, while encouraging them to act in concert to ensure that their own interest measures were passed into law.

The entire educational community met to hammer out general reform proposals, agreeing to sort out details later. Once the groups had developed positions, they proceeded, both individually and collectively, to negotiate with key legislators and Sanders. The majority of educational interest groups, however, remained surprisingly silent on the topic of reorganization. Many groups, such as the teachers' unions, were more concerned with issues more directly affecting their members. In other groups, the members were split on the issue, therefore making it difficult to present a unified front. There was also a general feeling that the imminent reforms were the most significant and promising events to happen in Illinois education for many years. The educational community did not want to risk jeopardizing the entire reform package by arguing too strongly on any one issue. It was also aware that any reorganization legislation likely to be included would be weak and permissive. All these factors allowed the interest groups to consider their "fence-sitting" posture a reasonable stance to adopt.

By mid-June 1985, literally hundreds of bills were circulating, all trying to become part of the reform package. In an attempt to pull the bills together, the governor and the legislative leadership decided on a limited "summit" conference. This involved an eight- to ten-day meeting between Sanders and the major education-oriented legislators. Their task was to decide the ultimate configuration of the reform legislation.

The summit meetings were rigorous but exciting. It was a time of intense negotiation as legislators, fed by various interests, fought for their proposals to be included. Negotiations and issues were so divisive and complicated that the General Assembly almost completely entrusted the formation of the reform package to the summit group. School district reorganization was frequently discussed at the summit meetings but the topic was so controversial, even in a soft, permissive form, that the group refused to make a decision on its inclusion, passing the final responsibility to Thompson and their legislative leaders. The answer came back in the affirmative—include an amended version of HB 935 in the reform package. The only mandatory remainder of HB 935 was the requirement that districts conduct reorganization feasibility studies. The consolidation section of the reform package received only scant attention from legislators not involved in the summit process. The entire final package had the support of all the major interest groups. When the landmark bill became PA84-126 (by a vote of 77 to 41 in the House, and 56 to 2 in the Senate), everybody involved was generally pleased with its content and support for education. Most considered the small reorganization section to be reasonable, largely stripped of the objectional dictatorial language that had characterized it when originally introduced in HB 935. The troublesome enrollment criteria were retained in PA84-126 but were now included only as possible guidelines, not mandatory minimums. The only opposition was expected to come from a small number of likely-to-be-affected school districts. Nobody was prepared for the huge public outcry that was about to occur.

PHASE 2: THE REACTIVE POLITICS OF CONSOLIDATION REFORM

At the same time as PB84-126 was passed, the General Assembly also passed House Bill 982 (HB 982), an event that added fuel to an already simmering controversy. HB 982 was originally intended to remove one financial barrier to the creation of unit school districts by eliminating the inequity in permissive tax rate authority between dual and unit districts of any size. The bill in its original form was quite acceptable to the General Assembly.[1] However, that support all but vanished when Governor Thompson amendatorially vetoed the bill to grant the new authority to tax at the increased rate only to unit districts who had more than 1,500 pupils. Quite simply, Thompson amended the bill for political reasons—in response to pressure from Douglas Whitley and TFI. Thompson informed his staff that the reason he had accepted Whitley's advice was to garner TFI support in the next gubernatorial election.

Hoffman strongly supported the governor's amendment, but Maitland, although he supported consolidation, opposed the concept. Maitland had always opposed the inclusion of any numerical enrollment criteria because of the divisiveness he predicted they would cause. He feared Thompson's tying of tax revenue access to enrollment standards would disadvantage low-population rural areas, and reinforce a general perception among small districts that the state was aiming for forced consolidation. The normally calm senator informed Thompson in no uncertain terms that his move could do irreparable damage to the consolidation process, but Thompson refused to budge. Because HB 982 elicited considerable controversy in the community, and consequently among legislators, Maitland had no shortage of supporters when he introduced House Bill 913 (HB 913), a measure whose sole purpose was to return HB 982 to its original form.

Maitland's campaign was successful, and Thompson was pressured into reinstating the original provisions of HB 982. Although Senator Maitland again threw his full weight behind consolidation reform, the position of many legislators was beginning to change from one of apathy to a concern that they could be politically harmed by the issue. Governor Thompson also seemed to be experiencing a slight change in attitude regarding his support for reorganization.

During the debates on HB 982 (PA84-1021) and HB 913 (PA84-1022) the controversy involving consolidation began to accelerate. Grassroots opposition began with the introduction of HB 935 and gained momentum as the year progressed. The anticonsolidation groups were mainly comprised of school superintendents, school board members, and parents drawn from small school districts in rural Illinois and the northern suburbs of Chicago.

They were distrustful of any form of consolidation legislation. By late 1985, the threatened districts decided it was time to organize more formally. An unusual coalition was forged between two geographic areas—rural Illinois and suburban Chicago—that historically shared few common interests. Rural districts generally organized under the unit structure, were hard pressed financially, and usually depended heavily on state aid for survival. They feared losing their state aid if they refused to consolidate. Conversely, the suburban districts were almost all dual districts that enjoyed high assessed valuation and received very little revenue from the state aid formula. They objected to the legislation because its preference for coterminous boundaries would cause them to lose their individual identities. These rich suburban areas were sometimes accused of opposing consolidation as a means of preserving their elite position, and of ignoring the growing educational, financial, and racial problems plaguing the remainder of the state. The factor that ultimately brought the two areas together was a fear of losing local control of their children's education.

The anticonsolidation groups were becoming increasingly well organized. They were developing an almost spiritual commitment to blocking any consolidation mandates. Nothing could placate their fears or convince them that, except for the required feasibility studies, the legislation was permissive. The reasons for this conviction are somewhat muddled. The general perception appears to be that the most vigorous reorganization opponents were school superintendents and school board members. These groups apparently had the most to lose should widespread reorganization eventuate. Many claims were made that these groups were more interested in keeping their jobs and their influence than they were in ensuring quality education. They were accused of deliberately providing misinformation in order to feed the fears of the local populace (Copley, 1985). Certainly much faulty information circulated during this period, but in retrospect it appears to have been more the result of misunderstanding and miscommunication than of deliberate distortion. The inaccurate interpretations of the consolidation legislation that abounded at this time can be traced to legislative vagueness over HB 935, PA84-126, PA84-1021, and PA84-1022; increased media attention; muddled pronouncements from politicians themselves; and lack of clarity in ISBE communications ("Consolidation of schools," 1985; "Schools reorganize," 1985; Winski & Hill, 1985).

As the controversy intensified, the press targeted Thompson, Sanders, and Hoffman as causing the problem and began applying pressure on all legislators, many of whom starting to look for ways of distancing themselves from the issue—an issue which they were on record as having supported as part of PA84-126. How could they now tell the voters they had not been fully aware of the bill's content and that they had left the decision up to "educational experts"—a decision many were beginning to regret?

While interest groups pressured and legislators scrambled, the ISBE, as required by law, proceeded to implement the legislation. Board staff traveled the state to explain the legislation and allay concerns, but succeeded only in eliciting increased opposition from local citizens. Staff members were widely accused of being arrogant and of presenting an inflexible, and, at times, inaccurate analysis of the legislation's intent. ISBE staff actually, and inappropriately, threatened to cut off access to state funds for districts that failed to consolidate and they would not entertain even slight variations from the legislated enrollment criteria—which were intended only as guidelines. It was certainly understandable that local citizens were becoming increasingly concerned that the state would force consolidation.

The attitude of and information provided by the ISBE enraged thousands of citizens to such an extent that Thompson and other reorganization proponents became concerned. The governor and key legislators contacted and/or met with Superintendent Sanders regarding the ISBE's handling of the dissemination process several times, but not before great damage had been done. The legislation's chances of successful implementation had been severely threatened, and a good deal of electoral support had eroded. The ISBE's handling of the issue was not only indelicate, but also confusing. It had generally been attributed to Sanders' newness to the state, his limited understanding of the Illinois educational system and ethos, and the loss of the extremely capable head of the ISBE's School Organization and Facilities section. These failures to organize and communicate accurately also placed an extra burden on Senator Maitland, who was being called on with increasing frequency to explain the consolidation initiatives in threatened districts.

While the political wrangling continued, the traditional educational interest groups maintained their ambiguous position. The anticonsolidation groups, however, were almost fanatical in their efforts, continually prophesying that mandated consolidation had arrived. They convinced citizens to withhold campaign contributions traditionally given to Republican coffers. They applied pressure to Republican lawmakers, especially in suburban Chicago and west-central Illinois. Spurred on by increasing community support, they managed to force the powerful Illinois Association of School Boards (IASB) to change its formal position from that of considered neutrality to one almost directly opposing the legislation presented in PA84-126 (Illinois Association of School Boards, 1985). This shift was a significant victory for the anticonsolidation groups: not only had they pressured one of the largest established educational interest groups to change their official position, but they also attracted a good deal of favorable press coverage in both rural and suburban districts.

Pressure Mounts to Soften Consolidation Reform

The anticonsolidation forces' victory in altering IASB's position prompted them to even more concentrated action. They wrote to newspapers, petitioned politicians, and pressured previously uninvolved legislators. Although Hoffman, Maitland, and Whitley continued to preach consolidation and communicate an accurate interpretation of PA84-126, Thompson and the majority of legislators began looking for a way out. Thompson was especially worried about the increasing flow of negative publicity and the effect it could have on his election campaign. He all too clearly recalled his narrow victory margin in the 1982 election. Thompson was also becoming increasingly antagonized by Sanders' handling of the issue. His staff suggested he publicly disassociate himself from any talk of forced reorganization. Accepting his advisors' recommendation, Thompson sent an open letter informing Sanders that he would veto any legislation that mandated consolidation (Dowling, 1985; J. Thompson to T. Sanders, 10 December 1985).

Thompson's letter to Sanders was a definite sign that he was backing off the issue and leaving other supporters out on a limb. Hoffman was not even aware of the letter until the day after it was sent. He wrote on his copy, "Letter not discussed w/[with] me—why? . . . was Maitland informed" (G. Hoffman to G. Hoffman 11 December 1985). The letter was symbolic of Thompson's growing electoral fears—the mentioned legislation involving forced consolidation did not even exist.

The governor's public reprimand of Sanders paved the way for legislators to actively retreat from the controversy and solidify their political positions before the 1986 election. The political backlash saw Republicans and Democrats scrambling over one another to suggest changes they would make in the legislation ("Reorganization fears," 1986; Johnson, 1986; Pfeifer, 1985). The controversy surrounding the issue became so potentially damaging that most legislators decided that they could no longer afford to support consolidation, even if they had wanted to.

The Democrats must have enjoyed seeing the incumbent Republican governor and his party writhe as the anticonsolidation forces continued to batter them. For although they too had been pressured, the bulk of public antagonism was aimed at key Republicans. By the end of 1985, the controversy, which had exposed a flaw in Thompson's election-time armor, continued to intensify. The Democrats, who were attempting to defeat a popular governor and increase their majority in the General Assembly, surveyed Governor Thompson's weakness with an exploitive eye.

Phase 3: Election–Time Politics and Consolidation Reform

By January 1986, the consolidation issue had become highly visible, easily dominating other reform measures in both political and educational circles. The Democrats, sensing Thompson's increasing discomfort with the reorganization issue, decided it would be politically beneficial to introduce the issue into the gubernatorial race. On January 8, Stevenson released a statement on reorganization criticizing both Thompson's position and the consolidation language included in PA84-126. He proposed new legislation that, not surprisingly, more closely resembled popular public opinion.

More specifically, Stevenson harshly criticized the minimum enrollment standards in PA84-126, calling for their elimination in favor of quality criteria (it is important to note that he did not oppose all consolidation legislation). He also accused Thompson of backtracking on the law (PA84-126) he had signed in July and of confusing the reorganization issue.

> The confusion peaked when Gov. Thompson recently "backtracked" from the law he had supported, saying he would veto any "minimum inflexible numbers of students in a district." Since the Governor's signature is on the legislation establishing "minimum inflexible" numbers, it is not clear what the law means. (Stevenson, 1986, p. 1)

There is general agreement among the actors in the reorganization saga that Stevenson's main motivation for presenting a consolidation position was similar to Thompson's more than a year earlier. Both men hoped to reap political advantage from educational reform. Rural and suburban superintendents and members of the Democratic Party (who had been carefully tracking the issue), in conjunction with other campaign advisors, advised Stevenson that he could use the issue to significant advantage in his gubernatorial quest. He was advised that consolidation in the state was very unpopular and his public opposition to it could win valuable votes away from Thompson.

The press immediately latched onto Stevenson's proposal, widely publicizing his position, while at the same time exposing Thompson's predisposition to backtrack on sensitive issues (Brody, 1985; Franklin, 1986; Pokorski, 1986). Legislators of both political persuasions rushed to submit legislation designed to disassociate themselves from any tie with mandated reorganization. Maitland, attempting to restore some sanity to the situation, called for restraint and common sense to prevail, but his voice seemed lost in the scramble.

Stevenson's attack on Governor Thompson gained him political points while at the same time arousing further anger about and resistance to consolidation (Sevener, 1986). Thompson was placed in a politically awkward position. He attempted to counterattack, but realized he was rapidly losing ground to Stevenson ("School consolidation," 1986). In an effort to recoup some electoral support he once again, publicly, contacted Sanders. Thompson openly chastized the ISBE for too narrowly defining the reorganization legislation, and for the first time he suggested that the quality of a district's program should be considered a "justifiable exception" in any case they might make against consolidation. This second public letter to Sanders completed the governor's "dumping" of any consolidation responsibility. As Representative Schaffer (R) joked to Sanders, "I think Governor Thompson's next letter will indicate that he has never met you" (Griffin, 1986, p. 2.2). Thompson's last move was a direct result of the favorable press given Stevenson's proposal. Just four months earlier he had used his amendatory veto to promote stronger consolidation legislation.

Stevenson's proposal was widely perceived as the major reason why the governor and the majority of legislators backed down on the issue (Armstrong, 1986; McMurray, 1986; Urbanek & Bross, 1986). However, it can more accurately be viewed as the catalyst creating the opening through which the massive retreat could surge. Thompson actually showed signs of recanting as early as September 1985 when he became the target of continual bombardment by interest groups, members of his own party, the press, and various grassroots organizations. Stevenson's proposal simply represented the peak of a highly visible anticonsolidation movement that had often been fueled by deliberate misinformation and widespread miscommunication. If it had not been an election year focusing on educational reform, Stevenson's proposal might never even have been presented.

The Democrats' proposal and subsequent reactions by Thompson, however, did have a number of consequences. First, it presented legislators in affected districts with the excuse they had been looking for to totally back away from the issue. Second, Stevenson's stand further accelerated press involvement. Once it became part of the gubernatorial campaign, it became "big news." Finally, it threw the ISBE and its regional committees into "limbo" as to how the proceed with the already enacted legislation. Despite Hoffman's assertion that the movement was "alive and necessary," the reorganization process was effectively stalled (Griffin, 1986). Hoffman, along with Maitland and their few remaining supporters, did all they could to retain at least some of the basic tenets of the legislation—but slowly saw their chances slipping away.

Although it has been established that Stevenson released his proposal to gain political advantage, even he did not anticipate how much reaction it would solicit. Immediately after it was released, his position began to be oversimplified and misconstrued. The anticonsolidation groups began to treat the issue in stark contrasts, and they tried to adopt Stevenson as their figurehead. Stevenson began to feel that he was losing control of the issue, for, as mentioned earlier, he was not opposed to consolidation *per se* but only against the size criteria. To his credit, he substantially backed away from the issue, considering it irresponsible to exploit it to its full political potential when his position was being misinterpreted and misused (Lawrence, 1986). Regardless of his partial withdrawal, the misinterpretation of his position served to intensify the anticonsolidation group's campaign and they were using the specter of the upcoming election to great effect (Stiers, 1986; Ognibene, 1986).

As the pressure campaign continued, many legislators introduced bills to exhibit their anticonsolidation stance to their constituencies. In an effort to bring some sanity to the whole process, and extract Governor Thompson from a political quagmire, Senator Maitland, at the request of Thompson, introduced Senate Bill 242 (SB 242). This bill was to be used as an agreed vehicle for both parties to consider and to reach compromise on the school district consolidation issue (Straus, 1986). On 10 February 1986, the House of Representatives passed an amended SB 242 by a near unanimous vote, handing the anticonsolidation forces virtually everything they sought (Keen, 1986). The final version of SB 242 included the following amendments: modified and extended timelines for the submission of regional plans; elimination of the criteria regarding enrollment preference for unit districts and coterminious boundaries; the establishment of educational opportunity (not minimum enrollment) as the primary consideration for reorganization; and provision for allowing regional committees to submit binding decisions that no reorganization was needed.

However, when the bill reached the Senate, Maitland refused to pass it. He blocked the bill, which he had only supported originally because of pressure from Thompson, because the Democrats had included an amendment that not only mutilated the bill but gave it a distinctly Stevenson-Democrat flavor. This move only provided the Democrats with more ammunition and disturbed an already impatient Thompson, who badly wanted the issue settled before the March primary election. Eventually, solely to support his governor in an election year, Maitland agreed to allow the bill to pass with all its amendments intact. He was disappointed that the issue had become so politicized and blamed the Democrats for the ultimate failure of the bill—although he acknowledged that Thompson had played a major role in the "backdown."

Before the Senate voted on the bill (SB 242), Thompson sent a letter to the General Assembly. He told the legislators that "If you send the legislation to my desk, I will sign it quickly. . . . School reform is too important to be allowed to flounder on this metaphorical rock" (Thompson, 1986, p. 1). On March 5, 1986, SB 242 became Public Act 84-1115 (PA84-1115) by a near unanimous vote in both houses. Only a few stalwarts such as Hoffman opposed the bill.

The signing of PA84-1115 effectively emasculated the reorganization legislation, turning it into little more than a political mud-slinging match (see Sanders, 1986). The press was quick to point out the lack of courage displayed by elected officials, accusing legislators of going too far in response to political pressures. One journalist wrote, "It seems the lawmakers, many of them up for re-election this year, believed the ability to claim credit for changes was more important than the impact on the state's educational system or treasury" (Camire, 1986). Don Sevener, commenting in the *Illinois Times*, was particularly hard on Thompson. He wrote, "the Sanders school consolidation law touched off such an uprising in rural Illinois so threatening that the Governor, whose backbone sways in the political winds, quickly backed away from the idea" (Sevener, 1986).

The signing of PA84-1115 brought tremendous sighs of relief from both legislators and small district educators and citizens. The anticonsolidation forces congratulated themselves on a victory for democracy, for the "little people." The grassroots groups had risen and defeated the consolidation-minded politicians and the ISBE at a time when national trends seemed to be lending support for reorganization and increased state-level control of education.

PHASE 4: THE AFTERMATH OF A FAILED REFORM

The death of the consolidation issue left the politicians free to concentrate on the other aspects of their political campaigns. Thompson promptly forgot the issue and concentrated on his "Build Illinois program." He was easily re-elected and no doubt swore to stay away from school district reorganization in the future. Adlai Stevenson III had more than enough problems within his own party to give consolidation another thought (for some explanation of this, see Barone & Ujifusa, 1987 and Wheeler, 1986). Rural and suburban districts ended their coalition and returned to concentrate on their own unrelated problems. Small district school board members and superintendents, once again feeling safe in their jobs, returned to worrying about the severe financial problems that plagued many of their districts.

Hoffman, Maitland, Sanders, and Whitley remained strongly in favor of consolidation. Both Hoffman and Maitland were easily re-elected . In fact, by the time the election was held the consolidation controversy had been almost completely forgotten. Whitley continued to preach the necessity of a more efficient educational delivery system. Sanders remained in his job, surviving his year-long baptism of fire and certainly being more aware of the educational and political workings of Illinois.

The impotence of the repealed legislation became obvious after regional committees submitted their reorganization plans. Of the fifty-nine regional plans required by PA84-1115, fifty groups submitted final decisions of "no reorganization" (Brown, 1987). Despite this dismal result, some optimists saw some positive conditions resulting from the controversy. They argued that the legislation had forced districts to sit down and talk, sometimes for the first time ever. They also noted that some districts thought they had come so close to losing their schools that they had begun examining, through their own initiative, possibilities for improving their schools—including consolidation. Although another episode in the consolidation battle in Illinois was over, few doubted that it would return sometime in the future.

CONCLUSIONS

The school district reorganization issue in Illinois in 1985–86 dominated and in many ways distracted from what was targeted as a year of substantial educational reform in the state. It is difficult to predict what the outcome of the consolidation battle might have been if it had not transpired so close to a state election, or if the two parties had not adopted educational reform as the major campaign issue. This examination of the issue does, however, provide some information regarding the pursuit of controversial educational reform measures at a stage level (see also Walker, 1987). It should be re-emphasized that the conclusions generated were drawn from a particular case.

The events involved in the school district reorganization issue in Illinois indicate that the passage of a controversial policy change may be easier if pursued within a crowded, legislative, bargainning environment and if promoted by a small group of focused decision makers. However, a policy change seems much less likely to be enacted if its aims and intent are miscommunicated, misinterpreted, or misconstrued; if those responsible for introducing and promoting the policy have varying goals; and if it is debated during the middle of a state election. The issue examined also seemed to indicate that a policy attempting to alter historically entrenched behaviors will be difficult to implement, especially under the aforementioned conditions.

The reorganization controversy in Illinois also showed that despite the increasing influence of the state legislature and executive in educational policymaking, small, homogeneous, grassroots pressure groups, can substantially influence the outcomes of the decision process. When they believe that their rights are threatened, such groups can neutralize politicians and traditional interest groups. The politicization of the issue was perhaps not surprising, considering the strong feelings involved and the increasing role of the state in educational policymaking. The events comprising the issue showed the power of committed citizens and local educators to negate moves toward increased state control by consciously manipulating political processes.

For all intents and purposes, this latest consolidation controversy in Illinois ended before the 1986 state election, but the issue continues to be discussed. The commitment of both opponents and supporters seems to indicate that the issue will be resurrected some time in the future—whether or not educational reform remains a political priority.

NOTE

1. The purpose of HB 982 was to promote the formation of unit districts, through financial incentive. The bill aimed to provide unit districts with access to equivalent property tax revenue for educational purposes as those enjoyed by separate elementary and high school districts. Before the proposal of HB 982, separate primary and secondary districts had access to higher property tax revenue than they would if they combined to form unit districts. HB 982 was to redress this inequity, thereby encouraging the formation of unit districts of any size. When Thompson amended the bill to make the equalized tax rate available only to districts of more than 1,500, he was in effect threatening financial sanction against districts who could not, or would not, meet the enrollment criteria. The governor's decision did little to reassure the doubting anticonsolidationists, who had very recently been told that the enrollment criteria in PA82-126 were only guidelines.

REFERENCES

Armstrong, E. (1985, 20 May). Rural districts vs. consolidation. *Springfield State Journal Register*, p. 5.

Armstrong, E. (1986, 13 January). Consolidation becomes hot issue. *Springfield State Journal Register*, p. 5.

Barone, M., & G. Ujifusa. (1987). Illinois. In M. Barone & G. Ujifusa, eds., *An almanac of American politics* (pp. 333–389). Washington, DC: National Journal.

Brody, J. (1985, 5 January). Adlai stresses curriculum over school size. *Springfield State Journal Register*, pp. 9, 16.

Brown, G. (1987, 19 February). *Results of 1985 school district reorganization act*. Springfield: Illinois State Board of Education.

Camire, A. (1986, 9 April). Heart is ripped out of reform legislation. *Rockford Register Star*.

Consolidation of schools a "hot issue." (1985, 4 September). *Elmhurst Press*, pp. 1–2.

Copley, P. (1986, 5 January). Howls greet school reform plan. *Waukegan News Star*.

Cullen, K. (1985, 14 June). School consolidation: State board recommends mandatory mergers. *Danville Commercial News*, pp. A-1, A-8.

Dowling, J. (1985, 12 December). Thompson: I'll veto forced school district mergers. *Springfield State Journal Register*, p. 3.

Education reform faces long haul. (1985, 29 April). *Farm Week*, p. 5.

Evenson, W. (1969). Illinois. In J. B. Pearson and E. Fuller, eds., *Education in the states: Historical development and outlook*. A Project of the Council for Chief State School Officers. Washington, DC: National Education Association of the United States.

Franklin, T. (1986, 9 January). Stevenson says he's cool to school consolidation. *Chicago Tribune*.

Geske, T., & G. Hoke (1985). The national commission reports: Do the states have the fiscal capacity to respond? *Education and Urban Society*, *17*(2), 171–185.

Glaub, G. (1985). Taking aim at small schools. *Illinois School Board Journal*, *53*(3), 5.

Governor's Commission on Schools. (1973, March). *Opportunities for excellence*. Final Report of the Commission on School Reorganization. Springfield, IL: Governor's Commission on Schools.

Grant, W., & T. Snyder. (1986). *Digest of educational statistics 1985–86*. Washington, DC: U.S. Department of Education.

Griffin, J. (1986, 17 January). Opposition to school consolidation gains among lawmakers. *Chicago Tribune*, Section 2, p. 2.

Hoffman, G. (1985, 9 November). Voice of the people: DuPage and the "rule of the Republicans." *Chicago Tribune*.

Holmes, B. (1985, June). *Senate Republican analysis of HB 935*. Springfield, IL: Senate Republican Staff.

Humphreys, L. (1985). A critique of "student achievement in Illinois: An analysis of student progress 1984." Unpublished manuscript, Department of Psychology, University of Illinois, Champaign-Urbana.

Illinois Association of School Boards (IASB). (1985, 23 November). *Transcription of debate on school district reorganization: Resolution No. 14*, pp. 47–76. Springfield: Illinois Association of School Boards.

Illinois Commission on the Improvement of Elementary and Secondary Education. (1984, July). *Excellence in the making: A preliminary report*. Springfield: Illinois Commission on the Improvement of Elementary and Secondary Education.

Illinois State Board of Education. (1985, May). *School district organization in Illinois*. Springfield: Illinois State Board of Education.

Johnson, T. (1986, January). Johnson: School consolidation mandates ignore some realities. *State Representative Tim Johnson reports from Springfield*. Urbana, IL: T. Johnson.

Keen, E. (1986, 27 February). *House Republican analysis of the current status of school district reorganization*. Springfield, IL: House Republican Staff.

Lawrence, M. (1986, 19 January). Stevenson sidesteps schoolyard mud puddle. *Decatur Herald Review*.

League of Woman Voters of Illinois. (1985). *Public education in Illinois: Achieving equity and excellence*. Chicago: League of Women Voters of Illinois.

Mabry, R. (1985, 23 May). High schools fuming over state report *Champaign-Urbana News Gazette*, Section A, pp. 1, 3.

McLure, W., & J. Stone. (1955, January). *A study of leadership in school district reorganization*. Urbana: Bureau of Educational Research, College of Education, University of Illinois.

McMurray, D. (1986, 11 January). School consolidation crops up as first substantive issue in the governor's race. *Alton Telegraph*, p. 3.

Nowland, J. (1986). Arbitrary school consolidation idea flunks. In J. Nowland, ed., *Illinois: Problems and promise* (pp. 44–45). Galesburg, IL: Lee Public Policy Press.

Ognibene, E. (1986, 4 February). *School reorganization under Senate Bill 730*. Oak Brook: Illinois Citizens Against Reorganizing Education.

Pfeifer, S. (1985, 29 December). De Angelis to urge change in school reform package. *Oak Forest Star Herald*, Section A, pp. 1–2.

Phipo, C. (1985). School district reorganization and family choice: Illinois moves to consolidate school districts. *Phi Delta Kappan*, 67(3), 182.

Pierman, S. (1985, 22 November). Donahue: Sanders "scaring" districts into reorganization. *Quincy Herald-Whig*, Section A, p. 3.

Pokorski, D. (1986, 9 January). Politics hinders planning for school consolidation. *Springfield State Journal Register*, pp. 9, 16.

Reorganization fears. (1986, 5 January). *Chicago Heights Star*.

Ross, D. (1985). A few words from the governor. *Illinois Issues*, 11(3), 6–19.

Sanders, T. (1986, 7 March). *Letter to reorganization committee members*. Springfield: Illinois State Board of Education.

School consolidation new victim of politics. (1986, 13 January). *Champaign-Urbana News Gazette*, Section A, p. 4.

Schools reorganize. (1985, 31 October). *Roseville Independent*.

Sevener, D. (1986, September) Reveries: Oil and Water. *Illinois Times*.

State of Illinois 84th General Assembly, House of Representatives. (1985, 20 June). *Transcription of debate on HB 935*, (pp. 85–94). Springfield: State of Illinois 84th General Assembly, House of Representatives.

Stevenson, A. (1986, 8 January). *Stevenson's statement on school reorganization*. Chicago: Stevenson for Governor.

Stiers, M. (1986, 3 February). Legislators, candidates attend anticonsolidation rally. *Galesburg Register Mail*.

Straus, F. (1986, 27 February). *House Republican analysis of school consolidation*. Springfield, IL: House Republican Staff.

Thompson, J. (1986, 4 March). *Letter to members of the General Assembly re: Reorganization*. Springfield, IL: Office of the Governor.

Thurston, P., & J. Clauss. (1985, October). CPR for rural school districts: Emerging alternatives in curriculum, program and reorganization. Paper presented at school reorganization conference in Decatur, IL. Available from P. Thurston, College of Education, University of Illinois, 1320 South Sixth Street, Champaign, Illinois 61820.

Urbanek, D., & D. Bross. (1986, 13 January). School consolidation law drawing fire. *Arlington Daily Herald*, p. 3.

Walker, A. (1987). The politics of school district reorganization and consolidation reform in Illinois in 1985 and 1986. Unpublished doctoral dissertation, University of Illinois, Urbana.

Weber, J. (1985). Superintendents concerned about Sanders' proposals. *Illinois School Board Journal*, 53(3), 18–19.

Wheeler, C. (1986). Adlai's candidacy. *Illinois Issues*, 12(5), p. 2.

Winski, J., & J. Hill. (1985, Winter). Illinois: A case of too much government. *Illinois Business*, pp. 8–12.

Conclusion

CHAPTER 15

An Overview of Education Reform Since 1983

William Firestone
Susan Fuhrman
Michael Kirst

Crisis is a constant in U.S. education. Scholars, university educators, businesspeople, and legislators regularly find major problems with elementary and secondary schools and propose substantial reforms to solve those problems. Two mechanisms have been used to encourage educators to make the changes that outside experts want. Until mid-century, the preferred approach to galvanizing action was symbolic, relying on the commission report or other authoritative pronouncement by respected sources. The Report of the Committee of Ten in 1893, *The Cardinal Principals of Secondary Education* in 1918, and *The American High School Today* in 1959 have been followed most recently by *A Nation at Risk* in 1983 (see Ginsberg and Wimpelberg, 1987, for a review). Since the 1950s, governmental action has become more prevalent and includes National Science Foundation (NSF) grants for curriculum development, court action to effect desegregation, and Title I and Chapter I and other federal programs to improve educational opportunity.

Two things are notable about these frequent efforts to reform U.S. education. First, the agendas for reform fluctuate dramatically. While the Committee of Ten sought to standardize secondary education for precollegiate students, *The Cardinal Principals* was geared to students who would take jobs directly after school (James & Tyack, 1983). The 1950s curriculum reforms were aimed at the future scientific leaders of the nation, while the 1960s reforms stressed equity for children of all races and achievement levels. Many reform reports in the 1970s recommended humanizing education, while those of the 1980s stress tightening standards (Passow, 1984).

Second, the reformer's targets are rarely met in practice. A recent review of a century of national commission reports proposes a "trickle-down" theory. It suggests that commissions make strong dramatic gestures to call attention to the problems of concern but make ambiguous recommendations and give too little attention to implementation problems. Recommendations can be interpreted in a variety of ways or even ignored. As a result, their impact on school and classroom life is meager (Ginsberg & Wimpelberg, 1987). Similarly, the most frequently cited study of the implementation of federal legislation highlights "mutual adaptation" where external requirements are adapted to local conditions, and local institutions change only slightly in response to those requirements (Berman & McLaughlin, 1975). Although it is possible, with great difficulty, for court-ordered desegregation to change who goes to which school, it is more difficult to change what goes on when they get there.

The reform efforts of the 1980s have been characterized by national commission reports and state legislative and executive action. The commission reports established a series of targets and directions for change. State action provided the mandates, incentives, and resources to ensure local action. Actual changes in practice, of course, take place at the local level.

Commission Reports and Reform Targets

Of the twenty-nine books and reports issued in and around 1983, *A Nation at Risk* had the most lasting significance. Table 15-1 summarizes the recommendations in that report and gives some idea of its breadth. In the succeeding five years, three themes have been apparent in efforts to reform U.S. education:

- *Increased academic content* through a curriculum more focused on major academic areas. The exemplar report for this theme is *A Nation at Risk* itself. The preferred vehicles for providing access to more content are increased course requirements; increased student testing; the establish-

Table 15-1
Recommendations from *A Nation at Risk*

I. Content
  A. High school graduation requirements raised; five new basics:
     1. Four years of English, including extended reading and writing skills and knowledge of our literary heritage.
     2. Three years of math:
        a. Higher-order mathematics such as geometry, algebra, and statistics
        b. Estimation, approximation, measurement, and accuracy testing
        c. A curriculum for those not planning college immediately
     3. Four years of science:
        a. Higher-order sciences, scientific reasoning, and inquiry
        b. Application of scientific knowledge and technology
     4. Five years of social studies:
        a. Studies of selves and others in the continuum of time and culture
        b. Understand social, economic, and political systems
     5. A half-year of computer science:
        a. Basic computer literacy and use of computers in other subjects
        b. Comprehension of electronics and related technologies
        c. Foreign languages, arts, and vocational education for college-bound students
  B. Upgrade elementary curriculum—foreign language, English development in writing, problem-solving skills, science, social studies, and the arts
  C. Outside experts to improve and disseminate quality curricular materials: Evidence of text quality and currency from publishers
II. Standards and Expectations
  A. All educational institutions to adopt more rigorous academic standards: Grades to be indicators of achievement
  B. Standardized tests of achievement at transition points
III. Time
  A. More learning time: efficient time use, longer day, or longer year
     1. More homework and instruction for study skills
     2. Districts to consider seven-hour days and 200- to 220-day school years
     3. Efficient management of the school day and class organization
     4. The strengthening of attendance incentives and sanctions
     5. Reduction of administrative and discipline burdens, and intrusion on teachers
IV. Teaching
  A. Improve preparation for and desirability of teaching
     1. Higher standards for incoming teachers; judge programs by quality of graduates
     2. Competitive, market-sensitive, and performance-based salaries; career decisions based on evaluation
     3. Career ladders and 11-month contract

(continued)

Table 15-1 (*continued*)
Recommendations from *A Nation at Risk*

4. Alternative credentialing, grants, and loans to attract teachers
5. Master teachers' plan programs for probationary teaching and supervision

V. Citizen and Federal Involvement and Fiscal Support
  A. Citizens oversee reform and provide financial support.
  B. Administrative and legislative officials provide stability and finance for reforms.
  C. Federal government identifies national interest, provides leadership, and supports states and local districts.

Source: National Commission on Excellence in Education, *A nation at risk: The imperative for educational reform* (Washington, DC: U.S. Government Printing Office.)

ment of curriculum standards; and the alignment of curriculum frameworks, tests, and textbooks.

- *Teacher professionalization* was introduced by *A Nation at Risk* (National Commission on Excellence in Education, 1983), which stressed changes in licensure requirements and compensation to recruit and retain the best. By 1986 the emphasis shifted to "restructuring" education to give teachers a greater role in such decisions as hiring, staff evaluation, and curriculum. A substantial redistribution of authority was envisioned by *A Nation Prepared* and the work of the Holmes Group, among others (Carnegie Forum on Education and the Economy 1986; Holmes Group, 1986).

- A reprise of *equity* theme was given passing attention in *A Nation at Risk* but was the central concern in *An Imperiled Generation: Saving Urban Schools* (Carnegie Foundation for the Advancement of Teaching, 1988). There are fewer clear action recommendations in this area, but the interest in measuring and reducing the dropout rate, providing services for at-risk youth, expanding early childhood education, and attending to urban schools all reflect this concern.

State Reforms

The last five years have seen a level of state policy activity in education that may be unprecedented since the formation of the common school system. The Center for Policy Research in Education's (CPRE's) tracking of state education reform suggests seven conclusions about this activity.

1. *States have been most responsive to providing more academic content and to those aspects of professionalization dealing with changes in certification and compensation.* The effort to provide more academic content has been substantial across the nation. All six states in CPRE's sample increased their high school graduation requirements, as did a total of forty-five of the fifty states in the nation. Student-testing requirements have also increased substantially. Some states, such as Pennsylvania, introduced statewide mandatory testing for the first time; others, such as Georgia and Florida, expanded existing programs. California has been notable for its effort to coordinate state-mandated tests, state textbook adoption, and curriculum standards in order to move instruction to a higher cognitive level. By contrast, a few recommended reforms have not been so popular. The most striking is the suggestion to increase the school year to 200–220 days. Although thirty-seven states considered such action and nine states actually took action, none lengthened the number of student contact days beyond 180 (Bennett, 1986). Other suggestions that received relatively little state attention were to lengthen the school day, upgrade the elementary curriculum, and change homework policies.

The most pervasive changes in teacher policy have been those modifying certification requirements and increased teacher salaries. Entrance requirements have been increased, although it is not clear how these will hold up if teacher shortages become more severe. Arizona, Florida, and California are among the twenty-seven states with a minimum grade-point average for entering teachers, and forty-six states require some kind of certification test. At the same time, the proliferation of alternative routes to certification creates the possibility that the role of teachers' colleges in training educators will decline. Over twenty states have some alternative route to certification that allows people with a liberal arts background to go into teaching. Along with changes in entrance requirements have come changes in incentives. Teachers' salaries increased 22 percent in real terms between 1980 and 1987 (Odden, 1987). Although not quite back to earlier levels, they still grew faster than those for the average worker (Darling-Hammond & Berry, 1988).

Reforms to restructure the organization of instruction or revise decision-making roles within schools have received less attention. Until very recently when a number of districts and states undertook restructuring experiments, the most discussed reforms aimed at enhancing the teaching profession were merit pay and career ladder programs. In 1986, eighteen states had or were planning such efforts (Cornett, 1986). Florida and Tennessee were among the few to try implementing such programs on a massive basis. Florida rescinded its program, and Tennessee's has been heavily modified. Some of the programs that continue lead to only minor changes in teaching roles, like California's mentor teacher program, or are being implemented only on a limited basis, like Arizona's pilot career ladder, which affects only 15 of the over 200 districts in the state. Although states continue to experiment with career ladders, they are doing so more carefully, often through pilot programs or with more intensive participation during planning. Much of the initiative in this area has shifted from the state to the district level.

2. *States' responses to national reform targets reflect local political culture.* In spite of the national press for reform, state content affects the process of passing reform, the kinds of reforms adopted, and the way they were implemented (Fuhrman, 1988). For instance, CPRE's three states that have a history of turning to large-scale policy fixes did so again. California's SB 813 of 1983 is in the tradition of its early childhood legislation of 1972, school finance reform in the same year, and school improvement program of 1979. Florida also has a history of major reforms that was repeated in 1983. As in earlier efforts, leadership came from the speaker of the House and the Senate president. In this case, the governor was also a major player, but he had had experience in the legislature.

The states that lacked experience with comprehensive reform did not initiate it in the 1980s. Pennsylvania's reforms were organized by the governor and came largely, as in the past, through state board action. Arizona has a history of modest legislative reforms, such as its pilot career program, which affects very few districts.

The reform policy mechanisms also reflect state context. For instance, state policymakers in Georgia often distrust the 187 county districts, especially the 117 with elected superintendents. This mistrust encouraged the state to rely heavily on mandates. California, in contrast, is very large and has a constitutional requirement that the state must pay for all mandated changes. Because these changes could become prohibitively expensive, California stressed incentives.

The implementation process itself often reflected state culture. For instance, in Arizona, the Republican legislature distrusted the executive, which was run by an elected Democratic chief state school officer. This partisan concern contributed to the decision by the two education committees to administer the pilot career ladder directly. Pennsylvania's legislature has a history of serving as a court of appeal for interest groups objecting to legislative action. Thus, when the teachers' association objected to newly mandated continuing professional development requirements, it turned to the House of Representatives.

3. *States tended to focus on the more manageable recommendations.* In Chapter 6, Firestone pointed out that policies become difficult to implement when they are

- Expensive
- Make a large quantitative addition to what already exists
- Complex (in that they require new administrative arrangements, new

technologies or inventions, or new behaviors from teachers and administrators)

- Redistributive (in that they transfer money, status, or authority from those in a more advantaged position to those in a more disadvantaged position)

The most popular reform of the last five years—increasing graduation requirements—avoids most of these problems. There are rarely direct costs to adding courses although sometimes teachers specializing in particular areas must be added. Educators understand how to add courses to the curriculum. Often the ones added were very similar to those that had already been on the books before the proliferation of electives in the 1970s. If not, teachers often had ideas about what they wanted to teach. Moreover, in many states, most districts' graduation requirements already met the increased state requirements. Finally, although there was some reallocation of opportunities from vocational to academic teachers to accommodate changed course requirements, there was no major redistribution, because all those teachers affected were already at the same level.

The reforms that have not been adopted or have been underadopted have the opposite characteristics. Increasing the school day and year can be extremely expensive; a massive addition to teacher salaries would be needed to cover the time. Career ladders are also expensive, because they require adding to the salary pool, to avoid divisiveness. They are complex because the task of creating fair and reliable assessment instruments strains existing technology. Finally, introducing neophyte and mentor teacher roles can lead to a major redistribution of authority both among teachers and between teachers and administrators. When states ventured into these more complex areas, they often constructed the reforms in ways that made them more manageable. For example, they began with pilot programs on a small scale.

Other reforms have fallen between the extremes. All states increased student testing but most stayed within the existing technology. Only California seriously tested that complexity by intentionally developing tests of higher-order cognitive thinking. Three states increased teacher salaries but only by raising minimums.

4. *The sets of reforms adopted by most states lacked coherence.* When reforms are designed as coherent packages with mutually reinforcing parts, they should have greater impact. Each part will facilitate the other, and the set will send a more coordinated message to local educators. As a rule, such coherence was missing from the recent round of reforms. Specific provisions were rarely in conflict; but they were often unrelated, sending a barrage of signals to districts and requiring complex decisions about where to allocate time and money.

The prevalence of unrelated reform provisions is probably typical of reform efforts of the last century. It reflects in part the inconsistent thinking behind some of the reforms. For instance, teaching reforms have been motivated by concerns about both quality and quantity of teachers. Yet some reforms, such as tightening certification requirements designed to enhance the quality of the teaching force, could very well increase shortages. Similarly, depending on how they are implemented, policies such as alternative certification routes risk increasing the number of teachers but watering down the quality. Moreover, the compromises required to get omnibus legislation passed often encouraged the inclusion of specific provisions advocated by individual leaders and groups.

Where coherence increased, it was because of the efforts of state leaders to integrate existing provisions rather than to create new ones. Thus, California's State Superintendent orchestrated existing requirements for student testing, state textbook selection, and state curriculum guides to place greater stress on higher-order cognitive thinking.

5. *States are continuing to work on reform but this is no clear shift in direction.* The rhetoric of reform portrays two waves: a first wave, from approximately 1982 to 1986, that concentrated on standardization through minimum requirements for students and teacher certification and a second wave, beginning about 1986, that focuses on moving beyond standards to quality improvements designed at the school site. Designated the "restructuring" movement, the second wave is concerned with rethinking the organization of instruction to improve teaching and learning for understanding; more depth of content, as compared to coverage; and more emphasis on higher-order thinking. It also has governance aspects, including school site autonomy, shared decision making, enhanced roles for teachers and parents, and regulatory simplicity (Sizer, 1984).

Elements of the second wave are finding their ways into practice in a number of district-level experiments and in several state programs that provide planning and implementation grants to schools and/or districts through a competitive process (David, 1989). However, examination of state actions in the 1986–1988 period leads to the conclusion that states are continuing to enact policies more characteristic of the first wave; there is no clear demarcation or shift to a second-wave agenda in practice. For example, Florida tightened teacher certification requirements again in 1988 and Pennsylvania began in that year to develop statewide testing at the high school level. Minnesota, whose 1985 and 1987 choice programs make it a pioneer in elements of the second-wave agenda, instituted a basic skills exam for teachers in 1987. At this point, it is more accurate to think of the reform movement as a broad set of policy recommendations that states consider in a time frame reflecting their own needs than as a set of successive waves marked by changes in direction.

6. *The easy reforms that were adopted have stayed in place.* For the most part, the reforms adopted in the 1983–85 period of extensive legislative and executive activity have been maintained. Few if any have been rescinded. The biggest exception within the CPRE sample is the Florida master teacher program. Originally, just under $10 million was allocated to this program to give qualifying teachers an annual $3,000 bonus. However, the major teachers' association objected to a program that would reward some teachers over others. The program was rushed into place in such a way that the complex administrative demands of scheduling teacher tests and evaluations were not met. Applications were lost or disqualified on technicalities. The state's teacher of the year and runner-up to be the first teacher in space did not qualify to be master teachers. Although some of the administrative problems were later rectified, the fairness of the program was never established; and it was repealed in three years. This was an extremely complex redistributive program.

7. *Expansion of the economy facilitated reform but was not a complete explanation of it.* The period from 1981 through 1984 was one of rapid economic expansion. Most of the more aggressive reform states benefited financially from this upturn and had more funds that could be committed to education. The economic expansion in some of CPRE's states, for instance, contributed directly to reform in those states. Georgia's governor mounted a major reform effort, but pledged not to raise taxes. Business interests in both Georgia and Florida lobbied hard for reform in part because new costs would be at best relatively small.

However, economic factors do not completely explain the distribution of reform efforts. It is not surprising that among those states with weak economies, several did not participate in the reform movement. Yet a substantial number—including Arkansas, South Carolina, Tennessee, Texas, and West Virginia—did initiate reform programs even though doing so required raising educational expenditures faster than inflation.

Whatever the cause, there has been a significant increase (about 17 percent after inflation) in expenditures between 1983 and 1988. States vary greatly in their increases for education, and the state share fell in twenty states.

It is unclear how much of the new money went for "reform" as against higher salaries and other expenditures that did not change curriculum, school structure, or other variables. Jordan and McKeown's study (chapter 4 of this book) suggests that state officials do not think much money was spent on "reform," but the definition of "reform" is unclear and difficult to calculate in terms of categories of expenditures.

Despite increases in state aid that far exceeded inflation, the property tax remains an important source of increased school revenues. The share of state revenue from sales and income taxes has risen at an uneven rate, while taxes on severance, gas, and cigarettes have declined since 1978.

New ideas and concepts are needed to justify another large-scale increase in state aid. At this point, public concern and willingness to pay more taxes is not matched by consensus on new programs or approaches with high payoff for school improvement.

District Action

As might be expected, the variation in district response to state reforms has been substantial. Nevertheless, the following three descriptive conclusions about district activity appear warranted from the data.

1. *There was very little resistance to the reforms related to increased academic content. In fact, in some cases districts exceeded state requirements* (Fuhrman, Clune, & Elmore, 1988). There has been very little organized resistance to the current round of reforms, especially those having to do with curriculum intensification. Many districts actually welcomed these changes. Some increased graduation requirements before relevant state action was formalized. There are a number of reasons for this positive response. First, in many cases the reforms legitimated existing practices. That is, in several states district requirements met or exceeded those newly established by the state. Second, even where state policy required changes, these were well within the capacity of local educators. Teachers and administrators knew how to add, without a great deal of difficulty, the courses they were required to introduce. Finally, there was often widespread support for the changes introduced in the 1980s, unlike the more politically unpopular redistributive changes of the 1960s.

2. *Much of the progress on the restructuring agenda has resulted from district initiatives.* Although a few states such as Washington, Arkansas, Maine, and Massachusetts have initiated newer programs to encourage restructuring, these programs usually take the form of seed money for local experimentation. A great deal of creative development is still being done by school districts. The earlier pioneers, such as Rochester, New York; Miami, Florida; and Cincinnati, Ohio, are being joined by others such as Santa Fe, New Mexico. In addition, some smaller districts in the CPRE states are also experimenting with new strategies without the same level of publicity or state support. Elements of programs in these districts included provisions for site-based management, usually including teachers; shared decision making at the district level; and sometimes innovative approaches to inservice. Where such experiments are taking place, they usually rest on the foundation of an unusually cooperative relationship between district administrators and the teachers' association (Elmore, 1988).

3. *Some districts are actively orchestrating various state policies around local priorities in order to achieve local priorities.* Past research on reform implementation

emphasizes that the local level typically minimizes responses to mandates and responds to grants with mutual accommodation rather than extensive change. These patterns were found among the CPRE districts, but so was another pattern—sometimes referred to as "See you and raise you five"— where the district exceeds the state requirements. One major urban district coordinates almost all state teacher policies to meet its prime objective of hiring large numbers of new teachers. Two districts in another state are using a merit schools program to support their own efforts to promote site-based management; one district is even putting in additional money. A fourth district is using state teacher policies to overcome teacher attrition problems encouraged by the competitive salaries offered in neighboring districts. At least six districts exceeded changes in graduation requirements mandated by the state. In some cases, districts had already begun aligning curriculum frameworks, tests, and texts before the state took action. In others, district leaders saw the state requirement as an opportunity to do something constructive, rather than as a constraint.

Looking to the Future

We have defined several distinct types of reform, as a way of analyzing future possibilities. After presenting these types, we point out some potential combinations that appear promising and that flow from the 1983–1988 policies discussed earlier.

Intensification of Existing Service Delivery System. The focus on intensification of the existing delivery system would emphasize more of the 1983 priorities, such as academic courses, staff development, and a revamped curriculum that stresses higher-order skills. For example, a major overhaul of U.S. science curriculum would include new curriculum, texts, tests, and a staff development effort similar in scale to the 1960s under the NSF. Using this approach, the basic structure of schooling may remain unchanged, but there is even more centralized curriculum alignment, cross-role teams to help implementation, and long-term staff development to help teachers implement higher-order skills. This approach assumes that the current school structure is adequate but needs to be intensified.

Output Performance Strategy. The output performance approach is a subpart of intensification because it does not change the existing model or structure. It would stress state payment for results, based on an index of indicators that includes test changes plus increases in other relevant outcomes. Some feasibility issues concern (1) the precision of the output measures and (2) how to link financial aid formulas to increases or decreases of an index that included dropouts, achievement, attendance, course-taking patterns, and others. The output strategy would focus on the school site as the unit for financial aid distribution, rather than on the school district. Florida has such a program entitled "merit schools" that allows local districts to establish different performance criteria. Schools that do not increase outcomes and that are at the bottom of state achievement tests would be candidates for "state takeover." President Bush has proposed a $500 million "merit schools" program to be phased in starting in 1990.

Reorganization and Professionalism. The approaches in Dade County, Florida, Toledo, and Chicago are encompassed by the restructuring and professionalism strategy, including the "restructuring of schools" to include more teacher decision making, peer review of teacher effectiveness, and an end to the 50-minute, six-period lockstep school day. This approach assumes that the current model or structure of schooling is fundamentally flawed and needs basic change. This strategy has featured governance changes such as school site decision making.

A potential subpart of professionalism is the *technology* strategy, whereby major increases in computers, VCRs, and other electronic devices would drastically revamp the teacher's role. Technology would also enable us to reconfigure the teaching force to use more aids with fewer but much more highly paid professionals who manage the technology. At this point, the technology strategy is not moving ahead in many schools.

Consumer-Driven Strategy. The consumer-driven strategy—a potentially radical change—includes a broad-based voucher system; vouchers only for particular groups, such as the disadvantaged in low-performing schools; and expanded choice *within* the public system, including eliminating all boundaries between public school districts. Choice strategies that include a private school option do not have enough political support. However, Minnesota has recently passed a version of state-mandated public school open enrollment that is attracting the interest of other states. Open enrollment bills have passed in Arkansas and Iowa and are under consideration in fifteen other states. Although these state requirements for open enrollment increase demand for choice, they do little to increase supply. The states are not proposing to pay for student transport or other local expenses.

The Comprehensive Student Services Strategy. Several analysts and policymakers contend that the bottom one-third of the achievement band needs drastic change in the current children's services delivery system and an overall attack on out-of-school influences that inhibit school attainment. This "comprehensive student services strategy" might include expanded choice as well as closer linkages with employers to impart work skills. National reports such as the Committee for Economic Development's *Investing in Our Children* (1985) highlight the need to improve and coordinate such things as children's health, attitudes, child care, income support, and protective services if we are to make a major impact on children with multiple needs. The schools can not provide all these integrated services, but they can do a better job at brokerage for individual children who are particularly at risk. Schools could be funded to provide case managers to bring fragmented services together for individual children. Out-of-school influences are crucial to improving performance in school, and new, integrated service delivery systems could be a part of this. For example, some chief state school officers have proposed an Individualized Teaching and Learning Plan (ITLP) for at-risk youth, based on the Individualized Education Plan (IEP) for "special-education students." The ITLP would include linkages among schools and other service delivery agencies in the same way that an IEP does for a physically handicapped child.

An analysis of alternative strategies should focus on which mix is optimal for which types of pupils. In general, the top two-thirds of the achievement band can benefit from the intensification strategy because changing the content that these pupils study may result in enhanced academic attainment. For example, state legislators reason that most students who complete three years of mathematics know more about mathematics than students who take only one or two years of mathematics.

Ironically, the lowest one-third of school achievers are the most threatened by the impending changes in the labor market. According to the U.S. Department of Labor, the average level of education needed for the lowest-level jobs is rising. The at-risk youth are needed to fill many jobs that require more than repetitive low-skill operations. The inner-city at-risk youth may need such approaches as residential schools, like the Jobs Corps, or a service delivery system that today exists almost nowhere, coordinated between public and private organizations.

Promising Combinations of Strategies

These strategies are clearly not water-tight compartments, and the most effective approaches probably combine these strategies. For example, some scholars have suggested ways to combine intensification with restructuring (Smith & O'Day, 1989). The state would provide a broad but explicit curriculum framework to guide teachers' choice of content to be covered. This state curricular strategy would also achieve coherence through careful alignment of similar content in state curricular frameworks, tests, texts, and accreditation standards. This alignment component would be reinforced with state-funded, in-depth staff development, and preservice preparation. The restructuring part comes in through new roles and rules for teachers to design and implement pedagogical strategies that cover the state curricular framework. Teachers at the school site would have more flexibility than they currently do to meet the needs of their students by adapting state frameworks to local contexts. Such flexibility is important because it allows teachers to adjust those frameworks to the local context and culture.

In a restructured setting, teachers could choose to use peer and cross-age tutoring, cooperative learning, and new ways of grouping students. These pedagogical strategies would proceed with the state curriculum framework and graduation standards in mind.

Another alternative combination is to combine restructuring with accountability for performance. School site management and teacher decision making should be expanded by reducing regulation of educational and organizational processes. This would be done by reducing rules, regulations, and curriculum content specifications. Instead of regulating these processes, outcomes would be monitored more closely by increasing performance reporting at the school site level. The continued state deregulation would depend on progress on the outcome performance indicators at the school level. This approach is a version of the merit schools idea and could be supplemented with cash rewards for outstanding school site performance.

The Economics and Political Environment for Reform

The future of education reform depends primarily on the growth of the U.S. economy and how this growth is distributed among the various states. Without continued economic growth, state governments will focus more on efficiency, performance incentives, and evaluation of the 1983–1988 changes. Education remains a priority issue for politicians, but they are searching for a specific set of initiatives that would be similar in scope to the 1983–1988 reform wave. In short, as of late 1988, there is no clear consensus concerning the next stage of education reform. The concern about at-risk youth has resulted in a few state token dropout and preschool programs, but nothing very substantial or widespread as yet. A recent report by MDC, Inc., reports that

> Some 45 states report having legislation that addresses the problems of at-risk children. But most of it is piecemeal in nature, typically supporting a limited number of pilot programs.

> With awareness has come a good deal of casting about by the states, almost all of it characterized by a certain haphazardness, not necessarily indicating lack

of direction as much as lack of central planning purpose . . . no single state has an overarching policy addressed to at-risk, school-aged youth (Olson, 1988).

The large expenditures built up from 1983–1988 (about 17 percent after inflation) cannot continue indefinitely. Cycles in school finance correlate roughly with periods of economic growth or recession. The probable slower growth in the U.S. economy during 1989 is not the best time for major new and costly reforms. But the issue of at-risk youth remains linked in many state policymakers' minds with economic competitiveness and is building political momentum. Significant political advances for disadvantaged children depend primarily on trends and upheavals in the economy and major social or political movements (Kirst & Meister, 1985). The depression of the 1930s galvanized huge federal efforts to relieve the suffering of the poor. The civil rights movement's success in the 1960s was a crucial event that created a climate of opinion favorable for government programs targeted at disadvantaged children. Recent changes in job requirements and labor force upgrading stimulate continued concern for the productive potential of disadvantaged children. This concern may translate into large-scale government interventions designed to upgrade the skills of those who do not meet the minimum threshold for employment skills in a rapidly changing economy.

References

Bennett, W. (1986). *American education: Making it work*. Washington, DC: U.S. Government Printing Office.

Berman, P., & M. McLaughlin. (1975). *Federal programs supporting educational change, Vol. 4: The findings in review*. Santa Monica, CA: Rand Corporation.

Carnegie Forum on Education and the Economy. (1986). *A nation prepared: Teachers for the 21st century*. Hyattsville, MD: Carnegie Forum on Education and the Economy.

Carnegie Foundation for the Advancement of Teaching. (1988). *An imperiled generation: Saving urban schools*. Princeton, NJ: Carnegie Foundation for the Advancement of Teaching.

Committee for Economic Development. (1985). *Investing in our children*. New York, N.Y.: Committee for Economic Development.

Cornett, L. (1986). *1986–incentive programs for teachers and administrators: How are they doing?* Atlanta, GA: Southern Regional Education Board.

Darling-Hammond, L., & B. Berry. (1988). *The evolution of teacher policy*. Santa Monica, CA: Rand Corporation.

David, J. L. (1989). *Restructuring progress: Lessons from pioneering districts*. Washington DC: National Governors' Association.

Elmore, R. (1988). *Early experience in restructuring schools: Voices from the field*. Washington, DC: National Governors' Association.

Fuhrman, S. (1988). State politics and education reform. In J. Hannaway & R. Crowson, eds., *The politics of reform and school administration*. New York: Falmer Press.

Fuhrman, S., W. H. Clune, & R. F. Elmore. (1988). Research on educational reform: Lessons on the implementation of policy. *Teachers College Record*, *90*(2), 237–258.

Ginsberg, R., & R. K. Wimpelberg. (1987). Educational change by commission: Attempting "trickle down" reform. *Educational Evaluation and Policy Analysis*, *9*(4), 344–360.

Holmes Group. (1986). *Tomorrow's teachers: A report of the Holmes Group*. East Lansing, MI: Holmes Group.

James, T., & D. Tyack. (1983). Learning from past efforts to reform the high school. *Phi Delta Kappan*, *64*(6), 400–406.

Kirst, M. W., & G. R. Meister. (1985). Turbulence in American secondary schools: What reforms last? *Curriculum Inquiry*, *15*(2), 169–186.

National Commission on Excellence in Education. (1983). *A nation at risk. The imperative of educational reform*. Washington, DC: National Commission on Excellence.

National Governors' Association. (1986). *A time for results*. Washington, DC: National Governors' Association.

Odden, A. (1987). Financing education in an era of excellence. Paper prepared for the Mid-Continental Regional Educational Laboratories, Kansas City, Missouri.

Olson, L. (1988, 21 September). States and the at-risk issue. *Education Week*, p. 14.

Passow, A. H. (1984, June). Tackling the reform reports of the 1980s. *Phi Delta Kappan*, *65*, 674–683.

Sizer, T. (1984). *Horace's compromise: The dilemma of the American high school*. Boston: Houghton Mifflin.

Smith, M., & J. O'Day. (1989). Teaching policy and research on teaching. New Brunswick, NJ: Center for Policy Research in Education.